The Company Democracy Model

Engineering Management Series

Series Editor: Timothy Kotnour, University of Central Florida, and Waldemar Karwowski, University of Central Florida

The series focuses on transforming, leading, and managing the project-based organization. Project-based organizations include organizations focused on delivering projects (construction, spec hardware, new military systems, research and development efforts). Current project-based organization books primarily focus on project management. This series will provide a foundation for integrating important topics such as business and enterprise transformation, strategic management, portfolio management, and project delivery. Project-based organizations are struggling to deliver projects. This series will pull together authors and their knowledge on the core disciplines for transforming, leading, managing, and delivering solutions within the project-based organization.

Transforming Organizations
Strategies and Methods
Timothy George Kotnour

Systems Life Cycle Costing
Economic Analysis, Estimation, and Management
John V. Farr

Modeling and Simulation-Based Systems Engineering Handbook
Edited by Daniele Gianni, Andrea D'Ambrogio, and Andreas Tolk

The Company Democracy Model
Creating Innovative Democratic Work Cultures for Effective Organizational Knowledge-Based Management and Leadership
Evangelos Markopoulos and Hannu Vanharanta

For more information on this series, please visit: https://www.routledge.com/Engineering-Management/book-series/CRCENGMANSER

The Company Democracy Model

Creating Innovative Democratic Work Cultures for Effective Organizational Knowledge-Based Management and Leadership

Evangelos Markopoulos and Hannu Vanharanta

Routledge
Taylor & Francis Group

A PRODUCTIVITY PRESS BOOK

First published 2022
by Routledge
605 Third Avenue, New York, NY 10158

and by Routledge
2 Park Square, Milton Park, Abingdon, Oxon, OX14 4RN

Routledge is an imprint of the Taylor & Francis Group, an informa business

© 2022 Evangelos Markopoulos & Hannu Vanharanta

ISBN: 9780367745639 (hbk)
ISBN: 9780367745622 (pbk)
ISBN: 9781003158493 (ebk)

DOI: 10.4324/9781003158493

Typeset in Garamond
by Deanta Global Publishing Services, Chennai, India

This book is dedicated to:

the future of my wife Olga, children Panagiotis, and Georgios,
and
the next generations.

Evangelos Markopoulos

the future of my wife Brita, children Outi, Mari, Sakari, and Lauri
and
the next generations.

Hannu Vanharanta

Contents

SECTION 1 APPLIED PHILOSOPHY

1 Science and Theory Precede Practice: A Scientific Framework for the Applied Philosophy Approach in Management and Leadership

14   Human Perception, Interpretation, Understanding, and Communication of Company Democracy: Building Co-opetitive Ecosystems

15   The Company Democracy Model for Human Intellectual Capitalism and Shared Value Creation: Toward Added Value and Circular Economies

List of Figures

List of Tables

Preface

Through the allegory of the cave, Plato teaches that people stay imprisoned in darkness and can't see reality with their own eyes. In Plato's allegory, human senses perceive the real world through the images on the cave wall, which are the shadows of reality. Plato's other world, the World of Ideas, consists of an ideal form of tangible things and abstract concepts. That is to say, when opening people's eyes to the multi-variety of different forms and ideas, we arrive at the modern notion of degree, where all the ontologies and models of reality contain several constructs, concepts, and thoughts. This belief follows the Aristotelian thinking that everything is part and parcel of the ultimate ideal of goodness. The totality of goodness describes well, for us humans, how to behave in the viable, dynamic living system in which we live. To convert this problem formulation, i.e., "opening people's eyes" to modern business management and leadership, we have to operate with a real human workforce, with business investments and many-faceted business constructs, concepts, and variables. These business characteristics, traits, and features are not so clearly defined and often without sharp boundaries. They can be perceived and understood as degrees of past, current, and future business situations and activities.

Using Plato's worldview, words, and sayings and applying the worldview of other philosophers (cf. Pythagoras, Socrates, Aristotle, Bacon, Descartes, Smith, Pascal, Locke, Leibniz, Voltaire, Rousseau, Kant, Heraclitus, Russel, Democritus, Epicurus, and Thales), we end up with human-centric thinking. Therefore, our aphorism for the business world starts naturally from individuals, humans, people, and the workforce. Thus, we have to focus first on working people and understand how it is possible to tap the full potential of their intellectual capital in the business context (i.e., their capacity, skills, ability, capability, competence, past and current experience, knowledge, and wisdom) by stating:

"Business is a prisoner of money – Release business to people."

Our aphorism means that we have to challenge the whole workforce by giving them opportunities, possibilities, and priority to think freely. People have to develop companies together to create added value activities through products and services and promote growth, profitability, productivity, and overall performance: first those of the company they are working for and then, ultimately, those of the society to which they belong. This book has used many philosophical views on business to release business to people and give people more room to think about their company's ultimate purpose and goal.

The world is changing in leaps and bounds to become more marketing-oriented and, simultaneously, more human-focused. Governmental systems in many countries accept markets as the determinants of current and future change, but they also allow more and more individual human decision-making and participation. This recent trend means that companies have to develop in this direction. We have to understand that the democratic way, as it has already existed for hundreds of years, might be the right and convenient solution in the new company context if it is applied to create added value and shared added value for societies.

Now we are ready to present our ideas of the Company Democracy Model, in which philosophy is the first supporting science. Our book's starting point is to develop the two essential dimensions in business, i.e., management and leadership. The content of the book supports the ideas of many philosophers, and we, therefore, call this management and leadership approach:

"The Applied Philosophy of Management and Leadership"

For this reason, this approach has a scientific background and nature, i.e., Episteme. It also contains other scientific areas to create new understanding, knowledge, and wisdom in the business context. Applied Philosophy shows us in many ways how important it is to use gathered theoretical knowledge, i.e., Sophia. It also shows the technocratic way, i.e., Techne, to use modern methods and tools to identify current and future business situations. Applied Philosophy brings us down to earth by showing the practical side, i.e., Phronesis, through many lenses, and gives us possibilities to grasp in new ways how to approach management and leadership issues in collaboration with the workforce. All the areas of our management and leadership approach help to perceive, understand, and boost the basic principles of the Company Democracy Model.

The book describes the model from academic, industry, trade, governmental, and practical perspectives. Its background lies in the wisdom of the ancient Hellenic Delphic maxims, primarily on 'Gnothi Seauton: Know Thyself,' 'Metron Ariston: Moderation is best,' and 'Miden Agan: Nothing in excess.' The model consists of a framework in which an evolutionary, organizational, and spiral approach supports and maintains the creation and execution of knowledge-based democratic cultures for effective corporate knowledge-based management and leadership. The Co-Evolutionary Spiral Method and processes in the model contribute toward identifying and achieving the capacity, capability, competence, maturity, and wisdom needed to turn information, data, and knowledge into insights and innovations. In this context, the spiral process is based on the degree of democracy in organizations. The Company Democracy Model is complemented by the Co-Evolute approach and its different applications. These organizational development tools support creating a strong corporate knowledge-based culture for management and leadership purposes. These methods' main idea is to evolve the organization by transforming tacit organizational business knowledge into explicit knowledge and wisdom.

In a broad context, the Company Democracy Model is a technique and methodology for creating business data, information, and knowledge, contributing to developing insights, ideas, and innovations, making it possible to achieve competitive advantage leading to extroversion and modern entrepreneurship. It is a model for managing and leading innovation work inside a company so that both individual and collective views of the innovation activity come to each participant's awareness. Data, information, and knowledge transformation thus flow actively into business processes and activities. The innovation engine of the company harnesses human intellectual assets.

The fundamental concept of our book lies in the metaphorization of the world around the human being. We use metaphors and ontologies from human and business activity's essential components in a democratic company context. One purpose of the symbolic and ontological structure is to facilitate a robust conceptual framework as the theoretical basis for a corporate strategy that promotes its continuous, sustainable, and democratic improvement. Another purpose is to enable people to find analogies for, clarify the differences between, and emphasize the importance of human-related and capital-related business issues in company development and the formation of shared value, added value, profitability, productivity, and performance. The third purpose is to use the basic metaphorical structure to generate a robust democratic design system inside the company to serve continuous business development and progress.

We hope that company members and readers will begin to think about themselves and their own business in a new democratic way. People should not let money talk only or too much, but help themselves to perceive, understand, and express their insights, ideas, and innovations so that they can be proud of being part of their own company. People should also be eager to improve their company's competitive position with many qualitative and quantitative business features and characteristics and show commitment, engagement, and motivation in their work. The Company Democracy Model presented in this book will enable and boost this evolution.

This book will give the readers new ideas on developing their company in a collective, modern, democratic manner.

"One Voice and Many Insights"

London, UK   **Helsinki, Finland**
Evangelos Markopoulos   *Hannu Vanharanta*

Acknowledgments

This book summarizes many of our research papers and articles over the past ten years of working together. Both of us have worked in the industry and academic institutions for several years, which means we have got a lot of our experience and knowledge from academic research, lecturing, and live companies and projects where we have worked. We are indebted to all those coworkers we have had the opportunity to work with locally, nationally, and internationally in the countries we have worked and lived. We cannot thank by name everyone who has contributed to the work we present here, but we would like to express our gratitude to those close friends and coworkers we have had during this innovative time we have spent together. We have separated our acknowledgments into several groups. The first group is our research colleagues from universities and other academic institutions. These team members are those coworkers who have helped us get this book ready during the past two years when we have tried to conceptualize our ideas, insights, innovations, and the model in the form of a book. The second group is the Evolute researchers. The third group is the editorial team, the fourth group is our international friends, the fifth group is our international students, and the sixth group is our family members.

Academic Research Team

Our academic research team has helped us in many ways, and mostly they have given us positive criticism and support. The group consists of the following persons:

Jarno Einolander, PhD, Vaasa University; Jussi Kantola, Professor, PhD, University of Turku; Waldemar Karwowski, Professor, PhD, University of Central Florida;

Tero Reunanen, MSc, Head of E&R, Turku University of Applied Sciences; Tapio Salminen, MSc, Lecturer, Tampere University; Ari Sivula, PhD, R&D Manager, Seinäjoki University of Applied Sciences; Ari Visa, Professor, PhD, Tampere University.

Thank you very much for your help, work, and support.

Evolute Application Team

Our research's application side and the book's empirical results come mainly from our Evolute team members' work. The team consists of the following people: Antti Piirto, PhD, Managing Director, AP-Safety; Petri Paajanen, PhD, Managing Director, Pori Energia Oy; Markku Salo, PhD, Manager, Valmet Oy; Tero Hanhisalo, MSc, Evolute LLC Researcher; Mikko Tuomainen, MSc, Evolute LLC researcher and Key account manager, Vahterus Oy; Kirsi Liikamaa, PhD, University of Turku; Sibel Kantola, CEO/ Graphic designer.

Thank you very much for your help in conceptualizing and applying complex management and leadership ontologies.

Editorial Team

We are grateful to CRC Press and Taylor & Francis Group for accepting our book proposal for publication. We appreciate the great help and patience from editor Michael Sinocchi, Taylor & Francis Group, editorial assistant Samantha Dalton, Taylor & Francis, Vijay Bose, Deanta Global, and others who were patient with us and coached us through this demanding publication process. Without them, this book would have been impossible. Michael Sinocchi has been the vital link for us to start writing this book, and Samantha Dalton has kept us on track in each phase of the publication process. We also got valuable support, assistance, and suggestions from Sue Pearson and Mike Jones to revise and proofread all the chapters' manuscript versions. We are also very grateful to all those who have contributed to complete this management and leadership book but who we don't know by name.

Thank you for your help and assistance during the publication process.

Our International Students' Support Team

During our lecturing in Finland, Greece, UK, and Poland, we had students world-wide. They have learned to use the Evolute applications, and they have also described their understanding and perception of company democracy in their own countries. These countries are many like Brasil, Nigeria, Morocco, Spain, Italy, Portugal, Italy, Germany, Slovakia, Russia, Egypt, Palestine, Israel, Iran, Iraqi, Nepal, India, China, Greece, Finland, Sweden, UK, Thailand, Sri Lanka, Pakistan, Bangladesh, Ruanda, Turkey, Algeria, Azerbaijan, Kenya, Poland, Mongolia, France, Cameron, Vietnam, Jordan, etc. The information and students' own work experience in their countries have given us ideas of what these companies in different countries lack and how to develop them collectively. These talks, changing information, comprehending, and listening have supported our efforts to continue our development work, and we are very grateful for our international students. With this perception of how companies behave and develop in these countries and how managers and leaders support their workforce has considerably changed our perception and understanding.

All students, thank you very much for your information and experience you gave us concerning these local and global companies' democracy and leadership issues. Thank you very much for your support and kindness, which you have shown to our academic research efforts.

Our International Friends' Support Team

We have picked to this group all those who have supported us during this heavy writing process. They have helped us think out of the bubble we have been in during these years. These persons are Panagiotis Tsafaras, Mr., *The Economist*; Asher Yuval; Mr. *Methoda*; George Kalkanis, PhD, CEO Pro-Action; Elena Panaritis, Ms, CEO T4Action; Nicos Karapittides, Mr.; Prof. Harris Makatrosis, UK; Prof. Yoon Chang, Korea; Prof. Peter Odrakiewicz, Poland; Prof. Stefan Trzcieliński, PhD, Poland; Pawel Krolas, PhD, Poland; Prof. Barbro Back, Finland; Adjunct Prof. Tomas Eklund, PhD, Sweden; Stefan Marsina, PhD, Slovakia; Aappo Kontu, PhD, Finland.

Thank you for your support, seeing this kind of work necessary for managers, leaders, and companies worldwide. We appreciate high your local and global perception of company development.

Our Family Members

Our families deserve heartfelt appreciation for their help, support, encouragement, and positive attitude during this long writing process. Critical comments and questions have forced us to think repeatedly about different management and leadership issues from a convenient and practical viewpoint. "Why Not this way" and "Why you believe this to be important" are the words we heard all the time and which our inner voices and our joint meetings have processed further. We appreciate very high these questions, critique, support, advice, and your curiosity. They all show us your interest in our work. We apologize in retrospect for not being present in our homes' various duties and keeping our work too important. We have not been 'on stage' so consciously as we should have been.

_____

During the intensive writing process, the problematic issue was the COVID-19 pandemic, which has already lasted over one year. It made it impossible to travel to the UK, Greece, Poland, the USA, and Finland to discuss in more detail the many specific issues belonging to this work. However, technology has served us very well, and the daily contacts through video connections with Teams, Zoom, or Skype calls have enabled us to work very closely. The test runs with various computer applications have also been possible with modern computer technology. So we are delighted that technology has helped us so much during these busy and challenging times writing this book.

With gratitude to everyone,
Evangelos and Hannu

Authors

The photo was taken in the Greek archipelago at Messinia.

Dr. Evangelos Markopoulos was born in 1967 in Kalamata, Greece. He is a scholar and an entrepreneur with expertise in Knowledge Management, Enterprise Engineering, Process and Project Management and Innovation & Entrepreneurship. He holds a BA in Computer Science with a minor in Mathematics, from the City University of New York, an MSc in Computer Science and Artificial Intelligence from New York University, and a Ph.D. on ICT Project and Investments Management from the University of Piraeus (Greece). He worked as a computer scientist in the USA at IBM (applications development), Siemens (systems engineer), and Bell Laboratories of AT&T (artificial intelligence and systems researcher). For nearly 20 years he was the CEO of EMPROSS Strategic IT consultants where he delivered projects in Software Engineering, Quality, and Project Management around the world. He invented and applied the ARIADNE Software Project Management Methodology for Software Development and Software Acquisition projects. As an academic, he taught, and still teaches, in universities such as the University College London (UCL), Queen Mary University of London (QMUL), Turku University of Applied Sciences (TUAS), City University New York, (CUNY), University of Essex, Royal Holloway University of London, SOAS-School of Oriental & African Studies, and Hult International Business School. He won the 2018 and 2020 HULT Prize Global Social Innovation competition at the UN with his UCL and QMUL students respectively. He is also part of the Clinton Global Initiative University (CGI-U) for sustainable and social innovation. Since 2018 his research is focused on the integration of advanced technologies with strategic management and corporate digital transformation. He works with technologies such as Metaverse,

Virtual Reality, Serious Games and Gamification, Artificial Intelligence, Expert Systems, Neural Networks, and Cognitive Science in business applications. He has over 150 articles and papers published in international journals and conferences.

The photo was taken in the Finnish archipelago at Taivassalo.

Dr. Hannu Vanharanta was born in 1949 in Pori, Finland. He enrolled in 1967 at Åbo Akademi University, Turku, Finland, where he earned an M.Sc. degree in Chemical Engineering. He began his professional career in 1973 as a technical assistant at the Turku office of the Finnish Ministry of Trade and Industry. He then entered the engineering industry and gained valuable practical experience in many fields of industrial management. During 1975–1992 he worked for several Finnish international engineering companies, including Jaakko Pöyry (now AFRY), Rintekno, and Ekono as a process engineer, section manager, and leading consultant. During 1992–1995 he was a researcher at the Institute for Advanced Management Systems Research. In 1995 he earned his Ph.D. degree in Industrial Management at Åbo Akademi and started his academic career. From 1995–1996 he was a professor in Business Economics at the University of Joensuu, Finland. In 1996–1998 he served as professor in Purchasing and Supply Chain Management at the Lappeenranta University of Technology, Finland. From 1998 to 2016 he was a professor of Industrial Management and Engineering at the Tampere University of Technology, Pori Campus, Finland. Since retiring from the Tampere University of Technology, he has held visiting professorships at Poznan University of Technology, Poland, and Vaasa University, Finland. His research interests are Strategic Management, Human Resource Management, Knowledge Management, Financial Analysis, Decision Support Systems, and Executive Information Systems. His particular interests are in knowledge discovery and data mining. He has published many articles on financial analysis as well as text analysis as a result of his research experience. The ultimate goal of his research is to synthesize quantitative and qualitative/linguistic data/information/knowledge for strategic decision-making. He has had over 300 articles and papers published in international journals and conferences.

Book Structure

The Company Democracy Model, as a model and practice, is based on the concepts of Applied Philosophy and living systems. Applied Philosophy, driven by the Delphic maxims, forms the wisdom cube, creating the theoretical framework needed to establish a Co-Evolutionary organizational culture. Living Systems, in turn, are practical extensions of Applied Philosophy. Building on self-awareness, the holistic concept of a man and the circles of mind metaphors harness intellectual capital in a cross-scientific approach creating hyper-knowledge through ontology-driven human-compatible systems. Therefore, the Living Systems have a prerequisite in Applied Philosophy, and the Company Democracy has as a prerequisite in the Living Systems. Democracy is based on systematic approaches based on practical and ethical philosophical ideas and values. Figure A demonstrates the relationship of the three concepts that form the three sections of the book.

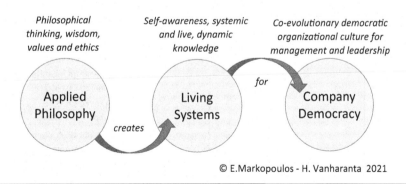

© E.Markopoulos - H. Vanharanta 2021

Figure A   The Company Democracy pillars and sections of the book.

The Company Democracy Model is the practical utilization of the self-aware intellectual capital deriving from human-driven living systems under philosophical wisdom, ethos, values, thinking, and reasoning. Company democracy is the knowledge-based organizational culture for management and leadership.

The book contains a preface, 19 chapters in three sections, and an epilogue/conclusion. Figure B presents the contents of the book in sections and chapters.

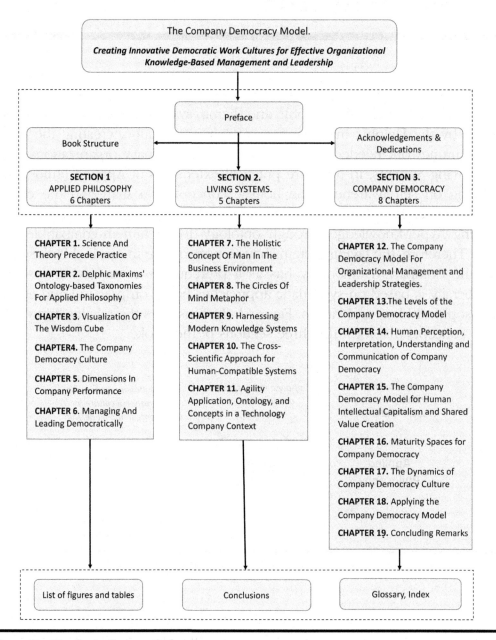

Figure B   Book sections and chapters.

All chapters begin with an introduction and end with a summary and the related references.

Chapters 1–17 are supported with a number of questions (minimum 10), which can test the readers' knowledge, ignite debates and discussions, and serve as food for thought for thinking individuals or group activities.

Each chapter of the book is designed to function as an autonomous topic that delivers specific and factual knowledge to the reader. All the chapters follow a natural flow but are not necessarily or strictly connected. It helps to read from Chapters 1 to 19, but the reader can still receive much value by reading the chapters in the order of interest.

Under the same thinking, the book chapters can also be used as academic lectures that can be delivered sequentially from Chapters 1 to 19, or powers section, or any combination the academic decides to compose.

Therefore, the book is a practical resource that introduces a new management and leadership model to the manager and a textbook that can be used for academic-level education in the disciplines of Business Management, Knowledge Management, and Innovation and Entrepreneurship.

As a textbook, the book can be used in courses/modules such as Organizational Culture, Human Resource Management, Innovation Management, Corporate Entrepreneurship, New Product Development, Strategy, Leadership, and other knowledge or business management topics.

Academics who wish to adopt the book or parts of the book for their lectures can contact the authors for supporting material such as video recordings, slides, teaching notes, quiz questions, examination questions, answers to the chapter questions, class activities, and other teaching and learning support resources.

A synopsis of the book chapters is presented in the following sections.

Section 1. Applied Philosophy

Chapter 1

Science and Theory Precede Practice: A Scientific Framework for the Applied Philosophy Approach in Management and Leadership

Humans must be in focus when companies improve their business productivity, profitability, and performance. The Applied Philosophy approach in management and leadership places humans in the company context as living entities aligned with business management and leadership objects in the conscious experience of the company workforce. Starting from the Hellenic philosophy and drawing on more modern philosophies relevant to everyday business, the Applied Philosophy approach in management and leadership can harness business ontologies, taxonomies, classes, and other knowledge classification techniques to create added value in companies. New theories, approaches, and practices can be generated by interpreting knowledge from the Delphic Maxims as the basis for many new and alternative management and leadership objectives. The Holistic Concept of Man and the Circles of Mind metaphors open up the human mind and redefine Situationality by giving unique, alternative ways to understand how humans, as decision-makers, behave in a company context. This chapter introduces the Applied Philosophy approach for management and leadership and provides the philosophical background needed to better understand the Company Democracy Model.

Chapter 2

Delphic Maxims' Ontology-Based Taxonomies for Applied Philosophy: An Interpretation of the Ancient Hellenic Philosophy in Business and Governance Management

Knowledge analysis and representation define situations before activities get executed. Knowledge engineering precedes knowledge management to construct the knowledge elements that can be used in the management. Over the years, various techniques have been developed for knowledge recognition, elicitation, acquisition, analysis, engineering, and management. As problems become more complex over time, the synergies of knowledge disciplines become critical and necessary. To tackle this complexity, it is also essential to seek knowledge in non-trivial sources via root cause analysis models on philosophical challenges that usually hide the answers to societal and economic problems. This chapter presents a triadic categorization approach of the Delphic maxims based on ontologies, taxonomies, and classes. It reveals their contribution to modern business and governance management through the Hellenic contribution to the global economy, civilization, and humanity.

Chapter 3

Visualization of the Wisdom Cube: Wisdom Space for Management and Leadership

The philosophers of the Ancient World (700 BCE–250 CE) have inspired us by their writings to start thinking more deeply about the visualization of wisdom and knowledge. These basic principles are now placed in such a form that it is possible to show, in a practical way, how knowledge and wisdom are intertwined. This chapter aims to show how the definitions of the dimensions of wisdom give us the means to go further in our thinking to perceive and understand the essential relationships between scientific, theoretical, technical, and practical knowledge. This can be seen as a journey toward knowledge creation and wisdom. The starting point has been the ancient Hellenic philosophers and their thinking, logic, and reasoning. This chapter indicates the beneficial impact of the philosophers' essential thinking and provides a practical understanding of knowledge creation and wisdom for management and leadership purposes.

Chapter 4

The Company Democracy Culture: Understanding Culture and Dynamics

The development of a dynamic democratic company culture inside an organization follows a systemic approach. This chapter presents an overall model, utilizing Miller's living system model; Samuelsson's model of inputs, processes, and output; Nonaka and Takeuchi's spiral knowledge creation model; and Markopoulos and Vanharanta's spiral model on focusing, perceiving, and understanding to reveal the overall ontology and to construct concepts and variables for dynamic democratic company culture. This comprehensive systemic approach can be considered as a learning and knowledge creation system for democratic cultural change. In the presented systemic view, humans are the activators, and time is the primary change variable that measures how fast the company is implementing a new democratic culture. After that, organizations can start to utilize the dynamic democratic company culture.

Chapter 5

Dimensions in Company Performance: The Power of Co-Evolution

Intellectual capital can significantly impact the transformation of a company's position from its current state to a future one. However, such human assets cannot be reflected clearly in financial statements or balance sheets. The growth of a company depends significantly on the intellectual capital produced from its human assets, which positively impacts the present and future operations. Important human intellectual capital assets can be considered innovation capital, process capital, organizational capital, customer capital, human resources capital, and knowledge capital. As long as these human asset components cannot be demonstrated directly or indirectly, the company's real value cannot be estimated or predicted sufficiently. This chapter presents the basic principles of how human performance can be integrated into company performance and how Company Democracy can be applied and harnessed to promote the human dimension's effectiveness through a Co-Evolutionary approach.

Chapter 6

Managing and Leading Democratically:
Achieving Democratic Balance

A significant challenge in today's managers seems to be the lack of time and opportunities to gather all the necessary data, information, and knowledge they need on how to behave or how to lead people in different occupational work roles while, at the same time, managing the company or organization. Several issues arise from this problem formulation, such as what managers should do and how they should manage and lead. This chapter provides a literature review on identifying the necessary information, knowledge, understanding, and rules to be covered in different business situations. It also introduces the Management Windshield, a powerful ontology-based metaphor for finding the proper tools for management and leadership purposes from the individual point of view. Overall Windshield's ontology has already been evolved into an applied practical process framework that supports daily management and leadership. The combined ontology gives managers and leaders the content they should use to pay attention to different management and leadership objects; to focus their leading and management efforts on these objects; to perceive the contents of the objects; to understand the meanings, relationships, and interrelationships of the objects; and then in practice to use the created knowledge in the final decision-making. The metaphor is also intended to guide managers and leaders to find a way to democratic company management and leadership.

Section 2. Human Focus in Living Systems

Chapter 7

The Holistic Concept of Man in the Business Environment: The Concepts We Live By

Over the past 20 years, new management and leadership concepts have started being developed around the individual, i.e., human beings. It is the employees who must know first who they are (know yourself), how they can develop their personal growth, and what methods they can use to do so. Today new requirements have arisen, and further questions are evolving on how an individual can be the added value creator in a business context. The Holistic Concept of Man can illustrate these new conceptual management system requirements with a robust metaphorical method. Its nature is not so self-evident because people think and act automatically in different business situations. However, new conditions lead to new thinking and provide a unique view of how people see the modern human being as part of a living system, working in occupational roles for added-value purposes inside the complex business environment.

Chapter 8

The Circles of Mind Metaphor: Actors on the Stage of Consciousness

Metaphors help people understand what they know about their physical and cognitive experiences in the world. They are also used to understand complex phenomena and ideas, mental activities, feelings, and the passing of time and people's existence. The world can be described as a theater stage with all the people actors, where each one is playing their role. This kind of perception helps people understand themselves and improve their productivity, latency, and performance on their stage. All the actors can form a mental theater to show their conscious experience on the stage. Inner and outer senses describe how they see their current reality, and future ideas can come suddenly by changing their own 'play' in their Situationality. By explaining it in this way, as a Cartesian theater, people can enter a new type of mind metaphor with certain circles around the stage. The players with inner and outer senses and ideas, the unconscious audience, the context operators behind the scenes, the director, and the spotlight controller create the live conscious experience on stage for every actor. The Circles of Mind metaphor helps people understand themselves better and gives them support and guidance in their Situationality when managing and leading companies and organizations. The target of the analogy is to understand yourself better and support people to understand each other better.

Chapter 9

Harnessing Modern Knowledge Systems: Applying Knowledge Frameworks

In the design, development, and use of modern computer-based decision support systems and applications, the ultimate challenges and goals are arranging and organizing successful interaction between the active human being, the computer interface, the different areas of knowledge, and the computer itself. This chapter examines the fusion of hyper-knowledge frameworks, the Holistic Concept of Man, and the Circles of Mind metaphors in decision support systems and applications to emulate individual and collective human behavior simultaneously with cognitive processes and unity. Modern computer systems and computing have replaced data processing with knowledge processing and information creation with knowledge creation. Getting new knowledge from data and information leads to the generation of new human wisdom. This chapter represents an emerging paradigm for achieving emulation and synergy between human decision-making processes and computer configurations. Such an approach is enormously important when managing and leading change steadily toward virtual work, virtual teams, complex business ontologies, constructs, concepts, and objects. This change substantially impacts how companies should organize, lead, and manage both intellectual and financial assets to continuously support the development of democratic company cultures where organizational knowledge begins.

Chapter 10

The Cross-Scientific Approach for Human-Compatible Systems: Acting with Modern Decision Tools

People grow and live in relations and interrelations within their internal and external working or personal environments. This coexistence can be described with systems and processes designed to promote evolutionary and Co-Evolutionary human development. Evolution and co-evolution offer new challenges, opportunities, and possibilities to address many business operations and strategies with creative human relations and interrelations. This chapter presents a cross-scientific approach, with which many human-compatible systems have been created, tested, verified, and validated, either concerning subjective introspection or objective extrospection. Top-down and bottom-up views can be combined to improve organizational productivity and individual performance and competencies in a democratic way.

Chapter 11

Agility Application, Ontology, and Concepts in a Technology Company Context: Agility Boosts Collective Wisdom

Agility is a multidimensional, complex ontology that needs adequate scientific, theoretical, technical, and human resources to find the right practical solutions in the company context. The main target is to generate significant added value in products, services, projects, and organizations. Because the ontology and concepts can have fuzzy nature, agility must be understood in detail throughout the whole organization and used according to the basic priciples of its concept. Agility evaluation needs, however, computer tools. Such a tool to measure the degree of agility in an organization has been developed by the author's international research group to be used in any size and type of organization. The software development used a democratic approach to finalize the application's content of the ontology. The application's development process started from a small, intuitive idea, but it got a sizeable collective understanding and support in a real business context. The positive usability, verification, and validation results indicated the application's potentiality during the evaluation of current and future agility trends in a Finnish company. The results also showed that this kind of collaborative development approach suits ontology-based management and leadership very well.

Section 3. The Company Democracy Model

Chapter 12

The Company Democracy Model for Organizational Management and Leadership Strategies: Democratic Innovation for Competitiveness and Extroversion

Democracy is one of the most powerful words. It is a word that indicates freedom, equality, rights, fairness, respect, justice, development, prosperity, and many other significant concepts. It is pronounced very similarly in many different languages, expresses the same meaning. However, managing, leading, achieving, and sustaining democracy in its true meaning can be challenging, if not almost impossible. This chapter presents the researched and developed democratic company culture model and reveals its principal components with the Co-Evolutionary Spiral Method. Such a democratic culture creation approach helps organizations develop new data, information, and knowledge to initiate, innovate, understand, perceive, and apply management and leadership results to achieve innovation, competitiveness, and extroversion. The overall process adopted in this model is based on previous works on human and company performance improvements. First, the actuality is viewed in detail through the current democratic behavior, and then, the capability and potentiality of the organization are examined. In this process, indicative critical concepts are being addressed and answered, such as actuality, potentiality, and capability. What are we planning to do for our company's democratic behavior? What could we do to develop our organization's democratic behavior? What could we achieve by developing democratic behavior in our organization? This chapter presents answers to these questions with an approach that identifies and defines the degree of Company Democracy.

Chapter 13

The Levels of the Company Democracy Model: A Spiral Co-Evolution

The Company Democracy Model is characterized by its pyramid structure and the number of levels that compose it. The pyramid indicates that the journey to the top is a challenge that cannot be achieved without commitment, dedication, and hard work. It also signifies the journey of knowledge creation. The lower levels mostly generate information rather than actual knowledge. However, as the levels rise, the information is transformed into knowledge, products/services, innovations, competitive advantages, and extroversion strategies. The pyramid also indicates the effort required for each level to be reached. The lower levels are time-consuming as they set up the base and infrastructure for the model to be applied. In contrast, the upper levels are less time-consuming since they utilize the previous levels' output. Another way to see the pyramid is the involvement of the people concerned. The lower levels are open to all company employees, while the upper levels are continuing with those who have evolved through the Company Democracy Model processes. There are many ways to interpret the Company Democracy Model structure related to effort, benefits, participation, complexity, and goals. Still, the most critical way to see this evolutionary path is its openness to the participation of all the employees in a company. Democracy provides the opportunity, not the outcome. Both the employees and the company should work together to co-evolve toward achieving the best, but this cannot happen unless the opportunity is given to everyone, unbiased and unconditionally.

Chapter 14

Human Perception, Interpretation, Understanding, and Communication of Company Democracy: Building Co-opetitive Ecosystems

New trendy buzzwords come up every few years in management and leadership, attempting to refresh and maintain old practices. In fact, management and leadership progress frequently end up in significant failure or zero contributions by those who manage and lead with old constructs and concepts, unable to research and innovate. Modern management gurus and consultants are fast on making up new buzzwords to reinventing old practices for immediate, quick, and measurable organizational profitability and productivity. The rapid changes in the business environments impact organizational management to follow the markets effectively. This leads to failure from not understanding global business situations properly. Organizational change is made by knowledge workers who succeed in today's environments and shape the future ones. They demonstrate knowledge-driven leadership and accept responsibility, provided that the organization adequately supports them. They are people with experience and expertise, seeking only a responsive environment to perform, create ideas, innovate, implement, test new products and services, and run the business efficiently and effectively. When identifying and utilizing knowledge-driven employees with modern management and leadership skills, capabilities, and competencies, democratic company culture must be in place to help and protect their freedom of thought and speech and help them contribute with their knowledge and insights.

Chapter 15

The Company Democracy Model for Human Intellectual Capitalism and Shared Value Creation: Toward Added Value and Circular Economies

People face difficulties in understanding and applying democracy and Company Democracy in practice. Democracy, as such, is difficult to define because it is so laborious to understand and perceive. Incomplete definitions, democratic rules, and regulations can have catastrophic results leading to anarchy, populism, and demagogy. Therefore, democracy and Company Democracy need protective and applicable frameworks, although too much protection runs the risk of making it less democratic. Metron Ariston (moderation is best), a Delphic maxim, may contribute to a reasonable definition of democracy and give better options for applying it effectively in practical contexts like Company Democracy. Democracy and Company Democracy in speech, actions, and different practical contexts can be demonstrated based on the shared added value produced. Shared value in business has been defined as the balance of economic value creation for the company. The target and the ultimate goal is to achieve financial success through company activities for all stakeholders. Such shared value can be seen as a creative means for meeting social requirements and a tool to develop Company Democracy. However, this activity needs continuous initiatives, insights, ideas, and innovations to respond to the risks, challenges, and requirements of a fast-changing world. Shared value is the added value created inside companies that reach society. This chapter combines the ideas of shared added value with the Company Democracy Model to present the company–society synergistic effects in a business context.

Chapter 16

Maturity Spaces for Company Democracy:
The Seven Clouds of Glory

Space is a vitally important element in a system for developing any business initiative. It defines the freedom needed for knowledge to mature, evolve, and be applied. Organizations are living systems obliged to give space to new management and leadership initiatives, theories, and practices; otherwise, they will not see any progress. The Company Democracy Model provides the space in which people can act in a democratic environment. This space can lead to meritocracy, valid knowledge, innovation, competitiveness, extroversion, and other organizational and personal advantages and development. Democracy, in turn, can be annoying to those who resist it by reducing its space, freedom, and the opportunities people deserve to have. This chapter presents a comprehensive approach to why organizations fail to learn from their mistakes. It provides a democratic Co-Evolutionary and co-opetitive framework that can significantly contribute to organizational development, as long as the minimum space is given for freedom of speech and action.

Chapter 17

The Dynamics of Company Democracy Culture:
Enlightening the Black Hole in Knowledge Management

Democracy offers the freedom for knowledge and opinions to be expressed unbiasedly, with justice and equality. However, this knowledge must be accurate, well-thought-out, and justified with facts, logic, common sense, and truth. The adaptation of the Company Democracy Model creates dynamic democratic cultures that identify and utilize the knowledge people have. More than that, it contributes to understanding what knowledge is, what true knowledge is, and how the proper knowledge grows and evolves through the Company Democracy Model levels. The model, however, can fail not due to lack of organizational knowledge and ideas or improper use of its processes but due to the lack of correct understanding or ideas and knowledge with unreasonable expectations and justification. This chapter extends beyond the Company Democracy Model and attempts to define what true knowledge is in the knowledge management discipline in which the Company Democracy Model belongs and operates.

Chapter 18

Applying the Company Democracy Model: From Theory to Practice

The Company Democracy Model comprises six levels, and its adaptation follows the Spiral Approach in a staged evolutionary process. However, the model can be adopted in several other ways based on organizational capability, maturity, management, leadership, strategy, priorities, and commitment. Therefore, the Company Democracy Model cannot impose or strongly suggest a specific adaptation process but can only recommend several from which an organization can select or combine the one to follow. Regardless of the chosen adaptation approach, it must be noted that the Company Democracy Model creates and impacts the organizational culture. Therefore, time, commitment, and support are needed to build this new culture or enhance the existing one. Change management practices can be applied in the adaptation of the Company Democracy Model but are not required. It is the leadership's power and charisma to deliver effective and inspirational management that will motivate the people and the organization toward building and functioning in a democratic organizational culture for the benefit of all.

Chapter 19

Repetition Is the Mother of Studying, Learning, and Internalization: Concluding Remarks with the Company Democracy Model and Applied Philosophy for Management and Leadership

At the beginning of the book, we have concentrated on introducing humans as part of the living system and showing with examples how it is possible to use their capacity in the best possible way. Our target has also been to show the reader the challenges and possibilities that the Company Democracy Model (CDM) can give first for individuals, groups, teams, and the whole organization. We understand that the Company Democracy Model has its potential when companies apply it continuously, as presented in Chapters 1–18. The CDM is based on our thinking with the Applied Philosophy for Management and Leadership. The model itself is constructed as a visual tool that contains many methods of using it and how to utilize it in practice. Many of the questions at the end of each chapter may be challenging to answer. It would be good if the reader of this book has a current practical situation to interpret the company's challenges and possibilities to use the Company Democracy Model inside the company. It would be even better if a project team has the right to apply the Company Democracy Model inside the company first as a pilot project and then in an actual project. We have demonstrated the benefits of using the systematic approach and applying it in practice. We have also thought that it may be an excellent way to learn if the team members go through all the three sections, ponder all their collected answers once again, and then see how new ideas emerge in their current company situation. We rely a lot on the team-based working methodology together with the Company Democracy Model.

In this chapter, we have presented six different ways to start thinking the Applied Philosophy way, and we have followed the same principles as we have shown at the end of each chapter –Chapter 19 is the bonus chapter for the reader.

APPLIED PHILOSOPHY 1

Chapter 1

Science and Theory Precede Practice: A Scientific Framework for the Applied Philosophy Approach in Management and Leadership

Executive Summary

Humans must be in focus when companies improve their business productivity, profitability, and performance. The Applied Philosophy approach in Management and Leadership places humans in the company context as living entities aligned with Business Management and Leadership Objects in the conscious experience of the company workforce. Starting from the Hellenic philosophy and drawing on more modern philosophies relevant to everyday business, the Applied Philosophy approach in Management and Leadership can harness business ontologies, taxonomies, classes, and other knowledge classification techniques to create added value in companies. New theories, approaches, and practices can be generated by interpreting knowledge from the Delphic Maxims as the basis for many new and alternative management and leadership objectives. The Holistic Concept of Man and the Circles of Mind metaphors open up the human mind and redefine Situationality by giving unique, alternative ways

DOI: 10.4324/9781003158493-2

to understand how humans, as decision-makers, behave in a company context. This chapter introduces the Applied Philosophy approach for management and leadership and provides the philosophical background needed to better understand the Company Democracy Model.

1.1 Introduction

For a long time, creating a democratic company culture has been regarded as ideal for companies that try to achieve harmony in management and leadership. Over time, this ideal has come closer for many business people and company executives searching for a democratic company culture that can be applied in practice. Bennis and Slater wrote two articles for the *Harvard Business Review Classic* series, which claim that democracy is inevitable as it has solid fundamental effects in societies (Slater, Bennis, 1990). They describe democracy as the only system that can successfully manage contemporary civilization's changing business and government demands. They also see that democracy contains the ability to prosper and provides a fresh and modern way to survive in a continuously changing society.

Bennis and Slater provide many examples of companies moving toward democratization and consider this progress to be based on a system of values, such as the following: (1) full and free communication (regardless of rank and power); (2) a reliance on consensus (rather than coercion or compromise when managing conflicts); (3) the idea that influence is based on technical competence and knowledge (rather than on the vagaries of personal whims or prerogatives of power); (4) an atmosphere that permits and even encourages emotional expression (as well as task-oriented behavior); (5) a fundamental human bias (one that accepts the inevitability of conflict between organizations and the individual, but is willing to cope with and mediate this conflict on rational grounds) (cf. Slater, Bennis, 1990).

Applying such values to an ordinary business world can be complex and problematic. The main point is that companies have to create a democratic company culture first, which will help their employees behave democratically after that. Leaders must perceive, interpret, understand, and internalize the democratic company culture before applying it in the organization. Likewise, employees must first learn what democracy means and how to use it in their daily activities.

Democracy in a business context does not have to be an ideological concept. It can only be a way of working together by sincerely respecting one another. Respect is an easy way to communicate because it effectively allows everyone to share visions, ideas, knowledge, and solutions democratically.

The practical meaning of democracy must be understood at all company levels, outside the business world, and throughout society.

The system of values that forms the basis of democratization in Bennis and Slater's description is connected partly to the systemic view of a living system (Miller, 1978). Their reports raise many how-do-you-do-it (implementation) questions, such as:

- How do you keep the system in operation through full and free communication, regardless of rank and power?
- How do you reach and improve the reliance on consensus in the decision-making process?
- How do you appreciate how technical competence and knowledge can influence change without any whims or prerogatives of power?
- How do you encourage people to express their emotional intelligence and their task-oriented behavior?
- How do you minimize the inevitable conflict between organizations and individuals? (cf. Slater, Bennis, 1990)

According to Bennis and Slater, democracy is the only organizational system compatible with perpetual change (Slater, Bennis, 1990). All the values that characterize an organization are based on individual behavior. Therefore, this chapter starts by regarding the human being as a holistic system in a situation. According to Rauhala, human beings can be described through a metaphor, viz., the Holistic Concept of Man (HCM) (Rauhala, 1995), and can be regarded as a living system within another living system, i.e., a living company or organization (Miller, 1978, Samuelson, 1978, Osterlund, 1994, Markopoulos, Vanharanta, 2015). Therefore, this chapter presents how basic democratic principles and other essential democratization issues are applied to various organizations and companies. It also explores how management and leadership used in philosophy can support the practical description of the Company Democracy Model (CDM). The CDM is the first outcome of the Scientific Framework of Applied Philosophy in Management and Leadership. Other results presented in this chapter are based on the above fundamental principles.

1.2 Creation of the Scientific Framework

The scientific framework covers the general areas of 'Episteme,' 'Sophia,' 'Techne,' and 'Phronesis.' It applies various sciences, creates a robust theoretical framework based on different management and leadership theories, uses available technical experience and skills, and produces, in the end, a practical understanding of democratic business management and leadership.

1.2.1 Scientific Background ('Episteme')

Episteme provides the creation of a solid, human-focused base to exploit the knowledge that derives from philosophy wisely. The ancient Hellenic civilization gave humanity essentially constructive elements and materials to perceive and understand human behavior and the ideal image of a man. Likewise, the ancient Hellenic philosophy continued to be developed through the ages and extended with several modern philosophies' contributions toward a much broader understanding of humanity. This chapter uses Hellenic philosophy and contemporary philosophy to create a kernel for democratic management and leadership (cf. Parke, Wormell, 1956, cf. Buckingham et al., 2011), and the scientific background places the human decision-maker in the living system as an entity. Taking this 'episteme' as the basis of this thinking results in new teachable knowledge regarding management and leadership efforts. In this context, we call this approach the Applied Philosophy for Management and Leadership.

1.2.2 Theoretical Background ('Sophia')

'Sophia' helps develop the reasoning concerning the universal truth. This chapter uses mainly the theories of living systems, systems thinking, behavior, motivation, management, leadership, economics, knowledge creation, and learning. These theories have been selected to construct a stable kernel for the Company Democracy Model to be understood and applied effectively. The theoretical methods used belong mainly to qualitative research. Ontologies have been created by using metaphors to understand better the different Business Management and Leadership Objects (BMLOs). Reasoning with this approach is supported by soft systems thinking when evaluating ontologies, taxonomies, and construed facts with multiple concepts inside each other. In this way, we, the authors, have used the currently available literature, retrieved information, knowledge discovered, and wisdom acquired/captured from all the theories mentioned above to develop the Company Democracy Model implementation framework.

1.2.3 Technological Background ('Techne')

Through 'techne,' we understand that, in this stage, specific skills are needed without the use of any particular technology. Technology-based ideas and results can easily be applied and evolved later with modern computer technology, decision support purposes, expert systems, and artificial intelligence. The Internet, big data, fuzzy logic, neural networks, simulation, and situation-aware computing can help this purpose today and in the future.

1.2.4 Practical Background ('Phronesis')

'Phronesis' combines practical wisdom with skills, capability, and competence concerning rational thinking. This chapter also draws heavily on the authors' experience with the above-mentioned scientific, theoretical, methodological, and technical skills, the capability, and the competence to understand BMLOs in a company context. This approach leads to actions that can provide the desired effects, i.e., to help managers and leaders in their essential decision-making activities.

1.3 Background Philosophy

An essential source of knowledge, which has contributed significantly to humanity's development, is found in Hellenic civilization's Delphic maxims. The Delphic maxims are aphorisms said to have been handed to the god Apollo at Delphi (Parke, Wormell, 1956). The maxims are 147 commandments, composed in the sixth century BCE at the Oracle of Delphi. They convey much of the wisdom and teachings of ancient Hellenes in concise and laconic sentences. The Delphi Oracle, on the slopes of Mount Parnassus, said to be home to Pegasus, was built at the place considered to be the 'Navel of the Earth' or the center of the world. The maxims themselves are also known as the 'Commandments of the Seven Wise Men' written by ancient Greece's seven sages (Solon of Athens, Chilon of Sparta, Thales of Miletus, Bias of Priene, Cleobulus of Lindos, Pittacus of Mytilene, and Periander of Corinth). The 147 maxims, which consist of no more than four words each, carry deep philosophical meanings, making their classification quite complicated depending on how they are interpreted.

The Delphic maxims analysis generates practical knowledge, characterized as the origin of the Applied Philosophy for Management and Leadership. In the same sense, the Holistic Concept of Man (HCM), a philosophical metaphor described by the Finnish philosopher and psychologist Rauhala (Rauhala, 1995), integrates the meanings of the Delphic maxims with a definition of a mentally oriented 'knowledge-based engine.' The HCM metaphor consists of body, mind, and situation (Rauhala, 1995). Thus, the three dimensions of the HCM, representing the actor or decision-maker's modes of existence, are (1) Corporeality, (2) Consciousness, and (3) Situationality (Figure 1.1).

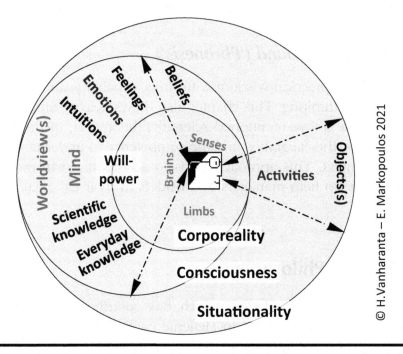

Figure 1.1 The HCM metaphor with mental/physical contrast (cf. Rauhala, 1986, 1995, Vanharanta, 2003, 2021).

The three modes of existence are intertwined with each other, forming a holistic entity, where the wholeness of interactive methods builds up a "regulative situational circuit" (Rauhala, 1995). *Corporeality* maintains the fundamental processes of emergent existence, expressed as the physical activities of a human being. In particular, the human brain and sensory organs are essential in conveying objects and concepts to the decision-maker as meanings in a specific situation. *Consciousness* stands for experiences and perceptions. It enhances the understanding of various phenomena, both inside and outside of oneself. Human beings use their outer and inner senses to receive physical signals from the environment in a particular situation, providing the Consciousness with meaningful content, i.e., a conscious experience. Perceiving and understanding the object–concept relationships leads to the emergence of a set of meanings available for use in the decision-making process. *Situationality* is the decision-maker's relevant relations with the outer world in its multifaceted plural dimensionality. The situational components are concrete or ideal; the former includes the external world, i.e., nature, buildings, technological equipment, hardware, and software. The latter consists of the inner world, i.e., human values, norms, and experienced social relationships.

However, the idea of the human being in a specific situation as a totality (Rauhala, 1995) is not a good metaphor on its own within the management and leadership context. The metaphor lacks the latest research findings on the unconscious part of the human brain, while it is also too simple for further use in terms of specific targets. However, it has a vital Situationality component describing the many connections and relationships in human life. Baars (1997) has combined psychology with brain science and the old conception of the human mind to create "the workspace of the mind." This totality is explained through the metaphor of the theater, where the self as an agent and an observer behaves as if on the stage. Close to the theatre stage is the brain's unconscious part ('the audience') divided into four main areas: the motivational system, the automatic systems, the interpreting system, and the memory system.

The spotlight controller, context, and theater director also belong to the totality in this metaphor. A combination of the HCM and Baars' theater metaphor has led to a new and comprehensive/useful metaphor, viz., the Circles of Mind (CoM) metaphor (Vanharanta, 2003, 2014). The CoM metaphor was also redesigned/updated in 2014 as a physical entity for many practical purposes (Figure 1.2).

The metaphor and the physical entity have led to the idea of brain-based systems that contain the physical body, following the Cartesian mind–body relationships, i.e., as a thinking substance and an extended substance (cf. Maslin, 2001, cf. Vanharanta, Kantola, Karwowski, 2005).

'Res Cogitans' ('thinking substance') was evident, consisting of the four main parts of the critical brain processes that affect the conscious experience on stage. In turn, 'Res Extensa' ('extended substance') represents the other physical dimension of the human being (i.e., the body) used on the stage. Vanharanta, Pihlanto, and Chang have shown how the decision-maker's holistic concept can be applied in strategic decision support systems in a hyperknowledge environment (Vanharanta, Pihlanto, Chang, 1996). Vanharanta and Salminen, in turn, used the metaphor in computerized decision support design (Salminen, Vanharanta, 2007) to explore its abilities and applications.

This chapter brings the different BMLOs to the conscious experience on the stage, to be perceived and understood from different angles and viewpoints, thereby giving a holistic view of both the current and anticipated future conscious experience. Adding many of these personal, individual views and perceptions results in the collective understanding of these BMLOs, which are also fundamental challenges for individuals and organizations developing a democratic company culture.

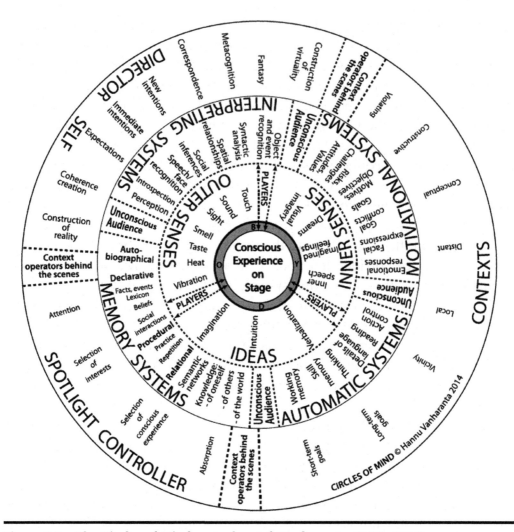

Figure 1.2   The Circles of Mind metaphor (cf. Vanharanta, 2003, 2014).

When the human being's conscious experience on the stage consists of BMLOs, we refer to this combination as a situation-based Applied Philosophy for Management and Leadership.

1.4 The Delphic Maxims and the Circles of Mind

The Delphic maxims provide content and commandments to 'Res Cogitans' *and* 'Res Extensa' when these two different philosophical perspectives are brought together. The three main maxims of ancient Hellenic wisdom can easily be part of the conscious experience on stage. The most famous of these maxims is 'know thyself,' which focuses the thinking substance on the person himself or herself. For someone to understand and apply the Delphic maxims, it is vital first to understand him/herself, that is, to seek 'Gnothi Seauton,' the Delphic maxim for self-awareness. People must 'know themselves'; indeed, this is the most important factor for managers and leaders to understand themselves better over time.

Through this thinking, the whole brain capacity should be used, i.e., each of the four different sections of the human brain's unconscious part, together with the conscious part, created by the human's inner and outer senses. Thus, the situation or reality is understood and perceived holistically. The Delphic maxims also provide commandments on how people should behave in different situations. 'Nothing in excess' offers fundamental recommendations on how people should see both 'Res Cogitans' and 'Res Extensa' so that the whole entity operates effectively in a sustainable way. 'Everything in moderation,' / 'Be careful what you promise/wish for,' which is the third central construct in the Delphic maxims, can be translated in many ways. However, this construct presents an overall recommendation for different situations in which people find themselves in management and leadership.

In situations involving managers and leaders, BMLOs are always part of their Situationality. In turn, business situations change according to the decisions that managers and leaders make in their activities. First, managers and leaders pay attention in a certain way, then focus on the BMLOs at hand, make perceptions, interpret the situation regarding the objects, understanding them and their relations and interrelationships, and cultivate knowledge before finally making their decisions. Through their conscious experience, they gain daily expertise and increase their long-term wisdom in business management and leadership. All activities happen in their future accessible area through their productivity activities and their use of latency (cf. Markopoulos, Vanharanta, 2017).

The Delphic maxims' three basic statements open up a window for each manager and leader: 'know yourself,' 'nothing in excess,' and 'everything in moderation' (the Aristotelian Golden Mean). Ideal managers and leaders do not exist, but the path to an ideal is worth following. The Finnish philosopher von Wright clearly describes in his book titled *Freedom and Determination* that everything depends on personal characteristics: capacity, skills, capability, willpower, competence, maturity, duties, and wants (von Wright, 1980).

1.5 Applied Systems Science

Systems science offers the possibility to integrate essential viewpoints of inputs, processes, and outputs into the management and leadership context (cf. Jackson, 2004). In a living system, there is only information, material, and energy as inputs. Then, there are the system processes whose outcome is also information, material, and energy. The vital factor to note is what is inside the system boundary. There are various systems and subsystems, with their inner variables controlling the activities. A system boundary is operated by (1) information and communication, (2) command and control, (3) maintenance and support, and (4) operational and production sections. Inside the command and control section is the decider (cf. Miller, 1978, Samuelson, 1978, Osterlund, 1994).

In management and leadership, all these supporting activities within the boundary must remain very clear in managers' and leaders' hands and minds. We have adapted the living system and its components to the business context and created a model similar to the live systems model with inputs, processes, and outputs (Figure 1.3).

According to Figure 1.3 and the democratic viewpoints of Bennis and Slater, the following vital issues should be considered:

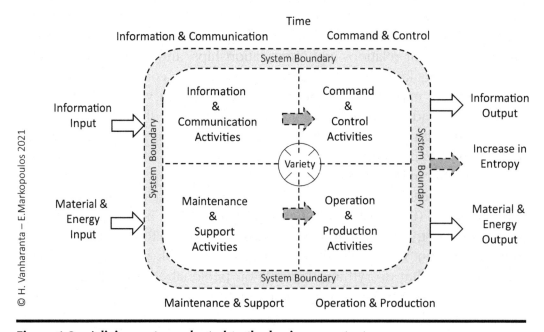

Figure 1.3   A living system adapted to the business context.

- The information flow must be kept active, i.e., communication should be clear, free, and accessible (cf. Slater, Bennis, 1990: "full and free communication, regardless of rank and power").
- Command, control, and decision-making in all activities through democratic processes (cf. Slater, Bennis, 1990: "reach and improve the reliance on consensus in the decision-making practice").
- Ensure adequate maintenance and support concerning the workforce (cf. Slater, Bennis, 1990: "encourage people to express their emotional intelligence and their task-oriented behavior").
- See that all operations and actual production activities are efficient and effective, with high overall performance and low entropy (cf. Slater, Bennis, 1990: "appreciate technical competence and knowledge to influence change processes without any whims or prerogatives of power").

Everything is observed in the system with time. Time is the most critical asset, together with the company personnel. Over time, the object, i.e., the company, changes due to decision-makers' decisions.

1.6 The Compiled Methods with Applied Philosophy

The Applied Philosophy approach has a significant socioeconomic impact, which is not easy to measure and evaluate quantitatively. It takes much more than business sense to identify the tremendous benefits that philosophy can offer to society and the economy, once effectively transformed into business management and leadership processes and practices. The great civilizations of the past contributed to the most fundamental elements on which organizations can build today's and tomorrow's achievements. Anything created in the past was for a reason, a cause, practicality, a justification, and a return, not only for the creators but also for society and the economy. Humanity evolved due to philosophy-driven thinking in the community's progress and prosperity under shared drives and ideals.

Shared value has been high on the list of expected outcomes on everything that has ever been attempted, designed, and developed. Therefore, trying to understand the thinking of the Hellenic civilization and others is very important when developing sustainable business models that can stand the test of time. Advances in developing classification techniques, processes, and models utilize the legacy left to us by our ancestors and provide a deeper understanding of integrating this knowledge and wisdom in today's society and economy.

Using such a magnificent wealth of expertise from the past can only be achieved if the mindset of those analyzing and using it, turning it into business practices, and applying it, is not far from the philosophy of their ancestors. Without such an attitude, this knowledge and wisdom, which could solve many of the problems in the modern economy and society, will not be utilized effectively despite the advances in technology and communications. Today's managers and leaders value business more than they value our society, without recognizing that society is an integral part of the economy. In such a case, no classification of any such knowledge and wisdom will be achieved effectively for everyone's benefit. However, in Figure 1.4, we share our thinking about how we can systemically integrate Applied Philosophy from Delphic maxims into the generation of wisdom and shared value creation for society. The integrators are always humans with their capacity, skills, capability, competence, maturity, duties, and wishes/needs.

The main idea of the process revealed in Figure 1.4 is that people first have to develop themselves to show their skills, competencies, and wisdom. The three Delphic maxims are the starting points for Applied Philosophy in Management and Leadership. The Holistic Concept of Man (Rauhala, 1995) supports ideas from the Hellenic philosophy, by introducing the human being's critical Situationality. The Workspace of the Mind (Baars, 1997) and the Circles of Mind (Vanharanta, 2003), in turn, provide the conscious experience of diverse management and leadership objects for shared decision-making. In the end, managers and leaders show how competent and wise they are in their decision-making and how well they served and supported their society, organization, company, and co-workers, i.e., their workforce, inside the Co-Evolutionary democratic environment.

To "Know yourself" follows the basic ideas of focusing, interpreting, perceiving, understanding, creating, activating skills and capabilities to reach high-level competence and wisdom. The content of the Circles of Mind metaphor extends "the deep understanding" of human behavior. The third dimension, "Nothing in excess," supports the systemic view, feedback, variety, low entropy, sustainable growth and development, high quality, lean and agile activities, added value, and shared added value creation.

With variety, it is possible to measure complexity (number of possible states in a system), and with entropy, it is possible to describe the created disorder in a system. The overall target is to minimize complexity and reduce confusion to create an effective organization (cf. Stafford Beer, 1993).

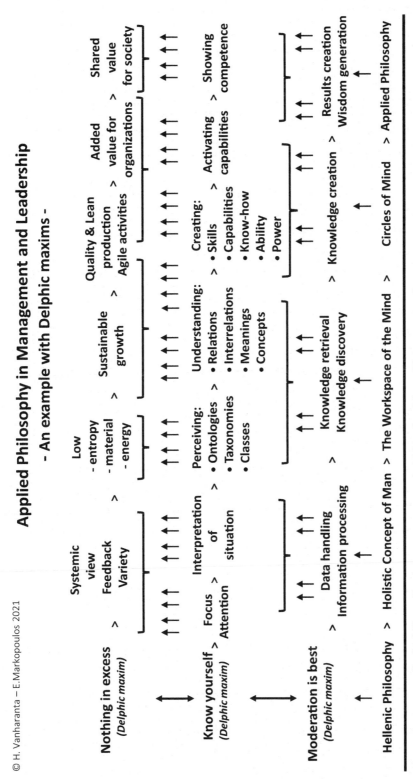

Figure 1.4 Applied philosophy in management and leadership with an example.

1.7 Summary

The Applied Philosophy approach for management and leadership shows practical ways to use philosophy as a start-up framework for human growth in a Co-Evolutionary way within the business context. Company democracy, however, is a challenging philosophical concept. Therefore, evaluating the extent of Company Democracy utilizing several different characteristics can only be done using many methodologies and practices, as democracy is, by nature, relative and situational.

This chapter presented how Applied Philosophy can benefit management and leadership. More than that, it demonstrated how this philosophical approach could be applied to the democratization process inside companies and organizations. It also addressed issues related to democratization processes, concluding that the only way to start developing democracy within business management and leadership is to apply the ancient Hellenic culture and philosophy.

This chapter also demonstrated how to reach and improve the reliance on consensus in decision-making practice by using the three fundamental statements of the Delphic maxims and adding a situational understanding of the Business Management and Leadership Objects in managers' 'conscious experience on stage.' Furthermore, the chapter showed how to inspire the workforce to innovate and rethink business processes through their skills, capability, competencies, leading to the creation of new knowledge and wisdom using the workforce's technical skills to benefit the company's targets, objectives, and goals. It also described how to keep democratic cooperative management and leadership system operational through full communication between all employees, regardless of their position, rank, and power.

Being part of a democratic system, managers and leaders activate all the systemic processes inside a company or any organization for the benefit of all. For both humans and company or organizational strategies, the systemic view refers to the beginning of Applied Philosophy thinking in a democratic context. Applied Philosophy offers people the right to express their emotional and intellectual intelligence and assets while benefiting themselves and their company. Applied Philosophy for Management and Leadership positively supports this kind of orientation. Through the described methodology, it is self-evident that the slogan "One Voice and Many Insights" accurately represents that each person working in a democratic company can give his/her ideas and understanding for the common good.

Questions for Review and Discussions

The system of values that forms the basis of democratization in Bennis and Slater's description is connected partly to the systemic view of a living system. Their views raise many how-do-you-do-it (implementation) questions.

How would you answer the following questions?

1. Does your company keep its business system in operation through full and free communication, regardless of rank and power?
   1.1 If YES, how is this done? Explain the process, give some success stories, and what do you think can be improved.
   1.2 If NO, please explain why that is and what can be done to reverse this situation.
2. Does your company attempt to improve the reliance on consensus in the decision-making process?
   2.1 If YES, how is this done? Explain the process, give some success stories, and what do you think can be improved.
   2.2 If NO, please explain why that is and what can be done to reverse this situation.
3. How do you appreciate how technical competence and knowledge can influence change inside your company without any whims or prerogatives of power? Justify your answer and provide examples.
4. Does your organization encourage people to express their emotional intelligence and their task-oriented behavior?
   4.1 If YES, how is this done? Explain the process, give some success stories, and what do you think can be improved.
   4.2 If NO, please explain why that is and what can be done to reverse this situation.
5. Does your company have processes/mechanisms to minimize the inevitable conflict between organizations and individuals?
   5.1 If YES, how is this done? Explain the process, give some success stories, and what do you think can be improved.
   5.2 If NO, please explain why that is and what can be done to reverse this situation.
6. Can you give an example of 'Situationality'? Explain how, when, and why.
7. Can you give an example of 'Corporeality'? Explain how, when, and why.
8. On a scale of 1 (low) to 10 (high), can you define/measure how committed your company's workforce is?

8.1 If the score is under 7, what are the reasons for this, and what can be done to improve it?

8.2 If the score is above 7, what are the reasons for this, and what can be done to sustain it or improve it?

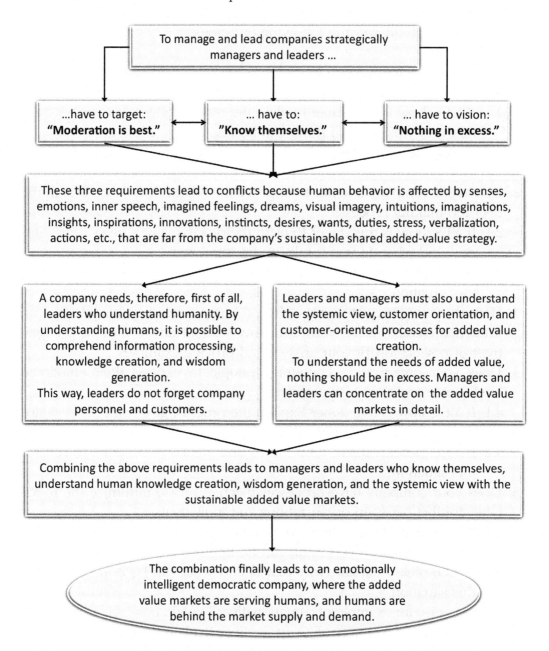

To manage and lead companies strategically managers and leaders …

…have to target: **"Moderation is best."**

… have to: **"Know themselves."**

… have to vision: **"Nothing in excess."**

These three requirements lead to conflicts because human behavior is affected by senses, emotions, inner speech, imagined feelings, dreams, visual imagery, intuitions, imaginations, insights, inspirations, innovations, instincts, desires, wants, duties, stress, verbalization, actions, etc., that are far from the company's sustainable shared added-value strategy.

A company needs, therefore, first of all, leaders who understand humanity. By understanding humans, it is possible to comprehend information processing, knowledge creation, and wisdom generation.
This way, leaders do not forget company personnel and customers.

Leaders and managers must also understand the systemic view, customer orientation, and customer-oriented processes for added value creation.
To understand the needs of added value, nothing should be in excess. Managers and leaders can concentrate on the added value markets in detail.

Combining the above requirements leads to managers and leaders who know themselves, understand human knowledge creation, wisdom generation, and the systemic view with the sustainable added value markets.

The combination finally leads to an emotionally intelligent democratic company, where the added value markets are serving humans, and humans are behind the market supply and demand.

© Vanharanta H., Markopoulos, E., Applied Philosophy for Management and Leadership, 2021.

Figure 1Q   Chart for Question 13.

9. Does your company apply individual holistic thinking in the business context?

   9.1 If YES, how is this done? Explain the process, give some success stories, and what do you think can be improved.

   9.2 If NO, please explain why that is and what can be done to reverse this situation.

10. Is it possible for you to place yourself with the Circles of Mind metaphor, and why?

    10.1 If YES, can you describe a journey?

    10.2 If NO, what prevents you from this?

11. How do you understand the fundamental three Delphic maxims in practice? Give examples of personal or professional experiences.

12. Do you think a scientific framework can help you understand the systemic view in business better than before?

    12.1 If YES, what makes you think that, and how will it help you?

    12.2 If NO, what makes you think that and why it won't help you?

13. An emotionally intelligent company does not study what people say but finds out the main motives: how people behave, what interests and inspires them, what are their wants and duties, or what scares them. The board, managers, and leaders of the company should be interested in the people who are in the company and also how people and customers behave in the market.

    13.1 Utilize the chart of Figure 1Q to evaluate the Holistic Concept of Man and Circles of Mind metaphors in the business context. How is it possible to create an emotionally intelligent company?

References

Baars, B. J., 1997. *In the Theater of Consciousness: The Workplace of the Mind.* Oxford University Press, New York.

Beer, S., 1993. *Designing Freedom.* House of Anansi Press Limited, Toronto, Canada.

Buckingham, W., King, Peter J., Burnham, D., Weeks, M., Hill, C., and Marenbon, J., 2011. *The Philosophy Book.* Dorling Kindersley Limited, London.

Jackson, M. C., 2004. *Systems Thinking: Creative Holism for Managers.* Wiley, England, UK.

Markopoulos, E. and Vanharanta, H., 2015. The Company Democracy Model for the Development of Intellectual Human Capitalism for Shared Value. Elsevier, *Procedia Manufacturing*, 3, 603–610. https://doi.org/10.1016/j.promfg.2015.07.277.

Markopoulos E. and Vanharanta H., 2017. Delphic Maxims Based Applied Philosophy for Business and Governance Management. In: Kantola J., Barath T., Nazir S., Andre T. (eds.) *Advances in Human Factors, Business Management, Training, and Education. Advances in Intelligent Systems and Computing*, Vol. 498. Springer, Cham, Springer, July 2016, 33–45. https://doi.org/10.1007/978-3-319-4 2070-7_4.

Maslin, K. T., 2001. *An Introduction to the Philosophy of Mind.* Blackwell Publishers, Inc., Malden, MA.

Miller, J. G., 1978. *Living Systems.* McGraw-Hill Inc, New York.

Osterlund, J., 1994. *Competence Management by Informatics Systems in R&D Work.* Royal Institute of Technology, Stockholm.

Parke, H. and Wormell, D., 1956. *The Delphic Oracle*, Vol. 1. Basil Blackwell, Oxford.

Rauhala, L., 1986. Ihmiskäsitys ihmistyössä (Finnish Edition), trans: *The Conception of Human Being in Helping People.* Gaudeamus, Helsinki.

Rauhala, L., 1995. Tajunnan itsepuolustus (Finnish Edition), trans: *Self-Defence of the Consciousness.* Yliopistopaino, Helsinki.

Salminen, T. and Vanharanta, H., 2007. The Holistic Interaction between the Computer and the Active Human Being. In: Jacko, J. (ed.) Proceedings of the 12th International Conference on Human-Computer Interaction (HCI), Beijing, China, Part I. LNCS 4550. 252–261.

Samuelson, K., 1978. General Information Systems Theory in Design, Modeling, and Development. *Information Science in Action*, 304–320. NATO Advanced Study Institute. Nijhoff, Boston – The Hague.

Slater, P. and Bennis, W., 1990. Democracy is Inevitable. *Harvard Business Review*, 68 (5), 167–176.

Vanharanta, H., 2003. Circles of Mind. In: Identity and Diversity in Organizations: Building Bridges in Europe Programme, the XI European Congress on Work and Organizational Psychology, Lisbon, Portugal. 14–17.

Vanharanta, H., 2014. Redesign of the Circle of Mind Metaphor.

Vanharanta, H., 2021. Redesign of the Holistic Concept of Man Metaphor.

Vanharanta, H., Pihlanto, P., and Chang, A-M., 1996. Strategic Decision Support Systems in a Hyperknowledge Environment and the Holistic Concept of the Decision-Maker. In: *The Art and Science of Decision-Making, Turku.* Abo Akademi University Press, Turku, Finland. 243–258.

Vanharanta, H., Kantola, J., and Karwowski, W., 2005. A Paradigm of Co-evolutionary Management: Creative Tension and Brain-based Company Development Systems. In: 11th International Conference on Human-Computer Interaction, Las Vegas, Nevada.

von Wright, G. H., 1980. Freedom and Determination. Amsterdam: North-Holland Publishing Company, *Acta Philosophica Fennica*, 31 (1), 13–85.

Chapter 2

Delphic Maxims' Ontology-Based Taxonomies for Applied Philosophy: An Interpretation of the Ancient Hellenic Philosophy in Business and Governance Management and Leadership

Executive Summary

Knowledge analysis and representation define situations before activities get executed. Knowledge engineering precedes knowledge management to construct the knowledge elements that can be used in management. Over the years, various techniques have been developed for knowledge recognition, elicitation, acquisition, analysis, engineering, and management. As problems become more complex over time, the synergies of knowledge disciplines become critical and necessary. To tackle this complexity, it is also essential to seek knowledge in non-trivial sources via root cause analysis models on

DOI: 10.4324/9781003158493-3

philosophical challenges that usually hide the answers to societal and economic problems. This chapter presents a triadic categorization approach of the Delphic maxims based on ontologies, taxonomies, and classes. It reveals their contribution to modern business and governance management through the Hellenic contribution to the global economy, civilization, and humanity.

2.1 Introduction

Knowledge is the keyword for success, development, prosperity, achievement, progress, creativity, wealth, and happiness. Knowledge is a crucial success element through which people know, recognize, accept, and understand their power. Knowledge drives all progressive activities, initiatives, projects, processes, and anything that can be considered a step ahead in professional and personal development (Markopoulos, Vanharanta, 2014).

Furthermore, fundamental knowledge is power, and power is freedom compared to ignorance, which can be seen as slavery. Those who know are free to reach the truth and create with the truth, far from illusions. Humans cannot possess anything that they do not understand. As the circle of knowledge grows, so does the circumference of darkness around it, verifying Socrates' words, "This one thing I know, that I know nothing" (Bowden, 2005) and, on the other hand, knowing and knowledge alone are not enough. Knowledge is nothing more than a tool, and tools can only be useful in the hands of the person who holds them wisely. Knowledge can contribute both creatively and destructively unless developed and used ethically, and not only legitimately (Markopoulos, 2013).

Although knowledge is undoubtedly the recipe for success for anything people do, it has always been challenging to define what knowledge is and what it is not. Once such a distinction can be achieved, even to a degree, then anything related to knowledge can be significantly improved, starting from the knowledge elicitation process to the knowledge utilization and capitalization. The distance between knowledge creation and knowledge utilization is tremendous. Many steps interfere in knowledge interpretation for its transformation into something that can indeed be capitalized on successfully, effectively, and rewardingly (Markopoulos, Vanharanta, 2015). Developing more effective classification models and methods to understand humanity by understanding various civilizations and generating the proper knowledge is more than necessary. The progressive continuation of the modern society and economy needs to learn from past knowledge and utilize it to progress in the future.

2.2 Analyzing the Delphic Maxims

A significant source of knowledge that contributes remarkably to humanity's development is found in the Delphic maxims (Parke, Wormel, 1956) of the Hellenic civilization. The Delphic maxims are a set of 147 aphorisms (Table 2.1), providing a framework for an honest, worthy way of living. They are suggestions for righteous living, not quite commandments as others call them but rather strong recommendations. They are guidelines and advice, but no absolutes.

Table 2.1 The 147 Delphic Maxims in Greek and English

No.	Greek	English
1.	Ἕπου θεῷ	Follow God
2.	Νόμῳ πείθου	Obey the law
3.	Θεοὺς σέβου	Respect the Gods
4.	Γονεῖς αἰδοῦ	Respect your parents
5.	Ἡττῶ ὑπὸ δικαίου	Be ruled by justice
6.	Γνῶθι μαθών	Know by learning
7.	Ἀκούσας νόει	Listen and understand
8.	Σαυτὸν ἴσθι	Know yourself, also, γνῶθι σεαυτόν
9.	Γαμεῖν μέλλε	Set out to be married
10.	Καιρὸν γνῶθι	Know your opportunity
11.	Φρόνει θνητά	Think mortal thoughts
12.	Ξένος ὢν ἴσθι	Know when you are an outsider
13.	Ἑστίαν τίμα	Honour the hearth
14.	Ἄρχε σεαυτοῦ	Be in control of yourself
15.	Φίλοις βοήθει	Help your friends
16.	Θυμοῦ κράτει	Control your temper
17.	Φρόνησιν ἄσκει	Exercise prudence
18.	Πρόνοιαν τίμα	Honour forethought
19.	Ὅρκῳ μὴ χρῶ	Do not use an oath
20.	Φιλίαν ἀγάπα	Embrace friendship
21.	Παιδείας ἀντέχου	Cling to education
22.	Δόξαν δίωκε	Pursue honour
23.	Σοφίαν ζήλου	Be eager for wisdom
24.	Καλὸν εὖ λέγε	Praise the good

(Continued)

Table 2.1 (Continued)   The 147 Delphic Maxims in Greek and English

No.	Greek	English
25.	Ψέγε μηδένα	Find fault with no one
26.	Ἐπαίνει ἀρετήν	Praise virtue
27.	Πρᾶττε δίκαια	Practice what is just
28.	Φίλοις εὐνόει	Show favor to your friends
29.	Ἐχθροὺς ἀμύνου	Ward off your enemies
30.	Εὐγένειαν ἄσκει	Exercise nobility of character
31.	Κακίας ἀπέχου	Shun evil
32.	Κοινὸς γίνου	Be impartial
33.	Ἴδια φύλαττε	Guard what is yours
34.	Ἀλλοτρίων ἀπέχου	Shun what belongs to others
35.	Ἄκουε πάντα	Listen to all
36.	Εὔφημος ἴσθι	Be fair of speech
37.	Φίλῳ χαρίζου	Look after your own
38.	Μηδὲν ἄγαν	Nothing in excess
39.	Χρόνου φείδου	Save time
40.	Ὅρα τὸ μέλλον	Look to the future
41.	Ὕβριν μίσει	Despise insolence
42.	Ἱκέτας αἰδοῦ	Have respect for suppliants
43.	Πᾶσιν ἁρμόζου	Be accommodating to all
44.	Υἱοὺς παίδευε	Educate your sons
45.	Ἔχων χαρίζου	If you have, give
46.	Δόλον φοβοῦ	Fear deceit
47.	Εὐλόγει πάντας	Speak well of everyone
48.	Φιλόσοφος γίνου	Be a seeker of wisdom
49.	Ὅσια κρῖνε	Choose what is holy
50.	Γνοὺς πρᾶττε	Act from knowledge
51.	Φόνου ἀπέχου	Shun murder
52.	Εὔχου δυνατά	Pray for what is possible
53.	Σοφοῖς χρῶ	Consult the wise
54.	Ἦθος δοκίμαζε	Test your character
55.	Λαβὼν ἀπόδος	If you have received, give back
56.	Ὑφορῶ μηδένα	Look down on none
57.	Τέχνῃ χρῶ	Make use of expertise
58.	Ὃ μέλλεις, δός	Give what you aim to give

(Continued)

Table 2.1 (Continued)   The 147 Delphic Maxims in Greek and English

No.	Greek	English
59.	Εὐεργεσίας τίμα	Honor generosity
60.	Φθόνει μηδενί	Envy no one
61.	Φυλακῇ πρόσεχε	Be on your guard
62.	Ἐλπίδα αἴνει	Praise hope
63.	Διαβολὴν μίσει	Despise slander
64.	Δικαίως κτῶ	Gain possessions justly
65.	Ἀγαθοὺς τίμα	Honor good people
66.	Κριτὴν γνῶθι	Know who is the judge
67.	Γάμους κράτει	Control your marriages
68.	Τύχην νόμιζε	Recognize fortune
69.	Ἐγγύην φεῦγε	Don't make risky promises
70.	Ἁπλῶς διαλέγου	Speak plainly
71.	Ὁμοίοις χρῶ	Associate with likeminded people
72.	Δαπανῶν ἄρχου	Control your expenditure
73.	Κτώμενος ἥδου	Be happy with what you have
74.	Αἰσχύνην σέβου	Revere a sense of shame
75.	Χάριν ἐκτέλει	Repay favors
76.	Εὐτυχίαν εὔχου	Pray for success
77.	Τύχην στέργε	Embrace your fate
78.	Ἀκούων ὅρα	Listen and observe
79.	Ἐργάζου κτητά	Work for what you can own
80.	Ἔριν μίσει	Despise strife
81.	Ὄνειδος ἔχθαιρε	Detest disgrace
82.	Γλῶτταν ἴσχε	Restrain your tongue
83.	Ὕβριν ἀμύνου	Shun violence
84.	Κρῖνε δίκαια	Make just judgments
85.	Χρῶ χρήμασιν	Use what you have
86.	Ἀδωροδόκητος δίκαζε	Judge incorruptibly
87.	Αἰτιῶ παρόντα	Make accusations face to face
88.	Λέγε εἰδώς	Speak from knowledge
89.	Βίας μὴ ἔχου	Have no truck with violence
90.	Ἀλύπως βίου	Live free of sorrow
91.	Ὁμίλει πράως	Have kindly interactions
92.	Πέρας ἐπιτέλει μὴ ἀποδειλιῶν	Complete the race and don't chicken out

(Continued)

Table 2.1 (Continued)   The 147 Delphic Maxims in Greek and English

No.	Greek	English
93.	Φιλοφρόνει πᾶσιν	Deal kindly with everyone
94.	Υἱοῖς μὴ καταρῶ	Do not curse your sons
95.	Γυναικὸς ἄρχε	Control your wife
96.	Σεαυτὸν εὖ ποίει	Benefit yourself
97.	Εὐπροσήγορος γίνου	Be courteous
98.	Ἀποκρίνου ἐν καιρῷ	Respond in a timely manner
99.	Πόνει μετ' εὐκλείας	Struggle for glory
100.	Πρᾶττε ἀμετανοήτως	Act decisively
101.	Ἁμαρτάνων μετανόει	Repent your errors
102.	Ὀφθαλμοῦ κράτει	Control your eye
103.	Βουλεύου χρόνῳ	Give timely counsel
104.	Πρᾶττε συντόμως	Act without hesitation
105.	Φιλίαν φύλαττε	Guard friendship
106.	Εὐγνώμων γίνου	Be grateful
107.	Ὁμόνοιαν δίωκε	Pursue harmony
108.	Ἄρρητον κρύπτε	Keep secret what should be secret
109.	Τὸ κρατοῦν φοβοῦ	Fear what rules
110.	Τὸ συμφέρον θηρῶ	Pursue what is profitable
111.	Καιρὸν προσδέχου	Accept due measure
112.	Ἔχθρας διάλυε	Dissolve enmities
113.	Γῆρας προσδέχου	Accept old age
114.	Ἐπὶ ῥώμῃ μὴ καυχῶ	Do not boast about power
115.	Εὐφημίαν ἄσκει	Exercise (religious) silence
116.	Ἀπέχθειαν φεῦγε	Shun hatred
117.	Πλούτει δικαίως	Acquire wealth justly
118.	Δόξαν μὴ λεῖπε	Do not abandon honour
119.	Κακίαν μίσει	Despise evil
120.	Κινδύνευε φρονίμως	Take sensible risks
121.	Μανθάνων μὴ κάμνε	Never tire of learning
122.	Φειδόμενος μὴ λεῖπε	Never cease being thrifty
123.	Χρησμοὺς θαύμαζε	Admire oracles
124.	Οὓς τρέφεις, ἀγάπα	Love those whom you rear
125.	Ἀπόντι μὴ μάχου	Do not fight an absent foe
126.	Πρεσβύτερον αἰδοῦ	Respect the old

(Continued)

Table 2.1 (Continued)   The 147 Delphic Maxims in Greek and English

No.	Greek	English
127.	Νεώτερον δίδασκε	Instruct the young
128.	Πλούτῳ ἀπίστει	Do not put your trust in wealth
129.	Σεαυτὸν αἰδοῦ	Respect yourself
130.	Μὴ ἄρχε ὑβρίζειν	Do not initiate violence
131.	Προγόνους στεφάνου	Crown your ancestors
132.	Θνῆσκε ὑπὲρ πατρίδος	Die for your country
133.	Τῷ βίῳ μὴ ἄχθου	Do not live your life in discontent
134.	Ἐπὶ νεκρῷ μὴ γέλα	Do not make fun of the dead
135.	Ἀτυχοῦντι συνάχθου	Share the load of the unfortunate
136.	Χαρίζου ἀβλαβῶς	Gratify without harming
137.	Μὴ ἐπὶ παντὶ λυποῦ	Have no grief
138.	Ἐξ εὐγενῶν γέννα	Beget good from good
139.	Ἐπαγγέλλου μηδενί	Make promises to none
140.	Φθιμένους μὴ ἀδίκει	Do not wrong the dead
141.	Εὖ πάσχε ὡς θνητός	Do as well as your mortal status permits
142.	Τύχῃ μὴ πίστευε	Do not put your trust in chance
143.	Παῖς ὢν κόσμιος ἴσθι	As a child be well-behaved
144.	Ἡβῶν ἐγκρατής	As a youth be self-disciplined
145.	Μέσος δίκαιος	As a middle-aged person be honest
146.	Πρεσβύτης εὔλογος	As an old man be sensible
147.	Τελευτῶν ἄλυπος	At your end be without sorrow

The universal meaning of the Delphic maxims can be revealed through multidisciplinary practices and techniques. Ontologies can be used to define the space in which maxims can move and change, per instance, interpretation, and usage. Taxonomies can also describe the maxims' categorization, and classes can be used to define the relationships between the elements of a category (taxonomy). Interpreting the Delphic maxims as Applied Philosophy for business management and governance can significantly contribute to the global economy and society. Ontologies can be used to analyze the maxims' contribution and impact in decision-making, strategy, human resources management, goal setting, organizational commitment, ethos, leadership, management, and entrepreneurship disciplines.

Such an analysis can develop new management frameworks influenced by concepts and values for organizational performance based on the best utilization of the skills, capability, competence, and knowledge of corporate human resources as described in the knowledge-creating company framework by Ikujiro Nonaka and Hirotaka Takeuchi (cf. Nonaka, Takeuchi, 1995). Organizations suffer not because they cannot solve their problems but because they cannot identify them. Lack of problem identification derives from a lack of corporate communication due to a lack of corporate culture due to a lack of corporate philosophy on values based on humanity and civilization's elemental principles.

2.3 Ontologies, Taxonomies, and Classes

The term 'ontology' (Bonacin, 2004) derives from the Hellenic word 'on' (ὄν), genitive 'ontos' (ὄντος): 'of being,' neuter participle of 'eine' (εἶναι): 'to be,' and 'logia' (λογία): science, study, theory. The term 'taxonomy' also derives from the Hellenic word, 'taxis' (τάξις), meaning 'order' or 'arrangement,' and 'nomos' (νόμος), meaning 'law' or 'science' (cf. Spideltech, 2015). The break-down of these Hellenic meanings are:

- Ontology = science of being
- Taxonomy = arrangement science

Therefore, taxonomy is the simple hierarchical arrangement of entities with a parent–child relationship (Oberle, Guarino, Staab, 2009, Tulu, Chatterjee, Maheshwari, 2007). On the other hand, ontology is a more complex taxonomy variation as it defines the taxonomies spaces (Figure 2.1).

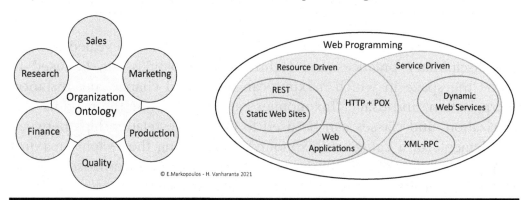

Figure 2.1 An ontology diagram (left) and a taxonomy diagram (right).

The purpose of taxonomies is knowledge classification, whereas ontologies extend into knowledge representation. Classes are taxonomical ranks, indicating interrelationships (including inheritance, aggregation, and association), operations, and attributes (Ambysoft Inc., 2015). The representation of classes can be in a tree or relationship arrangement based on the properties or characteristics of a particular class's behavior types.

An example of the Ontology–Taxonomy–Class relationship could be given with the following example. "To be, or not to be?" could be an ontological question for living creatures, in which "you're one of the humans" is a taxonomy of the living creatures, and "you are a Hellene" is a class for all the Hellenes. Therefore, the ontology is the description, the taxonomy is the classification, and the level is the rank or category within a taxonomy of the ontology (Figure 2.2).

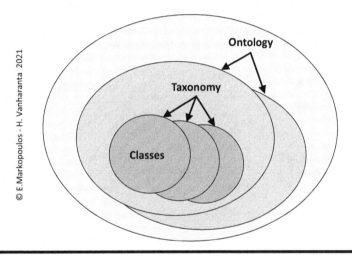

Figure 2.2   Ontology–taxonomy–class relationship.

Viewing this triadic classification relationship from a distance, a holistic knowledge representation can be achieved by understanding large sets of information and exploring their relationships in various paths and behaviors. According to Aristotle, knowledge can also be obtained and analyzed by observation (Aristotle, 1999).

2.4 Ontologies, Taxonomies, and Classes of the Delphic Maxims

2.4.1 Ontologies

The Delphic maxims' wisdom can be quite profound; therefore, its classification can be approached using ontologies to define the knowledge worlds they create. Many maxims can ignite different classification knowledge paths in various directions that can be interpreted, analyzed, and applied effectively to society and the economy. The core ontologies that can be derived from the Delphic maxims are the following: Self-control, Communication, Respect, God, Justice, Knowledge, Work, Finance, Family, Honor, Care, and Education.

Each ontology presents several concepts that can be developed as distinct knowledge categories with their interpretation to be based on their dependencies and usage. The way each ontology and its structure is applied develops different management approaches under different philosophical thinkings (Figure 2.3).

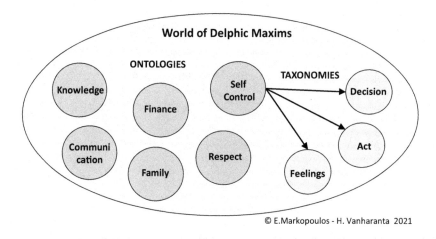

© E.Markopoulos - H. Vanharanta 2021

Figure 2.3   Delphic maxim ontologies and indicative taxonomies.

An example of such different approaches can be: 'God' provides 'Love/Care' that can generate 'knowledge,' and thought, 'respect,' and 'work' can deliver ethical 'financial' management. Another way to interpret this ontology relationship is that 'knowledge' generates 'self-control' where 'work' and 'care' can deliver ethical 'financial' management. The first approach is based on the triptych 'God–Love–Knowledge,' where the second one is based on the 'Knowledge–Self-control–Work.' They both end in ethical financial management and the benefits thereof, but the approach is different as the first one is more abstract while the second is more concrete.

This chapter does not intend to analyze all the ontologies derived from the Delphic maxims in the business, economy, and society context, but to point out a way to understand them practically.

2.4.2 Taxonomies

Numerous taxonomies can be generated from each of the ontologies of the Delphic maxims. The 'Self-control' ontology can engage several taxonomies related to self-control activities based on that ontology's maxims. Such taxonomies could be the following: Feelings, Acts, Thoughts, Decisions, Advice, and others.

Taxonomies can have similar representation structures to ontologies based on the way knowledge is analyzed. Taxonomies can also lead to the development of different management approaches under different types of philosophical thinking. 'Feelings,' for example, activate 'Thoughts' which execute 'Acts' based on 'Decisions.' Another way to see this taxonomical representation of knowledge can be that 'Decisions' are based on 'Feelings' and 'Acts' triggered by 'thoughts' (Figure 2.3). In the first case, the maxims drive a proactive management approach where 'Thinking' precedes 'Acting.' In the second case, the maxims drive a reactive approach where 'Acting' precedes 'Thinking.' Both processes result in different strategies for a common goal through different philosophical paths people have. The relationships between the taxonomies are not only linear but may also be conditional.

This chapter does not intend to analyze all the taxonomies that can derive from the interpretation of Delphic maxims in the business, economy, and society context, but to point out a way to understand them in practice.

2.4.3 Classes

The Delphic maxim taxonomies can generate several classes for each taxonomy. The 'Feelings' taxonomy of the 'Self-control' ontology can include maxims related to the 'control of feelings.' Some of such maxims are: 'Be grateful,' 'Control yourself,' 'Pursue harmony,' and others.

Likewise, the 'Decision' taxonomy of the 'Knowledge' ontology can include maxims related to the 'decisions based on knowledge.' Some of such maxims are: 'Tell when you know,' 'Act when you know,' 'Venture into danger prudently,' and others.

The classes contain elements with the information presented as processes or as decision/control mechanisms for a broader strategy. Several maxims relate to each other for a specific purpose, revealing knowledge in a process-oriented approach or method.

For example, the following class is developed with several elements from one or more taxonomy or ontology.

Class: 'Act Wisely' =

Maxim: Be/Know yourself (Taxonomy: Feelings; Ontology: Knowledge) >
Maxim: Foresee the future (Taxonomy: Feelings; Ontology: Self-Control) >
Maxim: Perceive what you have heard (Taxonomy: Act; Ontology: Knowledge) >
Maxim: Nothing to excess (Taxonomy: Decision; Ontology: Finance) >
Maxim: Act without repentance (Taxonomy: Act; Ontology: Self-Control) >
Maxim: Work for what you can own (Taxonomy: Act; Ontology: Finance)

The elements, Delphic maxims, in the above class create the process called 'Act Wisely.'

This process states the following:

Be/Know yourself > Foresee the future > Perceive what you have heard > Nothing to excess > Act without repentance > Work for what you can own.

Interpreting this class in structured English, the following Applied Philosophy is generated:

Know yourself first, foresee the future correctly, then utilize what you hear and with no exaggerations, start acting without looking back to work on what you can own.

The 'Act Wisely' class derived from elements (maxims) of three ontologies and three taxonomies forms a unique relationship and gives a specific process for acting toward a goal.

This chapter does not intend to analyze all the classes that can derive from Delphic maxims' interpretation in business, economy, and society, but to point out a way to understand them in practice.

2.4.4 A Triadic Classification of Knowledge

The representation of any type of information and precisely the structured information that generates knowledge based on how it is interpreted and analyzed cannot be classified correctly with only one specific classification technique (Brachman, 1978). Ontologies, however, provide a high-level representation of knowledge grouped in micro-worlds of information, connected with various relationships and dependencies (Mizoguchi, 2004).

Likewise, taxonomies are derived from ontologies and classify their information based on more specific categorization schemas, which probably overlap with other taxonomies and ontologies (Jackson, 2004). The discrete line between what type of information can be classified with either ontologies or taxonomies is based on the type of information, the meaning, and the depth of the analysis that can be given.

Classes, on the other hand, are groups of elements that define the behavior of the information. Classes can be formed with information from one or more taxonomies without representation restrictions. Classes can be analyzed using trees and other relationship-oriented techniques. Information that represents knowledge can generate classes that practically turn this knowledge into applied knowledge, composed of elements from different taxonomies and ontologies (Ades et al., 2007). In the Delphic maxims, classes are applied philosophical processes in small or large procedures (Figure 2.4).

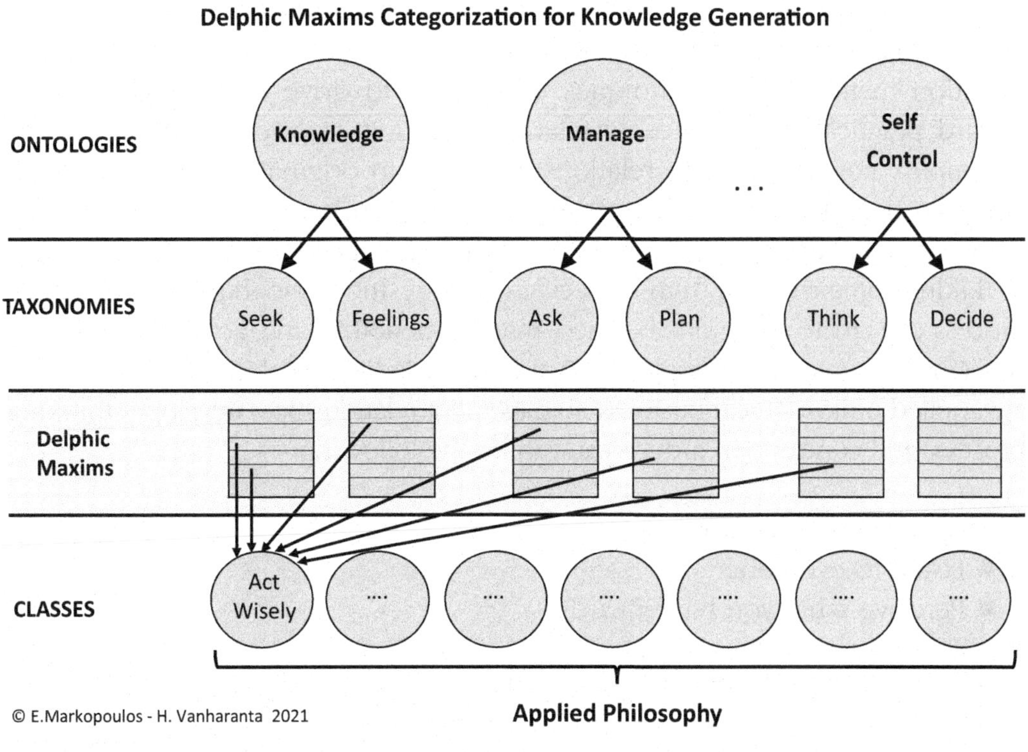

Delphic Maxims Categorization for Knowledge Generation

© E.Markopoulos - H. Vanharanta 2021   **Applied Philosophy**

Figure 2.4   Delphic maxims categorization for knowledge generation.

In this case, the natural source of knowledge, the Delphic maxims, is placed between the high-level classification and the applied interpretation through this triadic classification approach, making learning practical and useful. This approach allows knowledge to stem from the classes' elements, from one specific taxonomy, and one particular ontology. However, this serial classification type of information can restrict the interpretation of knowledge and the generation of cross-taxonomy and cross-ontology knowledge and wisdom.

This unbounded triadic representation of knowledge can be considered fuzzy and hypothetical in the knowledge classification interpretation. On the other hand, it can be advantageous if common sense is common indeed and approached more openly with unbiased and transparent thinking, avoiding personal barriers, formality, and political correctness.

2.4.5 Business Management and Leadership Relationships

Knowledge needs to be interpreted in a way that can add value to science, the economy, and society (Guibert, Laganier, Volle, 1971). Applied knowledge interpretation is the most significant issue in knowledge engineering and management (Freigenbaum, McCorduk, 1983). To achieve this, the classification methods and techniques used need to drive knowledge analysis toward practical and applicable relationships that must continuously evolve to simplify complexity. The relationships that can originate from the Delphic maxims' classification can be effectively applied in business management by complex or straightforward analysis within a classification technique.

Taking some maxims from a specific ontology, the 'Wise thinking and acting' process can create and guide business management thinking, acts, and decisions. A set of maxims, for example, from the 'Knowledge' ontology that can generate applied philosophical business management relationships, develop a thinking process, and conclude in a decision, can be the following:

- Know your opportunity
- Listen to everyone
- Perceive what you have heard
- Think as a mortal
- Tell me when you know

Another business management knowledge relationship derived from the maxims of the 'Self-control' ontology can be:

- Foresee the future
- Use your skill

- Act quickly
- Act without repenting
- Do what you mean to do

Likewise, maxims from the 'Finance' ontology can generate the following business management relationship and thinking process:

- Govern your expenses
- Nothing to excess
- Work for what you can own
- Pursue what is profitable
- Benefit yourself

The examples given are only one per ontology but can be extended to all ontologies. Each one of the 147 maxims encapsulates the Hellenic civilization's wisdom, i.e., the knowledge that can be turned into the Applied Philosophy approach in business management and leadership must be considered highly valuable in this process. Furthermore, the maxims' analysis can be extended using a triadic knowledge classification, enabling the creation of business practices with the interconnection of maxims from different ontologies and taxonomies. In that case, the combinations of the applied business concepts and processes that can be generated will be sufficient to address any challenge.

2.5 Beyond the Delphic Maxims

This classification of the existing knowledge in humanity through techniques, methods, and models that can turn this knowledge into applicable contributions to the modern economy and business management needs to be continued. The Delphic maxims are one set of expertise that can generate significant business management value, but it is not the only one in the Hellenic philosophical contributions to the world. This work can be extended to specific Hellenic philosophers whose life, values, and work can be characterized close to vertical business management needs and practices.

For example, Socrates's knowledge can help understand the requirements elicitation process that causes significant difficulties in all projects in all sectors today. Inadequate specifications drive tremendous financial and operational costs for organizations when they are not defined and handled correctly in the tendering, acquisition, and development stages of a project or investment. Plato's knowledge can be considered when developing change management and reengineering practices. Pericles's knowledge suits well project and product management processes. Aristotle's knowledge is applicable to organizational strategy development. Thucydides's knowledge can be useful for extroversion and internationalization. Isocrates's knowledge is very well suited for teamwork management and leadership. Heraclitus's knowledge is suitable for human resource management and Homer's for design and production management. Herodotus's knowledge, in turn, is appropriate for the tactical management process. Pythagoras's knowledge supports innovation management. Democritus's knowledge can be used for engineering management and leadership. Solon's knowledge provides organizational leadership methods and many others for multiple current and critical business needs and challenges. Similarly, knowledge from other significant civilizations such as the Roman, the Egyptian, or the Chinese can be analyzed with this triadic knowledge representation approach or other classification methods.

This work on the Delphic maxims has been extended toward supporting the Applied Philosophy approach by optimizing the classification process through the creation of new classification terminology, notation, and diagramming techniques to capture concepts with relative interpretation applicability to the business, society, and economy.

2.6 Summary

A black hole in knowledge management may be the definition of knowledge itself. What is knowledge, and what is not, is a very fuzzy concept. Knowledge can be generated by properly analyzing any information to obtain results that can be applied either in practice or in theory for further research. The difference between data, information, and knowledge is that data and information are unprocessed knowledge.

Today, people try to generate knowledge through several complex approaches and scientific disciplines without much certainty on the results' quality. It seems that any scientific approach toward creating knowledge can contribute to the evolution and progression of the economy, society, and humanity, but this is not entirely true. Knowledge cannot be produced in artificial environments, biased, or directed. Knowledge is a living entity that grows by nature in many forms and sources and is free for all who seek it.

Instead of investing in knowledge engineering efforts using artificial intelligence technologies, neuro-management (Satpathy, 2012), cognitive science

(Mischel, 2013), and other state-of-the-art technologies, it might be wise to consider that knowledge, in probably much more valuable forms, can be found in the roots of the civilizations who lived before on this planet. With the proper classification techniques, methods, and models, the knowledge extracted by analyzing historical events and situations can surpass, in value and return to the society and the economy, the knowledge that is attempted to be generated through today's efforts to artificially read people's minds (Piccinini, 2004).

The Applied Philosophy approach is not science but merely common sense, a common understanding that does not seem that common after all. The Delphic maxims are 147 simple statements that can redefine the business management, leadership, operations strategies, and practices once classified correctly and studied using common sense. The wisdom of the Delphic maxims is only a part of our existing global knowledge heritage. All nations have contributed to humanity, and therefore in all countries, there is information and wisdom that can be turned successfully into valuable modern knowledge and practices.

Questions for Review and Discussions

A significant source of in-depth knowledge that contributes considerably to humanity's development can be found in the Delphic maxims. Ponder and give thought to Delphic maxims and find relevant statements from the 147 Delphic maxims (see Table 2.1 at the end of the chapter), which belong to the decision-making process of leaders and managers and significantly how they can minimize anxiety and fear in organizations.

We have modified a figure from *The Philosophy Book* (Buckingham et al., 2011), where philosopher Sören Kirkegaard's philosophical thinking process helps envisioning the Applied Philosophy approach in management and leadership. Below are questions for review and discussions.

1. Based on the Dephic maxims
    1.1 Which Delphic maxims are related the most with each thinking stage of the process in Figure 2Q?
    1.2 Please explain why you selected each proverb (maxim) and how you would describe it with each step.
2. Create an ontology defining the world of the industry your organization (or a random organization) operates in.
    2.1 What could be the ontological elements, and why?

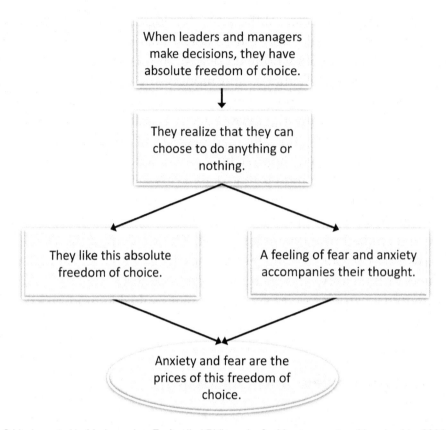

Figure 2Q   Chart for Question 1 (c.f., Buckingham, et al., 2011, Sören Kirkegaard, p. 194).

3. Create a set of taxonomies related to one of the ontologies in the industry's business world in which your organization (or a random organization) operates.
   3.1 What could be those taxonomies?
   3.2 Why, and what are the relationships between them?
4. Using the Word of Delphic maxims (Figure 2.3) and by combining any Delphic statements listed in the Table 2.1 at the end of the chapter, answer the following questions:
   4.1 Create another class on management and leadership wisdom (similar to the one presented in Section 2.4.3).
   4.2 How would you call it, and why?
   4.3 Can you explain in structured English the wisdom that derives from this new class?

4.4 When would you use this class? Under what conditions? What would help you deal with it?

5. Select 12 of the 147 Delphic maxims and prioritize them according to your values.

5.1 What do you learn about yourself as a human being?

5.2 How close are you to what the maxims and their meaning represent?

5.3 What changes could you have made to reflect more on who you think you are?

5.4 What changes could you have made to meditate more on who you want to be?

6. Select 12 of the 147 Delphic maxims and prioritize them according to your professional values.

6.1 What do you learn about yourself as a professional?

6.2 How close are you to what the maxims and their meaning represent?

6.3 What changes could you have made to reflect more on who you think you are?

6.4 What changes could you have made to meditate more on who you want to be ?

References

Ades, Y., Ben-Oman, F., Poernomo, I. and Tsaramirsis, G., 2007. Mapping ontology charts to class diagrams. In: The International Conference of Organisational Semiotics. ICOS2007, May 2007.

Ambysoft, Inc., 2015. UML 2 class diagrams: An agile introduction, www.agilemodeling.com /artifacts/classDiagram.htm, Cited: Aug. 20. 2015.

Aristotle, 1999. *Nicomachean Ethics*. Translated by Ross, W. D., Batoche Books, Kitchener, ON, Canada, Book VI. 91–105.

Bonacin, R., Baranauskas, M.C.C., and Liu, K., 2004. From ontology charts to class diagrams: semantic analysis aiding systems design. In: The 6th ICEIS, Porto, Portugal. 389–395.

Bowden H., 2005. *Classical Athens and the Delphic Oracle: Divination and Democracy*. Cambridge University Press, Cambridge.

Brachman, R., 1978. A Structural paradigm for representing knowledge. *Bolt, Beranek, and Neumann Technical Report (3605)*.

Buckingham, W., Burnham, D., King P. J., Hill, C., Weeks, M. and Marenbon, J. 2011. *The Philosophy Book*. DK Publishing. ISBN-10: 978-0-7566-6861-7,0756668611.

Feigenbaum, E. and McCorduk, P., 1983. *The Fifth Generation*. Addison-Wesley, Reading, MA.

Guibert B., Laganier J., and Volle, M., 1971. An essay on industrial classifications. *Économie et statistique*, 20, 1–18.

Jackson, J., 2004. Taxonomy's not just design, it's an art. *Government Computer News*, September 2, Washington, DC, 243–258.

Markopoulos, E., 2013. The Kapodistrian principles for freedom through knowledge and education. In: Ioanis Kapodistrias Conference, 30. Athens, Greece.

Markopoulos, E. and Vanharanta, H., 2014. Democratic culture paradigm for organizational management and leadership strategies: The company democracy model. In: Charytonowicz J. (ed.), *Advances in Human Factors and Sustainable Infrastructure*. Proceedings of the 5th International Conference on Applied Human Factors and Ergonomics (AHFE), Kraków, Poland 19–23 July 2014, 20, 190–201.

Markopoulos, E. and Vanharanta, H., 2015. Company democracy model for the development of shared value. In: The 6th International Conference on Applied Human Factors and Ergonomics (AHFE), Las Vegas.

Mischel, T. ed., 2013. *Cognitive Development and Epistemology*. Academic Press, Cambridge, MA.

Mizoguchi, R., 2004. Tutorial on ontological engineering: Part 3: Advanced course of ontological engineering. *New Generation Computing*, Ohmsha & Springer-Verlag, 22 (2), 193–220.

Nonaka I. and Takeuchi H., 1995. *The Knowledge-creating Company: How Japanese Companies Create the Dynamics of Innovation*. Oxford University Press, New York.

Oberle, D., Guarino, N., and Staab, S., 2009. What is ontology? In: *Handbook on Ontologies*. Springer, New York, 2nd Edition.

Parke, H. and Wormell, D., 1956. *The Delphic Oracle*, Vol. 1. Basil Blackwell, Oxford.

Piccinini, G., 2004. The First computational theory of mind and brain: A close look at McCulloch and Pitts's "logical calculus of ideas immanent in nervous activity. *Synthese*, 141 (2), 175–215.

Satpathy, J., 2012. Issues in neuro-management decision making. *International Journal of Business Management*, 2 (2), 23–36. http://phd.meghan-smith.com/wp-content/uploads/2015/09/neuromanagement-decision-making.pdf

Spideltech.com, 2015. Software engineering taxonomy diagram. *Spidel Tech Solutions, Inc. - Introduction. [online] spideltech.com*. Available at: http://spideltech.com/. Sited: August 20, 2015.

Tulu, B., Chatterjee, S., and Maheshwari, M., 2007. Telemedicine taxonomy: A classification tool. *Telemedicine and e-Health*, 13 (3), 349–358.

Chapter 3

Visualization of the Wisdom Cube: Wisdom Space for Management and Leadership

Knowing yourself is the beginning of all wisdom.

– Aristotle

Executive Summary

The philosophers of the Ancient World (700 BCE–250 CE) have inspired us by their writings to start thinking more deeply about the visualization of wisdom and knowledge. These basic principles are now placed in such a form that it is possible to show, in a practical way, how knowledge and wisdom are intertwined. This chapter aims to show how the definitions of the dimensions of wisdom give us the means to go further in our thinking to perceive and understand the essential relationships between scientific, theoretical, technical, and practical knowledge. This can be seen as a journey toward knowledge creation and wisdom. The starting point has been the ancient Hellenic philosophers and their thinking, logic, and reasoning. This chapter indicates the beneficial impact of the philosophers' essential thinking and provides a practical understanding of knowledge creation and wisdom for management and leadership purposes.

DOI: 10.4324/9781003158493-4

3.1 From Pythagoras to Socrates, Plato, and Aristotle

The concept of Applied Philosophy has its roots back in the ancient Hellenic civilization. It started with the Greek philosopher Pythagoras (born in Samos, Greece, c. 570–495/7 BCE) (Buckingham et al., 2011, Magee, 2016), who combined philosophy and mathematics. His most important discovery was the relationship between numbers and proportions, finding the way to numerical harmonies. Pythagoras's theorem reveals that shapes and ratios are governed by principles that can be discovered and shown by mathematical and graphical methods (Buckingham et al., 2011). Pythagoras was the first man who applied arithmetic to geometrical concepts like the "square" and the "cube" (Magee, 2016). Therefore, many graphs can be seen as harmonies, inspiring innovation across all industries.

Socrates (born in Athens, Greece, c. 469–399 BCE) has been referred to as the founder of moral philosophy and one of the founders of Western philosophy. He has also been called the most remarkable and best-known philosopher of them all. He developed the dialectic Socratic questioning method as a dialog between opposing views and understanding during his active time. He challenged people in philosophical discussions with fundamental questions concerning morality and politics. One of his pupils was Plato, who recorded the most important works of Socrates (Buckingham et al., 2011, Magee, 2016).

Plato (born in Athens, Greece, c. 427–347 BCE) described in his famous work *The Republic*, with his "Allegory of the Cave," that understanding lies inside our minds as a world of ideas, or forms, which have nothing to do with the material world, and that our understanding and perception of this world are possible only through reason. According to Plato, this world of ideas is the actual "reality," not the world perceived by our senses (Buckingham et al., 2011, Magee, 2016).

Aristotle (born in Stagira of Macedonia, Greece, 384–322 BCE), in turn, took a huge step forward by saying that Plato's theory of forms was wrong. Aristotle refuted Plato's view with the Third Man argument by saying that if a man is a man because he has the form of a man, then a third form would be required to explain how man and the form of man are both men, and so on ad infinitum. Plato's background was in mathematics, and Aristotle's as a researcher in the biological sciences. Aristotle based his thinking almost totally on observation, not on abstract concepts as Plato did (Buckingham et al., 2011, Magee, 2016).

According to Aristotle, by relying on our experiences of the world around us, we get an idea of the world's characteristics through our senses. Thus, we can also understand the inherent characteristics. After that, there are possibilities to study particular things and issues and conclude universal and immutable entities and truths (Buckingham et al., 2011). All of the above concepts are somehow difficult for people to perceive, comprehend, and apply to obtain a holistic view of scientific, theoretical, practical wisdom, and knowledge generation. One view is that everything is in people's minds; however, when it is articulated the other way around, i.e., that there are many different areas of knowledge that can be retrieved from data and information, people understand better how to create knowledge and where real knowledge exists.

We have to go back and analyze what these philosophers and their thinking can teach them, especially on how they view the different scientific, theoretical, methodological, technical, and practical knowledge needed to understand the world around them. Their thinking also helps us see how people can challenge their perception, understanding, current experience, and knowledge creation, and how their new knowledge changes their way of thinking and how it progressively contributes to management and leadership challenges.

The creation of the wisdom space and the planes of wisdom with the Wisdom Cube formation can provide a practical way of understanding knowledge and wisdom. The starting point is the four dimensions of wisdom.

3.2 The Dimensions of Wisdom

Wisdom is difficult to define both thoroughly and briefly. Wisdom is somehow internal as well as external. When it is in humans, it is internal, i.e., implicit, and when it is external, it is explicit knowledge that exists somewhere. It is also essential to understand what wisdom is not. It is certainly not data or information. Wisdom gets created and derives from processing data and information through reasoning, logic, and observation. Thus, it is systematically connected to humans, as humans are living systems (Miller, 1978). Often, however, human processes seem intuitive and automatic, based on the human brain's structure and operation.

Episteme, Sophia, Techne, and Phronesis are the main dimensions of wisdom defined and articulated by the ancient philosophers (Buckingham et al., 2011). Each dimension has its specific content, but the boundaries with the others are fuzzy by nature, and it may be better to describe them in terms of degrees (cf. Trillas, 2011).

A certain harmony can be achieved with the nature of these wisdom and knowledge concepts. By placing Episteme on the Y-axis, Sophia on the X-axis, and Techne on the Z-axis, a three-dimensional cube is obtained in which the diagonal represents the dimension of Phronesis, i.e., it has relationships and interrelationships with each of the three other dimensions and their components, concepts, and sub-concepts.

The Episteme dimension on the Y-axis contains all scientific knowledge and can be defined as the scientific dimension of wisdom. Sophia on the X-axis includes all theoretical knowledge and shows the theoretical dimension of wisdom. In turn, Techne on the Z-axis represents technical knowledge and can be defined as the technical dimension of wisdom.

The fourth (diagonal) dimension is the practical dimension of wisdom, i.e., Phronesis, which has connections, relationships, and interrelationships with each of the previous three wisdom dimensions (Baehr, 2014).

The graphical presentation of the four dimensions, shown in Figure 3.1, defines the Wisdom Cube. The Cube, with its components, will be delineated and depicted in more detail in this chapter.

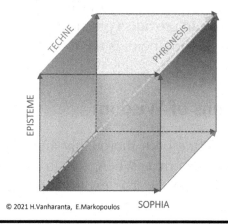

© 2021 H.Vanharanta, E.Markopoulos

Figure 3.1   The Wisdom Cube with the four dimensions of wisdom.

3.2.1 Episteme – The Scientific Dimension of Wisdom

As Aristotle said in his *Nicomachean Ethics* (Aristotle, 1999):

> Scientific knowledge is about things that are universal and necessary, and the conclusions of demonstrations and all scientific knowledge follow from first principles (for scientific knowledge involves the apprehension of the rational ground). This being so, the first principle

from which what is scientifically known follows cannot be an object of scientific knowledge, of art, or practical wisdom; for that which can be scientifically known can be demonstrated, and art and practical wisdom deal with things that are variable.

This means that what is scientifically known can be demonstrated, and so variable things belong more to art and practical wisdom. The above can lead us to conclude that taking Episteme as a basis demands a new type of teachable knowledge regarding management and leadership. This must be demonstrated better to obtain more universal and necessary knowledge for management and leadership purposes. This can be very demanding in social sciences; however, it is both natural and practical to consider the Episteme dimension, particularly if the other wisdom dimensions of Sophia, Techne, and Phronesis are used (Figure 3.2). A better scientific touch supports and improves the different areas of knowledge and wisdom.

EPISTEME
The Scientific Dimension of Wisdom

Scientific knowledge attributes:
- Universal
- Necessary
- Invariable
- Context independent
- Based on general analytical rationality
- "Justified true belief"
- To know

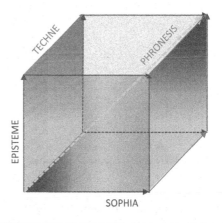

© 2021 H.Vanharanta, E.Markopoulos

Figure 3.2   Episteme – the scientific dimension of wisdom.

In the management and leadership context, Episteme, the scientific dimension of wisdom, is therefore essential; however, since valid principles cannot be followed as in the natural sciences like physics, chemistry, etc., scientific knowledge is only applied in this management and leadership context, and it is assumed that what people know is not capable of being otherwise (cf. Aristotle, 1999). Therefore, the aspiration of scientific knowledge, Episteme, is also a necessity in this context. However, it must be understood that there are difficulties finding context-independent, invariable, necessary, and universal knowledge. The knowledge created is primarily based on general analytical rationality. The target is to know and create knowledge, i.e., "justified true belief," that is as close as possible to the demands of Episteme.

3.2.2 Sophia – The Theoretical Dimension of Wisdom

The Ancient Greek word 'Sophia' (σοφία, sophía) is the abstract noun of σοφός (sophós), which has been variously translated into the words "clever, skillful, intelligent, wise," all of which characterize humans. Sophia has also been described with a broader conception as the theoretical dimension of wisdom (Baeher, 2014). Theoretical knowledge, in turn, has been defined as knowledge of "why" something is true. This means that it is necessary to find explanations to state why certain truths are true. A deep understanding is then required, which expects reasoning concerning universal truths. Abstract concepts and different contexts make this reasoning difficult, and many times the results do not fulfill the requirements (Figure 3.3).

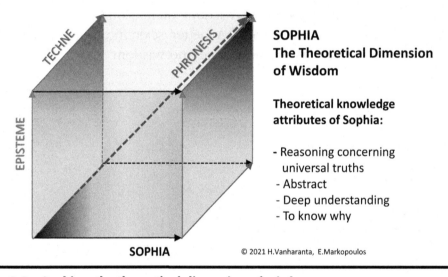

SOPHIA
The Theoretical Dimension of Wisdom

Theoretical knowledge attributes of Sophia:

- Reasoning concerning universal truths
- Abstract
- Deep understanding
- To know why

© 2021 H.Vanharanta, E.Markopoulos

Figure 3.3   Sophia – the theoretical dimension of wisdom.

In business management and leadership, the question "why" is crucial. Many cause-and-effect relationships and interrelationships are challenging to observe without smart, skillful, intelligent, and wise managers and leaders. However, this is not enough because knowledge also needs background theories, methodologies, and methods to establish connections to quantitative data and qualitative information.

3.2.3 Techne – The Technical Dimension of Wisdom

An excellent definition of what Techne means comes from Aristotle's texts, where he sees it as "representative of the imperfection of human imitation of nature" (Aristotle, 1999). Many examples describe Techne as an activity that is concrete, variable, and context-dependent. Carpentry has been mentioned in Aristotle's texts as an example of Techne and science like medicine and arithmetic. Often, Techne is thought of as more productive than theoretical, but Techne reveals its nature when people wish to obtain information concerning how to do something, i.e., technical know-how. It is also interesting that it fulfills the requirement of Episteme that it can be taught. This is related to the people behind this knowledge and wisdom. Techne has connections to people who can make things, know what is needed, know when the need exists, and the context where something is required. Techne is, therefore, very close to Phronesis, the practical dimension of wisdom (Figure 3.4).

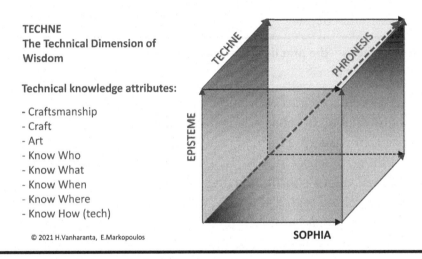

Figure 3.4 Techne – the technical dimension of wisdom.

Techne is also connected with communication since people are connected through their cultures and communicate what they are doing or making. Human ability, capacity, commitment, and motivation show what a person will do and make. Techne aims at deeds where activity or "making" leads to an end or an end product. Techne is close to the terms 'technique,' 'technical,' and 'technology,' resulting in production activities, processes, and other mechanical or material components of the real world (cf. Aristotle, 1999).

3.2.4 Phronesis – The Practical Dimension of Wisdom

Practical wisdom, Phronesis, is the fourth dimension of wisdom in the Wisdom Cube. It is an Ancient Greek word for a type of wisdom or intelligence (Ancient Greek: φρόνησῐς, translation 'phrónēsis'). In his book *Nicomachean Ethics*, Aristotle approaches Phronesis separately as one crucial area of wisdom (cf. Aristotle, 1999). This is a more action-oriented approach but also includes the capability of rational thinking (Figure 3.5).

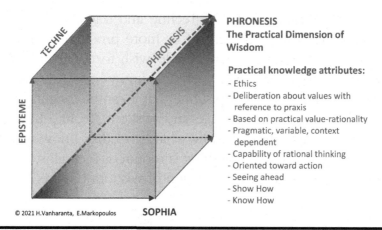

PHRONESIS
The Practical Dimension of Wisdom

Practical knowledge attributes:
- Ethics
- Deliberation about values with reference to praxis
- Based on practical value-rationality
- Pragmatic, variable, context dependent
- Capability of rational thinking
- Oriented toward action
- Seeing ahead
- Show How
- Know How

© 2021 H.Vanharanta, E.Markopoulos

Figure 3.5 Phronesis – the practical dimension of wisdom.

Phronesis is based on practical value-rationality, and the created knowledge is variable (not invariable) because it is very much a context- and situation-dependent dimension of wisdom. Phronesis emphasizes deliberation about ethics and values concerning practical needs. In business management and leadership, added and shared values constitute increased value, which the organization can produce for humankind with its human and fixed assets. One sub-dimension of Phronesis is looking ahead to the future, i.e., the "power of foresight" (Aristotle, 1999), which people trust to be important in their current situation. Many times this wisdom emerges when people know how and also when they are capable of showing how. Much of this wisdom and knowledge is connected to intuitive thinking in a specific context and situation, and so we understand that Phronesis is connected to Episteme, Sophia, and Techne. Its pragmatic nature serves people well, and deliberation of ethics and values keeps it close to daily life. Therefore, this wisdom dimension is crucial in day-to-day management and leadership when deep understanding and reflection are needed.

> Practical wisdom, on the other hand, is concerned with things human and things about which it is possible to deliberate; for we say this is above all the work of the man of practical wisdom, to deliberate well, but no one deliberates about things invariable, nor about things which have not an end, and that a good that can be brought about by action. (Aristotle, 1999)

Aristotle also teaches that practical wisdom needs a fundamental understanding of "particulars" or details. This wisdom lies in people who have experience and are more valuable than those who only emphasize universal knowledge and understanding (Aristotle, 1999). This means that good and high-level practice should also focus on particulars. On the practical dimension of wisdom, it is worth referring to Aristotle when he comments that learning is called understanding when exercising the faculty of knowledge (Aristotle, 1999).

3.3 The Planes of Wisdom

The Planes of Wisdom, presented in Figure 3.1, have been created with three vectors of wisdom and the cube concept. Each plane of the cube represents different wisdom areas, with the vector giving two planes with the same content. The planes of the constructed Cube of Wisdom are the following: the Plane of Scientific and Technical Wisdom, the Plane of Scientific and Theoretical Wisdom, and the Plane of Theoretical and Technical Wisdom (Figure 3.6).

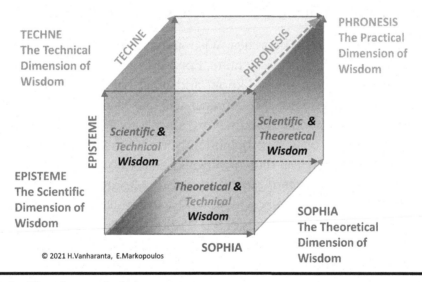

Figure 3.6   The planes of wisdom.

Inside the Planes of Wisdom, there is the current Universe of Wisdom, i.e., all the wisdom humans have created during their existence. This is the wisdom and knowledge that humankind has, and it also describes the Space of Wisdom with its system boundaries and content. The Space of Wisdom is expanding and growing continuously in three directions (Figure 3.6). Outside the Space of Wisdom is the unknown, which is not yet available to people.

Aristotle described this unknown in *Nicomachean Ethics*, Book VI, 3, as follows:

> We all suppose that what we know is not even capable of being otherwise; of things capable of being otherwise we don't know, when they passed outside our observation, whether they exist or not. (Aristotle, 1999)

This unknown may be revealed to people in the future if they work hard and observe the unknown. What then becomes known can be taught and will become the object of new learning and understanding. The Wisdom Space of Management and Leadership has its boundaries, planes, and dimensions of wisdom regarding management and leadership. The categories and contexts of the Wisdom Space shape and frame many areas of wisdom and knowledge, depending on the context in question. In the following, a short description of each of the planes of wisdom is presented.

3.3.1 The Plane of Scientific and Theoretical Wisdom

The Plane of Scientific and Theoretical Wisdom has two different wisdom dimensions and directions, i.e., the scientific Episteme and the theoretical Sophia. Scientific wisdom is what people know and what has been revealed through observations and experiments. Theoretical wisdom is more of a deep understanding that utilizes answers to many "why" questions. Knowing 'why the world is like what it is' reveals basic facts behind universal truths and the reasoning concerning them. This theoretical dimension can be abstract or concrete. Perceiving and understanding the content demands remarkable capacity from the people who create more theoretical knowledge and wisdom. This kind of knowledge can be imagined through the planes of the Wisdom Cube, where real facts, truths, and theories give a new profound understanding of the world. They also help to understand that interpreting problems with the help of reasoning in a given situation and with a good theory can provide many new opportunities to find meaningful solutions to the questioned issues. In social sciences, and particularly in management and leadership, it should be considered that true knowledge might be difficult to achieve because the theories of management and leadership are often fuzzy and not as accurate as strict theoretical requirements demand. In physics and chemistry, and other natural sciences, the situation is different. Within the scientific content, the Plane of Scientific and Theoretical Wisdom has a different nature and characteristics (Aristotle, 1999).

3.3.2 *The Plane of Theoretical and Technical Wisdom*

The Plane of Theoretical and Technical Wisdom also has two dimensions: the theoretical 'Sophia' and the technical 'Techne.' Both dimensions and directions create an essential area of wisdom and knowledge. Many technological discoveries are based on valid theories; in addition, the Techne dimension's craftsmanship thinking provides possibilities to understand the practical side of theories. Questions like know who, know what, know when, and know where, know-how, etc. fit exceptionally well with the theoretical reasoning concerning universal truths and abstract concepts. Craft and art aspects are different in Techne, but they activate and describe this direction very well (Aristotle, 1999). Deep understanding through theoretical discussions and empirical tests can widen the Plane of Theoretical and Technical Wisdom.

3.3.3 *The Plane of Scientific and Technical Wisdom*

The third plane is the Plane of Scientific and Technical Wisdom. There are also two dimensions and directions here, i.e., Episteme and Techne. The increase of scientific knowledge has given the technical side vast new opportunities in the modern world. Facts from scientific knowledge help craftsmanship and engineering to flourish, generating innovative and ever better products and services for humankind. In the modern era, we have experienced many new scientific discoveries, which have been turned into everyday products or services. Computer sciences have taken the leading position to change the world and solve complex multivariable problems in many scientific, theoretical, and practical areas and contexts.

3.4 The Space of Wisdom

All three planes are components in building the Space of Wisdom. It is understood that an ample space can be constructed with a vast number of connections and interconnections by determining each plane's characteristics and faculties. This network is maintained and supported by the data and information that people, freely and democratically, put into the system that uses the data and information to extract knowledge. To obtain a holistic view of the dimensions, planes, and the Space of Wisdom, all the planes and their concepts are integrated into Figure 3.7.

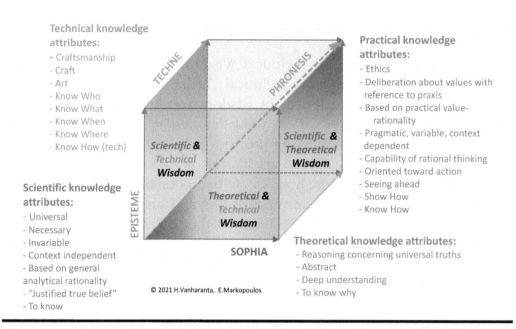

Technical knowledge attributes:
- Craftsmanship
- Craft
- Art
- Know Who
- Know What
- Know When
- Know Where
- Know How (tech)

Scientific knowledge attributes:
- Universal
- Necessary
- Invariable
- Context independent
- Based on general analytical rationality
- "Justified true belief"
- To know

Practical knowledge attributes:
- Ethics
- Deliberation about values with reference to praxis
- Based on practical value-rationality
- Pragmatic, variable, context dependent
- Capability of rational thinking
- Oriented toward action
- Seeing ahead
- Show How
- Know How

Theoretical knowledge attributes:
- Reasoning concerning universal truths
- Abstract
- Deep understanding
- To know why

TECHNE — PHRONESIS — EPISTEME — SOPHIA

Scientific & Technical Wisdom — Scientific & Theoretical Wisdom — Theoretical & Technical Wisdom

© 2021 H.Vanharanta, E.Markopoulos

Figure 3.7 The space of wisdom with the dimensions and planes of wisdom.

Figure 3.7 shows that breaking down the construct into different characteristics helps to understand the nature of wisdom. It also shows how important it is to use this created knowledge for teaching purposes in management and leadership context. Figure 3.7 helps to further penetrate deeper into the secrets of business knowledge in the specific context selected. Humans behave as active members inside this Space of Wisdom as entities, i.e., living systems (Miller, 1978).

The Planes and Space of Wisdom show that the ancient Hellenic philosophers reached a level of understanding, offering great humanity opportunities to see ourselves as members and owners of that 'big wisdom.' However, it is crucial to realize the extent of wisdom, as Socrates understands it:

> The only true wisdom is in knowing you know nothing.
>
> **– Socrates**

The degree of wisdom in each plane can describe an individual's position in the overall universal Wisdom Space. A vital scientific, theoretical, and technical education throughout the Planes of Wisdom is crucial for managers and leaders to attain a strong position in their organizations. For cross-scientific purpose teams, teaming, and teamwork, it is essential to concentrate on a verified and validated education, which increases knowledge creation in all dimensions. This process leads to high-level outputs in daily work at the individual and collective levels.

3.5 Summary

This chapter has scientific, theoretical, technical, and practical content for management and leadership purposes. The ideas came from discussions between the authors over several years and from writing about the new management and leadership concepts in different areas. The authors have had a keen interest in philosophy as well as management and leadership issues. The three-dimensional model, the Wisdom Cube, has been an integral part of our thinking for several years now. We consider that three-dimensional thinking has helped us understand many new business ontologies, real business constructs, and concepts.

The construct of the Wisdom Cube with the Dimensions of Wisdom and the Planes of Wisdom has helped us demonstrate the concepts of knowledge areas in Episteme, Sophia, Techne, and Phronesis. The construct has also provided a strong base for further analysis of what it means in management and leadership.

As a scientific contribution (Episteme), we can conclude that the Wisdom Cube visualization helps in understanding the creation of scientific knowledge. Scientific knowledge attributes clarify the requirements of "justified true belief," which are precise demands for knowledge creation in management and leadership. The theoretical contribution (Sophia) in this chapter helps us to understand the attributes of theoretical knowledge. The attribute "know why" focuses the reasoning process on answering why management and leadership constructs, concepts, and variables produce essential information for knowledge creation in specific business situations. The technical dimension of wisdom (Techne) and its relations to the other wisdom dimensions can be seen as enablers. Many new scientific theories see the light of day through developed technologies. Techne transforms scientific and theoretical discoveries and innovations for practical use. During recent years, we have experienced many new technology services and products which help humankind in many ways. We can say that Techne converts human wisdom into practice. The practical visualization of wisdom, the Dimension(s), and the Plane(s) of Phronesis can be used first for educational purposes. The attributes of Phronesis are highly suitable for advanced trainees in business management and leadership.

As a whole, the Wisdom Cube is a clear metaphor, which can be remembered easily. The Cube is also relevant for managers and leaders already working in the business. It shows how important it is to increase personal and collective knowledge creation in their organizations continuously. The Phronesis attributes focus on a detailed deliberation about values from many directions. They also cover a large area of knowledge creation to understand what to do now and how to do it and see into the future so that decision-makers can support, lead, and decide the best possible paths for their own company. Essential questions in perceiving, in deep understanding, and in knowledge creation are: Where are we now? Why are we here? Where should we be? and Are we getting there?

Wisdom is an intuitive reason combined with scientific knowledge.

– Aristotle

Questions for Review and Discussions

The philosophers of the ancient world (700 BCE–250 CE) have inspired us by their writings to start thinking more deeply about the visualization of wisdom and knowledge.

These basic principles are now placed in such a form that it is possible to show, in a practical way, how knowledge and wisdom are intertwined. Ponder and give thought to the dimensions and planes of the Wisdom Cube through the following questions:

1. If you were to replace one or more of the Wisdom Cube dimension/s, which one/s would it/they be? and for what reason?
   1.1. What could have been the elements of that/those new dimension/s?
2. Rank your company (or a company you select) against the Wisdom Cube dimensions. On a scale from 1 (lowest) to 10 (highest), how would the company score? and why?
   2.1 What are the scores by each dimension?
   2.2 What could you do to increase scores below 7?
3. How do you see the justified true belief in the management and leadership context?
4. Do management and leadership theories help your company find out why specific issues exist?

    4.1 Are you aware of any such theory your company proactively uses?

    4.2 If No, explain why.

    4.3 If Yes, explain which theories have been used, often on what challenges, and with what results.

5. How much does technology help your company reveal complicated and complex business issues? Please give examples of any such cases.

    5.1 Explain the case, the challenge, and the outcome.

    5.2 What are the new technologies you would like to use?

6. What are the relevant technological applications which help decision-making in your company?

    6.1 Please describe each one by giving examples and explaining how they work, how often they are used, and how they benefit the company.

    6.2 Is your company proactive in leveraging technology?

7. What kind of new technology applications are needed to support the decision-making process?

    7.1 How shall they work (operate/function)?

    7.2 What would you expect from each one?

8. List five important moral issues in your company and prioritize them (most to least important to you).

    8.1 Explain why you selected them.

    8.2 What do you think the company shall do to improve them or sustain them?

9. How much time do you discuss in your company ethical and moral issues?

    9.1 Do you have any programs for that (workshops, thinking groups, open forums, etc.)?

    9.2 If Yes, how do they work? are they enough?

    9.3 If No, what do you think the company shall do and how?

10. How much do you see together ahead (see to the future)?

11. How much effort does your company place into trying to find new knowledge through different planes of wisdom? Explain and justify your answer, please.

12. How can you place intuition in the Wisdom Cube? Explain, please.

13. Is it possible that your understanding of your product and service positions is wrong? Justify your answer with arguments.

    13.1 If something is wrong, what do you propose?

14. Ponder how you can understand your products and services' current and future state with the chart of Figure 3Q?

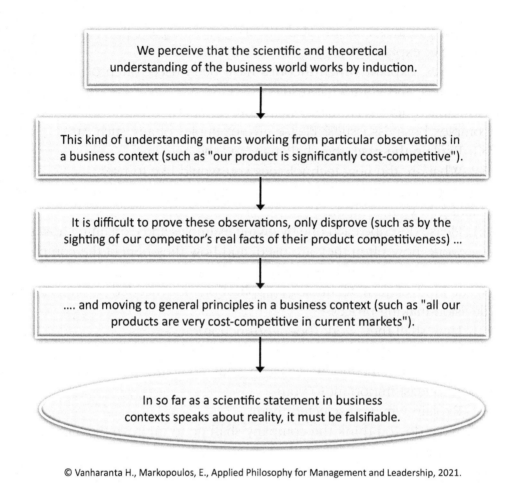

© Vanharanta H., Markopoulos, E., Applied Philosophy for Management and Leadership, 2021.

Figure 3Q Chart for Question 14 (c.f., Buckingham, et al., 2011, Karl Popper, p. 263).

References

Aristotle, 1999. *Nicomachean Ethics*. Translated by Ross, W. D., Batoche Books, Kitchener, ON, Canada, Book VI. 91–105.

Baehr, J, 2014. SOPHIA: Theoretical wisdom and contemporary epistemology. In: Timpe, K., Boyd, C. (eds.) *Virtues and Their Vices*. Oxford University Press, Oxford. 303–323.

Buckingham, W. King, Peter J., Burnham, D., Weeks, M., Hill, C., and Marenbon, J., 2011. *The Philosophy Book*. Dorling Kindersley, Ltd., London.

Magee, B., 2016. *The Story of Philosophy*. Dorling Kindersley, Ltd., London.

Miller, J.G., 1978. *Living Systems*. McGraw-Hill, Inc., New York.

Trillas, E., 2011. Lotfi A. Zadeh: On the man and his work. *Scientia Iranica*, 18 (3), 574–579.

Chapter 4

The Company Democracy Culture: Understanding Culture and Dynamics

Executive Summary

The development of a dynamic democratic company culture inside an organization follows a systemic approach. This chapter presents an overall model, utilizing Miller's living system model; Samuelsson's model of inputs, processes, and output; Nonaka and Takeuchi's spiral knowledge creation model; and Markopoulos's and Vanharanta's spiral model on focusing, perceiving, and understanding to reveal the overall ontology and to construct concepts and variables for dynamic democratic company culture. This comprehensive systemic approach can be considered as a learning and knowledge creation system for democratic cultural change. In the presented systemic view, humans are the activators, and time is the primary change variable that measures how fast the company is implementing a new democratic culture. After that, organizations can start to utilize the dynamic democratic company culture.

4.1 Introduction

Democracy in a societal context is always a dynamic learning process. While transitioning into a democracy, many countries have achieved high living

DOI: 10.4324/9781003158493-5

standards. Some countries that tried, but failed, did not internalize the content enough to produce the expected welfare for their citizens and society. Many revolutions and wars have been recorded since the existence of democracy, indicating the ethical challenges of living and learning.

Company democracy is also a dynamic learning and knowledge creation process with its early versions applied in many countries and companies without formalizing from the individual employee's perspective. Naturally, some opportunities have been given to the working class; however, laws, rules, and cultures have often restricted learning, forcing the general education to apply a complex version of Company Democracy. For many years, Sweden, for instance, has used the term "medbestämmande lag" (co-deciding law), which has proved to be very successful. Finland followed Sweden and applied the so-called "YT" laws in companies, although they have mainly been used for corporate layoff and restructuring programs.

Understanding the differences between sociopolitical democracy and Company Democracy starts by observing that political democracy follows the principle of "one man – one vote" in elections. The results of constitutional democratic elections guide society. In Company Democracy, however, the basic tenets cover much more meaningful learning, educational, and knowledge creation processes that can develop individuals in their daily occupations to create added value for themselves, the company, and the society. That is why it is essential to emphasize employees' collective understanding and conditions. Measuring the degree of democratic culture in the company benefits the company employees and the overall organization as well.

The individuals as the collective workforce must know who they are and what the company is strategically targeting. It is also crucial for them to see the company's objectives and goals to create a robust democratic company culture for a healthy and viable company. This chapter intends to reveal the company's democratic culture ontology with several different structures, constructs, and characteristics. The democratic culture forms a collective understanding of what this is all about and how it can create new value-added functions and activities. The dynamics of the company are based on its people and their collective activity and actions.

4.2 The Company Democracy Culture System and Sub-Systems

In the Company Democracy Culture System, the systemic view is followed. The system consists of the following sub-systems:

Information – Communication Sub-system	(Section 4.2.1)
Command – Control Sub-system	(Section 4.2.2)
Operation – Production Sub-system	(Section 4.2.3)
Maintenance – Support Sub-system	(Section 4.2.4)

The four sub-systems contain 20 sub-ontologies within the Company Democracy Culture Ontology (CDCO). In the following sections, the concepts of each sub-system are briefly described.

4.2.1 Information and Communication Sub-system

In the information communication sub-system, there is only one primary ontology with two separate sub-ontologies, i.e., information sharing, and conversation and listening.

i. Information Sharing Ontology

An organization's strategy can contain the basic principles of information sharing and exchange; however, information flow and sharing are often not described in companies' strategic plans. This is contradictory as knowledge creation and discovery are considered essential issues in strategic decisions, documentation, and communication. Employees appreciate high levels of information sharing. This is one of the most important concepts in creating a responsive environment inside a company. Information exchange externally and internally is a crucial component for successful company performance. It is also critical to the productivity, profitability, and overall performance of an organization. Through information exchange, people create new meanings and new knowledge. Information sharing and interaction construct groups, teams, departments, the whole organization, and the entire business supply chain, in which the company is creating added value. From the Company Democracy point of view, information sharing and exchange among employees require the free flow of information, which strongly influences transparency, openness, and equality. Information flow, sharing, and exchange are important in coordinating supply chain partners and processes. This also contributes positively to customer experience and satisfaction. Information in the company system is the feed for knowledge creation and knowledge discovery sub-systems (cf. Hatala, Lutta, 2009, cf. Li, Lin, 2006, cf. Moberg, Cutler, Gross, Speh, 2002).

ii. Conversation and Listening Ontology

In all organizations, the company workforce places a high value on conversation and listening. Inside these concepts are the fundamental democratic concepts of freedom of speech, debate, and decision-making. People should have the possibility to express their ideas, insights, and innovations. People also need the freedom to come together and feel and understand that they are being heard and valued. Conversations and listening help people to gain a conscious experience of responsive company culture. These concepts are an integral part of feeling and understanding the democratic company culture.

Listening is an important skill, capability, and competence for every employee, especially for managers and leaders. When listening is active, people have to pay attention, provide feedback, respond appropriately, wait the proper time to ask questions, understand the nonverbal communication (body language), respect mutual conversation, and learn to use progressive dialog. Listening requires people first to pay attention, then focus. Only after that will they be able to understand what they hear. Listening competence also involves noticing facts about opinions, understanding the meaning of the message, and remembering the main points from the conversation (cf. Cooper, 1997). The question here may be 'How can people improve their listening skills so that the level of organizational listening can be improved?' There are several quick techniques to improve the organizational level, but the change must happen individually. It is always good to start with knowing oneself, self-awareness, commitment, focusing, curiosity development, being fully present, and asking several right questions.

It is also possible to categorize organizational listening. One category is information seeking. The second category is the evaluation of others, and the third is responding to others. The company culture and managerial attitudes also have an impact on listening. Management and leadership must be committed to supporting effective listening inside the organization. This makes listening part of the decision-making process. Listening helps managers and leaders grasp the discussions' true meaning before entering the final decision-making stage (cf. Helms, Haynes, 1992).

Communication is an open, equal, two-way, and unbiased feature in the democratic company culture. Good reliable communication between parties is difficult to achieve, and people must work hard to achieve it. Organizational communication is always a dynamic and rapid phenomenon, and therefore a difficult concept to measure (cf. Muchinsky, 1977). Communication is often grouped into formal and informal and consists, in this context, of four types of message flows. These are membership negotiations, organizational self-structuring, activity coordination, and institutional positioning (cf. Putnam, Nicotera, 2009). Furthermore, communication requires a common language within an organization as this helps information and knowledge sharing and comprehension among people.

4.2.2 Command and Control Sub-system

The second sub-system is command and control, which contains six different ontologies.

i. Leadership Ontology

Leadership is an essential part of the command-and-control sub-system. It has a direct connection to leaders and the workforce. Leaders must have a purpose in their leadership style and be competent at activating people and using practical focusing skills.

ii. Trust Ontology

In leadership, mutual trust between leaders and employees is one of the key concepts for company success. There are three different types of meaning for the trust concept, according to Galford (cf. Galford, 2003): strategic trust (faith in how the business is run), personal trust (the bond between employees and leaders), and the organizational trust that both leaders and employees have in the company.

Trust is a qualitative measure of all human connections, i.e., between people, groups, team members, and organizations. It is characterized as the conscious and unconscious bond between parties. Hurly has identified ten factors with which to manage trust in organizations: (1) levels of communication, (2) relative power, (3) security, (4) risk tolerance, (5) alignment of interest, (6) benevolent concern, (7) capability, (8) several similarities, (9) integrity, and (10) predictability (cf. Hurley, 2006). According to Bartolomé, trust development depends on the following main concepts: respect, fairness, predictability, competence, support, and communication (Bartolomé, 1989).

In the ontology of the company's democratic culture, trust is an essential concept in the command-and-control sub-system. The concept of trust is highly appreciated and valued by company employees. The strategic, personal, and organizational types of trust are complicated to measure due to their content and fuzzy boundaries. Therefore, they are described as a measurement degree.

iii. Motivation Ontology

Theoretically, motivation can be described in many ways. The most critical concepts are intrinsic and extrinsic factors on how managers can design motivating tasks and jobs (cf. Herzberg, 1987). Many people who have intrinsic motivation to develop skills, capabilities, and competencies manage the current business challenges and requirements better. In Company Democracy Culture, these characteristics need to be learned so that the whole company can benefit from this kind of positive attitude and activity. The intrinsic factors are related to job satisfaction, while extrinsic factors are related to job dissatisfaction (cf. Herzberg, 1987).

Motivation can be defined as the processes connected to an individual's intensity, direction, and persistence in achieving a goal. Intensity means the effort a person puts into achieving the goals. Direction, in turn, means the kinds of benefits there are for the organization. The persistence variable represents for how long a person can maintain the effort of goal achievement (cf. Robbins, Judge, 2010).

In the company's democratic culture, it is crucial to understand the workforce's motivation. It is also essential to see and evaluate how to improve the motivation of the whole organization. This means that careful analysis needs to be made of each specific company's leading motivational drivers and everyone's Situationality in the company.

iv. Management Ontology

Managing a company demands having a clear picture of its purpose, the focus that must be maintained, its main activities, the problems it is trying to solve, and how to lead it. Therefore, managing a company has a direct link to objectives and evaluation activities.

v. Objectives Ontology

One of the main factors that need to be clarified to the employees is the company's purpose, as this is why the company exists. The company must have a clear mission, many visions, goals, and objectives. It must also have specified daily tasks and activities for added-value creation. In the Company Democracy context, this ontology covers its main objectives, which may also contain some of the concepts mentioned above that belong to the company's purpose.

vi. Evaluation Ontology

Evaluation is a critical process in management and leadership. Companies need to know where they are, why they are there, where they came from, and where they are heading. This kind of information is helpful for strategic planning as well as for general and specific decision-making. The company has to know how the previous actions, events, and prior decisions have affected its position, what added value the company has gained, and what added value the company is creating today. From a leadership perspective, it is essential to review the workforce's overall performance and recognize the degree of intellectual capital and its value. New insights, ideas, innovations, new products, and service development are crucial for the future. Most of this information is derived from an in-depth evaluation of the company's performance. Many problems arise when companies do not have a robust performance evaluation feedback system (Hersey, Blanchard, Johnson, 2001). According to Buchanan and Huczynski, feedback evaluation of the business performance positively affects employee behavior (cf. Buchanan, Huczynski, 2010).

Any kind of feedback culture and system seems to impact employee behavior positively, and therefore, feedback evaluation systems help the democratic culture development. Conversely, a democratic company culture allows company management to create a strong and effective evaluation system. Through an influential feedback culture, employers can see their positive contribution to the performance of their company. Suitable feedback methods help the employees understand the key performance figures and indicators dynamically, the improvements that need to be made in that regard, their impact on the company's added-value creation, and the overall company performance.

4.2.3 Operation and Production Sub-system

The operation and production sub-system has eight different sub-ontologies.

i. Participation and Collaboration Ontology

Participation and collaboration are discussed in the human resource management literature from both the individual and collective points of view. The degree of collaborative employee involvement has been characterized by the following categories: normative, disorganized, organized, consultative, negotiated, participative, and controlling.

The degree of involvement starts from the obligation to do the work through the moral norms and under the eyes of authority control and guidance. The degree ends with the controlling category, in which employees acquire control of the employees' cooperation. In Company Democracy, a strong focus on individual participation creates a collaborative atmosphere. That is why participation and collaboration start from the Delphic maxim statements and ideas. The main point is that each employee shall know him or herself to the maximum degree.

Employee participation has both negative and positive effects on organizational outcomes. When several employees participate in and collaborate on decision-making activities, the operational costs can quickly increase (cf. Schwochau, Delaney, Jarley, Fiorito, 1997). Participation somehow helps fulfill employees' higher-order needs, which leads to increased morale and satisfaction allowing change-making to be easier (cf. Miller, Monge, 1986).

Collaboration means a positive employer–employee relationship in the work environment. Internal collaboration can bring potential benefits in innovative cross-unit product and service development, increase sales through cross-selling, and adopt best practices to reduce production's operational costs. Collaboration indicates that market productivity, in particular, can grow, but also capital productivity can change. These changes have a positive effect on overall company performance. Added-value collaboration is the most effective way to improve company performance. (cf. Chapter 5). Therefore, cooperation should be focused on suitable added-value activities, and the employees should understand the added-value creation mechanisms. Bottom-up, top-down, and middle top-down activities must support strong employee participation and collaboration. Approaching collaboration with the wrong actions will destroy added-value creation (cf. Hansen, 2009).

ii. Commitment Ontology

Organizational commitment refers to the extent to which individuals regard themselves as corporate persons. It is the relative strength of an individual's behavior, i.e., "the relative strength of an individual's identification and involvement in a particular organization" (cf. Porter, Steers, Mowday, Boulian, 1974). O'Reilly has another view that brings Situationality into the picture by defining organizational commitment as "an individual's psychological bond to the organization, including job involvement, loyalty, and belief in the values of the organization" (cf. O'Reilly, 1989). Meyer and Allen (Alen, Meyer, 1990, Meyer, Alen, 1991) defined organizational commitment through three components: affective, continuance, and normative commitment. They state that these components reflect distinct psychological states of employees. Employees, in turn, can experience each of these states to varying degrees. First is affective commitment, which refers to employees' Situationality, i.e., how strongly an employee identifies with, is involved in, and enjoys membership in an organization. Second is the continuance commitment, related to the employees' own decisions concerning sacrifices and investments, namely, a cost-related commitment aspect. The third is the normative commitment, where organizational commitment, a component of Meyer and Allen's model (cf. Allen, Meyer, 1990, cf. Meyer, Allen, 1991), is based on internalized loyalty norms, i.e., feelings of obligation to remain with an organization. The described "bonds," in different ways, determine how much a person is committed to their work role to the organization.

As indicated, organizational commitment has been defined in various ways, but the following common three-dimensional theme can be found in most of these definitions:

1. Committed employees believe in and accept organizational objectives, goals, and values.
2. Committed employees are ready to provide considerable effort on behalf of their organization.
3. Committed employees are willing to stay in their organization (cf. Mowday, Steers, Porter, 1979, cf. Steers, 1977).

However, the main question is how to gain strong commitment in organizations. Organizational commitment has been interpreted as a mediator variable in several causal models of employee behavior. It has been related to employees' performance, absenteeism, and company turnover. Many correlations have also been recognized for job involvement and job satisfaction behaviors. It can be concluded that commitment is an essential, complicated, and extensive concept in the democratic culture.

iii. Diversity Ontology

During the last years, diversity has been extensively discussed in management and leadership. In many countries, the phenomenon has been caused by globalization; the workforce may represent several different nationalities, races, ethnicities, religious and political beliefs, sexual orientations, etc. Diversity requirements have changed; therefore, the working culture has changed too. The concept of diversity in business means respect and acceptance of any differences that employees might have. There are still many other characteristics of diversity like gender, socioeconomic status, age, physical abilities, and different ideologies that belong to the concept of diversity.

Managing and leading diversity require an understanding of the different views and perspectives presented by the company. It also means respecting each other and understanding the individual characteristics of each member of the company. These characteristics can be divided into three main groups, i.e., primary, secondary, and tertiary characteristics. Primary features show such identities through the following dimensions: gender, ethnicity, race, sexual orientation, age, and mental or physical abilities and traits. Secondary dimensions offer backgrounds like education, geographic location, religion, first language, family status, work styles, and work experience. Tertiary dimensions are the core of individual identity, which is more profound in the brain's unconscious part, like values and beliefs. Diversity has power, which can create a competitive advantage and increase productivity and profitability (cf. Mazur, 2010). Diversity management and leadership mean that every workforce member can perform according to their real potential. The main goal is that diversity is managed in the same manner as every homogenous workforce (cf. Thomas, 1990).

By applying the Company Democracy principles, the full potential of diversity in the organization can be embraced. This also means that the change toward the company's democratic culture through open and unbiased communication, education, and learning must support diversity.

iv. Equality Ontology

Equality can be considered a significant variable in diversity. The equality concept also presents several degrees in each organization. Some people praise equality as an essential aspect of an organization, and some entirely disagree and disparage equality (cf. Dworkin, 2002). In politics, equality is seen as the first principle of democracy, which gives equal fundamental liberties to all citizens. The second and third principles cover the right to work and how social cooperation should be available for all (cf. Rawls, 1971). Frequently, equality is seen from the inequality point of view. Inequality means that every kind of discrimination belongs, thus, to the degree of equality. It arises from many issues like religion, gender, class, race, age, and the organizational hierarchy's steepness (cf. Acker, 2006).

Lately, modern management and leadership have been directed toward equality and striking against inequality. These are concepts that management and leadership need to focus on as well. Many companies proceed with organizational changes to improve the degree of equality. Such changes have supported many women who have been placed in organizations in a similar distribution to men (cf. Acker, 2006). The same phenomenon is seen when every employee is regarded as impartially, i.e., regarding rights, opportunities, and treatment.

Furthermore, gender-neutral decisions are starting to take a more central role. Equality contains several essential variables in democratic company culture. It is firmly positioned within the concept of diversity, covering all its characteristics.

v. Justice Ontology

Conscious experience in a business situation and the workforce's emotional behavior lead to individual reactions if employees are not treated fairly in a specific case and situation. Greenberg has described "justice" with a broader term, viz., "organizational justice," which refers to employee perceptions and understanding of the reactions to fairness in the workplace (Greenberg, 1987); justice means that actions and decisions are morally right and can also be defined according to law, fairness, equity, ethics, and religion (cf. Tabibnia, Satpute, Lieberman, 2008).

Organizational justice has several sub-concepts, making it a multidimensional concept. The most critical sub-concepts are procedural and dimensional justice. Procedural justice concentrates on the perceived fairness of the process itself, which determines the outcome. Two crucial areas of procedural justice are process control and explanations. Dimensional justice conceptualizes the perceived fairness of the work. As a business concept, organizational justice behaves in a systemic way. A third sub-concept is interactional justice which describes the perceived degree to which people are treated with dignity and respect. Distributive justice is strongly related to satisfaction with the outcomes and organizational commitment (cf. Robbins, Judge, 2010). All these justice sub-concepts belong to everyday life. The workforce gains a collective understanding and view of justice in the business context when managers and leaders make justice happen in their daily decision-making.

vi. Respect Ontology

In a business environment, employees strive to be respected by other company members. Respect can be grouped into two categories: recognition of respect and the appraisal of respect. Respect recognition entails the general acknowledgment of the equivalence of another person. This is a two-way recognition and can be seen as a metric between people. A person respects or has different degrees of respect for another person. Respect means that people make assessments of other people continuously and understand their behavior through many activities. They look at the role and also the business situation of the other person in question. Respect also belongs to the occupation, such as respect for a person's skills, capabilities, expertise, and competence in a specific career or work (cf. van Quaquebeke, Eckloff, 2010). Employees should understand and learn to respect each other to create a responsive environment and a positive organizational climate. Respect is essential in the Democratic Company Culture ontology. It begins by focusing on and noticing employees who contribute to creating a positive job attitude in any company.

vii. Openness Ontology

Openness, or transparency, has been defined in three different ways in management and leadership literature. The disclosure of personal information is an aspect of transparency in a business context. Nonpersonal information is the second way to see openness in a business context; in other words, vulnerability involves disclosing nonpersonal information. Non-personal information can consist of many business issues concerning work plans, objectives, goals, strategies, etc. The third type of openness is defined as supportiveness (cf. Eisenberg, Witten, 1987). Openness can develop in many other ways embedded in company activities like decision-making, communication, leadership, management, objectives, expectations, and the free flow of ideas.

Communicative openness results in positive dynamics inside the organization and dramatically influences the responsive work environment. It increases discussion and understanding of different organizational issues. It also enhances the preparation of corporate and business changes. It is argued that openness results in higher job satisfaction among subordinates and perceptions and understanding of communicative equity (cf. Wanguri, 1996). Openness holds an essential position in democratic company culture development. It might be challenging to create because of confidential company information. Companies need policies and rules to follow in this respect before a lively, responsive, and open company environment can be created.

4.2.4 Maintenance and Support Sub-system

The maintenance and support sub-system contains five different ontologies.

i. Organizational Structure Ontology

An organization can be structured, grouped, and divided in many ways, based on its objectives, goals, and activities. The structure of an organization defines the way it operates and performs. It also describes how employees' work, task allocation, and activities are formally divided, grouped, and coordinated in a company or organization. Seven different vital elements are included in the organizational structure: hierarchy, departmentalization, centralization, formalization, work specialization, control span, and command (cf. Buchanan, Huczynski, 2010). Essential activities connected to the organizational structure also include various coordination activities and their supervision.

Employees perceive and understand their position through the organization's structure. They also understand their responsibilities and the duties that are connected to their work roles and occupations. According to Toffler, the difference between industrial-style, centralized, top-down, bureaucratic planning and a more open, democratic, decentralized style is straightforward and can be called anticipatory democracy (cf. Toffler, 1983). The breakdown is different from a centralized to a more open decentralized structure; therefore, a more democratic company culture inside each organizational structure is also required.

Many new ways to manage organizational structures have emerged through the computerization of organizations. Hierarchies have been flattened, and networking possibilities have been improved. New media like social media offers new opportunities for internal and external activities, which have changed the traditional rigid organizational structures. What is seen today is the trend of more democratic systems and closer cooperation possibilities between employees and their supervisors. In short, the new organizational structures today seem to support democratic company culture development.

ii. Empowerment Ontology

In the postindustrial society, when the service sector started to generate more wealth than the manufacturing sector of the economy, more focus has been placed on human behavior in a business context. The traditional approach to empowerment means that employees believe that they play a crucial role in their progress and development. Authorization is, therefore, realized by granting power to the persons being empowered (cf. London, 1993).

Empowerment progresses through a complicated process. It is not an object but a complex management and leadership concept. As an abstract concept, it cannot be passed from one person to another, and from a management point of view, it needs a clear vision of how it will be implemented. The implementation requires the participation of both parties, i.e., management and employees. Empowerment can be consciously experienced in many ways in an organization. By trusting employees, management can give employees more decision-making power and make them feel responsible for their tasks and work (cf. Erstad, 1997).

Similarly, trust means that employees start to use their intellectual capital to become more creative and innovative in their occupational roles. Empowerment also means that employees invest more in cooperation instead of co-opetitive behaviors. Therefore, communication should be respectful in all its meanings (cf. Fabre, 2010). Empowerment is a strategic concept used in management and leadership. It is clearly related to Company Democracy Culture development.

iii. Team Spirit Ontology

An achievement-oriented company environment helps to create a strong team spirit. However, this spirit is connected to individual capacity, skills, capabilities, and competencies in an active company. Therefore, team spirit contains many deep individual factors like self-confidence, self-esteem, visionary thinking, positive attitude, etc. It also contains many collective factors. In the company context, it is also possible for companies to have several different types of team spirit (cf. Hersey, Blanchard, Johnson, 2001).

Since individuals can learn to work in teams, it is then a management and leadership challenge to make this happen. Managers and leaders can turn their organizations into team player organizations in several different ways. One way is to employ persons who have such an internal passion for working in teams. Some people who have this skill continue to develop it when they are in a positive company environment. A second way, but a slower process, is the education and training of people to become team players. A third way is to provide incentives for people to be good team players. This requires a Co-Evolutionary and co-opetitive way of thinking; the internal competition within a team can damage the outcome of team activities. Organizations should arrange reward systems to encourage working in teams, i.e., support more collaboration, cooperation, and co-opetitive behavior (cf., Robbins, Judge, 2010).

Team spirit belongs to the concept of learning. First, team spirit factors must be perceived and understood, and then it is possible to improve the skills, capabilities, and competencies to work in groups and teams. Membership in a team gradually creates a positive attitude toward achievements. This, in turn, makes a positive impact on the company's democratic culture.

iv. Innovation Ontology

Insights and new ideas lead to innovations. Innovations need a creative and responsive environment to encourage employees to think of and develop new products, services, and practices. Creativity means producing novel and valuable ideas, whereas innovation successfully implements creative ideas into practice within an organization (cf. Amabile, 1996).

Successful innovations start with the analysis of the sources of new challenges and opportunities. Design is conceptual and perceptual, requiring innovators to go out into the markets and look, ask, and listen to those who need new products and services. Innovation requires information, knowledge, equity, skills, and talent, but above all, focused and purposeful work (cf. Drucker, 2002).

Innovation is defined in many ways. A straightforward way is a new insight, idea, method, device, or application that fulfills new requirements and market demands. This has to be separated from invention because the invention is a product or service produced via engineering processes. Innovation is something that changes an old service or product into new, more effective products and services. Innovations can also cover new business models and technologies.

Activities around innovation are essential in democratic company culture. When employees are given the right to think for themselves and fully use their brain capacity to benefit their company's future, they are part of excellent democratic company culture.

v. Reward Ontology

Reward and recognition systems are nowadays widely used in business and all types of organizations. Reward and recognition systems and programs are applied to motivate employees to work harder and change their work habits to benefit their companies and organizations. Armstrong defines this concept as "how people are rewarded in accordance with their value to the organization." There can be both non-financial and financial rewards connected to achievement, recognition, responsibility, influence, personal growth, etc. (cf. Armstrong, 2002). All reward and recognition systems are essential to employees as they create a positive job attitude and working conditions. In a democratic company culture, reward and recognition systems are part of empowerment and responsive company culture.

4.3 Democratic Company Culture Ontology Structure, Space, and Dynamics

4.3.1 Structure of the Company Democracy Culture Ontology

It is possible to build a combined ontology for the Company's Democratic culture from the Company Democracy Culture system ontologies. The overall system consists of the information and communication sub-system, command and control sub-system, maintenance and support sub-system, and the operation and production sub-system. The ontology has a total of 20 ontologies, i.e., features, which have been described in detail in this chapter. The overall structure of the ontology is presented in Figure 4.1.

Company Democracy Culture Sub-Systems

Information – Communication Sub-System

- Information sharing ontology
- Conversation and listening ontology

Maintanance and Support Sub-System

- Organization structure ontology
- Empowerment ontology
- Team spirit ontology
- Innovation ontology
- Reward ontology

Command – Control Sub-System

- Leadership ontology
- Trust ontology
- Motivation ontology
- Management ontology
- Objectives ontology
- Evaluation ontology

Operation and Production Sub-System

- Participation and collaboration ontology
- Commitment ontology
- Diversity ontology
- Equality ontology
- Justice ontology
- Respect ontology
- Openness ontology

© H. Vanharanta – E.Markopoulos 2021

Figure 4.1 Company Democracy Culture Ontology structure.

4.3.2 The Space and Dynamics of the Company Democracy Culture Ontology

The systemic view of the Company Democracy Culture is shown in Figure 4.2, in which all four sub-concepts have been combined into one entity. The arrows inside the figure describe the viable dynamics of the system. The timer indicates the time when the culture is changing.

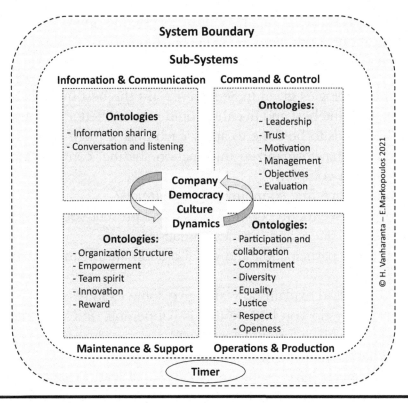

Figure 4.2 Dynamic Democratic Company culture development.

4.4 Summary

The Democratic Company culture dynamics help managers and leaders to understand the current and potential future trends of the democratic company culture. With the information generated for the adaptation of such a culture, it is possible to analyze quantitative data and qualitative information according to the current and target state of the company's democratic culture progress. The combined synthesis gives managers and leaders a transparent metric system on this complex concept, applied in any organization. Company Democracy Culture is a comprehensive management and leadership concept that should be measured continuously. By measuring the degree of the company's democratic culture, it is possible to educate the employees on the ontologies' concepts to improve and strengthen the democratic culture.

Questions for Review and Discussions

The development of a dynamic democratic company culture inside an organization follows a systemic approach. The following four different sub-systems support the company culture's systemic approach: Information – Communication; Command – Control; Operation – Production; and Maintenance – Support.

1. From the ontologies given in Section 4.2, list the best five that your organization uses the best and five that could be used better or not used at all.
   1.1. What needs to be done to apply each one of them later?
2. How do you have organized information sharing, conversation, and listening in your company?
   2.1 Do you have free communication channels?
   2.2 Do you have the freedom to speak and present your ideas about the current business and business situation?
3. Do you think participation and collaboration are organized well in your company?
   3.1 If Yes, please explain how and give some examples.
   3.2 If No, why do you believe this is happening, and what needs to be done to achieve a satisfactory level?
4. Do you have real team spirit inside your company?
   4.1 If Yes, please give examples of cases that lead to success. What has been done well? What was the win? How did the team function?
   4.2 If No, why is this happening? And what could be done to achieve effective and successful teams and teaming?
5. How well have you organized innovation possibilities, and how do you reward individuals' innovativeness in your company?
   5.1 If Yes, please give examples of the process followed and the types of rewards offered.
   5.2 If No, or not well enough, what should be done to do this better in both innovation possibilities and rewards? Please give examples.
6. Are the employees in your company culture treated with enough respect and openness to express their knowledge, ideas, and insights?
   6.1 If Yes, how is this achieved?
   6.2 If No, why has this not been fully completed yet? What degree is it achieved? What needs to be done to be achieved?
7. Ponder and give thought to your company's democratic issues in any of the company's operations and define the essential points you are ready to improve. Explain the issue, why it is an issue, and how you can apply democracy to solve it.
8. Think thoroughly with the chart of Figure 4Q on how you could create the purpose of your management or leadership occupation? Justify your answer with examples.

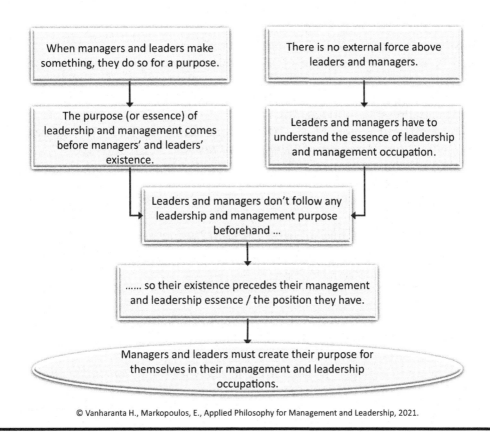

© Vanharanta H., Markopoulos, E., Applied Philosophy for Management and Leadership, 2021.

Figure 4Q   Chart for Question 8 (c.f., ref. Buckingham, et al., 2011, Jean-Paul Sartre, p. 269).

References

Acker, J., 2006. Inequality *regimes*: Gender, class, and race in organizations. *Gender & Society*, 20 (4), 441–464.

Allen, N. J. and Meyer, J. P., 1990. The measurement and antecedents of affective, continuance, and normative commitment to the organization. *Journal of Occupational Psychology*, 63 (1), 1–18.

Amabile, T. M., 1996. *Creativity and Innovation in Organizations*. Harvard Business School Publishing, Boston, MA, January 5. Note 9-396-239. 1–15.

Armstrong, M., 2002. *Employee Reward*. Chartered Institute of Personnel and Development, London.

Bartolomé, F., 1989. Nobody trusts the boss completely: Now what? *Harvard Business Review*, 67 (2), 135–142.

Buchanan, D. A. and Huczynski, A., 2010. *Organizational Behavior*. Pearson Education, Ltd., Harlow, UK.

Buckingham, W., King, Peter J., Burnham, D., Weeks, M., Hill, C., and Marenbon, J., 2011. *The Philosophy Book*. Dorling Kindersley Limited, London.

Cooper, L., 1997. Listening competency in the workplace: A model for training. *Business Communication Quarterly*, 60 (4), 75–84.

Drucker, P., 2002. The discipline of innovation. *Harvard Business Review*. 80 (8), 95–103.

Dworkin, R., 2002. *Sovereign Virtue: The Theory and Practice of Equality*. Harvard University Press, Cambridge, MA.

Eisenberg, E. M. and Witten, M. G., 1987. Reconsidering openness in organizational communication. *Academy of Management Review*, 12 (3), 418–426.

Erstad, M., 1997. Empowerment and organizational change. *International Journal of Contemporary Hospitality Management*, 9 (7). 325–333.

Fabre, J., 2010. The importance of empowering front-line staff. *Supervision*, 71 (12), 6–7.

Galford, R., 2003. The enemies of trust. *Harvard Business Review*, 81 (2), 88–95.

Greenberg, J., 1987. A taxonomy of organizational justice theories. *Academy of Management Review*, 12 (1), 9–22.

Hansen, M., 2009. When internal collaboration is bad for your company. *Harvard Business Review*, 87 (4), 82–88.

Hatala, J.-P. and Lutta, J., 2009. Managing information sharing within an organizational setting: A social network perspective. *Performance Improvement Quarterly*, 21 (4), 5–33.

Helms, M. M. and Haynes, P. J., 1992. Are you really listening? *Journal of Managerial Psychology*, 7 (6), 17–21.

Hersey, P., Blanchard, K. and Johnson, D., 2001. *Management of Organizational Behavior: Leading Human Resources*. Prentice-Hall, Hoboken, NJ.

Herzberg, F., 1987. One more time: how do you motivate employees? *Harvard Business Review*, 81 (1), 109–120.

Hurley, R., 2006. The decision to trust. *Harvard Business Review*, 84 (9), 55–62.

Li, S. and Lin, B., 2006. Accessing information sharing and information quality in supply chain management. *Decision Support Systems*, 42 (3), 1641–1656.

London, M., 1993. Relationship between career motivation, empowerment, and support for career development. *Journal of Occupational and Organizational Psychology*, 66, 55–69.

Mazur, B., 2010. Cultural diversity in organizational theory and practice. *Journal of Intercultural Management*, 2 (2), 5–15.

McGee Wanguri, D., 1996. Diversity, perceptions of equity, and communicative openness in the workplace. *The Journal of Business Communication* (1973), 33 (4), 443–457.

Meyer, J. P. and Allen, N. J., 1991. A three-component conceptualization of organizational commitment. *Human Resource Management Review*, 1 (1). 61–89.

Miller, K. I. and Monge, P. R., 1986. Participation, satisfaction, and productivity: A meta-analytic review. *The Academy of Management Journal*, 29 (4), 727–753.

Moberg, C. R., Cutler, B. D., Gross, A., and Speh, T. W., 2002. Identifying antecedents of information exchange within supply chains. *International Journal of Physical Distribution & Logistics Management*, 32 (9), 755–770.

Mowday, R. T, Steers R. M. and Porter, L. W. 1979. The measurement of organizational commitment. *Journal of Vocational Behavior*, 14 (2), 224–247.

Muchinsky, P. M, 1977. Organizational communication: Relationships to organizational climate and job satisfaction. *Academy of Management Journal*, 20 (4), 592–607.

O'Reilly, C., 1989. Corporations, culture, and commitment: Motivation and social control in Organizations. *California Management Review*, 31, 9–25.

Porter, L. W., Steers, R. M., Mowday, R. T., and Boulian, P. V., 1974. Organizational commitment, job satisfaction and turnover among psychiatric technicians. *Journal of Applied Psychology*, 59 (5), 603–609.

Putnam, L. L. and Nicotera, A. M. eds., 2009. *Building Theories of Organization: The Constitutive Role of Communication.* Routledge, New York.

Rawls, J., 1971. *A Theory of Justice.* Harvard University Press, Cambridge, MA.

Robbins, S. P. and Judge, T., 2010. *Essentials of Organizational Behavior.* Prentice-Hall, Hoboken, NJ.

Schwochau, S., Delaney, J., Jarley, P., and Fiorito, J., 1997. Employee participation and assessments of support for organizational policy changes. *Journal of Labor Research*, 18 (3), 379–401.

Steers R. M., 1977. Antecedents and outcomes of organizational commitment. *Administrative Science Quarterly*, 22, (1), 46–57.

Tabibnia, G., Satpute, A. B., and Lieberman, M. D., 2008. The sunny side of fairness: Preference for fairness activates reward circuitry (disregarding unfairness activates self-control circuitry). *Psychological Science*, 19 (4), 339–347.

Thomas, Jr, R. R., 1990. From affirmative action to affirming diversity. *Harvard Business Review*, 68 (2), 107–117.

Toffler, A., 1983. *Previews & Premises: An Interview with the Author of Future Shock and the Third Wave.* Black Rose Books, Ltd., Canada.

Van Quaquebeke, N. and Eckloff, T., 2010. Defining respectful leadership: What it is, how it can be measured, and another glimpse at what it is related to. *Journal of Business Ethics*, 91 (3), 343–358.

Chapter 5

Dimensions in Company Performance: The Power of Co-Evolution

Executive Summary

Intellectual capital can significantly impact the transformation of a company's position from its current state to a future one. However, such human assets cannot be reflected clearly in financial statements or balance sheets. The growth of a company depends significantly on the intellectual capital produced from its human assets, which positively impacts the present and future operations. Important human intellectual capital assets can be considered innovation capital, process capital, organizational capital, customer capital, human resources capital, and knowledge capital. As long as these human asset components cannot be demonstrated directly or indirectly, the company's real value cannot be estimated or predicted sufficiently. This chapter presents the basic principles of how human performance can be integrated into company performance and how Company Democracy can be applied and harnessed to promote the human dimension's effectiveness through a Co-Evolutionary approach.

DOI: 10.4324/9781003158493-6

5.1 The Human Intellectual Capital Paradox

Companies consciously invest in human resources and development; however, these investments are mostly considered as 'direct cost centers' since they are not visible enough to view profit centers. A company's market value is measured primarily from its existing assets and financial capital without considering the intellectual capital in the overall company valuation. This phenomenon creates a significant paradox. Companies praise the value of their human resources but grow without relating their intellectual capital in any financial statement. Even though some intellectual capital costs are mentioned, such as patent costs, goodwill, etc., the real value of a company's knowledge is not recorded for any valuation

The human intellectual capital that can be generated in a company with an engaged workforce can be tremendous. The employees' performance and contribution to the company's operations should be treated similarly to financial capital performance indexes such as the return on investment (ROI), the return on equity (ROE), the return on assets (ROA), and others. Company performance can be boosted with a collective way of thinking in a democratic company culture that can generate insights and knowledge from all the employees. Such a collective view can help companies understand in depth current markets and company positions and contribute to developing knowledge-based strategies instead of data-based strategies.

5.2 Co-Evolution in Human Performance

In his book *Brain of the Firm*, Stafford Beer presents that achievements can be defined with three levels of human performance: actuality, capability, and potentiality (Beer, 1995, First edition 1972).

- Actuality: What we manage to do now, with existing resources, under existing constraints.
- Capability: What we could achieve now, if we worked at it, with existing resources and under existing constraints.
- Potentiality: What we might be doing by developing our resources and removing constraints, although still operating within the bounds of what is already known to be feasible.

Furthermore, we define the crucial relations between the factors, according to Stafford Beer:

- Latency: The ratio of potentiality and capability.
- Productivity: The ratio of capability and actuality.
- Performance: The ratio of potentiality and actuality and also the product of latency and productivity.

Figure 5.1 presents the critical levels as factors for measuring human performance and illustrates the Co-Evolutionary management and leadership paradigm embedded in the human resource management area following the relationships deduced by Stafford Beer (Beer, 1995), which Jackson also examines in his book *Systems Thinking: Creative Holism for Managers* (Jackson, 2004).

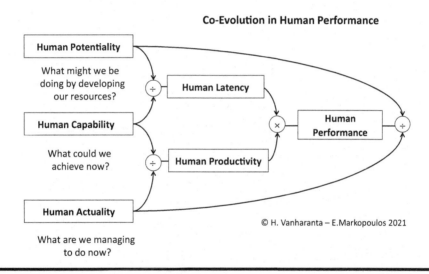

Figure 5.1 Measures of human performance (cf. Stafford, 1995, Jackson, 2004).

On the current level (actuality), it is essential to know the current management performance of a person, i.e., how the person performs at present and the constraints of such a performance. On the future level (potentiality), the employee's new targeted level is revealed. Moving toward a future state describes the individual's creative tension, which is the "autopoietic energy" the person needs to change in the current state to reach the targeted state, which is where the person wants to be. The capability to do something drives the best abilities or the best qualities a person could exhibit in a specific period. Human competence is the ability to do something well (high efficiency) and effectively (high effectiveness) in the immediate future (expanding on the potentiality). This indicates capabilities in action. By applying the time dimension to the equations of Figure 5.1, viable, dynamic systems and models are revealed, described through the co-evolution of the components and their relations and interrelations in time.

Figure 5.2 derives from Figure 5.1, with asymptotic curves of human productivity and human latency. It presents the relations and interrelationships of human performance. An individual's current performance position (C) and possible future performance position (F) can be depicted on the graph. The change in position is a function of time, shown with the time variable.

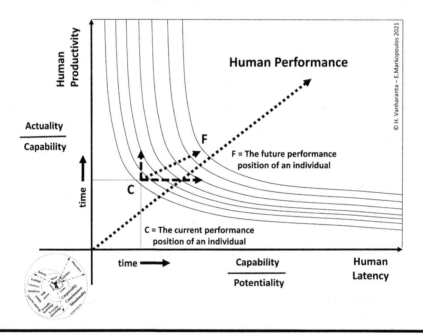

Figure 5.2 Human performance dimensions and variables.

The performance position can be improved either by changing the human productivity dimension or the human latency dimension. The human productivity path/method of improving the current performance rate is possible but difficult without considering the human latency dimension's possibilities. The equal performance curves indicate new performance rates if the existing position is above the equal vector. The position means that by developing the ratio capability/potentiality, fast new results can be achieved.

Similarly, if the current position is under the equal vector, it is better to operate with the human productivity ratio. Both ways indicate that the targeted future stage can be improved using the current performance stage of the human latency and human productivity dimensions. This change can be interpreted as the need to learn new ways by looking at the "theoretical" side and then applying the new knowledge in practice, i.e., to increase human productivity.

Figure 5.3 demonstrates the positioning of innovation performance and development with the presented method. In this example, innovation performance can be improved through the innovation productivity dimension or the innovation latency dimension, or both dimensions. It must be noted that both dimensions are essential as innovation performance improvement cannot be fully achieved theoretically but needs to be practically incorporated in different innovation methods.

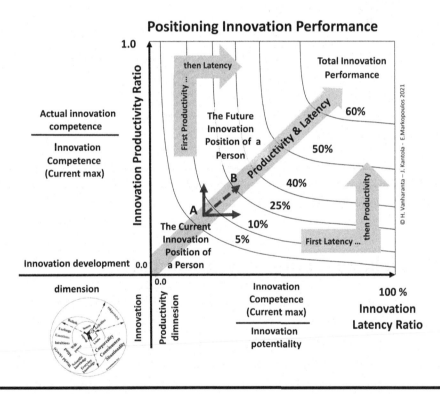

Figure 5.3   Ratios and dimensions of positioning innovation performance.

Figure 5.4 indicates the change from high innovation productivity efforts to a more innovation latency way of improving innovation performance. Faster rates of innovation performance can be reached by taking advantage of the latency dimension.

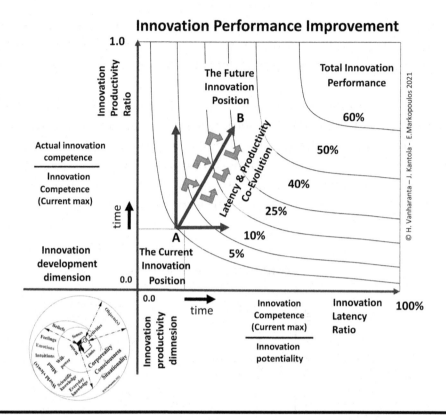

Figure 5.4 Innovation performance improvement through high innovation productivity impact and less innovation latency impact.

5.3 Co-evolution in Business Performance

Another example of the Co-Evolutionary management and leadership paradigm can be illustrated using the concept of productivity in company performance calculations (Figure 5.5). The critical operational attribute which influences the overall company performance is productivity (cf. Kidd, 1985, Kay, 1993). Capital productivity indicates how much capital is invested in added-value operations in the company, while market productivity shows how much profit is yielded in all added-value activities. Capital productivity is the added value divided by the total capital (total assets), while market productivity is the operating profit divided by the added value. Added value is the market price of products and services sold minus the market costs of purchased materials (or services) contained within them (cf. Kidd, 1985, Kay, 1993, Vanharanta, 1995).

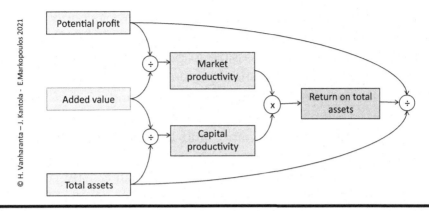

Figure 5.5   Measures of capital performance (cf. Kidd 1985, Kay, 1993, Vanharanta, 1995).

Figure 5.6 presents these performance patterns, as referred to in the case of human performance illustrated in Figure 5.1. It is crucial in this example to assure good overall profitability performance by keeping the ratios high. Before changing the ratios, the following questions should be answered: Where is the company now? How has it behaved in the past? And what are the current objectives and goals of the company?

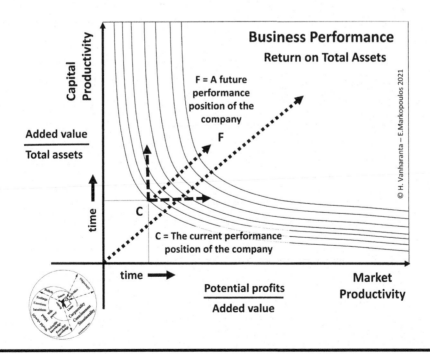

Figure 5.6   Business performance, capital productivity, and market productivity.

The company's position (situation) at present defines its current possibilities to grow and move ahead. After that, by understanding the company's present position (Situationality), it is possible to provide new guidance on how to increase the company's overall financial performance, i.e., return on total assets.

In practice, the notions illustrated in Figures 5.1 and 5.5 need to be understood and utilized simultaneously and concurrently to identify the capital profitability, i.e., financial performance and human performance at present, and the same in the immediate future.

These equations are similar, giving asymptotic curves. By combining the information in these equations, a possible new space can be determined to simultaneously handle both concepts, i.e., financial performance and human performance. The combination indicates essential relationships concerning the questions of how these ratios can be changed. It is the Co-Evolutionary way of thinking related to the two equations (not directly combined), which leads to the overall performance of financial and intellectual capital, i.e., the company's market value (cf. Edvinsson, Malone, 1997).

From the financial point of view, it has to be considered how the company's financial assets are harnessed to create added value and how its customers are willing to pay for that created added value. From the human point of view, it has to be considered which human characteristics (properties, traits, characteristics) provide the best possible human performance in each specific situation.

The business performance or company performance is usually calculated using the profit margin and the capital turnover rate. By multiplying these two characteristics at the end of a period, the profitability can be calculated. Capital productivity and market productivity result in the same equal profit curves when calculating profitability. The result is the same as the previous calculation; however, the current profitability position is slightly different. What is important here is the way the profitability is calculated. Capital productivity describes the added value divided by total assets without intellectual capital, and market potentiality is calculated by dividing potential profits by added value.

The existing position emerges by multiplying these two dimensions. This position reveals where the company is now and provides a detailed picture of where the company is headed in the future. It is also vital from the leadership perspective to ask: Is it more profitable to increase capital productivity or market productivity in the current position or business situation? If capital productivity is high and market productivity low, it is better to improve market productivity. When market productivity is high, the company has to operate in the capital productivity dimension.

This thinking changes the ratios in both dimensions/axes. Figure 5.6 presents the relationships between these two dimensions. All the profit curves can be calculated for the graph before entering the company position, giving good possibilities for analyzing the current position and indicating future trends in the development path.

As human intellectual capital is not included in the company valuations, Figure 5.6 cannot indicate the human dimension's intellectual capital contribution in business. However, this can be approached by taking the z-axis and viewing it as affecting the business performance in the third dimension. The managers' and leaders' conscious experience should see the risks and challenges of implementing a change in the company's position, exemplified by Figure 5.7.

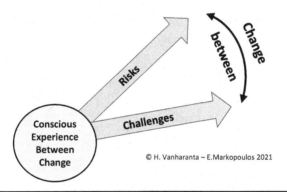

Figure 5.7   Conscious experience, risks, and challenges in the business change process.

Managers need to know their company's current position with qualitative and quantitative performance measures to make effective improvement decisions that will drive them to the desired position. It is crucial to identify the company's key characteristics and appreciate the intellectual capital generated to make the best possible impact on its market value, illustrated in Figure 5.8.

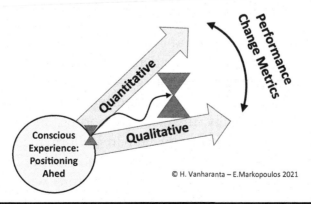

Figure 5.8   Quantitative and qualitative performance measures in the business change process.

Human performance changes should be managed over a certain period, which helps managers and leaders understand the relationships and interrelationships between human performance and intellectual capital. The organizational growth from the individual level to the collective level is a critical leadership issue interrelated with managerial topics such as productivity, profitability, and company performance.

The leaders' and managers' conscious experience, capacity, capability, and competence influence their decision-making process (Figure 5.9). The human dimension comes through the leadership function of the company development process on the intellectual capital side. Organizational growth is the way the human dimension is perceived through the Co-Evolutionary activities inside the company. Management aspects look at the profitability and productivity issues on the financial capital side. The overall performance of the company also belongs collectively to the workforce.

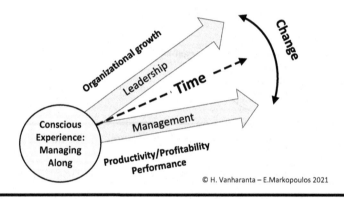

© H. Vanharanta – E.Markopoulos 2021

Figure 5.9 Leadership and management side of the change process.

5.4 Co-evolution in Collective Performance

Democratic behavior depends on the people inside the organization. Companies that create and maintain a democratic culture that bridges the distance between decision-makers and the workforce can explore new emerging spaces for performance attributes. Human performance is a product of potentiality, capability, and actuality, therefore supporting and developing future leaders' characteristics for more solid human performance. People need to understand and improve these ratios. Collective human performance can only be created through a company's democratic culture when each employee works for the expected targets, objectives, and goals.

It is vital to see the current, perceived reality from different perspectives in the proposed co-evolution context. It is also essential to understand the time dimension and the change processes inside the systems and subsystems. By increasing the viewpoints, it is possible to increase the variety of information in human brains, decreasing the potential errors in perceiving the current reality. From a human point of view, it is therefore essential to understand both people's inner world and the external environment in which they live.

Co-evolution applied to an internal perspective (introspection of their nature or characteristics) extends people's ability to evaluate and develop different personal attributes simultaneously. Co-evolution focused on the external world and different external processes (extroversion) provides a possibility to frame, categorize, conceptualize, understand, and perceive current reality in a diversified way. From the business point of view, the co-evolutionary process viewpoint helps identify the current position after the need for a change is felt, both in people and business processes. This kind of process can be considered to develop the company's democratic culture, i.e., many new views on the current business processes.

The notion of co-evolving processes is well-rooted in systems science, as well as in other sciences. Nothing can be perceived in isolation, and therefore a methodology that supports this kind of thinking seems to be a necessity. As a fundamental theory, the living systems theory by Miller (1978) can be used, which starts from the cell level and culminates in supranational systems (cf. the EU, UN, etc.). According to Miller, different systems in living systems contain similar systems and subsystems and unit processes. Control engineering focuses on feedback loops and comparators to maintain an optimal process flow in a system. Organizational and management theories also have a keen interest in holism and individual creativity to find new ways to handle complexity in contemporary business management and leadership. This systemic view has also gained ground from other areas, such as philosophy.

The whole complex functions through its parts. Progress and growth depend on the interaction between the elements and the created networks. Steady state in these systems and subsystems is impossible. Co-evolution seems to be the common denominator. It enables the timely progress of all the possible systems and subsystems through their relations and interrelations.

Co-evolution in collective performance needs the continuous "Bottom-Up and Top-Down" processes presented in Figure 5.10 to create meta-knowledge. These processes emphasize the "Incremental Bottom-Up View and

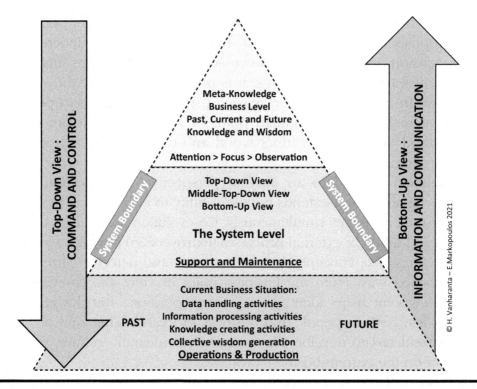

Figure 5.10 Collective meta-knowledge creation for understanding current reality and business situation.

Participation," which consists of attention, focus, perceiving, understanding, internalizing, and actions, and the "Analytical Top-Down Guidance and command" processes of communication, control, maintenance, support, production, and operations.

Incremental bottom-up actions and views reveal the current situation through collective understanding. Analytical top-down guidance, in turn, reveals the apparent synthesis of the change drivers in the current business situation and the qualitative and quantitative variables of business process features.

Democratic company culture behavior in business reveals the underlying human drivers for cooperation and co-evolution. Since nothing is made by itself, several difficult change situations must be experienced together and, at the same time, ignite a new future for the company. As these drivers of democratic behavior affect democratic performance according to the relationships described in Figure 5.11, a graphical presentation of the main drivers is presented in Figure 5.12 to illustrate the relationships between them, their dependency on each other, and ways to improve democratic performance.

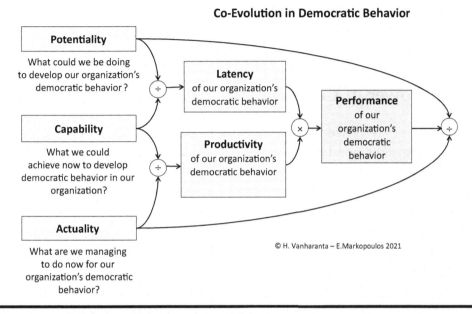

Figure 5.11   Performance characteristics of the organization's democratic behavior.

Figure 5.12 assumes that democratic performance can be measured with the democratic productivity and latency dimensions. Thus, performance can be calculated in the positions with asymptotic curves: the current performance position of the democratic activity and the possible future targeted position

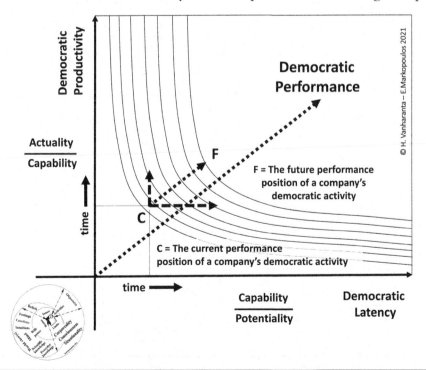

Figure 5.12   Measuring the degree of company's democratic performance.

of the democratic activity. The positions are relative, and so the measurement should be calculated to a certain degree.

5.5 The Power of Co-Evolution

Real knowledge is power, and power is freedom in contrast to ignorance. There is a constant need for freedom creation to enable learning and ideas developed with a Company Democracy framework. The combination of the human performance dimensions (cf. Figure 5.2), the business performance dimensions (cf. Figure 5.6), and the democratic performance dimensions (cf. Figure 5.12) can lead to modern organizational leadership and management models where company growth is associated with solid added-value and shared added value creation.

Intellectual capital drives new knowledge generation needed for company success, but this requires the support of financial capital to be achieved. On its own, intellectual capital is not enough for sufficient company growth without approaching it from the collective point of view of democratic company cultures, which bring these three different components together for the best possible results. Figure 5.13 demonstrates the progress path in

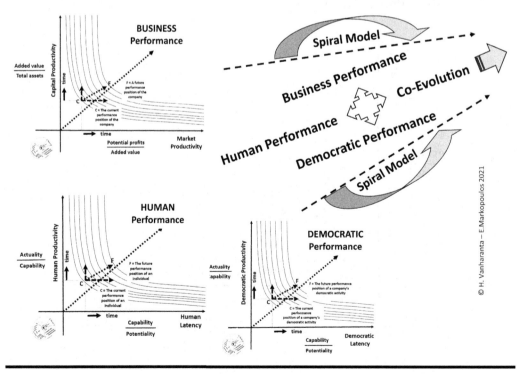

Figure 5.13 Co-evolution of human, physical, and democratic assets.

each dimension. The democratic company culture needs to be developed through the individual human development process, followed by its financial side, which controls the capital, and market productivity to meet the market demand. The integration of these three dimensions leads to new paths for company development and growth.

5.6 Summary

Human capital, Physical capital, and Semocratic capital are all real assets that lead to human performance, business performance, and democratic performance through co-evolution. This type of development process makes the co-evolution of these assets possible. By placing each of the assets in focus, it is possible to demonstrate how equal asymptotic curves can improve each asset's performance levels. It is essential to understand the capital productivity ratio and market productivity ratio when increasing the total business performance of financial assets. It is also necessary to know how to improve human performance through two critical dimensions: human productivity and human latency. The third component, i.e., democratic performance, can be enhanced by understanding its productivity and latency dimensions in a company context. Creating a democratic company culture is the key to a thriving democratic culture and the education and learning of the complex and challenging concepts inside. There is a demand for co-evolution in the company context if managers and leaders expect their company to grow in a balanced and harmonic manner.

Questions for Review and Discussions

This chapter presented the basic principles of how human performance can be integrated into company performance and how company democracy can be applied and harnessed to promote its effectiveness through the co-evolution approach. The co-evolution of human performance culminates in three different dimensions: Actuality, Capability, and Potentiality.

1. What are the significant constraints that impact your company's operations, development, and achievement?
   1.1 What has your company achieved with the current resources and under existing constraints? Please explain your answer and give examples.

1.2 What could your company achieve if it tries hard with the existing resources and under the current constraints? Please explain your answer and give examples.

1.3 How much can your company increase its resources' potentiality by developing resources and removing possible constraints? Please explain your answer and give examples.

2. How do you see the position of your company's innovation performance?

   2.1 What are the strong and weak factors?

   2.2 Why are they strong or weak?

   2.3 What can be improved?

   2.4 Please justify your answers and provide examples.

3. On a scale of 1 (low) to 10 (high), how do you consider your company's financial capital productivity level?

   3.1 If the score is under 7, what are the reasons for this, and what can be done to improve it?

   3.2 If the score is above 7, what are the reasons for this, and what can be done to sustain it or improve it?

4. On a scale of 1 (low) to 10 (high), how do you consider your company's intellectual capital productivity level?

   4.1 If the score is under 7, what are the reasons for this, and what can be done to improve it?

   4.2 If the score is above 7, what are the reasons for this, and what can be done to sustain it or improve it?

5. How do you define the term 'Democratic Performance' in your company? Are there any activities or operations related to this term?

   5.1 If Yes, what are those activities, how are they used, and are they practical (what are the results)?

   5.2 If No, why is this term or activities/operations related to it not used? What would you recommend? Please give examples.

6. On a scale of 1 (low) to 10 (high), how do you consider the degree of your company's democratic performance?

   6.1 If the score is under 7, what are the reasons for this, and what can be done to improve it?

   6.2 If the score is above 7, what are the reasons for this, and what can be done to sustain it or improve it?

7. Regardless of what your company does, if you were the CEO of a new company, what would you have done to create a democratic culture and improve the degree of your company's democratic performance? Please justify your answer. Be specific and give examples.

8. Please ponder on the chart of Figure 5Q depicting the propositions we make about your business positions.

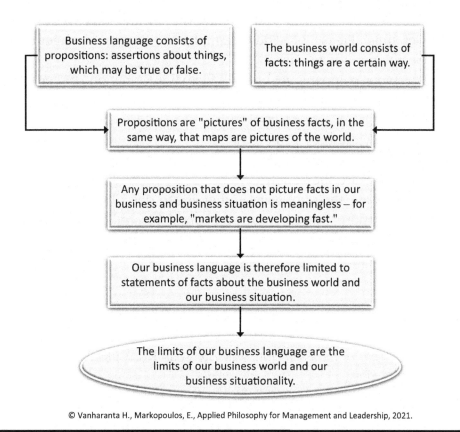

Figure 5Q   Chart for Question 8 (c.f., ref. Buckingham, et al., 2011, Ludwig Wittgenstein, p. 248).

   8.1 Does your company rely on the financial facts it gets to understand its financial situation?
       8.1.1 If Yes, what type of points give such confidence and understanding, and how?
       8.1.2 If No, what kind of financial data and analysis is needed?
   8.2 Does your company take any actions to identify its position on equal profit curves?
       8.2.1 If Yes, what are these actions? And how frequently they are executed (quarterly, semi-annually, annually, bi-annually)?
       8.2.2 If No, what alternative actions, if any, does your company take?
   8.3 Does your company balance the risks and challenges it faces? And how?

8.4 Based on what data your company generates any qualitative and quantitative analysis, does this give it enough support to synthesize its current position in the market?

8.5 How do your leaders and managers lead and manage the change over time? Please provides examples of change management over specific periods or cases.

8.6 Does your company get enough factual information concerning your business situation?

8.6.1 What are those facts?

8.6.2 How are they gathered?

8.6.3 Where/how are they produced?

8.6.4 How are they analyzed?

8.7 Do you have the right ways and words to describe your current business situation? Present your company's current operations status in 300 words using the concepts presented in this section.

References

Beer, S., 1995. *Brain of the Firm*. Jon Wiley & Sons Ltd, Chichester, West Sussex, England., 162–166.

Buckingham, W., King, Peter J., Burnham, D., Weeks, M., Hill, C., and Marenbon, J., 2011. *The Philosophy Book*. Dorling Kindersley Limited, London.

Edvinsson, L. and Malone, M. S., 1997. *Intellectual Capital: Realizing Your Company's True Value by Finding its Hidden Roots*. Harper Collins Publishers, Inc., New York.

Jackson, M., 2004. *Systems Thinking Creative Holism for Managers*. Wiley, Chichester.

Kay, J., 1993. *Foundations of Corporate Success*. Oxford University Press, New York.

Kidd, D., 1985. Productivity analysis for strategic management. In: Guth, W. (ed.) *Handbook of Business Strategy*. Gorham & Lamont, Boston, MA, 17/1–17/25.

Miller, J. G., 1978. Living Systems. McGraw-Hill, Inc., New York.

Vanharanta, H., 1995. *Hyperknowledge and Continuous Strategy in Executive Support Systems*. Abo Akademi, University Press. Turku, Finland.

Chapter 6

Managing and Leading Democratically: Achieving Democratic Balance

Executive Summary

A significant challenge in today's managers seems to be the lack of time and opportunities to gather all the necessary data, information, and knowledge they need on how to behave or how to lead people in different occupational work roles while, at the same time, managing the company or organization. Several issues arise from this problem formulation, such as what managers should do and how they should manage and lead. This chapter provides a literature review on identifying the necessary information, knowledge, understanding, and rules to be covered in different business situations. It also introduces the Management Windshield, a powerful ontology-based metaphor for finding the proper tools for management and leadership purposes from the individual point of view. The overall Windshield's ontology has already been evolved into an applied practical process framework that supports daily management and leadership. The combined ontology gives managers and leaders the content they should use to pay attention to different management and leadership objects; to focus their leading and management efforts on these objects; to perceive the contents of the objects; to understand the meanings, relationships, and interrelationships of the objects; and then in practice to use

DOI: 10.4324/9781003158493-7

the created knowledge in the final decision-making. The metaphor is also intended to guide managers and leaders to find a way to democratic company management and leadership.

6.1 The Management Windshield

The Management Windshield invokes a mental image of a workable metaphor that describes the basic concept behind it. However, such a concept must be explained and explored in detail for the metaphor's core meaning to be understood in context and content.

The Management Windshield metaphor is built up from three different viewpoints: the first is time, the second is leadership, and the third is management (Figure 6.1). All three perspectives and their contents have been placed on the driver's windshield. In this case, the driver, i.e., the leaders, managers, and executives, can see the content and the activities that form part of their work from the driver's seat. They can see the route ahead and the continuously running time of their journey. They also need to realize how the world is changing and understand how the changing environment affects their daily activities and decision-making.

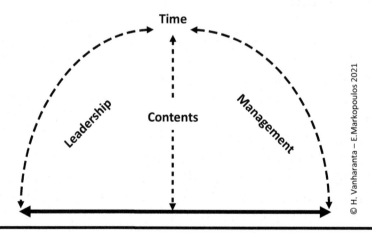

Figure 6.1   The elements of the Management Windshield metaphor.

The driver's (manager's and/or leader's) decision-making should generate the least amount of variety and entropy possible with the highest output, i.e., so that the vehicle (company) is on a constant, progressive, and successful path of change, able to answer complex questions such as: What is of the most significant importance to the drivers in the changing world? What do drivers have to see that those traveling with them don't see? How must drivers perceive the current state and the future? What must drivers say that is valid today but also tomorrow? How should drivers take care of their workforce? How do they have to balance their leadership and management competencies mentally? and also, How should drivers manage their time?

The Management Windshield metaphor is a simple support tool that helps decision-makers in situations where managers, leaders, and executives are in the conscious management and leadership 'stage.' Furthermore, the metaphor can lead to effective management and leadership concepts that can be stored on a software application or a process map to support day-to-day leadership and management and better serve the organization and business progress.

6.2 The Time Ontology

Time is not always an easy concept to handle. First, it is a unique resource, in short supply, unaffected by the demand for it, and impossible to store; second, there is neither a price nor a marginal utility curve for time; and third, it is perishable, irreplaceable, and has no available substitute (Drucker, 2005).

However, time can be managed to some extent if it can be divided and perceived differently. One way to understand time is to separate it into two different time concepts: chronological time and personally experienced time. Time can also be seen as a two-way arrow pointing to the future and the past. Between the arrows exists the present time in which we live. The economic value of time has been described by different expressions such as "time is money," "time is precious," "time matters," and others. Though different people judge time differently, when it comes to managerial positions, the importance of time and chronological order in managing various tasks gives structure to management and leadership strategies and actions.

To manage time, Bodil Jönsson uses the concept of time through a four-step metaphor (Jönsson, 2000). The first step is understanding that time can either be accepted or denied. The second step covers the discovery of more systematic ways to perceive our own time and its usage. By the third step, people have learned to describe their ideas and thoughts about time and how they relate to it. At the fourth step, the time concept can be mastered, with the possibility to compare and analyze one's way of thinking of time with other methods and thinking processes concerning time and its dimensions.

With a conscious experience of time, how people behave in time, with time, and how they understand the future, past, and present, there are possibilities to live in the present and prioritize different tasks according to how much preparation time they need. According to Jönsson, classifying tasks in these four different quadrants is already one step further in understanding how tasks can be categorized in the time dimension (Jönsson, 2000). Jönsson states that some tasks are easy and enjoyable, other tasks are easy and boring, others are difficult and enjoyable, while others are difficult and boring. People's achievement depends on the extent to which they reserve time for preparation, especially for difficult and demanding tasks. From the leadership and management perspective, routine tasks must be delegated to concentrate on demanding and challenging tasks. Jönsson's four-step time process metaphor indicates that the fourth step must be reached before progress is made in more demanding processes in terms of time management.

Concerning time, Drucker (2005) divides time management into a three-step process. The first step is recording time when influential executives and managers know how they are using their time. The second step of the process is managing time by organizing time and "cutting back on the unproductive demands on their time" (ibid.). In the third step, discretionary time is consolidated into significant activities. This three-step process is a practical management approach. It indicates that it is crucial to start with time and not with tasks. Effective managers and executives start their days by planning how to use their time. They try to have as much effective time as possible at their disposal. From Drucker's three-step process, the first time ontology can be designed by placing the critical management activities within each step of the process (ibid.):

A. Recording time: Actual recording of tasks and activities. Methods: Time log – once a week, every two weeks, or once a month; technology, tasks, and timely diagnosis.
B. Managing time: Time-wasters: Lack of system or foresight, overstaffing, disorganization, malfunction of information, wasting other people's time; things that do not need to be done at all.
C. Consolidating time: Consolidation of discretionary time. Priorities of management tasks: essential things, less critical things, unpleasant things.

Managers and executives must continuously evaluate their time and the tasks that their time is spent on and divided between. Preparation time calls for discretionary time, which is controlled by the managers and executives themselves. After analyzing time, a better grasp of how to manage time will ensue. Creating discretionary time requires excellent analysis and control of time usage. Depending on the managerial tasks, discretionary time is needed for different managerial purposes, especially for difficult and demanding tasks.

According to the literature, time must be scrutinized; it must be understood through each person's conscious experience of living in their time, i.e., the current present. Managers' time usage should also be examined by different task categories and recorded accordingly. Managers should reserve preparation time, prioritize their time for various tasks, and find or create more discretionary time. From the above, a simple ontology can be formed for the concept of time in a managerial position: chronological time, experienced time, preparation time, recording time, managing time, and discretionary time (Figure 6.2).

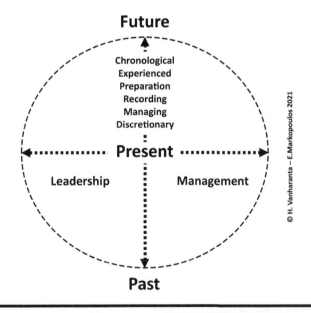

Figure 6.2 Time concept representation.

Each time category content must be internalized by the manager, leader, or executive to achieve the best possible results through effective time management.

6.3 The Leadership Ontology

Leadership is an abstract term that has been defined in many ways. It is generally characterized as a broader concept than management. Some people understand leadership as part of management. According to Hersey, Blanchard, and Johnson:

> leadership occurs whenever one person attempts to influence the behavior of an individual or group, regardless of the reason. It may be for one's own goals or the goals of others, and these goals may or may not be congruent with organizational goals. (Hersey, Blanchard, Johnsson, 2001)

Following the Holistic Concept of Man metaphor (cf. Salminen, Vanharanta, 2007), the leadership concept can also be considered from the situational, conscious experience, and managing viewpoints.

According to David Pardey, "Leadership is something that people see or experience, personally. It is above all about the relationship between the leader and those being led" (Pardey, 2007). People build relationships in conscious experience in a particular situation. Situationality is, therefore, an essential component of the leadership concept. The categorization of the leadership concept can build the leadership ontology components needed by dividing leadership into four main categories. The first category is the Purpose of Leadership, the second is Leadership Focus, the third is Leadership Styles, and the fourth is Leadership Activities. These leadership areas significantly impact the development of a company's democratic culture.

6.3.1 Purpose of Leadership

i. Organizational Success

Organizational success is one of the main goals of leadership. It is considered that successful leadership can be achieved as the success of an organization is positively related to leadership effectiveness in managing the organization's intellectual capital (Edvinsson, Malone, 1997). Intellectual capital can be separated into human capital and structural capital. In addition, customer capital and organizational capital are the essential components outside the human-dependent capital that affect an organization's development and growth (ibid.). The leaders are responsible for the development and growth of these assets. They must realize how these components can be addressed, as development and growth are essential to everyone in the organization. However, the core factor behind every organizational change is how people behave in their different work roles.

ii. Crafting the Future

There is intense and continuous pressure to create new markets, new products, and new services while at the same time keeping all of the customers satisfied. To achieve such a management goal, leaders need to understand their organization's past and current state. They also need to understand how the future is created. Organizational success starts at the individual level. Success requires a workforce that follows visions, challenges, and objectives; however, this progressive way also calls for discontinuities, lateral thinking, conceptual thinking, analytical thinking, integrative thinking, etc., to create a new future. Crafting and projecting the future is undoubtedly better than simply coping with the present. The creation of the future, and not just its projections, needs a new recipe with new ideas, new ways of producing, new products, and new services for current and future customers. Crafting the future that can lead to an organization's success is one of the critical purposes of leadership and should thus be part of the leadership ontology.

iii. Followers

Leaders should first contemplate who they are, what kind of competencies they have, how they behave now, and how they can improve, develop, and grow their leadership skills into leadership competencies. The focus then shifts more to how the leaders use their competencies within their organization and how they maintain and empower organizational development and growth. This will lead to the best possible overall productivity and latency development of the workforce, which will, in turn, deliver the best possible performance. Based on the above definitions, leadership seems to originate from the leader's initial influence on his/her direct subordinates. It is maintained by the leader's competence and the commonly understood goals supported by all participating parties. Leaders have specific attributes, skills, capabilities, and competencies to influence their direct subordinates. Pardey describes the creation of one particular meaning between the leader and the object/subject, i.e., the follower, as relationship building. He specifies the relationship as follows: "Leaders need followers, and one definition of leadership is that leaders are people who inspire others to follow" (Pardey, 2007).

iv. Individual Success

Leaders and managers should accept the coexistence of the mind and body first. This is very close to the idea concerning time, i.e., trying to understand what time means to each individual personally. In the same way, leaders must understand the deep structures and content of the body, mind, and situation before any individual success can be achieved. This basic understanding can help leaders create the solid background knowledge needed in the demanding lead role. After that, it is much easier to understand and coordinate all the essential leadership characteristics. This type of map or ontology helps people to understand the attributes of the leadership role. When these capabilities are in active use, they form competence. This process leads to individual success.

6.3.2 Leadership Focus

Pardey has compiled some of the most crucial leadership types (Pardey, 2007).

Transactional leaders have a keen interest in high productivity figures, specific short-term and long-term goals and objectives. Leadership is like a transaction between leaders and followers.

Action-centered leaders focus their activities on the task by supporting individuals and teamwork.

Transformational leaders try to create mutual trust and confidence among their followers.

Servant leaders go deeper into the human psyche, seeking to understand workers and their relationships and interrelationships more.

Emotionally intelligent leaders try to find their own most important competencies and social competencies to influence and inspire their followers.

6.3.3 Leadership Styles

The situational leadership model developed by Dr. Paul Hersey is an easy-to-use model to which different leadership styles can be applied in various occupational situations (Hersey, 1984). According to Hersey, the first aspect to understand is the current situation, the task orientation, and the relationship behavior needed in a specific situation. The conceptual model has two different perspectives, the leader-directed or follower-directed sub-concepts.

The model gives four different modes which can be applied in practice (ibid.):

1. Telling mode (telling, guiding, directing, establishing)
2. Selling mode (selling, explaining, clarifying, persuading, coaching)
3. Participating mode (participating, encouraging, collaborating, committing)
4. Delegating mode (delegating, observing, monitoring, fulfilling)

The leadership modes require different stages in follower-development and growth processes. In the telling mode, task behavior is high, and relationship behavior is low. The follower is incompetent and unwilling. Leaders and managers must tell the follower what to do. In the selling mode, both task and relationship behavior are high. The follower is still incompetent but has become willing to do the work. The participating mode requires high relationship behavior and low task behavior. In this readiness level, the follower has learned a lot but is still avoiding responsibility, i.e., is still a little unwilling. In contrast, in the last delegating mode, both relationship and task behavior are low, and the follower is competent and willing to participate and take responsibility. The model itself is simple and forms a curved metaphor that is easy to recall. The simplicity of Hersey's model makes it ideal for the Management Windshield metaphor and model.

6.3.4 Leadership Activities

i. Leading

Leading organizational resources necessitates a profound understanding of these assets and how market value can be created by allocating assets. Leading requires threshold skills, professional knowledge, and occupational role capabilities before competence in a specific leadership role can be shown. This means that role-specific occupational competencies must be developed. Leaders need to test their competencies to obtain an idea of their particular leadership style, which can cover both actual activities and potential activities, i.e., how personal competencies can be developed in and for the future.

ii. Visioning

Good leaders work a lot to create and develop their visions, which are essential for both the organization and the leader. In scenario thinking, it is possible to extract the workable visions for the realization process. Visions should be simple, imaginable constructs. Leaders also need followers and extensive knowledge to empower those followers to work toward critical objectives, goals, challenges, and visions.

iii. Guiding

Leaders must be able to communicate and describe their visions thoroughly so that followers can understand and internalize them. There are many different technologies and ways of understanding, such as metaphors, figures, discussions, talks, meetings, incentives, etc. It is advantageous for the organization if the leader's followers can sustain and relate to the organizational visions as the followers' ideas. Guiding visions is one of the most critical competencies needed in leadership.

iv. Empowering and Inspiring People

Change expects leaders to use all their competencies, especially the inspiring competencies, to set followers on their path to the future. This calls for an empowering organizational culture pre- "tuned or inspired" by the whole organization, especially the leaders.

v. Problem-Solving

Handling Conflicts: Nothing can happen quickly and easily. There are always those who resist change or new methods or new ways of doing new things. Therefore, conflict resolution is an essential leadership skill. As the leaders' strong opinions easily reverberate throughout the organization, they have to think in many different roles.

Making Change Happen: Leadership is actualized when leaders make the change happen outside and inside the organization, i.e., they turn their visions into real-life experiences. This overall process is perhaps the key difference between management and leadership. However, management and leadership are closely related, especially when real-world experiences obtain form and content.

6.4 The Management Ontology

According to Drucker, management as a discipline simply means "managers practice management" (Drucker, 1985). It is partly real work that managers do, but management also has other conceptual meanings. Drucker states that management is the organ of leadership, directions, and decisions on where these activities are practiced (ibid.). It consists of three crucial concrete tasks: giving direction, setting objectives according to the mission, and organizing resources to achieve results (ibid.). In this way, management covers abstract issues together with practical work. Constructing a comprehensive management ontology requires many different viewpoints, yet this is still not enough as management is a vast concept with many fuzzy components. However, we have created a basic idea of how an ontology for management can be constructed for the Management Windshield. The ontology categories are divided as follows: Purpose of Management, Management Focus, Management Work Styles, and Management Activities.

6.4.1 Purpose of Management

The management ontology should encompass the organization's purpose because each organization exists for a specific reason, as described in its mission statement, visions, and goals. Generally, this means that the organization has economic plans in a business context and strives to achieve high business performance levels (cf. Drucker, 1985). All businesses should first think about their purpose, then their mission, and only after that should they build the visions to structure objectives and near-term tasks. This output can be covered by the company strategy so that all organization members understand through their conscious experience why they do what they do and when to do it.

6.4.2 Management Focus

One highly valued concept in management is contribution, the offering of something meaningful inside the organization. Meaningful refers to a high level of efficiencies, such as increased productivity and profitability and high overall effectiveness rates. Part of the contribution process is attributable to the manager. One aspect is cooperation with direct reports, colleagues, etc., and another the usage of different management tools. However, management's main contribution can generally be divided into three main focus areas, which can then be taken from the manager or executive's viewpoint. These areas are as follows (cf. Drucker, Maciariello, 2006).

i. Focus on Getting Results

Managers and executives try to contribute to their organization's results and performance positively. They are responsible for making everything happen efficiently and effectively, in the best possible way, by targeting high overall performance levels.

ii. Focus on Values and Value Building

Each organization needs a purpose, a mission, several visions of the future, and the commitment to do something to achieve them. Essential values lie behind the purpose, mission, visions, etc. They are held and developed continuously. These values guide the organization into an unknown future. Managers and executives are responsible for these values and value-creating.

iii. Focus on Developing Human Resources

The workforce's inability to manage the natural change of the external and internal environment is always a concern. Building and developing people in their occupational roles to meet the future is one of the management's main tasks. An organization has to renew its human capital by steadily upgrading its human resources for tomorrow. Managers and executives are responsible for human capital improvement. They are also the ones who should support the development and growth of their workforce to accomplish the change needed in their productivity and latency levels.

6.4.3 Management Work Styles

Management work styles differ from leadership work styles. At certain times, managers can be very decisive, autocratic, and exercise high control. At other times the management work style can allow personnel more freedom to decide on their work. Based on the contents of theory X and theory Y (cf. Hersey, Blanchard, Johnsson, 2001), the pure forms of these two extreme management styles are seldom used in practice. A time- and place-sensitive combined style of management is seen in actual management situations. This integrated management method is fuzzier, where management is affected simultaneously by many different factors. The fuzzy management work style, therefore, gives management the needed flexibility.

6.4.4 Management Activities

According to Allen (cf. Allen, 1995), management activities can be categorized practically into seven essential categories. These categories are summarized below, and their activities are connected to the Management Windshield model.

i. Establishing Objectives

Organizational objectives must derive from the organization's strategy to be part of it. They describe the business at its present and in the future. The objectives must fit well with the operational and tactical levels of the organization. It should then be possible to find realistic near-term targets, tasks, and work role assignments for each member of the organization, using the objectives as a starting point. Drucker lists the following eight key areas where objectives need to be set (cf. Drucker, 2005): marketing, innovation, human resources, financial resources, physical resources, productivity, social responsibility, and profit requirements. Many objectives can exist simultaneously because so many areas have specific objectives. After collecting a set of main objectives, the common challenges can be identified, and the risks involved in them can be measured. However, knowing these key objectives is not enough for managers and executives. They must also organize people and motivate them to meet the challenges involved in reaching the objectives.

ii. Organizing

Organizing starts with objectives. The managers and executives must analyze the current situation and decide the target levels, human resources, and the schedule to reach the objectives. A detailed plan must be made so that everybody involved in the effort knows what to do and when to do it. Cooperation and teamwork are essential tools in this phase. Employees should know what the plan is, and they should also have the opportunity to discuss its content in more detail with their superiors.

iii. Motivating

Motivation is crucial to getting things done. Ford's motivational systems theory gives us a framework to follow based on three sets of phenomena that need consideration:

the selective direction of the behavior pattern, i.e., where people are heading and what they are trying to do; the selective energization of the behavior pattern, i.e., how people get "turned on" or "turned off"; and the selective regulation of behavior patterns, i.e., how people decide to try something, stick with it, or give up. (cf. Ford, 1992)

iv. Developing

Developing people is a management function that calls for concrete plans and programs. People usually are willing to learn more, create new knowledge, and be active partners. Creating a culture of competence in the organization is one of the main tasks managers and executives face in today's competitive environment (cf. Zwell, 2000).

v. Communicating

Allen (1995) provides some simple rules to follow in management concerning communication, which may be sufficient in many management situations. Communication requires exchanging information, all information to be obvious, perfect, and complete, containing meaning, being understood, and being delivered in many ways without losing its content.

vi. Controlling and Measuring

To determine whether the organization is achieving the objectives set by its management, continuous measurement and analysis are required. Specialists should control the measuring itself to be valid in practice. Measuring should also be done in due time to obtain current real data and information concerning the company's characteristics in every respect. All reports and analyses should target the same objective: to make corrective actions in time. The methods used must be easy to understand as well as meaningful for the organization. The action itself, i.e., the measuring, must also be economically feasible. All measurements should be kept as simple as possible, and they should be understandable to each partner who uses them.

vii. Problem-Solving and Decision-Making

Problem-solving and decision-making are the most demanding managerial and executive activities and require special attention. Many formal discussions are needed before managers and executives can get a picture of the real options and make decisions. It is crucial to understand whether a decision is possible, really necessary, and feasible. Decision-making is, however, a process of many phases. The priority is to find the problem(s), classify them, define their content, make particular specifications concerning each problem, and then decide what is right in light of the primary focal areas described above, after which comes the critical, final decision-making. Lastly, it is necessary to build action plans, follow up, and control how the decisions affect real life outside and inside the organization.

6.5 Management Windshield: The Combined Ontology

The Management Windshield is a combined management and leadership ontological framework that focuses on the idea of helping decision-makers with a simple support tool that can be used in situations where managers, leaders, and executives are at their conscious management and leadership 'stage.' The Management Windshield has been created with the content of the three most essential ontologies: time, leadership, and management. The combined ontology is now presented here as the Management Windshield metaphor (Figure 6.3).

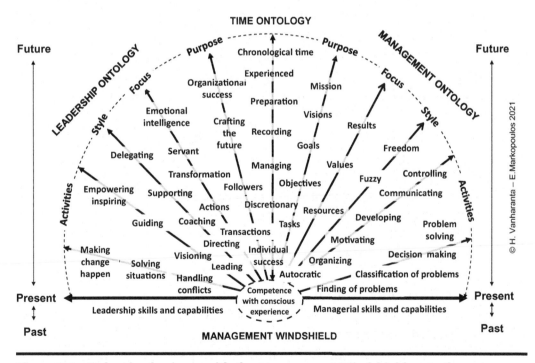

Figure 6.3   Balancing business with the Management Windshield metaphor.

The Management Windshield presents critical concepts in a simple, visual manner. It can analyze the current state of leadership, management, and managers' and leaders' conscious experience over time. Thus, the metaphor forms the workable "Management Windshield" with its many real-world application possibilities in management and leadership. Leadership is divided into four different parts: activities, style, focus, and purpose. Similarly, the management side is divided into activities, style, focus, and purpose. With the help of this management and leadership tool, it is possible to balance democratic activities in/within organizations.

6.6 Summary

To use the Windshield metaphor, the leader or manager must take initiatives to get things done with the organization s/he is serving. This way, there are possibilities to impact many areas mentioned in the metaphor on its right-hand or left-hand side. Before getting involved, managers and leaders must understand the different features of time and how time passes. At the start, managers and leaders must understand that relationships are significant in all active managerial and leadership roles, i.e., the right-hand side issues and the left-hand side issues. They must also use the Delphi maxims basis to strengthen their understanding of themselves (Know yourself). They should perceive what they can promise (Moderation is best; Be careful what you promise/wish) and see that everything is produced in harmony (Nothing in excess).

The critical basic principles of management and leadership are as follows:

A. Concerning individuals
   - Be responsible for the leadership role assigned.
   - Adhere to ethical principles in management.
   - Strive for selflessness.
   - Maintain self-control in all situations.
   - Develop maturity.
   - Confirm situational awareness.
   - Use experience intelligently, i.e., wisely, in different situations.
B. Concerning the organization/group/team
   - Take good care of interpersonal relationships at every turn.
   - Adhere to equality.
   - Be fair.
   - Tolerate errors in the performance of your subordinates.
   - Encourage and give recognition to your subordinates.
   - Be an example to others.

The ultimate goal is to help the individual in the driver's seat to develop leadership and management competencies on "the leadership and management stage." The Management Windshield has already been used successfully in several cases. One such case was the development of leadership and management practices in the Finnish health-care sector.

This chapter's managerial activities will help leaders and managers create an excellent company democratic culture and focus on the correct issues for balancing and controlling their demanding work roles.

Questions for Review and Discussions

This chapter described the challenge today's managers face when leading and managing their companies. They lack time and opportunities to gather all the necessary data, information, knowledge, and wisdom to behave or lead people in different occupational work roles while managing the company or organization. Several essential areas rise managing time, leading people, and addressing the critical issues inside the company. Leadership and management ontologies have the same focus: Activities, Style, Focus, and Purpose.

For questions 1–4 considering that you are the CEO of a company, please ponder and evaluate the following issues:

1. Leadership (for each sub-question, please justify your answer, expelling the process you follow and give examples)
   1.1 How I lead my organization?
   1.2 What kind of style I have?
   1.3 What is the focus of my leadership?
   1.4 Do I have a real purpose in my leadership?
2. Management (for each sub-question, please justify your answer, expelling the process you follow and give examples)
   2.1 How I manage my company?
   2.2 What kind of managing style I have?
   2.3 What are the focus areas I concentrate on in my managing?
   2.4 Do I have a real purpose in my management?
3. Time (for each sub-question, please justify your answer, expelling the process you follow and give examples)
   3.1 How I manage time?
   3.2 How can I have enough time to think?
   3.3 How can I have enough time to concentrate on critical issues?

4. Focus/Balance (for each sub-question, please justify your answer, explaining the process you follow, and give examples)
    4.1 How can I zoom in to particulars?
    4.2 How can I zoom out to see the big picture?
    4.3 How can I balance between leading and managing my company?
    4.4 How can I behave democratically in my leadership and management efforts?
5. Please find out the problematic areas in your business with the chart of Figure 6Q.

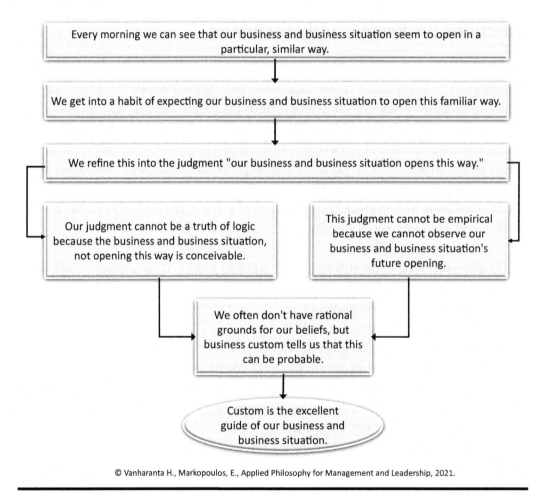

© Vanharanta H., Markopoulos, E., Applied Philosophy for Management and Leadership, 2021.

Figure 6Q   Chart for Question 5 (c.f., ref. Buckingham, et al., 2011, David Hume, p. 151).

5.1 Is "business as usual" a common phrase in your company?
    5.1.1 If YES please explain why? If NO, please explain why?
    5.1.2 Is this good or poor practice?

5.1.3 What are the results of such thinking?

5.2 Do you want to revert to the "business as usual" situation in your company?

    5.2.1 If YES, why and how?

    5.2.2 If NO, why?

5.3 Does your company have ideas that drive its business?

    5.3.1 If YES, where do the ideas come from? How do you get them? Explain the process? Can you improve this process, and how? Give examples.

    5.3.2 If NO, then why is this happening? What could you do to revert this situation?

5.4 Can you identify the enablers of your business?

    5.4.1 If YES, how do you specify? Who is behind? Can you have more enablers? And how?

    5.4.2 If NO, then why is this happening? What could you do to revert this situation?

5.5 Can you have foresight in your business situation?

    5.5.1 If YES, what can you foresee? How do you achieve this?

    5.5.2 If NO, then why is this happening? What could you do to revert this situation?

5.6 Do you think your company is more of a follower or leads and creates new business opportunities?

    5.6.1 Explain why the company is a leader or follower.

    5.6.2 If it is a leader, then how is this achieved and sustained?

    5.6.3 If it is a follower, is there any intention to be a leader?

        5.6.3.1 If YES, how will this be achieved?

        5.6.3.2 If NO, why is it acceptable to stay a follower?

References

Allen, R. E., 1995. *Winnie-the-Pooh on Management*. Penguin Books, London, UK.

Buckingham, W., King, Peter J., Burnham, D., Weeks, M., Hill, C., and Marenbon, J., 2011. *The Philosophy Book*. Dorling Kindersley Limited, London.

Drucker, P. F. and Maciariello, J. A., 2006. *The Effective Executive in Action*. HarperCollins, New York.

Drucker, P. F., 2005. *The Essential Drucker*. HarperCollins, New York.

Drucker, P. F., 1985. *Management Tasks, Responsibilities, Practices*. Harper & Row, Publishers, Inc., New York.

Edvinsson, L. and Malone, M. S., 1997. *Intellectual Capital: Realizing Your Company's True Value by Finding its Hidden Roots*. Harper Collins Publishers, Inc., New York.

Ford, M. E., 1992. *Motivating Humans, Goals, Emotions, and Personal Agency Beliefs.* Sage Publications, New York.

Hersey, P., 1984. *The Situational Leader.* Warner Books, Inc., New York.

Hersey, P., Blanchard, K. H. and Johnsson, D. E., 2001. *Management of Organizational Behaviour Leading Human Resources.* Prentice-Hall, Inc., New Jersey.

Jönsson, B., 2000. *10 Ajatusta ajasta.* Translated from "Tio tankar om tid." Karisto Oy, Hämeenlinna.

Pardey, D., 2007. *Introducing Leadership.* Elsevier, Ltd, Amsterdam.

Salminen, T. and Vanharanta, H., 2007. The holistic interaction between the computer and the active human being. In: Jacko, J. (ed.). Proceedings of the 12th International Conference on Human-Computer Interaction (HCI), Beijing, China. Part I. LNCS 4550. 252–261.

Zwell, M., 2000. *Creating a Culture of Competence.* Wiley, New York.

HUMAN FOCUS IN LIVING SYSTEMS

2

Chapter 7

The Holistic Concept of Man in the Business Environment: The Concepts We Live By

Executive Summary

Over the past 20 years, new management and leadership concepts have started being developed around the individual, i.e., human beings. It is the employees who must know first who they are (know yourself), how they can develop their personal growth, and what methods they can use to do so. Today new requirements have arisen, and further questions are evolving on how an individual can be the added-value creator in a business context. The Holistic Concept of Man can illustrate these new conceptual management system requirements with a robust metaphorical method. Its nature is not so self-evident because people think and act automatically in different business situations. However, new conditions lead to new thinking and provide a unique view of how people see the modern human being as part of a living system, working in occupational roles for added-value purposes inside the complex business environment.

7.1 Introduction

With the human focus, people refer to the many leadership concepts and issues in the management and leadership of organizations and companies,

DOI: 10.4324/9781003158493-9

i.e., business environments. The behavioral and human resource management literature focuses mainly on practical organizational behavioral and human resource management questions from the leadership and management perspectives. Management literature, in turn, has been concentrated many times on production, technology, productivity, and new technological solutions.

From a leadership point of view, there are many broad and complex leadership ontologies, constructs, and concepts that emphasize a new collective understanding of leadership issues such as individual differences, gender, skills, capabilities, competencies, motivation, job satisfaction, engagement, commitment, education, learning, stress tolerance, social interaction, group, and intergroup behavior, etc. From the management perspective, many issues and concepts also need new thinking: new computer systems, emerging technologies, alternative work design, control systems, structure, performance, productivity, managerial processes, change culture, safety culture, power, redundancy, variety, entropy, etc.

These different leadership and management areas, constructs, concepts, and issues raise more essential questions. However, they all lack the collective understanding and discussion of the critical starting points for human resource or intellectual capital management and leadership, such as discussing human beings and their existence. In the following sections, the Holistic Concept of Man metaphor is presented in the business environment and explores how metaphors can help identify the essential business constructs and concepts people live by. Lakoff and Johnson's view of people's conceptual system concerning how they think, act, and experience various activities supports this kind of holism in metaphorical thinking (cf. Lakoff, Johnson, 2003).

7.2 Know Yourself – Opening the Human Mind

There have been efforts in philosophy to understand human beings, their behavior, and the world around them. In management and leadership literature, authors and researchers rarely go far back in human history or back to the fundamental philosophical principles developed through hundreds of years to link the past with today and the future. *The Philosophy Book* provides condensed information on developing different intellectual trends from the ancient world to the modern contemporary era (cf. Buckingham et al., 2011).

There has been a strong emphasis on debate, dialog, knowledge management, knowledge creation, logic, language, morality, politics, reasoning, systems of thought, science, and society in each era. There has also been a focus on ideas, values, and beliefs, such as the fundamental problems of human existence and our understanding of the world. These areas of focus in philosophy have strongly supported modern management and leadership development. However, the basic understanding of the human and the human mind has primarily been in the background, not approached from a practical viewpoint for daily management and leadership (ibid.).

This chapter unlocks the human mind, especially for managers and leaders, to see themselves as active human beings in their current management and leadership roles. The aim is first to help managers and leaders see themselves clearly (know yourself). After that, the objective is to provide ideas on how they can actively develop their characteristics, and with some examples, to see different business management and leadership constructs, concepts, and objects in the complex company environment.

7.3 The Holistic Concept of Man Metaphor

The Holistic Concept of Man (HCM) is considered a metaphor whose basic dimensions consist of body, mind, and situation. The physical human being exists as part of the situation in which they are or have been for a certain period (cf. Rauhala, 1986, 1995). According to Rauhala, the three modes of existence of man form the holistic concept. They are as follows:

1. Corporeality or existence as an organism with organic living processes (the body), i.e., inputs, processes, and output. It is the physical body as an open system.
2. Consciousness or existence as a psychic-mental phenomenon: thinking, interpreting, perceiving, and experiencing human beings. Rauhala calls this the mind of the human being.
3. Situationality or existence concerning reality, i.e., the situation. A human being has relationships and interrelationships that characterize an individual's qualities in a specific situation or situations they have experienced in the past, are experiencing currently, or are anticipating in the future.

In this context, the Holistic Concept of Man metaphor is applied by considering an active human being in a work role situation who is a member of a company or organization. Engaged human beings can evaluate their relations and interrelationships through introspection and make other interpretations that characterize objects' external concepts or qualities in their conscious experience. Therefore, this kind of introspection and extrospection is an integral part of human activity, which connects human beings as a living system to the external or internal business environment.

The first mode of existence, Corporeality, maintains the fundamental processes of existence and implements the human being's physical activities. All the fundamental processes of human life are biological. These functions include evolution, metabolism, growth, respiration, digestion, excretion, reproduction, responsiveness, movement, activity, differentiation, and belongingness. All of these different processes are related and interrelated. The human brain and senses (internal and external) are needed when a human being first becomes aware of a situation, then focuses on a particular happening or observes the objects and concepts in a specific situation.

In Consciousness, an active human interprets, perceives, and understands the different phenomena, objects, and concepts they encounter. This is more than a dynamic thinking process because experiencing, focusing, perceiving, understanding, and interpreting are included. When human beings use their inner and outer senses, they continuously receive many physical signals from the external environment. The situation always provides meaningful content to the Consciousness, and a human being understands this content, i.e., perceives the corresponding object(s) or concept(s) as "something," i.e., having some meaning or meanings.

Situationality is the third dimension of human existence, highlighting that a human being exists not only "as such" in a vacuum or isolation but always in relation and interrelation to reality with its multitude of aspects in an open system. The world, or reality, exists concretely or ideally, i.e., the world to which people generally relate. Situationality (or the life situation) is that part of the world through which a particular human being forms relationships and interrelationships (cf. Vanharanta, Pihlanto, Chang, 1997).

In Figures 7.1, 7.2, and 7.3, the Holistic Concept of Man is formulated, and the three different modes of existence are presented simultaneously.

Figure 7.1 has been drawn so that the outer circle represents the situation and the Situationality of the human being. It contains, therefore, all the relations and interrelationships that the human being has. Consciousness is inside Situationality and helps one interpret what is happening in a situation. This Consciousness is formed inside the human mind by the processes of the brain. Inside Consciousness, Corporeality is depicted as the body with senses, limbs, and brains.

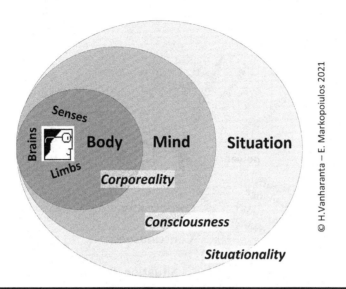

Figure 7.1 **Basic concepts of the Holistic Concept of Man (cf. Rauhala, 1986, 1995, Vanharanta, Pihlanto, Chang, 1997, Vanharanta, Markopoulos, 2021).**

Figure 7.2 indicates how an object is connected in the conscious part of the human mind. It demonstrates the content of the Holistic Concept of Man revealed more from the Consciousness point of view.

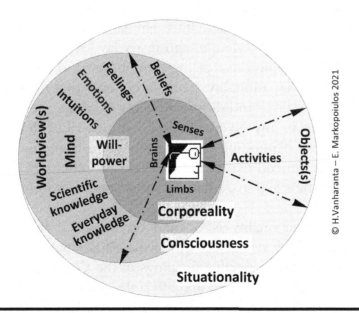

Figure 7.2 **Some essential concepts in the human mind (cf. Rauhala, 1986, 1995, Vanharanta, Pihlanto, Chang, 1997, Vanharanta, Markopoulos, 2021).**

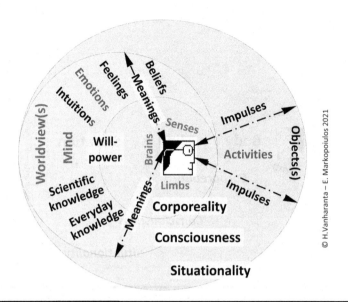

Figure 7.3 Objects activate impulses and meanings in the human brain (cf. Rauhala, 1986, 1995, Vanharanta, Pihlanto, Chang, 1997, Vanharanta, Markopoulos, 2021).

In the metaphor, Rauhala describes human will/willpower as the starting point for all activities. Behind that will, he describes the human mind's parts by stating that scientific information and everyday knowledge are the rational base for different activities. Human activities are not decided by willpower, scientific knowledge, and everyday knowledge, but they are influenced by beliefs, opinions, feelings, emotions, and the human being's intuition in a certain Situationality. Rauhala believes that many experiences affect how people behave, and different events in earlier life affect the decisions humans make in any given situation. He describes that people have different worldviews depending on where they are from and what kind of life they have experienced earlier in their lives. In other words, many various factors affect their actions, especially the behaviors humans display in a specific situation.

In Figure 7.3, Situationality is opened up to reveal how the different impulses from an object or subject inside the Situationality activate human brain processes and affect specific meanings in the Consciousness. All these impulses and meanings are related and affect the person's worldview, i.e., the human being. From the management and leadership perspective, managers and leaders must understand these basic principles of human Situationality, Consciousness, and body, and how people's senses, intuition, feelings, beliefs, emotions, and opinions are related and interrelated in many ways.

Each individual's situation awareness is always unique, and it creates their worldview – "the result of living." Different human beings can understand, in a unique way, the same concrete or abstract concept(s) in their situation. Understanding this phenomenon is critical when people introspect or evaluate business constructs, concepts, and processes.

7.4 Basic Steps to the Company Democracy Culture

The Holistic Concept of Man can demonstrate the creation of democratic company culture. The starting point then is human beings in their situation. The following information should be gathered first:

- What kind of democratic culture has the company had?
- What kind of democratic culture does it have today?
- What kind of drivers and variables are needed in the future to change the current democratic culture?

According to the previously presented ideas with the Holistic Concept of Man metaphor, attention is given first to the democratic behavior to send the human mind's impulses. Each individual receives their understanding by evaluating the processes around the company's democratic culture in different ways (Figure 7.4).

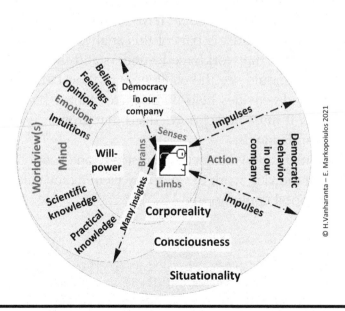

Figure 7.4 Human mind pondering democratic behavior inside a company (cf. Rauhala, 1986, 1995, Vanharanta, Pihlanto, Chang, 1997, Vanharanta, Markopoulos, 2021).

When the starting point is the Holistic Concept of Man, and the concept is the company democracy, a particular understanding comes through the human impulses (inner and outer), which then creates meanings in the human brain system. It is possible to understand how the workforce sees the overall Company Democracy collectively by capturing these human impulses and meanings through computer applications or process models. Such tools already exist, supporting this new thinking on understanding different management objects like democracy qualitatively. With these tools, it is possible to understand the broad democracy construct in the conscious experience "on stage" with many different concepts and sub-concepts.

Existing software applications and technologies, such as the Evolute, help each person create their image, picture, or opinion of the democratic company culture. Modern management and leadership tools help gain a collective and qualitative understanding of the current and future democratic company culture. It is also possible to ask people to describe what kind of culture they are willing to create in the future and how they prioritize different features of Company Democracy.

People with a democratic company culture application provide their opinions and understanding of how they perceive the company's situation through different actions and statements to the managers and leaders. Past information affects their analysis and also the current situation in which people are. The application results also show how the democratic company culture within an organization is changing and why. The results can strengthen, maintain, or weaken the current management and leadership decisions regarding democratic company culture changes. People have to create a new culture.

The mental/physical contrast is part of this analysis. Managers and leaders must work together with the workforce to understand the company's democracy concept. People should see the challenges in their behavior and that the scenarios, visions, and activities help them make change happen collectively inside the company. It must be acknowledged that growth is continuous and always starts with individuals.

It is not a one-man-one-vote method; instead, one man can bring many insights concerning the vital work of Company Democracy culture that should be done and developed continuously.

7.5 Summary

The Holistic Concept of Man in the business environment can explain many human concepts and management and leadership issues. It is the starting context where all the business activities happen on each person's stage. The democratic culture has been one example of the management and leadership objects in the workforce's conscious experience in a typical scenario. In this context, the democratic culture empowers people to reach continuously higher levels than previously. Therefore, it can be assumed that the collective way of viewing different management and leadership ontologies can further help analyze such complex management and leadership constructs and concepts.

In the coming chapters and sub-chapters, the combination of the Holistic Concept of Man, the Workspace of the Mind, and the Circles of the Mind metaphors provides possibilities for further developing the human focus in business management and leadership. This stepwise approach leads to a fundamental understanding of the natural processes for individuals' continuous co-evolution, development, growth, and maturity within an organization.

Questions for Review and Discussions

The Holistic Concept of Man illustrates new conceptual management system requirements with a robust metaphorical method. It contains the body, Consciousness, and Situationality. People think and act automatically in different business situations, so this kind of metaphor is not easy to understand. However, new conditions lead to new thinking and provide a unique view of how people see the modern human being as part of a living system, working in occupational roles for added-value purposes inside the complex business environment.

1. Write your definition of the Holistic Concept of Man (HCM) metaphor, in terms of the three dimensions of Situationality, Consciousness, and Corporeality, in simple words.
    1.1 Present it to ten different people and ask them if they understood the terms and your example.
    1.2 Evaluate the responses and identify the wrong ones.
    1.3 How would you redefine the terms to make them more understandable by all?
2. How does the HCM metaphor help better understand how people connect to society and other people?
    2.1 Justify your response and provide examples.
    2.2 Do you think that this metaphor fulfills the requirements of living systems? If Yes, why?

2.3 If No, why not? What does it need to make such fulfillment?

3. How do you see autopoiesis in the HCM (i.e., a closed system capable of creating itself)? Justify your response and provide examples.

4. In the HCM, how do you understand your worldview and willpower?

    4.1 Explain them in simple terms and provide examples.

    4.2 Why are they placed in the metaphor and in the specific places (locations) on the figure?

5. In the HCM, how do you rely on your beliefs, emotions, intuition?

    5.1 Should you rely on them or not? And in what way?

    5.2 What is the process to do this?

6. What is the role, and how do you see your duties and wants in the HCM?

    6.1 How do your role and duties impact the outcome of the metaphor?

7. Do you think your everyday knowledge could have changed if you had more scientific knowledge?

    7.1 If No, why not?

    7.2 If Yes, how would it change you? What kind of scientific knowledge do you think might help you in your case?

8. What kind of personal and company data, information, and knowledge do you store in your company?

    8.1 How do you access it?

    8.2 How do you integrate it?

    8.3 How do you process it?

9. The HCM metaphor has been designed to create wisdom. How do you understand your wisdom with this analogy?

    9.1 How is wisdom created?

    9.2 What is the process?

10. If you could have added/deleted, or changed, something on the HCM to improve it or simplify it, what would that be?

    10.1 Why did you select these additions/changes?

    10.2 How would they make the metaphor better?

11. Please follow the chart of Figure 7Q.

    11.1 Do you think this vision limits the current business world's vision and situation or not?

    11.2 Is it easy for you to focus, i.e., see the forest from the trees and trees in the woods with different business constructs, concepts, and variables to find the business's limits and problems, i.e., understanding the business situation better?

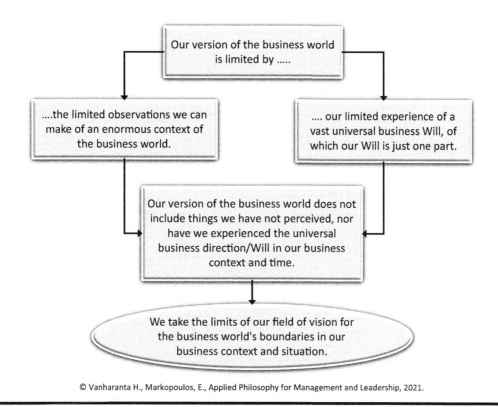

© Vanharanta H., Markopoulos, E., Applied Philosophy for Management and Leadership, 2021.

Figure 7Q   Chart for Question 11 (c.f., ref. Buckingham, et al., 2011, Arthur Schopenhauer, p. 187).

References

Buckingham, W., Burnham, D., King, P.J., Hill, C., Weeks, M. and Marenbon, J. 2011. *The Philosophy Book*. Dorling Kindersley Limited, London. https://freebooksmedical.com/the-philosophy-book-by-will-buckingham/

Lakoff, G. and Johnson, M., 2003. *Metaphors We Live By*. The University of Chicago Press, Chicago, IL.

Rauhala, L., 1986. *Ihmiskäsitys ihmistyössä* (Finnish Edition), trans: "The Conception of Human Being in Helping People." Gaudeamus, Helsinki.

Rauhala, L., 1995. *Tajunnan itsepuolustus* (Finnish Edition), trans: "Self-Defence of the Consciousness." Yliopistopaino, Helsinki.

Vanharanta, H. and Markopoulos, E., 2021. *Re-drawing of the Holistic Concept of Man Figure with New Information*.

Vanharanta, H., Pihlanto, P., and Chang, A.-M, 1997. Decision support for strategic management in a hyperknowledge environment and the holistic concept of man. In: Proceedings of the 30th Annual Hawaii International Conference on Systems Sciences, IEEE Computer Society Press, California. 5, 307–316.

Chapter 8

The Circles of Mind Metaphor: Actors on the Stage of Consciousness

Executive Summary

Metaphors help people understand what they know about their physical and cognitive experiences in the world. They are also used to understand complex phenomena and ideas, mental activities, feelings, and the passing of time and people's existence. The world can be described as a theater stage with all the people actors, where each one is playing their role. This kind of perception helps people understand themselves and improve their productivity, latency, and performance on their stage. All the actors can form a mental theater to show their conscious experience on the stage. Inner and outer senses describe how they see their current reality, and future ideas can come suddenly by changing their own 'play' in their Situationality. By explaining it in this way, as a Cartesian theater, people can enter a new type of mind metaphor with certain circles around the stage. The players with inner and outer senses and ideas, the unconscious audience, the context operators behind the scenes, the director, and the spotlight controller create the live conscious experience on stage for every actor. The Circles of Mind metaphor helps people understand themselves better and gives them support and guidance in their Situationality when managing and leading companies and organizations. The target of the analogy is to understand yourself better and support people to understand each other better.

DOI: 10.4324/9781003158493-10

8.1 Introduction

The Holistic Concept of Man theory was the first background metaphor in developing the Circles of Mind metaphor described in the previous chapter (Chapter 7). However, the Holistic Concept of Man was not a real open metaphor (cf. Rauhala 1986, 1995), as it does not contain the modern approach to human brain research. It would also be challenging to make it computer-simulated or automated.

On the other hand, the second background metaphor, the Circles of Mind, is closer to the Cartesian metaphor ideated by philosopher Rene Descartes, who believed in the power of innate ideas and supported rationalism in his philosophy to understand the world around us. However, his Cartesian dualism started from material and mind thinking as ontologically distinct substances, unlike the Holistic Concept of Man metaphor. These two concepts are immersed together in one causally operated unit. Descartes's philosophy culminates in his thinking, "Cogito ergo sum" (I think; therefore, I am), which opened a new dimension in European philosophy (cf. Buckingham et al., 2011) and has affected the development of the Workplace of the Mind and the Circles of Mind metaphors (Baars, 1997, Vanharanta, 2003).

Systemic thinking is the modern way to understand systems and their relationships. In such systems, everything is open and relational. They contain feedback loops to clarify the process-oriented way of natural living systems thinking. They have specific processes inside a system boundary, inputs, and outputs, giving the system feedback to fulfill its openness and freedom requirements.

The Holistic Concept of Man can be considered as a closed system. The Situationality in it describes a degree of openness, but the processes of how this works in practice are not entirely clear. On the other hand, in the Circles of Mind metaphor, the system's content is open with inputs, processes, and outputs. It contains a complex cognitive human system with infinite possible operating states. This kind of variety can be described, for example, as the degree of freedom people have in different occupational roles.

In these occupational roles, people have to perceive and understand their Situationality and their mental processes. They also have to understand what kind of freedoms are possible and how viable systems operate. From the individual point of view, it is essential to know yourself, to understand the organization you belong to, improve your performance, and master your profession in the best possible way. The following sections indicate how individual, meaningful relationships exist, how performance improvement can be achieved, and how to understand achievement in different occupational roles.

8.2 The Workspace of the Mind

Bernard J. Baars has used the Cartesian model of the human mind in a modern way by describing Consciousness and the activities in the brain's unconscious areas. In his book *In the Theater of Consciousness: The Workspace of the Mind,* he explains in detail how people can better understand the construct of the human mind, its concepts, and sub-concepts (Baars, 1997). The metaphor provides a helpful structure to understand the inputs, processes, and outputs of the human brain. It is an open systemic system, a human in a situation. All people are conscious and try to understand the world around them in a unique way. Consciousness continuously generates personal experiences, according to the Global Workspace Theory by Baars. The theory presents a "theater model" where the Consciousness has a central role on a theater stage (ibid.).

The Holistic Concept of Man or the idea of a human being in a specific situation as a totality is not the proper metaphor for developing management and leadership constructs, concepts, and decision-making tools. It lacks the new current research findings on the unconscious part of the human brain. Baars (ibid.) also combines psychology with brain science and unites the old conception of the mind to the mind's workspace. The totality can then be explained through the idea of the theater metaphor, where the self as an agent and observer behaves on the theater stage, i.e., 'Conscious Experience on Stage.'

The players, i.e., the outer and inner senses and ideas, contact both the external world and the inner world. The outer senses are the most well-known senses of touch, sound, sight, smell, taste, heat, and vibration. The inner senses are "inner speech," "imagined feelings," "dreams," and "visual imagery." The third area of senses is ideas like imagination, intuition, and verbalization. These ideas are activated automatically, but they also belong to the group of players in the conscious experience on stage. Not far from these players, close to the stage is the audience, i.e., the unconscious part of the human brain system, divided into several main areas: Motivational system, Automatic systems, Interpreting system, Memory system as well as Spotlight controller, Context (worldview), and the Theater director him or herself (ibid.).

8.3 The Structure of the Circles of Mind Metaphor

The Holistic Concept of Man thinking and the theater metaphor by Baars have given us a new idea and a convenient metaphor. The original metaphor was named the Circles of Mind metaphor (CoM) by Vanharanta (2003, 2014a, 2014b), based on Baars's theater metaphor. CoM contains ideas from both the HCM metaphor and the Cartesian way of thinking. The Circles of Mind metaphor was also designed as a physical object, which could be used for other research and development purposes in management and leadership contexts (Vanharanta, 2014a, 2014b). This physical object led to new ideas of brain-based systems containing the physical body following the Cartesian body–mind relationships, i.e., in Maslin's terms, a "thinking thing" and an "extended thing" (Maslin, 2001). One version of the physical CoM is presented in Figure 8.1.

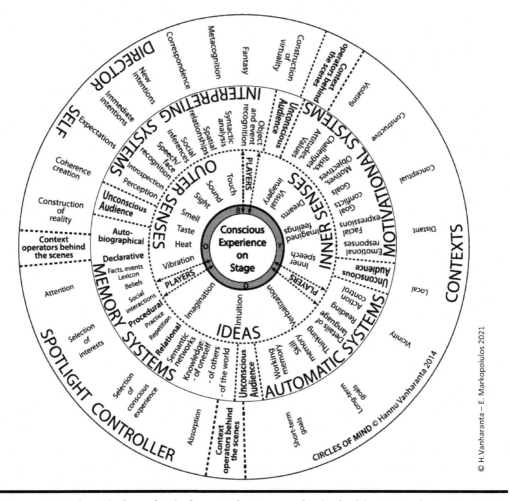

Figure 8.1   The Circles of Mind metaphor as a physical object (Vanharanta, 2003, 2014a, 2014b).

The physical CoM metaphor contains four different transparent discs, which are stacked and connected from the center. The center represents the Conscious Experience on Stage; i.e., it describes each person's real-world experience in their Situationality (cf. "Holistic Concept of Man metaphor" [Rauhala, 1986, 1995]).

The system is open (inputs/processes/outputs), and the senses around it are a natural part of the body (not separated). The players form the second disk, which contains the inner and outer senses and ideas. The third disk, the unconscious audience disk, contains Motivational systems, Automatic systems, Memory systems, and Interpreting systems. The fourth disk combines the Context operators behind the scenes and consists of the Spotlight controller, the Contexts (the worldview), and the Director self (see Figure 8.1).

All four disks contain many different concepts and provide a natural clarification of the many different combinations, creating a conscious experience at each stage. As people are different, the Circle of Mind only explains the main idea; i.e., there are endless possible combinations of content and many other ideas that can be activated in the human mind to be presented in the conscious experience on stage.

8.4 The Usage of the Circles of Mind Metaphor

'The conscious experience on stage' is presented in Figure 8.2, showing how it is formed by having experiences on stage and how the unconscious part of the human brain affects the conscious experience on stage. The process behaves like a heart-pumping experience up to the worldview, affecting the future new experiences on stage.

The combinations generated entail numerous and very complex processes that occur in the human brain. The result is the life lived. The way people can describe their past and the current experience on the stage is the path on which people live their lives within their Situationality. The life experience is the end product of this human activity and behavior. The dotted circles show how people pump information/their experiences via the senses into their unconscious part of the brain, up to the worldview. As directors of their own play, people decide how they act on their stage.

For management and leadership purposes, this kind of understanding of human beings is vital. It is also essential to understand the unconscious areas of the human brain. Some people may have problems in their motivation and commitment to their occupational role. Therefore, what do they have to do, and what kind of qualities and traits do they have to improve the current situation?

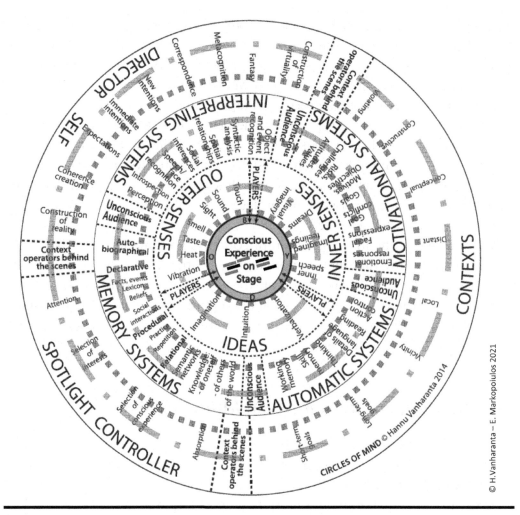

Figure 8.2   Use of the Circles of Mind metaphor as a physical object.

Some people have a good memory; others need real help in interpreting complicated management ontologies, constructs, and concepts. Others may have focus problems, i.e., attention, selection of interest, low absorption capacity, etc.

The following examples present the use of the Circles of Mind metaphor by looking at different combinations that can be found through the metaphor.

8.4.1 Returning to Your Roots

It is essential to know yourself. This means that it is good to "go" to your autobiographical memory and describe who you are and where you come from. You have to be confident in telling your background to your coworkers so that they can understand you better (Figure 8.3).

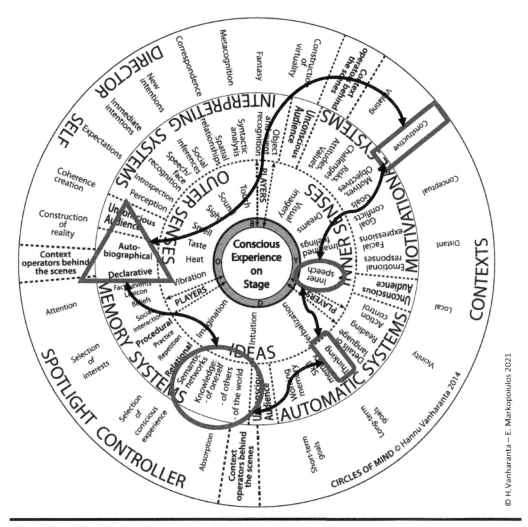

Figure 8.3 Returning to your roots.

8.4.2 Knowing Other People Better

It is essential to know people better in societies and organizations, understand what they do, and help or support other people in their lives or occupational roles. This kind of knowledge starts with the actors who know themselves better. They have to think about the situation of where they are and where they came from. They also have to understand that the worldview background affects their Situationality. The inner voice continually helps people to understand their Situationality. Figure 8.4 presents the active areas involved in knowing others better. The arrows indicate the activities people undertake when they try to understand other people more profoundly.

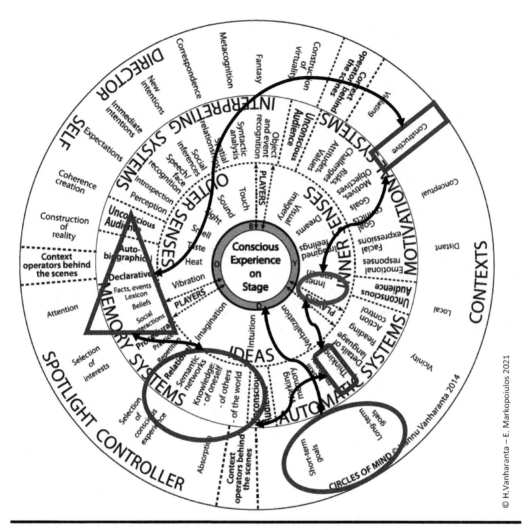

Figure 8.4 Knowing other people better.

8.4.3 Challenge Yourself, and Develop Your Skills

People need to challenge themselves and continuously develop their skills. They have to think about their strengths and improve their skills, capabilities, and competencies. Individuals are advised to make their SWOT (Strengths, Weaknesses, Opportunities, Threats) analysis and identify the strengths, weaknesses, opportunities, and threats. Figure 8.5 indicates some activities that people may use to help improve their traits and characteristics.

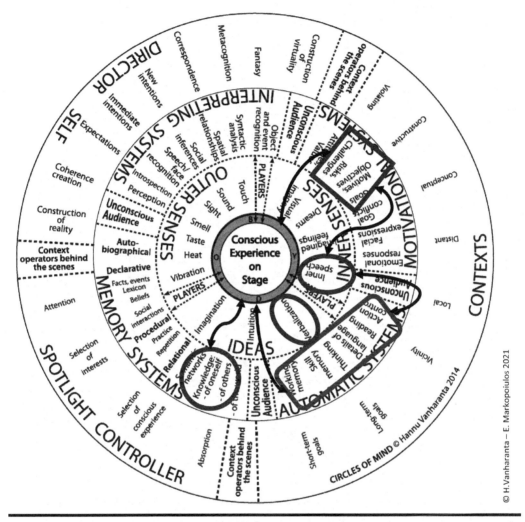

Figure 8.5 Challenge yourself and develop your skills.

8.4.4 Thinking and Acting

Before people act, they have to think. Intuition is fast, so people have to be very careful about the ideas from their brain system. It is good to focus on the correct issues and concepts, interpret the situation, remember the past situation, and then act in the best possible way (Figure 8.6).

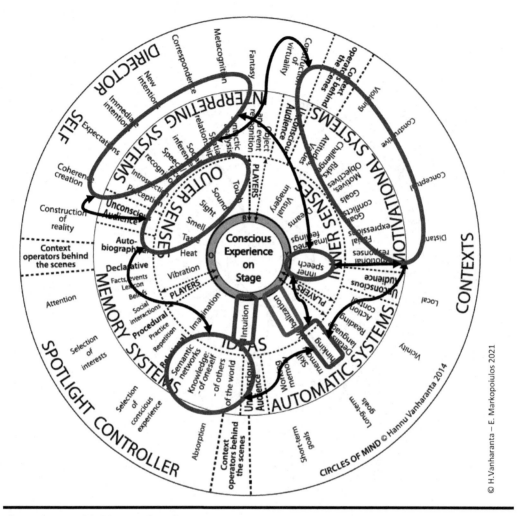

Figure 8.6 Thinking and acting.

8.4.5 Connecting to an Organization

Often, a hierarchical organization chart is not the right way to understand the organization that people belong to. Usually, the unofficial organization is the one that moves the company forward. To understand the operational organization well, it is suggested that people should ask a lot of questions and present themselves as accurately as possible for coworkers to know each other and understand each other's characteristics and traits.

Questioning others' work activities helps one interpret their coworkers' situations and see how their achievements add value to the organization. This kind of thinking and acting is essential, especially when people are new to the organization. They have to create links and network independently, become part of the organization, and increase their organizational commitment (Figure 8.7).

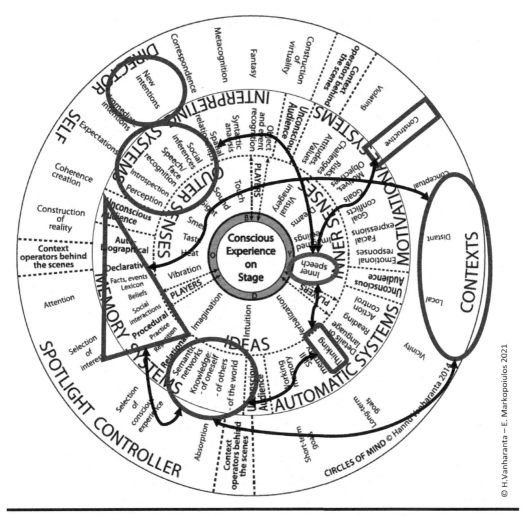

Figure 8.7 Connecting to an organization.

8.4.6 Networking Performance

It is not very well understood how to increase humans' overall performance and how it is possible to improve dynamic networking performance, for example. After understanding that persons like to act and improve their networking in the organization, it is possible to use the idea from Chapter 5 on the power of co-evolution. Figure 8.8 shows in a similar way how it is possible to improve networking performance through the productivity and latency dimensions, depending on the position of the person in question. It is essential to see that the productivity dimension can be activated immediately, but this is not easy because performance follows hyperbolic curves. The most effective way is to use both dimensions, i.e., latency and productivity. This

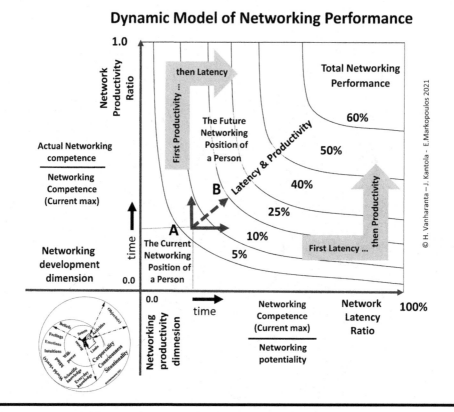

Figure 8.8   Networking performance improvement.

means that individual training or consultancy is a must before a real improvement can happen in networking performance.

The Circles of Mind has been used to describe human beings and help create management and leadership tools. It has also been used to describe fundamental past and current processes and further explain different management and leadership objects like occupational roles, learning, knowledge creation, safety, Company Democracy, etc. The previous examples have shown many vital areas in which individuals can directly use the physical Circles of Mind disk. It has also been demonstrated how, with other graphical methods, an individual's possibilities to improve their human traits and characteristics can be analyzed.

8.5 Improving Your Mastery

Personal mastery is a large ontology, i.e., construct, which contains many different concepts and sub-concepts. With the concepts, it is possible to create a mind map of personal mastery, which helps managers and leaders see different paths when considering improving their overall personal mastery. The starting point is first to understand the Circles of Mind constructs and concepts in it. After that, it is easier to follow the lines in the Personal Mastery mind map (cf. Nurminen, 2003) (Figure 8.9).

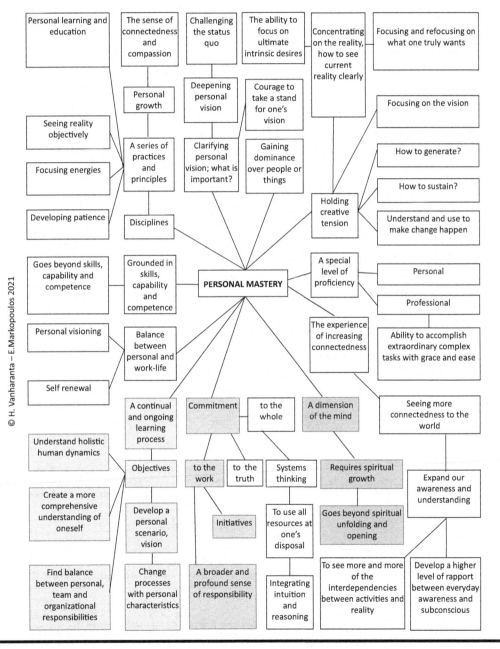

Figure 8.9   Personal mastery mind map. (Copyright 2003, K. Nurminen; new design by Vanharanta, Markopoulos, 2021; permission from K. Nurminen.)

Figure 8.9 marks three different paths, using different shades of gray. The *first path* (second column from left to right) is a continual and ongoing learning process with specific objectives such as personal scenarios and visions concerning learning. There are significant issues behind the purposes that affect them, such as understanding human dynamics (cf. Circles of Mind), understanding yourself, and balancing the personal, team, and organizational responsibilities. This requires changes in individual characteristics that the person must consider in detail before starting the continuous and ongoing learning process.

The *second path* is the commitment, which also depends on a broad and deep sense of responsibility, starting from human initiative. The *third path* is the mind's dimension, which is well perceived within the Circles of Mind metaphor's content. The Personal Mastery mind map is based on the content of the book *The Fifth Discipline: The Art & Practice of the Learning Organization* by Senge (cf. 1990). According to Peter Senge, "People with high levels of personal mastery are continually expanding their ability to create the results in life they truly seek. From their quest for continual learning comes the spirit of the learning organization" (ibid.).

Figure 8.10 indicates how competence improvement can be divided into four different sections, i.e., personal capacity, personal capability, personal competence, and personal mastery. People first have to identify their work-specific capabilities. They have to develop these capabilities and understand task-specific

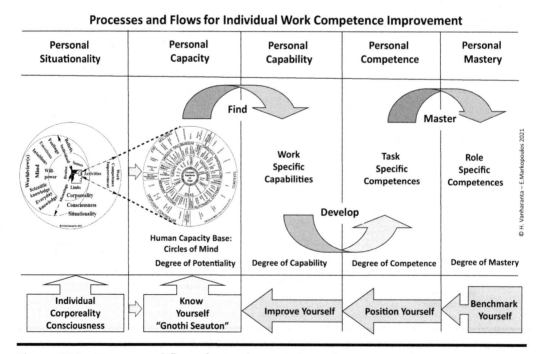

Figure 8.10   Process and flows for work competence improvement.

competencies before they try to master role-specific competencies. They start from a certain degree of personal potentiality, begin to understand the degree of their capabilities, then see the degree of their task-specific competencies, after which they can see the degree of their mastery in a specific work role.

The individual process starts when people understand themselves first, follow through with the other methods, and benchmark their role-specific competencies. When benchmarking is done, the feedback loop starts, i.e., positioning yourself, improving yourself, and starting from the beginning, again by understanding yourself. These four phases can also be described as degree of potentiality, degree of own capability, degree of competence, and degree of mastery.

According to Spencer and Spencer (1993), competencies can be divided into two categories: (1) Threshold competencies and (2) Differentiating competencies, where threshold competencies describe the essential characteristics needed in a job to be minimally effective. Differentiating competencies, in turn, distinguish superior performers from average performers. By concentrating on developing these differentiating, task-specific competencies, the leaders and managers can achieve personal mastery in role-specific competencies. Achieving this mastery level is very important when creating a balanced democratic company culture.

8.6 Emphasis on Working People for Organizational and Societal Shared Added Value

The Holistic Concept of Man, the Workplace of the Mind, the Circles of Mind metaphors, and the derived contexts are based on many scientific areas and disciplines. The main one is philosophy, but steps that follow to more practical application levels rely on computer science to reveal cognitive science and neuroscience-based research results. Applying the contents of these metaphors with further constructs and concepts from management and leadership areas results in an efficient environment where employees can understand themselves, increase their contribution to their organization, and grow together. As the emphasis is now shifted to the employees, the collective view of various management and leadership ontologies provides opportunities to analyze complex management and leadership constructs and concepts. Such analysis can deliver a numerical figure or a particular qualitative evaluation of employee performance that creates added value to the organization.

There have been attempts to find an equation that can help demonstrate how a responsive company environment in the employee's conscious experience on stage might affect this person's achievement or a group or team of people targeting specific work goals. It seems that the combination of Ford's Achievement Equation (cf. 1992) and the content from the metaphors described above can form an extended 'Achievement' equation. What is needed is personal agency beliefs, a certain tension/creative tension inside people, active sensing through sensory systems, and specific goals to target. These motives are one part of the achievement. By adding people's skills, capabilities, competencies, and aptitude with a responsive hands-on organization, the result will be the achievement obtained, i.e., the added value that a person or team brings to the organization (Figure 8.11).

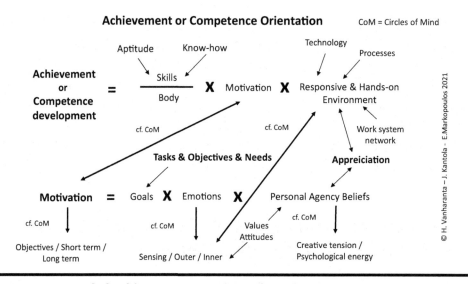

Figure 8.11   Extended achievement equation (cf. Ford, 1992).

All people are different physically and internally and have very profound characteristics, showing how differently they behave in practice. Understanding this kind of multi-variable equation in management and business might help leaders and managers create better working conditions for all the people they lead and manage (cf. Ford, 1992).

Many new management and leadership theories and methodologies target shared values as their primary focus. However, the metaphors mentioned in this chapter share added value by creating management and leadership activities that will first generate this value for the employees within their organization, extend it to the organization they are part of, and then the society their organizations serve. The critical element is respect for the employees through which their characteristics and traits can be developed to build their confidence and commitment to the organization they serve.

8.7 Summary

The Holistic Concept of Man in the business environment refers to the many human concepts and issues in organizations' and companies' management and leadership. It is the starting context where all business activities take place. This chapter introduced the Holistic Concept of Man, the Workspace of the Mind, and the Circles of Mind metaphors for creating responsive business environments where Company Democracy can be applied. The combination of these metaphors provides possibilities to further develop the human focus in business management and leadership. This stepwise approach aims to present the background that leads to a fundamental understanding of employees' continuous co-evolution and their organizations' natural processes. This Co-Evolutionary organizational development requires the creation of a new culture with the employees in leading roles. This will allow various management and leadership ontologies to generate a collective view for analyzing complex management and leadership phenomena, problems, ontologies, constructs, and concepts in detail.

Questions for Review and Discussion

The players with inner and outer senses and ideas, the unconscious audience, the context operators behind the scenes, the director, and the spotlight controller create the live conscious experience on stage for every actor, e.g., leaders and managers. The target of the metaphor is to understand yourself better and support people to understand each other better.

Why the Circles of Mind is called the "conscious experience on stage" or the "theater model"? What is the theater, and what is the stage? Who are the actors? How is the theater being played?

1. What kind of inputs can you understand in the CoM?
   1.1 What kind of processes exists?
   1.2 How do you see the output of these processes?
   1.3 Please justify your answer with examples.
2. How does each action in the conscious experience on stage affect our worldview?
3. Can you explain how the unconscious part of your brain capacity behaves like the "unconscious audience"? Please justify your answer with examples.
4. Show and describe the areas of the unconscious audience you activate when telling yourself about your past. What kind of activities do you perform when thinking and acting?

5. What is an "unofficial organization"?

    5.1 How important is it to understand the unofficial organization? And why?

6. How do you challenge yourself to develop your traits?

    6.1 What processes do you follow?

7. What are the methods to improve your networking performance? Explain the process and provide an example in a business context.

8. Personal mastery is an extensive and comprehensive concept. Do you have an understanding of how to improve your personal mastery?

    8.1 Draw a mind map with your specific personal mastery elements.

    8.2 Why did you select those elements?

    8.3 Where and how will they lead you?

9. How can you improve your role-specific competencies? Explain the way, the processes, and give an example in each stage.

10. Ponder on your situation with the Applied Philosophy chart of Figure 8Q.

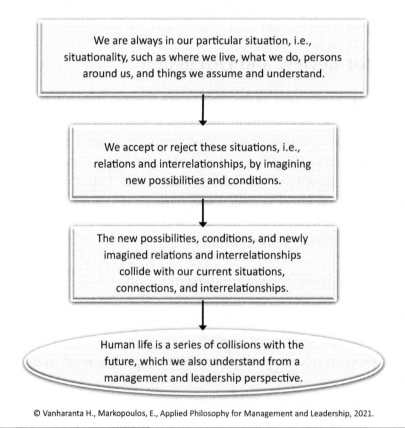

© Vanharanta H., Markopoulos, E., Applied Philosophy for Management and Leadership, 2021.

Figure 8Q   Chart for Question 10 (c.f., ref. Buckingham, et al., 2011, Jose Ortega-Gasset, p. 242).

Situationality means the many relations and interrelations which humans have in their lives. Please think about your Situationality from different perspectives; think about your possibilities and challenges in your occupation. Think also about all your current and future commitments and motivations. Do you have conflicting goals in your situation?

References

Baars, B. J., 1997. *In the Theater of Consciousness: The Workspace of the Mind.* Oxford University Press, New York.

Buckingham, W., King P. J., Burnham, D., Weeks, M., Hill, C., and Marenbon, J., 2011. *The Philosophy Book.* Dorling Kindersley Limited, London. https://freeboo ksmedical.com/the-philosophy-book-by-will-buckingham/

Ford, M. E., 1992. *Motivating Humans, Goals, Emotions, and Personal Agency Beliefs.* Sage Publications, New York.

Maslin, K. T., 2001. *An Introduction to the Philosophy of Mind.* Blackwell Publishers, Inc., Malden, MA.

Nurminen, K., 2003. *Deltoid: The Competencies of Nuclear Power Plant Operators.* Master of Science Thesis, Tampere University of Technology at Pori, Finland.

Rauhala, L., 1986. *Ihmiskäsitys ihmistyössä* (Finnish Edition), trans: "The Conception of Human Being in Helping People." Gaudeamus, Helsinki.

Rauhala, L., 1995. Tajunnan itsepuolustus (Finnish Edition), trans: "Self-Defence of the Consciousness." Yliopistopaino, Helsinki.

Senge, P. M., 1990. *The Fifth Discipline: The Art & Practice of the Learning Organization.* Currency Doubleday, New York.

Spencer, L. M. and Spencer, S. M., 1993. *Competence at Work: Models for Superior Performance.* Wiley, New York; Chichester.

Vanharanta, H., 2003. Circles of mind. In: Identity and Diversity in Organizations: Building Bridges in Europe Programme, the XI European Congress on Work and Organizational Psychology, Lisbon, Portugal. 14–17.

Vanharanta, H., 2014a. *Creation of the Physical Object of the Circles of Mind Metaphor.* Sibel Kantola, Kaarina, Finland.

Vanharanta, H., 2014b. *Redesign of the Circle of Mind Metaphor.* Sibel Kantola, Kaarina, Finland.

Vanharanta, H. and Markopoulos, E., 2021. *Re-drawn from the Original Figure in Kimmo.* Nurminen's Master's Thesis, 2003.

Chapter 9

Harnessing Modern Knowledge Systems: Applying Knowledge Frameworks

Executive Summary

In the design, development, and use of modern computer-based decision support systems and applications, the ultimate challenges and goals are arranging and organizing successful interaction between the active human being, the computer interface, the different areas of knowledge, and the computer itself. This chapter examines the fusion of Hyper-knowledge framework, the Holistic Concept of Man, and the Circles of Mind metaphors in decision support systems and applications to emulate individual and collective human behavior simultaneously cognitive processes and unity. Modern computer systems and computing have replaced data processing with knowledge processing, and information creation with knowledge creation. Getting new knowledge from data and information leads to the generation of new human wisdom. This chapter represents an emerging paradigm for achieving emulation and synergy between human decision-making processes and computer configurations. Such an approach is enormously important when managing and leading change steadily toward virtual work, virtual teams, complex business ontologies, constructs, concepts, and objects. This change substantially impacts how companies should organize, lead, and manage both intellectual and financial assets to continuously support the development of democratic company cultures where organizational knowledge begins.

DOI: 10.4324/9781003158493-11

9.1 Introduction

The Holistic Concept of Man (HCM) was the first background metaphor to develop the Circles of Mind (CoM) metaphor. However, the Holistic Concept of Man was a metaphor that lacked a modern approach to human brain research and cannot be supported much by computer applications. In contrast, the Circles of Mind metaphor provides more vital cognitive science elements that can be automated using artificial intelligence and advanced computing, especially Decision Support Systems (DSS).

The development of decision support systems has segmented technology into more varied organizations, user groups, and activities. The primary purpose of a DSS is to extend the decision-making skills, capabilities, and competencies of an individual to master computer usage, data, information, knowledge content, and creation. It is also intended for understanding the processing procedures and interpretations in any context in which the technology is used.

Software designers, developers, and users must understand and internalize the human actor's nature, the human brain's activities, theories, methodologies, decision-making methods, data processing, information retrieval, and knowledge creation.

This chapter focuses on the business dimension of a computer-based system design for user support beyond the mere retrieval and processing of data, information, and knowledge. It presents the extent to which the application of the hyper-knowledge framework developed by Ai-Mei Chang and the Holistic Concept of Man (HCM) developed by Lauri Rauhala have been combined and used. The Circles of Mind (CoM) metaphor developed by Hannu Vanharanta can be transformed into a decision support system to emulate better individual and collective human behavior with cognitive processes (Chang, Holsapple, Whinston, 1989a, 1989b, 1993, 1994, Rauhala 1986, 1995, Vanharanta, 1995). The chapter also presents an improved understanding and internalization of an active user's Situationality and a better experience of which objects, constructs, and concepts should be included in the design of computer systems and applications.

By combining the Hyper-knowledge framework with the Holistic Concept of Man framework and then integrating them with the Circles of Mind metaphor, a new software architecture can be developed. It can then be applied to many computer systems and new computer usage areas, where holism has an important role. Digitalization is both a challenge and a threat to civilized nations, companies, organizations, citizens, and employees. The target is to harness computers to support democratic knowledge creation and utilization principles ethically in a management and leadership context.

9.2 Philosophic Model of the User

The Holistic Concept of Man is a philosophical model that has been described in several books and articles by Rauhala, a Finnish phenomenological philosopher and psychologist (cf. Rauhala 1986, 1995). Rauhala's source material consists of the two well-known German philosophers Edmund Gustav Albrecht Husserl and Martin Heidegger (cf. Hussler in Husslerliana, 1963–1973, Heidegger, 1962). Compared to the theories presented by Husserl and Heidegger, the advantage of the Holistic Concept of Man is that it has a relatively simple construction and is understandable to non-experts.

The Circles of Mind metaphor (Vanharanta, 2003) opens up the mind and the following essential sectors: Memory system, Interpretation system, Motivation systems, and Automatic system. Computer systems can support furthermore these crucial human mind sectors to generate content and support the user's activities.

The Hyper-knowledge framework (Chang, Holsapple, Whinston, 1989, 1993) views a decision-maker as a person who possesses many diverse and interrelated pieces of knowledge (i.e., concepts) and sees them through a Graphical Computer Interface (GUI). The result is then a hyper-knowledge view of the underlying constructs, concepts, and content on the computer screen. When turned off, the knowledge creation disappears. The combination of these three views creates an architecture for computer applications and constructs.

9.3 The Hyper-knowledge Framework

The Hyper-knowledge framework views a decision-maker, i.e., an active computer user, as someone who cognitively possesses many diverse and interrelated pieces of knowledge (i.e., concepts). Some of this knowledge is descriptive, some procedural, some are concerned with reasoning, etc. The mind can deal with these pieces of knowledge in a fluid and inclusive manner via controlled attention. The decision-maker actively acquires (recalls, focuses) desired pieces of knowledge by cognitively navigating among the universe of available concepts. The user's interaction with the DSS that emulates such activities should be relatively 'friendly,' natural, and comfortable. The DSS can be regarded as an extension of the decision-maker's innate knowledge management capabilities.

The decision-maker can contact and manipulate the knowledge embodied in the DSS as a wide range of interrelated concepts. The decision-maker can navigate through the DSS's concepts directly or in an associative fashion, pausing to interact with them. Thus, the Hyper-knowledge framework regards a decision support environment ideally as an extension of the user's mind or as cognitive capabilities and faculties. The framework's map of concepts and relationships extends the user's mental map, pushing back the cognitive limits on knowledge representation. Furthermore, its knowledge processing capabilities augment the user's skills by overcoming cognitive limitations on human knowledge processing speed and capacity, i.e., power. This chapter summarizes, on a technical level, the actual content and functionality of a DSS specified as per the hyper-knowledge framework. For further details, readers can refer to Chang, Holsapple, and Whinston (1989, 1990, 1993) and also to the framework-based prototype applications (Vanharanta, 1995).

9.4 A Modern Human Knowledge System

According to the hyper-knowledge framework, the decision support system is defined, architecturally, in terms of a Language System [LS], Presentation System [PS], Problem Processing System [PPS], and a Knowledge System [KS].

The LS is the universe of all requests that the DSS can accept from the user, and the PS is the universe of all responses that the DSS can yield. The KS is the vast universe of all knowledge stored in the DSS. The PPS has a wide range of knowledge management capabilities corresponding to the wide range of knowledge representations permitted in the KS. The KS holds concepts that can be related to each other, definitionally and associatively. These concepts and their relationships can be formally expressed and processed in terms of database, formal logic, and model constructs. Associative and definitional relationships among KS concepts are the keys to creating a hyper-knowledge environment and navigating within it. The KS also contains more than just models and data. It has reasoning, assimilation, linguistic, and presentation knowledge. Figure 9.1 presents the human system metaphor developed by Dos Santos and Holsapple (1989).

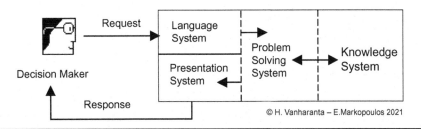

Figure 9.1   Structure of the decision support system (Dos Santos, Holsapple, 1989, Vanharanta, 1995). New design by Vanharanta, Markopoulos, 2021.

The DSS dynamics involve transforming messages from the user's language system to the decision support system. These transformations are carried out by the problem solving system (subject to the KS content) using three essential functions: assistance (a), functionality (f), and presentation (p). The user interface and functionality of a DSS specified as per the hyper-knowledge framework are depicted in Figure 9.2.

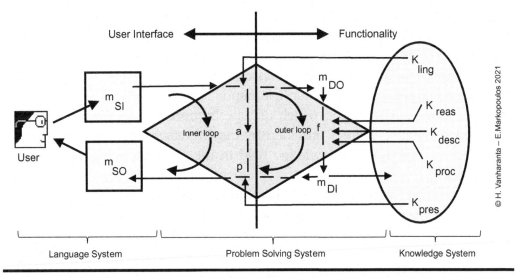

Figure 9.2   The user interface and functionality of the hyper-knowledge framework (cf. Chang, Holsapple, Whinston, 1989, 1990, 1993, Vanharanta, 1995). New design by Vanharanta, Markopoulos, 2021.

The knowledge symbols in the knowledge system signify the following available knowledge:

K_{ling} = Linguistic knowledge
K_{reas} = Reasoning knowledge
K_{desc} = Descriptive knowledge

K_{proc} = Procedural knowledge
K_{pres} = Presentation knowledge

The other symbols in Figure 9.2 signify following:

m SI = a surface input message, i.e., keystrokes, mouse movement, touching screen, etc.
m SO = a surface output message to the user
m DI = a deep input message; specifies what the problem processing system must do to satisfy the request expressed in m SI
m DO = a deep output message; derived knowledge produced by the problem solving system

When a decision-maker is working in the hyper-knowledge environment, a concept must be 'contacted' before it can be 'impacted' (affected) by or have an 'impact' on the decision-maker. Contact means recognizing a concept in the environment, and it entails sensing the concept's existence and bringing it into focus. Either implicitly or explicitly, the user is provided with a "concept map" as the basis for establishing contacts (cf. Vanharanta, 1995).

The concept map indicates what concepts are in the environment and what their interrelationships are. An implicit map is external to the DSS (e.g., in the user's cognitive environment, which may be burdensome as the KS becomes complex). A detailed map is provided by the DSS itself and can be regarded as a piece of descriptive knowledge held in the KS, describing its content's present state.

With a concept map as the original contact point within the environment, the user can make purposeful controlled contacts with any desired concept in the hyper-knowledge realm. A user can focus on any part of an image. Multiple windows can provide different views of parts of the same image, and different images of the same underlying concept can be seen in various windows. The result is extensive user interface flexibility, which is essential in a simple and adaptive interface design.

9.5 Emerging Paradigm and Its Functionality

Computer architecture has been developed based on co-evolution thinking by combining the Holistic Concept of Man metaphor, the Hyper-knowledge framework, and the Circles of Mind metaphor into a single design framework, i.e., a fusion framework. According to the ideas from modern brain science and cognitive science and the basics of the Holistic Concept of Man and the hyper-knowledge functionality, the key argument has been to map computer constructs and computer applications.

With the created fusion framework, various computer applications can be designed and can affect advanced knowledge and databases. First, all the developed applications are seen to contain the same systems as the human brain has. With these applications, business processes can be emulated in the same way that the brain imitates reality with its functions. The knowledge structure contains the same vital areas as the unconscious part of the brain.

Figure 9.3 represents the user (with their brain processes) touching the computer screen through the user interface. The functionality is described as hyper-knowledge functionality and the database construction as the human brain's unconscious part. In modern internet applications, it is possible to navigate the information and then combine it according to user needs, like the hyper-knowledge functionality that describes the active computer user. Again, in these applications, the idea is the same as supporting the current user through the user interface. They also try to support the basic human mind processes, i.e., interpretation, memory, motivation, and automatic activities.

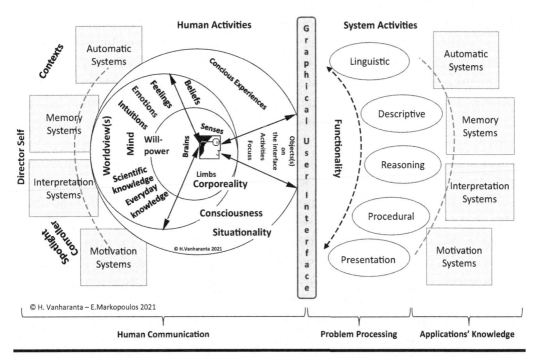

Figure 9.3 An emerging paradigm of a human compatible computer system. New design by Vanharanta, Markopoulos, 2021.

On the other hand, the combination possibilities are enormous. Therefore, the computer user must be brought to a specific context that increases efficient and effective computer content opportunities. These computer applications describe the content and objectives of the application itself. The creation of a context-specific ontology then becomes crucial.

The given paradigm indicates that system and application design must be more holistic. More comprehensive thinking on computer systems is required to cover new decision support systems to help managers and leaders reach a collective perspective, analyze knowledge in a democratic and unbiased way, and effectively use machine wisdom in their decision-making.

9.6 New Technology with the Fusion Paradigm

Hypertext, hyperlinks, World Wide Web technologies, etc., have changed computer usage significantly in the last two decades. Data and information are readily available through the computer, but getting authentic and valid knowledge remains a significant challenge, demanding more effort. Hyper-knowledge describes new knowledge on the computer screen that disappears when the computer is closed.

According to the Holistic Concept of Man, Workplace of Mind, and the Circles of Mind metaphors, knowledge permanently resides in humans, not in any external database. Therefore, the philosophical view supports hyper-knowledge creation but not the result of abstract knowledge outside computers. This is why it is crucial to widen human activities to concrete and abstract actions within a democratic culture framework. Figure 9.4 presents how the content of a DIKW table (Data, Information, Knowledge, Wisdom) is widened to cover human activities in concrete and abstract ways. The main activities are data handling, information processing, knowledge creating, and wisdom generation.

The DIKW table is composed of concrete (Table 9.1) and abstract (Table 9.2) human activities in wisdom generation.

This complete DIKW table (Table 9.3) depicts the ways humans process their activities and change their worldview in different situations. Individuals are, therefore, always the focus. In each category, there is always a particular demand and supply for these main activities. They are also in continuous flux, as they flow in different systems and subsystems. When new computer systems are designed, this kind of DIKW table helps understand the demand from human activities and provides new ways to design machine-based computer systems collectively.

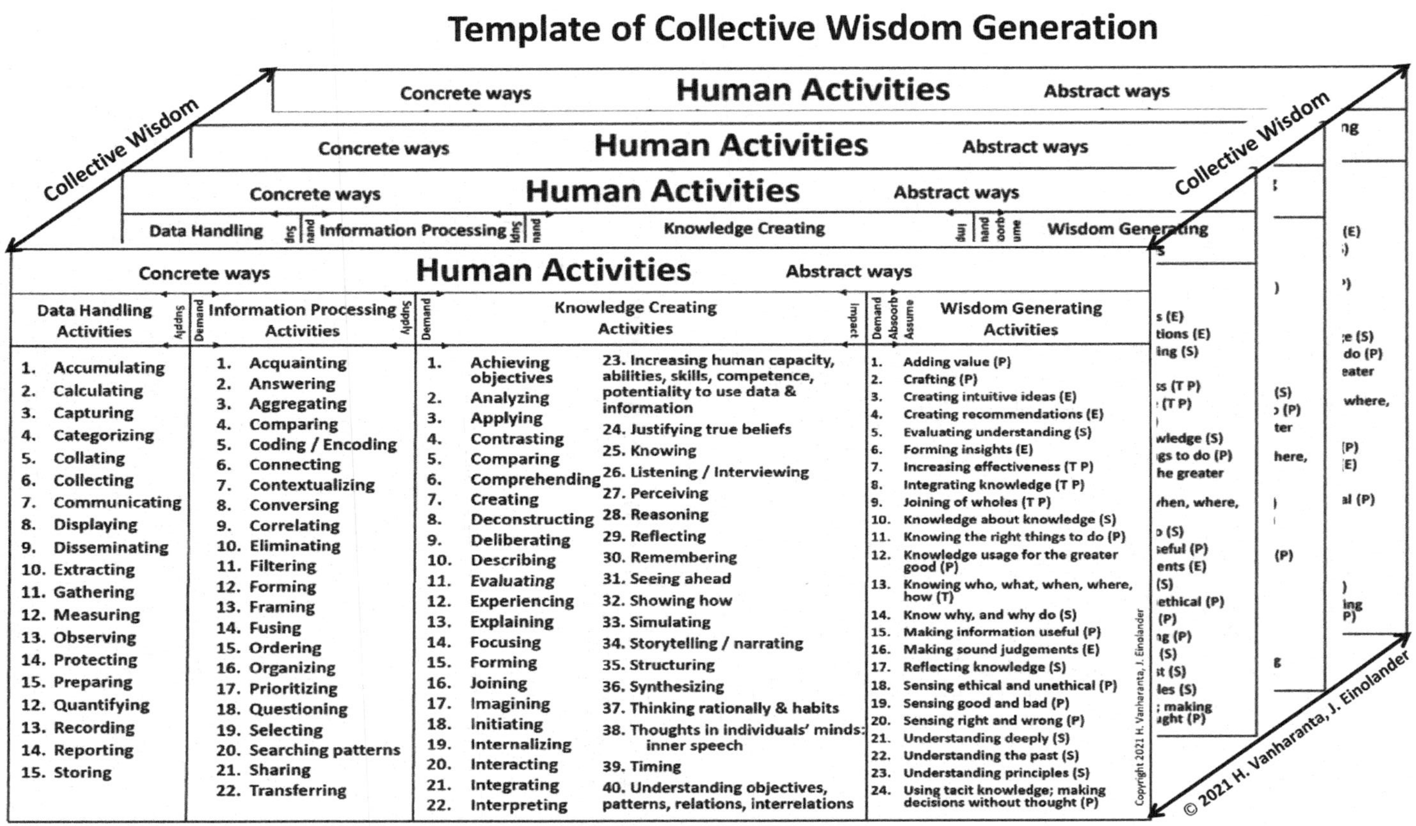

Template of Collective Wisdom Generation

Collective Wisdom — Human Activities — Abstract ways

Data Handling / Information Processing / Knowledge Creating / Wisdom Generating

Data Handling Activities
1. Accumulating
2. Calculating
3. Capturing
4. Categorizing
5. Collating
6. Collecting
7. Contextualizing
8. Communicating
9. Displaying
10. Disseminating
11. Extracting
12. Gathering
13. Measuring
14. Observing
14. Protecting
15. Preparing
12. Quantifying
13. Recording
14. Reporting
15. Storing

Information Processing Activities
1. Acquainting
2. Answering
3. Aggregating
4. Comparing
5. Coding / Encoding
6. Connecting
7. Contextualizing
8. Conversing
9. Correlating
10. Eliminating
11. Filtering
12. Forming
13. Framing
14. Fusing
15. Ordering
16. Organizing
17. Prioritizing
18. Questioning
19. Selecting
20. Searching patterns
21. Sharing
22. Transferring

Knowledge Creating Activities
1. Achieving objectives
2. Analyzing
3. Applying
4. Contrasting
5. Comparing
6. Comprehending
7. Creating
8. Deconstructing
9. Deliberating
10. Describing
11. Evaluating
12. Experiencing
13. Explaining
14. Focusing
15. Forming
16. Joining
17. Imagining
18. Initiating
19. Internalizing
20. Interacting
21. Integrating
22. Interpreting
23. Increasing human capacity, abilities, skills, competence, potentiality to use data & information
24. Justifying true beliefs
25. Knowing
26. Listening / Interviewing
27. Perceiving
28. Reasoning
29. Reflecting
30. Remembering
31. Seeing ahead
32. Showing how
33. Simulating
34. Storytelling / narrating
35. Structuring
36. Synthesizing
37. Thinking rationally & habits
38. Thoughts in individuals' minds: inner speech
39. Timing
40. Understanding objectives, patterns, relations, interrelations

Wisdom Generating Activities
1. Adding value (P)
2. Crafting (P)
3. Creating recommendations (E)
4. Evaluating understanding (S)
5. Forming insights (E)
6. Increasing effectiveness (T P)
7. Integrating knowledge (T P)
8. Joining of wholes (P)
9. Knowledge about knowledge (S)
10. Knowing the right things to do (P)
11. Knowledge usage for the greater good (P)
12. Knowing who, what, when, where, how (T)
13. Know why, and why do (S)
14. Making information useful (P)
15. Making sound judgements (E)
16. Reflecting knowledge (S)
17. Sensing ethical and unethical (P)
18. Sensing good and bad (P)
19. Sensing right and wrong (P)
20. Understanding deeply (S)
21. Understanding the past (S)
22. Understanding principles (S)
23. Using tacit knowledge; making decisions without thought (P)

Figure 9.4 The collective wisdom generation framework (cf. Vanharanta, Einolander, Kantola, Markopoulos, Sivula, 2020, Vanharanta, Einolander, New design 2021).

Table 9.1   Concrete Human Activities in Wisdom Generation

Concrete ways of Human Activities		
Data Handling Activities	Supply / Demand	Information Processing Activities
1. Accumulating 2. Calculating 3. Capturing 4. Categorizing 5. Collating 6. Collecting 7. Communicating 8. Displaying 9. Disseminating 10. Extracting 11. Gathering 12. Measuring 13. Observing 14. Protecting 15. Preparing 12. Quantifying 13. Recording 14. Reporting 15. Storing		1. Acquainting 2. Answering 3. Aggregating 4. Comparing 5. Coding / Encoding 6. Connecting 7. Contextualizing 8. Conversing 9. Correlating 10. Eliminating 11. Filtering 12. Forming 13. Framing 14. Fusing 15. Ordering 16. Organizing 17. Prioritizing 18. Questioning 19. Selecting 20. Searching patterns 21. Sharing 22. Transferring

© 2021 H. Vanharanta, J. Einolander

9.7 Individual, Collective and Machine Wisdom Generation

The DIKW table helps design a particular collective framework for data, information, knowledge, and wisdom generation. By collecting individual human activities together, it is possible to obtain a collective view of other concrete and abstract concepts and activities (Figure 9.4). This new computer framework can help managers and leaders gain knowledge and increase their wisdom in different business situations. It should also help managers and leaders to see how to go ahead democratically when designing new products and services through democratic knowledge elicitation processes.

When machine activities are emulated democratically, human–machine wisdom generation can be seen from a new perspective (Figure 9.5).

Figure 9.6 depicts the use of the Human and Machine Wisdom Generation framework. The example covers the data, information, knowledge, and wisdom links from the computer side (machine activities) to the decision-makers. It tries to present recommendations concerning the right things to do in a particular business situation.

Table 9.2   Abstract Human Activities in Wisdom Generation

Demand	Abstract ways of Human Activities				
	Knowledge Creating Activities		Impact	Demand / Absoorb / Assume	Wisdom Generating Activities
	1. Achieving objectives	23. Increasing human capacity, abilities, skills, competence, potentiality to use data & information			1. Adding value (P)
	2. Analyzing				2. Crafting (P)
	3. Applying				3. Creating intuitive ideas (E)
	4. Contrasting	24. Justifying true beliefs			4. Creating recommendations (E)
	5. Comparing	25. Knowing			5. Evaluating understanding (S)
	6. Comprehending	26. Listening / Interviewing			6. Forming insights (E)
	7. Creating	27. Perceiving			7. Increasing effectiveness (T P)
	8. Deconstructing	28. Reasoning			8. Integrating knowledge (T P)
	9. Deliberating	29. Reflecting			9. Joining of wholes (T P)
	10. Describing	30. Remembering			10. Knowledge about knowledge (S)
	11. Evaluating	31. Seeing ahead			11. Knowing the right things to do (P)
	12. Experiencing	32. Showing how			12. Knowledge usage for the greater good (P)
	13. Explaining	33. Simulating			13. Knowing who, what, when, where, how (T)
	14. Focusing	34. Storytelling / narrating			14. Know why, and why do (S)
	15. Forming	35. Structuring			15. Making information useful (P)
	16. Joining	36. Synthesizing			16. Making sound judgements (E)
	17. Imagining	37. Thinking rationally & habits			17. Reflecting knowledge (S)
	18. Initiating	38. Thoughts in individuals' minds: inner speech			18. Sensing ethical and unethical (P)
	19. Internalizing				19. Sensing good and bad (P)
	20. Interacting	39. Timing			20. Sensing right and wrong (P)
	21. Integrating	40. Understanding objectives, patterns, relations, interrelations			21. Understanding deeply (S)
	22. Interpreting				22. Understanding the past (S)
					23. Understanding principles (S)
					24. Using tacit knowledge; making decisions without thought (P)

© 2021 H. Vanharanta, J. Einolander

Combining these two frameworks gives computer design a new vision, challenge, and opportunity to support business leaders and managers in their daily work. The target can be the democratic individual view or collective views concerning specific business issues, constructs, concepts, and found problems.

9.8 Summary

The computer architecture and frameworks developed here are based on democratic co-evolution thinking. In this kind of overall system design, the computer has been shown to have identical subsystems as people have in their brains. The framework can be applied to many different technical applications. When knowledge is increased through computer interaction, hyper-knowledge is created on the computer screen. The construction of emerging human-compatible computer systems contains the basic co-evolution ideas where people develop through computer interaction.

Table 9.3 Concrete and Abstract Human Activities in Wisdom Generation (Vanharanta et al., 2020, Vanharanta, Einolander, New design 2021)

Human Activities

Concrete ways		Abstract ways	
Data Handling Activities	Information Processing Activities	Knowledge Creating Activities	Wisdom Generating Activities
1. Accumulating	1. Acquainting	1. Achieving objectives	1. Adding value (P)
2. Calculating	2. Answering	2. Analyzing	2. Crafting (P)
3. Capturing	3. Aggregating	3. Applying	3. Creating intuitive ideas (E)
4. Categorizing	4. Comparing	4. Contrasting	4. Creating recommendations (E)
5. Collating	5. Coding / Encoding	5. Comparing	5. Evaluating understanding (S)
6. Collecting	6. Connecting	6. Comprehending	6. Forming insights (E)
7. Communicating	7. Contextualizing	7. Creating	7. Increasing effectiveness (T P)
8. Displaying	8. Conversing	8. Deconstructing	8. Integrating knowledge (T P)
9. Disseminating	9. Correlating	9. Deliberating	9. Joining of wholes (T P)
10. Extracting	10. Eliminating	10. Describing	10. Knowledge about knowledge (S)
11. Gathering	11. Filtering	11. Evaluating	11. Knowing the right things to do (P)
12. Measuring	12. Forming	12. Experiencing	12. Knowledge usage for the greater good (P)
13. Observing	13. Framing	13. Explaining	13. Knowing who, what, when, where, how (T)
14. Protecting	14. Fusing	14. Focusing	14. Know why, and why do (S)
15. Preparing	15. Ordering	15. Forming	15. Making information useful (P)
12. Quantifying	16. Organizing	16. Joining	16. Making sound judgements (E)
13. Recording	17. Prioritizing	17. Imagining	17. Reflecting knowledge (S)
14. Reporting	18. Questioning	18. Initiating	18. Sensing ethical and unethical (P)
15. Storing	19. Selecting	19. Internalizing	19. Sensing good and bad (P)
	20. Searching patterns	20. Interacting	20. Sensing right and wrong (P)
	21. Sharing	21. Integrating	21. Understanding deeply (S)
	22. Transferring	22. Interpreting	22. Understanding the past (S)
		23. Increasing human capacity, abilities, skills, competence, potentiality to use data & information	23. Understanding principles (S)
		24. Justifying true beliefs	24. Using tacit knowledge; making decisions without thought (P)
		25. Knowing	
		26. Listening / Interviewing	
		27. Perceiving	
		28. Reasoning	
		29. Reflecting	
		30. Remembering	
		31. Seeing ahead	
		32. Showing how	
		33. Simulating	
		34. Storytelling / narrating	
		35. Structuring	
		36. Synthesizing	
		37. Thinking rationally & habits	
		38. Thoughts in individuals' minds: inner speech	
		39. Timing	
		40. Understanding objectives, patterns, relations, interrelations	

Supply / Demand   Supply / Demand   Demand   Impact   Demand / Absorb / Assume

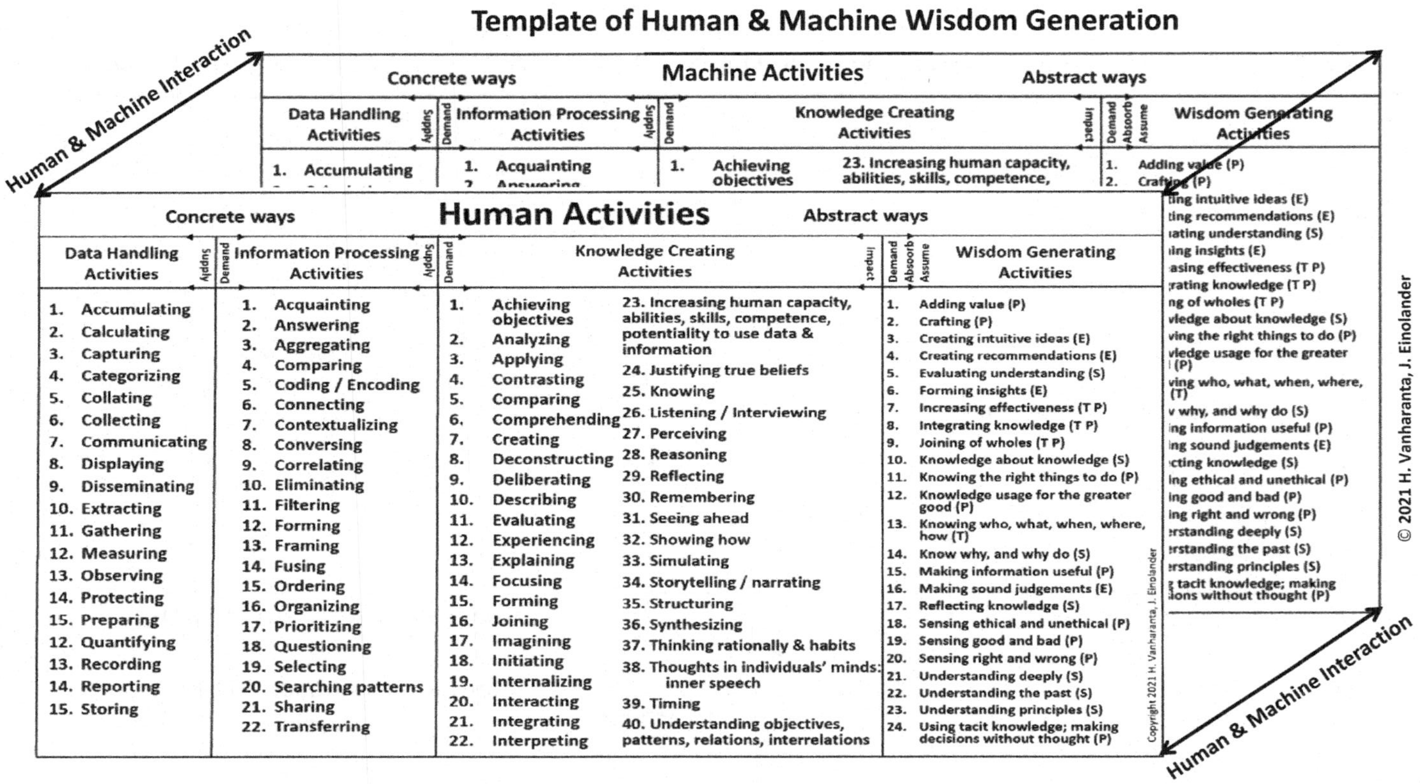

Figure 9.5 The human and machine wisdom generation framework (cf. Vanharanta, Einolander, Kantola, Markopoulos, Sivula, 2020, Vanharanta, Einolander, New design 2021).

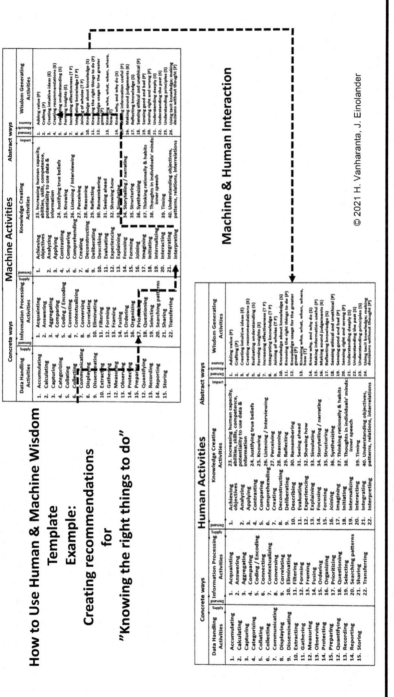

Figure 9.6 How to use the human machine framework as a decision support system (cf. Vanharanta, Einolander, Kantola, Markopoulos, Sivula, 2020, Vanharanta, Einolander, New design 2021).

Some information is brought to people automatically. Some applications extend their memory capacity. Other applications may help them interpret the current reality. Other applications may motivate their activities and efforts, and still other applications perform in all system areas. In this way, all applications somehow increase and support brain processes. In the same way, people can operate with concepts other than computers in humans' conscious experience.

Placing an object into the conscious experience, for example, different business processes, constructs, or concepts, can create these issues' extroversion. The actor can go around these issues and view the current and target business situations in detail with new knowledge. The change needs democratic thinking, supporting ontologies, concepts, and technology to determine the basic ideas of motivation, interpretation, memory, and automatic systems and how these different subsystems can be used in real-life applications. They also need other living system concepts, such as democratic cultures, to keep the processes up and running and make them more humane.

Questions for Review and Discussions

This chapter represented an emerging paradigm for achieving emulation and synergy between human decision-making processes and computer configurations. Getting new knowledge from data and information leads to the generation of new human wisdom. Such an approach is enormously important when managing and leading change steadily toward virtual work, virtual teams, complex business ontologies, constructs, concepts, and objects.

1. It's been said 'tell what computer you have, to tell you who you are.'
   1.1 What kind of requirements do you have for your computer?
   1.2 Does your compute support the work you do, or you can do, or is it closer to your lifestyle?
   1.3 Under what criteria you bought your computer?
2. Can your computer support you in your decision-making?
   2.1 Do you have the applications, the computing power, and the technology to run decision-making applications?
3. Do you think that your occupation and the market you operate in are covered with practical tools and applications (can you find in the market the applications you need)?
   3.1 Do you need better tools and applications in your profession?

3.2 If yes, what would those be? Describe each in 300 words.

3.3 If no, why not?

4. Is it possible to demand more from computers to support you as a living entity?

    4.1 To what extent does your work depend on computer applications (not emails, word processing, and spreadsheets)?

    4.2 How does this impact your life?

    4.3 How does this affect your skills, knowledge, and wisdom?

5. Expert systems advance artificial intelligence. Do you know what an expert system is?

    5.1 Give an example of an expert system and how it works?

    5.2 What expert system would you have developed if you could create one?

    5.3 How would your expert system work?

6. What is the difference between expert systems and decision support systems?

    6.1 To what extent are they both considered artificial intelligence?

    6.2 What are their differences?

7. Should computers have more of a human-compatible configuration and act as expert systems?

    7.1 What human–computer interaction or other artificial intelligence technologies would you add to an expert system, and why?

8. What is the difference between a database and a knowledge base?

    8.1 What knowledge would you prefer to collect related to your occupation?

    8.2 What kind of knowledge combinations could support you best?

9. How can abstract ways of human activities create more knowledge, and that way, more wisdom?

    9.1 How can this wisdom be stored on a computer?

    9.2 What form of artificial intelligence is needed for this?

10. Is it possible to create collective wisdom with computers?

    10.1 If yes, explain how. Provide examples.

    10.2 If no, why not? What stops this?

11. Do you think that machine wisdom is possible?

    11.1 Can we move from 'artificial intelligence' to 'artificial wisdom'?

    11.2 If yes, how can this happen?

    11.3 If no, why not?

12. See the statements in the chart of Figure 9Q.

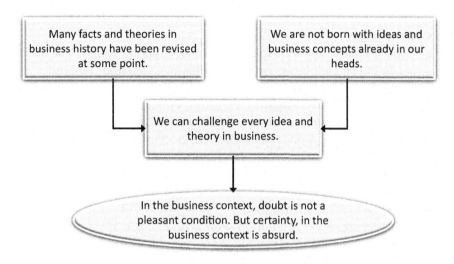

© Vanharanta H., Markopoulos, E., Applied Philosophy for Management and Leadership, 2021.

Figure 9Q   Chart for Question 12 (c.f., ref. Buckingham, et al., 2011, Voltaire, p. 146).

12.1 Do you challenge business theories, or do you think you are born with such knowledge that you can quickly master future business problems?

12.2 Do you see that you need profound scientific, theoretical, and practical knowledge and expertise continuously and absorb each new knowledge you find critically?

References

Buckingham, W., King, Peter J., Burnham, D., Weeks, M., Hill, C., and Marenbon, J., 2011. *The Philosophy Book*. Dorling Kindersley Limited, London.

Chang, A.-M., Holsapple, C. W., and Whinston, A. B., 1989b. *A Decision Support System Theory*, working paper. University of Arizona, Tuscon, AZ.

Chang, A.-M., Holsapple, C. W., and Whinston, A. B., 1989a. A decision support system theory. *Kentucky Initiative for Knowledge Management*, Paper (5).

Chang, A.-M., Holsapple, C. W., and Whinston, A.B., 1993. Model management issues and directions. *Decision Support Systems*, 9 (1), 19–37.

Chang, A.-M., Holsapple, C. W., and Whinston, A.B., 1994. A hyperknowledge framework of decision support systems. *Information Processing and Management*, 30 (4), 473–498.

Dos Santos, B. and Holsapple, C.W., 1989. A framework for designing adaptive D.S.S. interfaces. *Decision Support Systems*, 5 (1), 1–11.

Heidegger, M., 1962. *Being and Time*. Blackwell, Hoboken, NJ.

Hussler, E., 1963–1973. *Husserliana I-XVI, Gesammelte Werke.* Martinus Nijhoff, Haag, Netherlands.

Rauhala, L., 1986. *Ihmiskäsitys ihmistyössä* (Finnish Edition), trans: "The Conception of Human Being in Helping People." Gaudeamus, Helsinki, Finland.

Rauhala, L., 1995. *Tajunnan itsepuolustus* (Finnish Edition), trans: "Self-Defence of the Consciousness," Yliopistopaino, Helsinki, Finland.

Vanharanta, H., 1995. *Hyperknowledge and Continuous Strategy in Executive Support Systems.* Abo Akademi, University Press, Turku, Finland.

Vanharanta, H., 2003. Circles of mind. In: Identity and Diversity in Organizations: Building Bridges in Europe Programme, the XI European Congress on Work and Organizational Psychology. Lisbon, Portugal. 14–17.

Vanharanta, H., Einolander, J., Kantola, J., Markopoulos, E., and Sivula, A., 2020. Phronetic leadership style evaluation with a fuzzy logic application. *Theoretical Issues in Ergonomics Science*, pp. 317–337, Taylor & Francis Group, U.S.A. https://doi.org/10.1080/1463922X.2020.1768319

Vanharanta, H. and Einolander, J., 2021. *New Design.*

Vanharanta, H. and Markopoulos, E. 2021. *New Design.*

Chapter 10

The Cross-Scientific Approach for Human-Compatible Systems: Acting with Modern Decision Tools

Executive Summary

People grow and live in relations and interrelations within their internal and external working or personal environments. This coexistence can be described with systems and processes designed to promote evolutionary and Co-Evolutionary human development. Evolution and co-evolution offer new challenges, opportunities, and possibilities to address many business operations and strategies with creative human relations and interrelations. This chapter presents a cross-scientific approach, with which many human-compatible systems have been created, tested, verified, and validated, either concerning subjective introspection or objective extrospection. Top-down and bottom-up views can be combined to improve organizational productivity and individual performance, and competencies in a democratic way.

10.1 Introduction

Rapid changes in the internal and external business environment have made management and leadership more vulnerable than ever before. The

DOI: 10.4324/9781003158493-12

firm's growth theories and many other theoretical views help us understand and perceive corporate management and leadership and reveal many challenging constructs and concepts for practical management and leadership. Managers continue to strive for new methodologies and more practical tools to manage and lead in a fluctuating and chaotic business environment.

However, suppose the traditional management theories and their methods do not work in practice. In that case, the following questions arise:

- What can be done to make managerial and leadership work more efficient and significantly more effective?
- What can be extracted from different sciences to help management?
- What can be extracted from other non-management theories?
- What can be extracted from the newly available techniques, tools, and technologies?
- How could practical management be close to management theories and be supported by management and leadership sciences?

The traditional answer has been that intuitive managers and leaders must understand everything very extensively and sincerely before finding a new direction to drive their organization. They are forced to make decisions with any available data, information, knowledge, wisdom, and worldview they have in different business situations. However, managers do not always clearly understand the existing management and leadership science and theories. They have neither up-to-date data, information, and knowledge to correctly perceive the changing business climate and business situations locally, regionally, territorially, and globally.

10.2 Democratic Corporate Cultures

One way for managers and leaders to obtain the practical knowledge needed to communicate with the market and society is their employees' use of their organization's final ability at the grass-roots level. The employees face the natural world and experience the business environment daily in their workplace. They are close to the organization's actual problems. They have the information, knowledge, and wisdom from their daily activities to propose solutions and various points of view in chaotic, complex, and unstructured business situations. Knowing what they currently need, they can participate in change management initiatives, contribute to change requirements, and set near-term targets and goals to change the current business situation collectively. In other words, the employees are the people who can create the future together provided they are given the challenge and opportunity to participate and to be heard democratically.

By using employee knowledge, businesses can be more effective and responsive to daily fluctuations and changes. The change of intelligence capability in the employees' conscious experience can be turned into operational competence. This kind of management and leadership activity can help bring the employees closer to the theoretical side of management and leadership and support their managers and leaders in running the organization more effectively. To find out what is needed and the problems that have to be overcome, a particular type of cross-scientific approach is needed to connect people effectively to create human-compatible systems.

This chapter presents a framework that aims to help management and leadership in dynamic business environments, gather information from the organization's grass-roots levels, and provide a collective understanding of management and leadership purposes. Several computer-supported management and leadership applications have been developed with business ontologies for practical use. The goal now is to deepen this scientific, theoretical, methodological, and technological understanding to address the concept of democratic company culture and its derivatives.

This chapter presents the basic principles of the cross-scientific approach for human-compatible systems and the co-evolution theory and methodology framework's current status. It also approaches collective change and dynamics with the creation of ontology-based management and leadership constructs and concepts and the development of ontologies such as the Company Democracy Culture, Safety Culture, Agility Culture, etc., which can be turned into internet-based computer applications. Several case studies have indicated that a collective understanding of current and future situations can be successfully reached using applications that allow management and leadership to obtain fast, valid, and more in-depth information from the grass-roots level. This enables managers to enrich their knowledge and wisdom on the company's current position and get valuable data and information concerning its future growth. The management and leadership ontologies used in this chapter are the results of in-depth research and development work.

10.3 Current Situations in Managing and Leading

The cross-scientific approach and the research objectives address management and leadership problems based on management and leadership in different organizations. The following list summarizes the background thinking:

- Managers continuously need a holistic picture of the business situation.
- It is not easy to get a holistic picture of daily business through top-down processes alone.
- New and modern technology can help managers create a holistic view of business situations with bottom-up, middle-top-down, and top-down processes.
- People who face the real world and experience the business environment daily in their workplace can create a holistic view of the current business situation. They have all the data, information, knowledge, wisdom, and understanding to extract problems from chaotic, complex, and unstructured daily business situations. They are the people who know what they need in their occupational roles.
- The basic constructs, concepts, variables, relations, and interrelations can be defined and created to form business Management and Leadership Object Ontologies (MOOs and LOOs).
- The employees' actual business situation can be captured to make the business management and leadership ontologies dynamic.
- Managers need a scientific background, new theories, and methodologies to understand and manage these ontologies.
- Managers also need new technical tools to use management and leadership ontologies.
- By motivating the organization's grass-roots level to make a current and future analysis of the business, it is possible to get a more realistic view of the anticipated change.
- Asking about future trends at the grass-roots level of the organization is a very effective way to progress.
- The "Collective Mind" seems to be a potent activator of business development.
- The "Collective Mind" can work through business management and leadership object ontologies (MOOs and LOOs).
- People who face real-world issues can support the current business together with their managers and leaders. Top-down, middle-top-down, and bottom-up processes will be realized. Collective wisdom is generated.

These statements and propositions indicate the demand for grass-roots organizational knowledge and the supply sources to be used objectively in real terms and business situations. Suppose business object ontologies are derived from actual data and follow the current state of the business. In that case, dynamic business ontologies can be achieved, i.e., ontologies that contain current and anticipated future data and information. Such ontologies would help people increase their knowledge and generate practical wisdom from the business situations they handle. 'Dynamic' refers to creating new meta-knowledge for management and leadership purposes from the existing and evolving data and information. In this case, 'dynamic' also means that employees participate in specific qualitative evaluations by giving their beliefs and opinions on the current business situation and a future proactive vision of how it may change.

This qualitative method, i.e., the linguistic method, is based on meanings correlated in different business situations. There are many ways to put the statements mentioned earlier into hypotheses and propositions that can be used and analyzed with the cross-scientific approach.

10.4 Cross-scientific Approach

The integration of a scientific and a theoretical framework delivers a cross-scientific approach.

Scientific Framework

The scientific dimension of the cross-scientific approach lies in the research results from modern neuroscience, behavioral science, management science, and computer science that interplay in a Co-Evolutionary manner. The scientific approach is mainly based on the following areas:

- Philosophy
- Social science
- Neuroscience
- Motivational science
- Management science
- System science
- Computer science

These scientific areas define the targets from the scientific point of view. Philosophy has been the starting point, but many targets can change due to the other scientific areas in the scientific approach.

Theoretical Framework

The theoretical dimension of the cross-scientific approach consists of many old and new theories like Miller's Living Systems Theory (Miller, 1978), Rauhala's Holistic Concept of Man theory (Rauhala, 1986), Ford's Motivation Theory (1992), Senge's Creative Tension (Senge, 1990), etc.

The theoretical dimension consists of the following theories:

■ Living systems theory
■ Systems theory
■ Behavioral theories
■ Motivational theories
■ Management theories
■ Leadership theories

The theoretical approach requires many different views from different theories, mostly related to humans and human behavior as systems or active members in an organization.

Methodological Framework

The cross-scientific theory framework supports the development of Co-Evolute theory and methodology. Companies have essential characteristics that should be developed carefully within a co-evolution strategy.

According to the Co-Evolute methodology, all business parameters should be developed collectively. It is also apparent that situation-aware computing is gaining ground in management and leadership research. This change from static to more dynamic requirements demands more from decision support systems. Figure 10.1 illustrates the connection between ontology development, data handling, information processing, knowledge creation, and wisdom generation from the human perspective.

Quantitative and qualitative methods are two kinds of rigorous scientific methods. Both methods use modern information technology tools that help position, for example, company characteristics. Recent research indicates that neural networks can map different industrial sectors and measure their

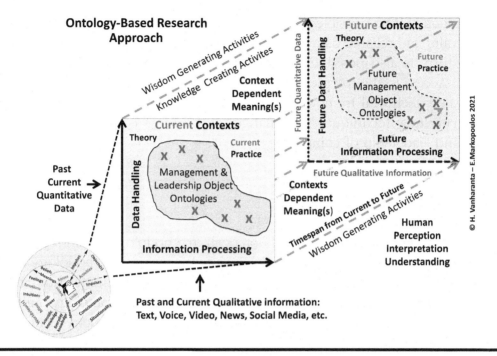

Figure 10.1 Ontology-based research approach.

employees' actual competence levels. New findings can be derived through qualitative linguistic methods, viz., fuzzy logic. Such methods can be applied to different business situations. However, the real challenge is to successfully combine the two methods (qualitative and quantitative) to operate simultaneously with the dynamic ontologies.

Meanings are widely believed to be created from data, from the available information, and from how people perceive, interpret, and understand what happens in their organization. Final decisions are made based on meanings generated from the qualitative and quantitative information at hand.

Technological Framework

Situation-aware computing is the start-up of the Evolute approach with different technologies and techniques. Modern artificial intelligence applications and tools like neural nets and fuzzy logic can bring new ways to see the current company position and its changes in the current competitive situation. Both numerical and linguistic methods are possible and also the synthesis with Hyperknowledge-type environments. Human–computer interaction with human and machine wisdom possibilities can make decision-making more straightforward and more secure. Many new ways to simulate complex phenomena will be possible and specific analysis helps managers and leaders create valid and reliable data and information analysis. Collective understanding, in turn, is also possible to make, which supports democratic company culture. Access to the internet and different internet applications (IoT) belong to this new technical framework. The new type of technological framework with many new techniques will change the business contexts, the management, and leadership of companies.

10.5 Co-Evolute Approach

By summarizing the scientific, theoretical, methodological, and technical frameworks and by presenting the Co-Evolute theory and methodology architecture depicted in Figure 10.2, the content of the overall framework can be achieved, from the supporting sciences through theories to ontology building, with different methods in the methodology section and modern technology usage (Kantola, 2016).

Co-Evolute architecture indicates many diverse areas where this scientific framework has already been applied. It supports the content engineering view on creating and constructing applications to be used in practice. This view also upholds the idea of the "Collective Mind," i.e., the actual people engaged in the specific business situations, who know more than others of the current state and can foresee the potential state as well. By measuring, for example, their current knowledge creation level and their "proactive vision," it is possible to use that data to create the present collective insight, the future proactive vision, and the meta-knowledge to be used in enhancing management and leadership within their work.

Emphasis and focus should be placed on developing core ontologies and how this kind of management content engineering can be technically enabled in the best possible way. For this, the Co-Evolute approach should be further described and tested in practice for its use to be clear to all users. Co-Evolute approach can help managers and leaders to realize that there are alternative ways to manage their companies and support their decision-making. Still, first, it is crucial to provide them with the necessary ontologies to help them understand more about their current business situation and influencing trends.

This chapter first introduces a paradigm of Co-Evolutionary management to shift the traditional focus of management science to the need for a fundamental understanding of the natural processes of continually evolving and co-evolving individuals and systems in which these individuals work.

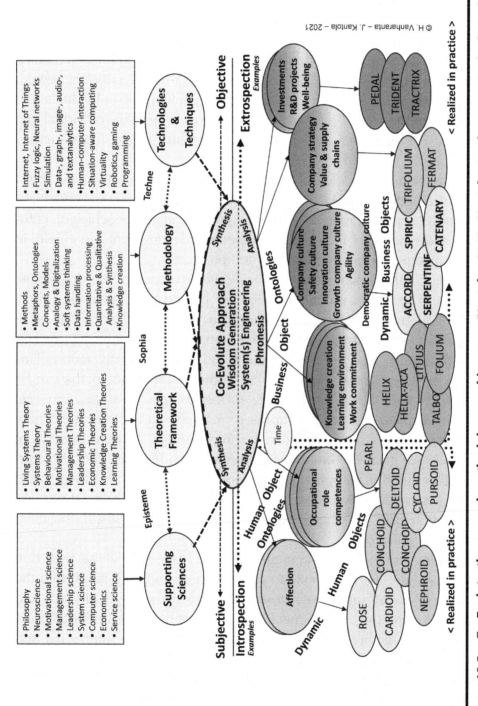

Figure 10.2 Co-Evolute theory and methodology architecture (Kantola, 2016, Kantola, Vanharanta, Revised Vanharanta, Markopoulos, 2021).

In this management paradigm, essential focus areas are raised, such as co-evolution in human performance, co-evolution in business performance, and co-evolution in human–computer interaction. All these specific focus areas can lead to a Co-Evolutionary design practice for human-compatible systems.

Despite this chapter's general nature, the new design construct is presented on a high conceptual level. This kind of theoretical cross-scientific framework has been created because the evolution and co-evolving of individuals and organizations are the critical requirements for developing both individual and organizational competencies, which are also necessary for business survival and success in our knowledge-dominated world.

The co-evolution methodology is introduced in the human mind by applying the Holistic Concept of Man and the Circles of Mind metaphors (Rauhala, 1995). This novel approach represents an emerging paradigm for achieving holistic mapping and synergy for individuals' competence development and growth in improving companies' business ontologies and processes.

The scientific human-compatible applications developed in the Co-Evolute architecture and technology competencies are limited to those critical for a specific occupational role. These applications uncover the individuals' creative tension related to their particular job. Based on the individuals' current and future visions, human resource development and other company action plans can then be made in a more targeted way. Future competence paths can be simulated. When the objects are business processes, it is possible to analyze current business processes from bottom-up perspectives to understand how these business process ontologies can be improved. A bottom-up view of business processes gives the emulated picture of each business process's current status. Through this mapping, it is possible to get an inverse model of the business processes and create new updated, relevant, and advanced models, i.e., a new action plan on what should be done about the existing business processes and Situationality.

By combining the top-down management and leadership views with bottom-up understanding, it is possible to control, steer, and command both the organization's financial and human resources toward the targeted goals and objectives. Therefore, the created meta-knowledge is the most important new knowledge made together with all the people involved. The individual and the collective, incremental bottom-up views help managers and leaders perform qualitative and quantitative analysis and understand its situation. This allows them to turn information into meta-knowledge through a potent synthesis of current and future trends.

The Co-Evolute activities are connected to keep the boundary of the company in a steady state. These activities are command and control, operations and production, support and maintenance, information input, and communication. Figure 10.3 presents the underlying paradigm and the methodology behind this thinking.

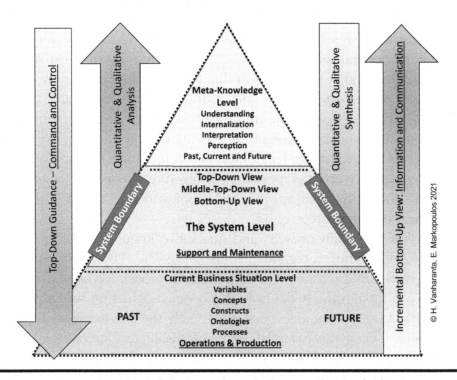

Figure 10.3   A systemic view of the meta-knowledge creation in the business management and leadership context.

Using the applications and methodology in this novel management and leadership practice helps present the current organizational stage and the future desired stage. All the applications support the company's democratic culture, which is the engine of organizational knowledge creation.

10.6 Application Context and Environment

The main areas of the Co-Evolute context that focus on the cross-scientific approach of human-compatible systems are the following: Strategic Management, Strategic Leadership, Human Resource Management, Knowledge

Management, Investment Management, Supply and Value Chain Management, Product and Service Development, Innovation Management, and Leadership, Company Culture Management, and Leadership, and of course the Democratic Company Culture.

All the areas presented are related to the management and leadership ontologies that have been created. Most of the work is directly on these topics, and some are close to the issues involved. Professor Jussi Kantola has gone further in his research and developed a method for constructing these ontologies in general terms (Kantola, 2016). During the first test runs of the co-evolution method, it became clear that the technique gives new collaborative research results qualitatively and quantitatively. Additionally, the Circles of Mind metaphor opens up the mind to its critical systems – memory, interpretation, motivation, and automation – giving new application opportunities for competence development in different occupational roles. Collaborative research groups have developed the Co-Evolute theory and methodology framework; therefore, it is approached from various scientific, theoretical, and practical backgrounds.

Combining quantitative results and qualitative/linguistic-based results from work done with technical computer tools is possible. These studies form part of the effort to develop a new cross-scientific approach for human-compatible systems. Even though the initial lack of a concrete structure was a problem in this area of management and leadership research, the cross-scientific framework indicates that having the essential elements inside can strengthen the cross-scientific approach. It is also possible to maintain and improve its content and the knowledge derived from the adaptation of democratic company culture.

10.7 Summary

This chapter introduced a paradigm of Co-Evolutionary management and leadership as a way to shift the traditional focus of management science from management, as a set of activities that includes planning and decision-making, organizing, leading and controlling, and the related management work (Griffin, 2002) to the need for a fundamental understanding of the natural processes of the continuous co-evolution of individuals within the organizations they work in.

The co-evolution between individuals and organizations is a critical requirement for developing an individual's competencies and organizational performance, both of which are necessary for business survival and success in this knowledge-dominated world. Collective views also give new fundamental ways to support company performance improvement and to generate knowledge and wisdom. The Company Democracy Model described in Section 3 of this book supports this cross-scientific approach for human-compatible systems.

Questions for Review and Discussions

This chapter presented a cross-scientific approach, with which many human-compatible systems have been created, tested, verified, and validated, either concerning subjective introspection or objective extrospection. Top-down and bottom-up views can be combined to improve organizational productivity and individual performance, and competencies in a democratic way.

1. Do you think that a holistic view helps leaders and managers to make better decisions than without holism?
   1.1 What are the benefits of a holistic perspective, and what are the risks or drawbacks associated with that?
2. Can a holistic view be achieved with a bottom-up process?
   2.1 If YES, how such a strategy would work? Justify your answer and provide an example. Then do the same example with a top-down approach.
   2.2 Compare the two methods. Which one was easier to do and why?
   2.3 Which one gave better results, and why?
3. Can you identify the introspection of your management and leadership traits and characteristics?
   3.1 How would you describe it?
4. How can business object ontologies and concepts get analyzed with extrospection?
   4.1 What would that process be? Justify your answer and provide examples.
5. Please comment on "people who face the real world and experience the business environment daily can help create a holistic view of the current business situation."
   What is your point of view on this?
   5.1 Is the workforce closer to daily business than leaders and managers? Justify your answer and provide examples.

6. Can wisdom be created collectively?
    6.1 If NO, why not?
    6.2 If YES, how can this be done?
    6.3 What is the process? If it is collectively collected, who owns this wisdom? Provide examples.
7. Can qualitative and quantitative data and information analyses be combined so that it is possible to synthesize?
    7.1 How can such a combination be achieved?
    7.2 By what means? Please provide examples.
8. How can companies understand and adopt the incremental bottom-up view with top-down guidance, command, and control?
    8.1 What would that process be? Provide an example.
9. Ponder the content in the chart of Figure 10Q. How does your company ensure that all members of your company are treated equally and fairly?
    9.1 Do people have the right to participate and explain the current business situation from their standpoint?
    9.2 What processes do you follow to achieve such a goal? Please provide examples.

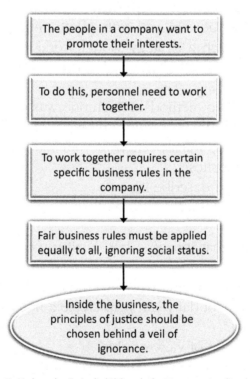

© Vanharanta H., Markopoulos, E., Applied Philosophy for Management and Leadership, 2021.

Figure 10Q Chart for Question 9 (c.f., ref. Buckingham, et al., 2011, John Rawls, p. 294).

References

Buckingham, W., King, Peter J., Burnham, D., Weeks, M., Hill, C., and Marenbon, J., 2011. *The Philosophy Book*. Dorling Kindersley Limited, London.

Ford, M. E., 1992. *Motivating Humans, Goals, Emotions, and Personal Agency Beliefs*. Sage Publications, New York.

Griffin, R., 2002. *Fundamentals of Management*. Houghton Mifflin Company, New York.

Kantola, J., 2016. *Organizational Resource Management, Theories, Methodologies, & Applications*. CRC Press, Taylor & Francis Group, Boca Raton, FL.

Kantola, J. and Vanharanta, H., 2021. Figure 10.2 revised.

Miller, J.G., 1978. *Living Systems*. McGraw-Hill Inc., New York.

Rauhala, L., 1986. *Ihmiskäsitys ihmistyössä* (Finnish Edition), trans: "The Conception of Human Being in Helping People." Gaudeamus, Helsinki.

Rauhala, L., 1995. *Tajunnan itsepuolustus* (Finnish Edition), trans: "Self-Defence of the Consciousness," Yliopistopaino, Helsinki.

Senge, P. M., 1990. *The Fifth Discipline: The Art & Practice of the Learning Organization*. Currency Doubleday, New York.

Chapter 11

Agility Application, Ontology, and Concepts in a Technology Company Context: Agility Boosts Collective Wisdom

Executive Summary

Agility is a multidimensional, complex ontology that needs adequate scientific, theoretical, technical, and human resources to find the right practical solutions to improve agility in the company context. The main target is to generate significant added value in products, services, projects, and organizations. Because the ontology and concepts can have fuzzy nature, agility must be understood in detail throughout the whole organization. After that it can be adequately used in practice. Agility evaluation needs, however, computer tools. Such a tool to measure the degree of agility in an organization has been developed by the author's international research group to be used in any size and type of organization. The software development used a democratic approach to finalize the application's content of the ontology. The application's development process started from a small, intuitive idea, but it got a sizeable collective understanding and support in a real business context. The positive usability, verification, and validation results indicated the application's potentiality during the evaluation of current and future

DOI: 10.4324/9781003158493-13

agility trends in a Finnish company. The results also showed that this kind of collaborative development approach suits ontology-based management and leadership very well.

11.1 Introduction

The Co-Evolute approach has a strong background in understanding human involvement, business objects, constructs, concepts, and variables in a real-world context. From a scientific background, developing a strong theoretical management and leadership base helps define and manage the multifaceted agility construct and the many concepts within it. In turn, the organizational co-evolution approach and philosophy suit the study of agility. Companies have to meet real-world problems and challenges, adapt themselves to the current and future situation, and see their future options.

The cross-scientific methodology used in the agility application revealed that one should be very cautious when thinking and speaking about agility. Many managers and leaders see agility as a trendy concept, a management tool for all cases, and an effortless way out for implementing anything, anytime, and anywhere. However, this is not an appropriate way to think and apply agility. On the contrary, agility is a multi-concept complex ontology that makes this holistic way of thinking and acting fuzzy and complicated to precisely define and apply it.

The concept of responsiveness is one of the most critical traits of agility. Organizations try to be more flexible and dynamic in a continuously changing world. However, these same organizations and companies must closely monitor their added-value creation in the whole value chain so they can continue to serve their customers and clients with adaptability and flexibility. The agility concept can be described with the combination of terms such as 'adaptability,' 'flexibility,' 'responsiveness,' and even 'yielding.' For agility to be comprehended appropriately, it is important to understand first that the world and the organizations are agile in many ways. In practice, this means that people within each organization should understand the different dimensions of agility similarly. In particular, managers and leaders who are called upon to apply agility must understand that agility starts from the people and culminates in the organizational goals. Therefore, making organizational changes too fast and without the employees' involvement to obtain agility in management and leadership can be quite risky.

To avoid misconceptions, it is suggested that it is wise to redefine the term using an ontology that can cover the areas and limits in a specific context. Ontology originally derives from philosophy and refers to the science of being. The term 'ontology' has recently also been used in information technology, where it is a conceptualization specification.

This chapter presents an agility case study and demonstrates an international Finnish technology company's ontology application to verify the ontology, construct, and concepts. The testing covered several test subjects, all of whom were the technology company's employees.

11.2 The Nature of Agility

The popularity of agility increased over the last two decades in almost all business, engineering activities, operations, and strategies. However, today's meaning of agility differs significantly from the initial definitions used before its adaptation from the software engineers and engineering industry.

The nature of agility concept can be described as "being gently rolling, light, flexible, witty and nimble, contrasted to rigidity." In practice, the term has a different meaning, as it stands mainly for adjustability. The agile concept became very popular through the software engineering discipline and communities to enhance the development process and bypass bureaucratic complexity in the software development efforts imposed by strict software development processes, tools, and structures (cf. Beck et al., 2001).

The problem agility aimed to solve was relatively straightforward. The software development industry needed structured methodologies and a process to assure its engineering quality. However, being very structured was more of a trouble than a solution in a fast-changing world. Technology constraints (continuous advancements), client constraints (varying and unstable requirements), and project constraints (unpredicted schedule and budget limitations) were considered obstacles in developing software within a fixed budget, time, and quality (Markopoulos, Panayiotopoulos, 2008).

The software industry had to bypass bureaucratic challenges in software development processes by adopting flexible processes without declining from the existing industry standards and processes (Markopoulos, Panayiotopoulos, 2005). To solve this challenge, the complex agile concept was invented, reinvented. The idea of agile software development is to apply software development best practices based on the environment, context, project constraints, challenges, goals, and objectives. Thus, software development on small-sized projects could avoid, for example, long design, testing, and documentation processes that create either an unnecessary or expensive overhead. On large projects, the processes could be adjusted according to the project goals. The processes could be strengthened with additional activities to reach the expected requirements and conditions on critical projects or applied with reduced activities to meet the expected schedule or budget. Agile methodology was based on the idea that there is not an actual implementation methodology and specific processes, but a framework that can flexibly adjust the existing processes and practices the desired project goals and objectives (Markopoulos et al., 2008). Therefore, agility turned out to be the "Lego-type" adjustment tool of the software development process. The results of applying agility in software development were very successful. For the engineers, software was developed with fewer processes and overhead, while for the clients, software developed incrementally, faster, and with tangible and continuous small results.

However, agility is very difficult to design and risky to apply without the related experience and expertise in the area it is called to be applied. Reducing the number of processes from an existing methodology requires high capability, competence, and maturity from those responsible for selecting which processes are needed, which are to be removed, and which are to be changed to achieve agility. The same applies to the management and leadership teams, which acting outside the development process use agility to bypass problems that require significant expertise to make the right decisions (Markopoulos, 2008).

Over the last two decades, many software engineering agile methodologies and methods have been developed. Some of them were successful, and others not that successful (Markopoulos, 2006). The ARIADNE Methodology, developed by the author professor Markopoulos at EMPROSS Strategic IT Consultants, was one of the first agile software engineering and project management methodologies (EMPROSS, 2002) launched in 1992. It was developed based on the concept of "Agile Lego," i.e., "build it yourself," to manage the various project constraints. The ARIADNE set of processes made the methodology compatible with 108 international project management and engineering methodologies. ARIADNE supports more than 15 different software development types such as waterfall, spiral, incremental, rapid prototyping, etc., offering agility in the implementation process and the implementation strategy (EMPROSS, 2003) (Figure 11.1).

Agile process engineering is not for everyone and not for every company to attempt. It requires the integration of management and engineering disciplines to select, design, and adjust the right processes that will deliver the agile

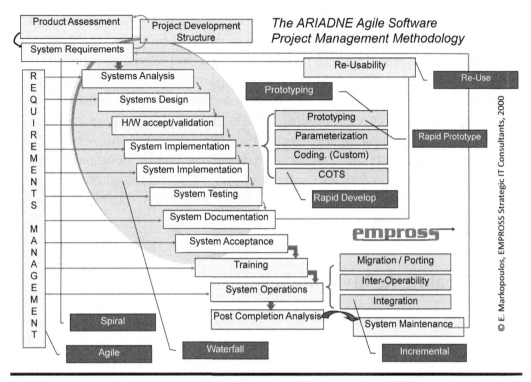

Figure 11.1 Methodological approaches supported by the ARIADNE Agile Software Engineering Methodology.

methodology to be used in a specific project. Agile methodologies provide significant flexibility that can be critical when needed, but they require tremendous expertise and discipline in the area in which they are being applied.

11.3 Defining Agility Ontology

The term 'ontology' derives from the Hellenic 'on' (όυ), genitive 'ontos' (όυτος): "of being," neuter participle of 'eine' (είυαι): "to be," and 'logia' (λογία): science, study, theory. Therefore, 'ontology' indicates the live and not static elements contained in it. These elements affect or get affected by the environment and context used (Oberle, Guarino, Staab, 2009). In the Stanford Encyclopedia of Philosophy, ontology is divided into two categories. The first defines the study of what exists in an entity, while the second defines the study of what is involved in settling the questions to identify what is in an ontology. Effingham (2013) claims that ontologies split the information they contain into the abstract and concrete. Osterwalder (2004) studied business model ontologies and developed practical ontologies through a theoretical approach derived from Information and Communication Technologies (ICT), proving that ontologies in practical life are primarily used in information technology business process modeling and related activities.

Similarly, Dietz studied enterprise ontology from his ICT background and point of view. He believes that enterprise conceptual models must be coherent, comprehensive, consistent, and concise (Dietz, 2006). These models are ontological. His example of the World Wide Web provides an everyday basis for a common understanding of some exciting area among people (Hansisalo, 2017). Furthermore, professors Vanharanta and Kantola have taken some steps toward more practical ontology approaches, although there is always an application in the background (Vanharanta, Kantola, 2012).

11.4 Creating Agility Ontologies

To achieve agility in ontologies creation, one must understand the relationship of the elements that compose the specific ontology. All ontologies have passive and active components that define a microcosm of activities, operations, and goals. This microcosm affects and gets affected by other ontologies based on the way they interact. Therefore, well-designed ontologies must be agile to achieve the desired flexibility and adjustability needed for their practical and rewarding use.

Furthermore, the ontology elements can also be characterized as the imports and exports of information in an ontology. They are the elements that collect the information to be processed in the ontology and export information after being processed in the ontology. Figure 11.2 presents an agile ontology with active, import, and export elements.

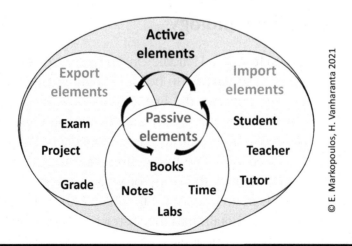

Figure 11.2   Agile 'Teach' ontology with relationships between elements.

There are two main challenges in creating agile ontologies. The first one is the careful and correct identification of the ontology elements and their relationships that can achieve agility, i.e., to be used with flexibility and adjustability on the maximum number of occasions. The second is the ontology designer's proper use when applying ontologies in processes, systems, and methods. To achieve ontology agility, the elements of the ontologies' taxonomies must also be identified with the same attention. An ontology can also be designed to include sub-ontologies, which are actual taxonomies of the ontology elements. The breakdown of the ontology elements into taxonomies defines the range of the ontology use.

Figure 11.3 presents the 'teach' and 'learn' ontology. It indicates that agility is related to the way teaching is done and the learning achieved. The degree of agility is based on the number of ways such combinations can be satisfied. One way to maximize agility is to treat both ontologies as taxonomies of a more comprehensive 'Teach–Learn' ontology that defines teaching and learning options within the ontology. These options determine the degree of agility in using the specific ontology.

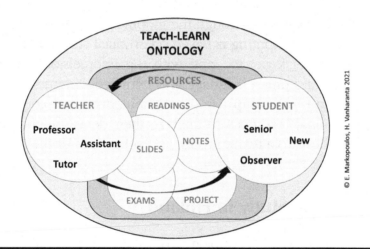

Figure 11.3   Taxonomies within ontologies for maximum ontology agility.

It must be noted that agility is not a practice, a method, a process, or a trend. Still, it is the art of understanding the real world and satisfying it continuously with adjustments on the continuous needs and operations environment. The use of agile ontologies significantly impacts the development of agile processes, methods, and practices. Agility resides in the ontology and not in the methodology. Methodologies include ontologies that drive and support the methodology execution. Once such a view is conceived, ontological agility can be obtained effectively.

11.5 Agility Application Catenary

Management and Leadership Object Ontology (MOOs and LOOs) applications can be found on the Evolute application platform (Evolute, 2016). The Evolute agility object ontology and its application are called Catenary. Catenary's name was given according to the mathematical equation: Catenary. The equation forms a curve like a chain hanging from two points or a free-hanging high-voltage power line.

The Evolute system has a methodological approach (Evolute, 2016, Kantola, 2016) and forms a platform supported with fuzzy logic-based computing. The Catenary for Organizational Agility application uses linguistic statements to describe the ontology's content. With the application, it is possible to visualize the meaning of the knowledge input democratically collected from stakeholders, allowing all employees to become involved and heard. Each person can present their opinions, feelings, beliefs, and understanding, indicating the existing and future organizational agility direction. The Evolute approach follows a modular process that involves individuals and stakeholders. Their perception and understanding of organizational resources are sought and collected one by one with the application. People must think, build meanings in their brains, and express this through the graphical computer interfaces (GUI). The Evolute's system computing is based on artificial soft-computing methods and algorithms (fuzzy logic) to cope with the imprecision and uncertainty embedded in natural human language and knowledge inputs.

Management and leadership use the computed current and future meanings of organizational resources to analyze their development. The analysis can be made of the whole team, group, and subgroups of the organization.

11.6 Agility Case Study in Finland

The case study tested the agile ontology, constructs, and all the concepts inside. The application was conducted with 24 test subjects who represented a Finnish technology company. The carefully created ontology statements were put into the Catenary application. The number of statements was 110, varying from the understanding of the term 'agility' to its implementation and control activities, including several subcategories, which are described in detail by Hanhisalo (2017).

Since these were just the first real-world test runs of the application, the number of participants was limited to 24 test subjects. Hence it is difficult to draw final scientific conclusions from this case study alone, but it provided good verification and validation for the application. Table 11.1 presents an example with 17 from the 110 statements to indicate the ontology structure.

Table 11.1 Example of Agility Ontology Statements in Catenary

High-Level Concept	Sub-concept	Indicators	Minimum	Maximum
General Concept	Agility aware-ness	I understand the term 'agility'	not at all	completely
		Most people in our organization understand the term 'agility'	not at all	completely
		Our organization has to be agile	not at all	definitely
		We do not need agility in our organization	not at all	definitely
		Our company is 'fast'	not at all	absolutely
		We understand our company strategy	not at all	completely
		I understand my company's strategy	not at all	completely
	Agility suitable	Agility is suitable for our organization	not at all	definitely
		We know how to utilize agility in our organization	not at all	absolutely
		Agility has helped our organization	not at all	totally
		We have to plan our things better	not at all	absolutely
		Our organization innovativeness is at a high level	not at all	definitely
		We have an organizational culture that encourages innovation	not at all	completely
	Innovation	Our organization innovativeness is at a high level	not at all	definitely
		We have an organizational culture that encourages innovation	not at all	completely
		We have facilities that promote innovation	not at all	completely
		We have a daily meeting where we can share our innovative ideas	never	always

11.7 Agility Case Study Results

The Catenary application results reflect the status of the respondents' organization, i.e., the Finnish technology company, and are taken as such. After the test runs, the company continued its internal thinking and development based on the results achieved. The aggregate results can be seen in Figure 11.4, which shows the summary by the main categories, while the detailed results by topic are presented in Figures 11.5 and 11.6. The general numerical results clearly show that the 'Investigation of Problems' category is in the best state (current states over 0.70). In contrast, the other three categories are lower between 0.58 and 0.63. The target state in each category means that a lot of development work is required.

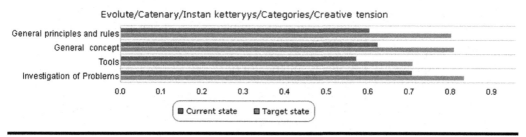

Evolute/Catenary/Instan ketteryys/Categories/Creative tension

Figure 11.4 Summary of agility study results in a Finnish technology company by main categories.

In Figure 11.5, the individual concepts are sorted by their current state "ranking."

The current state seems to be entirely satisfactory in the concepts of Delivery management, General, KPI Awareness and usage, Performance, and Communication implementation. The opposite is true for total productive maintenance (TPM), 5S, Agility software, Lean management, General knowledge about agility tools, etc. One cannot say whether the results are right or wrong. Nevertheless, they show the company's direction to develop its activities and reveal the agility concepts for management and leadership purposes. According to the future state, shown in Figure 11.6, the individual concepts are sorted by their "ranking."

The most critical points in Figure 11.6 are the categories: Delivery management, General, and Share knowledge. It is also possible to obtain an index from the system describing the current-to-target state ratio. This index is called the Evolute Index.

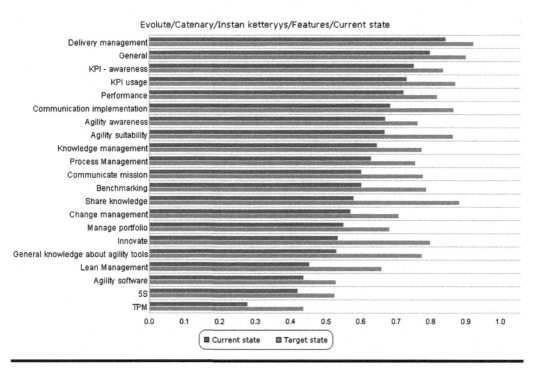

Figure 11.5 Concepts of agility in a Finnish technology company sorted by their current state.

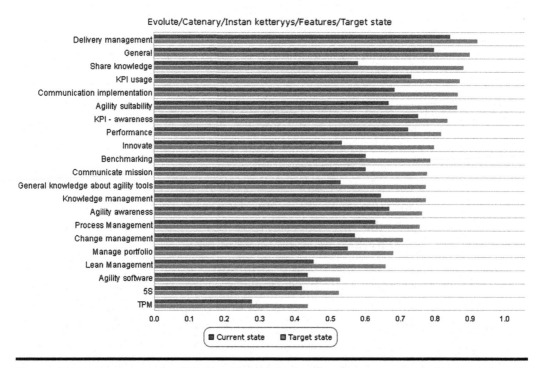

Figure 11.6 Concepts of agility in a Finnish technology company sorted by target state.

Figure 11.7 presents the concepts sorted by the Evolute Index. The highest index is in TPM issues, followed by the concept "share knowledge" as an essential innovation concept. In this index, the lowest concepts are KPI awareness and Delivery management.

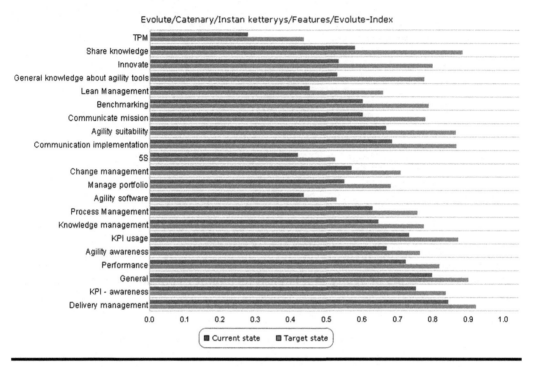

Figure 11.7 Concepts of agility in a Finnish technology company sorted by the Evolute Index.

According to the respondents, a high index tells us that the concept needs attention and improvement in that company. Figure 11.8 shows a simple statistical summary of the case. It shows the average values and the standard deviation of the concepts in the ontology.

Finally, it is essential to recognize that people understand and experience agility in their company very differently. However, the mean values give a good picture of how the sub-concepts have been perceived and understood and what is essential to develop at the current time.

This analysis also indicates that a company cannot develop all the sub-concepts simultaneously. This development requires the company's management and leadership to have more experience, capability, competence, and know-how. Specific priorities may lead to reasonable solutions, but as agility is a fuzzy concept, it requires careful teaming, teamwork decisions, and planning on what to do next and how to make progress with each concept.

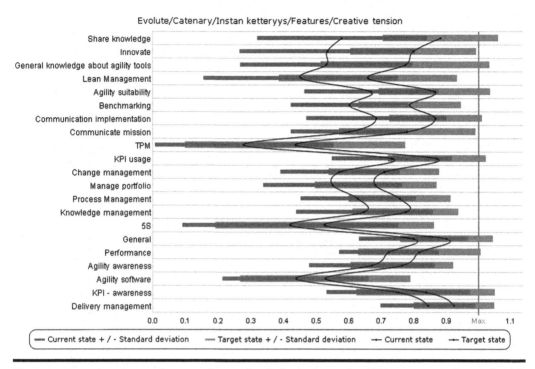

Figure 11.8 Average values and standard deviation of agility concepts in a Finnish technology company sorted by creative tension (target–current).

In Figure 11.9, we demonstrate how it is possible to get specific information from each feature. The figure reveals the target state deviation from the mean value and shows well how the test subjects have answered to the statements under each feature. In Total Productive Maintenance (TPM), we see that the term is perhaps not so well known among the test subjects, and the current knowledge is low. However, there is a keen interest to improve the current state. Lean management is a well-known concept, and test subjects want to improve the lean management concept from the current state. Communications need improvement, as well as how to share knowledge. Agility suitability and awareness show the need for improvement, and both are well positioned on the figure.

Figure 11.10 shows the summary of the agility research results by different topics in the Finnish technology company, sorted by creative tension. The results indicate the need to improve the perceiving and understanding of agility concepts. The application also reveals the main sub-concepts that should be developed immediately, such as "Share knowledge."

The statements in the application can be further developed but are adjusted from company to company. However, in this application, in contrast

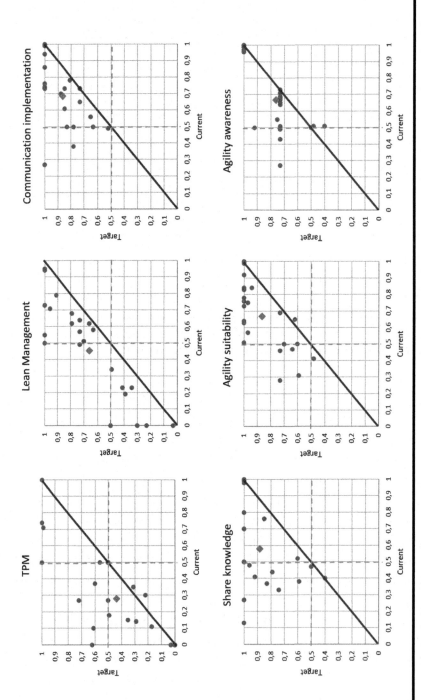

Figure 11.9 Detail analysis of the test subjects results with six different agility features in a Finnish technology company (target–current).

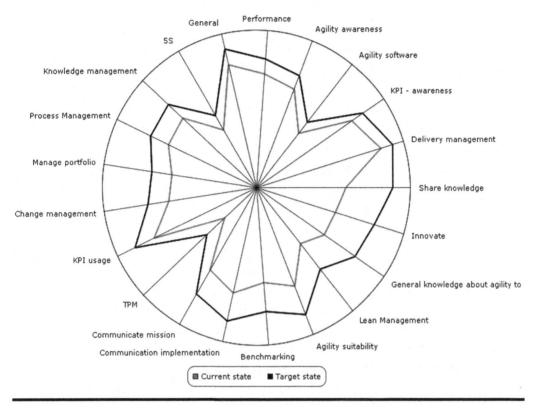

Evolute/Catenary/Instan ketteryys/Features/Creative tension

Figure 11.10 Summary of agility concepts in a Finnish technology company sorted by creative tension. (Start reading from 3 o'clock > Share knowledge.)

to applications that are closer to psychological tests, it is safe to say that there is no need to compare the results with similar applications, as there are no other applications currently available on the market for measuring organizational agility with a similar approach.

11.8 Summary

Beyond applications in the information and communications technology sector, from where the concept stems, ontology as a structured thinking practice is uncommon in the broader school of business thought and practice. Even if someone understands what ontology means, it remains a challenge to integrate this philosophical dimension properly in a business context. Philosophy must be applied more in the fast-moving and fast-changing business world. Hence easy methods need to be invented and taught to give the necessary help in understanding such concepts. The methodologies and tools developed by EMPROSS or Evolute LLC support this thinking in the agility area.

The agility created in many businesses' plans and strategies demands a level of caution from managers and leaders during the implementation processes. Agility can suit some companies, but not necessarily all of them. For instance, should governments be agile or not? How about many heavy industries – can they be agile? To what degree? Agility is well suited for software and electronics-related businesses like mobile phones, electronic components, computers, etc., where innovation cannot be controlled with a static structure and non-flexible management and leadership. However, adopting agile management in non-ICT organizations requires more in-depth thinking and well-justified decisions.

The agility/ontology application presented in this chapter is convenient and can be used in any organization for management and leadership purposes. It can indicate the status of agility, the degree of agility, and the organization's development needs. It is possible to find many similar areas, functions, and disciplines in non-ICT organizations to develop ontologies. Developing an ontology by using the application is not complicated. However, to achieve the significant development of such applications, a minimum set of research statements is required.

Ontologies are still heavily used in information systems and processes development to manage innovation effectively. Still, such thinking should be broader, as innovation does not only exist in the technology sector. Time will show whether ontologies will be used furthermore in practical business cases, processes, and operations, especially for management and leadership purposes. Ontologies can help structure this type of thinking, as they provide all the potential needed to support agile thinking in organizations.

Finally, management and leadership applications like the Catenary help extract information from the organization's employees to develop business processes and prioritize the changes derived from such analysis. To achieve these results and create more practical, feasible, and effective business processes and strategies, the agility concept can more effectively be applied in organizations with democratic culture and thinking where the knowledge of all can be used for the benefit of all.

Questions for Review and Discussions

The practical research results in Chapter 11 with agility application have shown that the collaborative development approach suits ontology-based management and leadership. Collective knowledge creation is possible to get from current company assets, and of the trend, these assets are moving in the future.

1. How can you define the term 'Agile organization'?
   1.1 What makes an organization agile, and how can this be measured practically?
2. What type of agility would you expect your organization to have?
   2.1 What kinds of operations in your organization can be managed with agility, and how?
   2.2 How would that help the organization perform better? Please provide examples.
3. Have you ever considered applying agility to a non-tangible business operation?
   3.1 How can agility be applied, and how could you measure it?
4. Scrum methodology is considered a leading agile practice and actually part of the agile concept.
   4.1 How can scrum be applied in agile leadership?
   4.2 How can scrum be used in non-tangible business operations?
5. Based on the agility case study presented in this chapter, how can you analyze the results to identify the organization's degree of agility?
6. Based on your judgment, can you prioritize the different management and leadership issues (of the case study) that impact organizational agility the most?
   6.1 Justify your answer. Provide an example.
7. Develop five agility features according to the current state, target state, and the Evolute Index (= the highest relative difference between the future and current stage).
   7.1 Compare them and explain how each one achieves organizational agility better.
   7.2 Which one do you think supports the concept best?
8. How can you interpret the average values and standard deviation on the agility concepts?
   8.1 What meanings derive from each reading?
9. Communication implementation and knowledge sharing are essential concepts from the democratic perspective in companies. How do you see these concepts?
   9.1 Can they provide enough information to start specific projects and improve knowledge sharing and communication? If YES, justify your answer and give an example.
   9.2 If NO, what do you suggest for improving this methodology?
10. Please ponder this chapter with the chart of Figure 11Q and think about how scientific, theoretical, and technical knowledge can change the world.

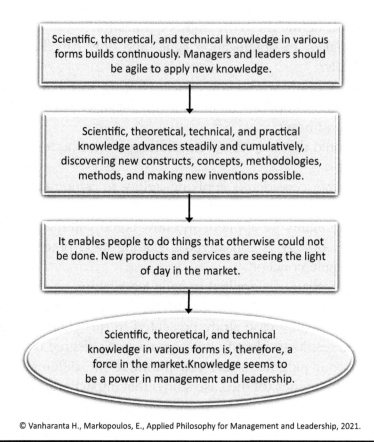

© Vanharanta H., Markopoulos, E., Applied Philosophy for Management and Leadership, 2021.

Figure 11Q Chart for Question 10 (c.f., ref. Buckingham, et al., 2011, Francis Bacon, p. 110).

10.1 Do you follow how new knowledge penetrates your business?

10.2 Do you see how new technology can change your products or services?

10.3 Are you ready to invest in knowledge creation?

10.4 Do you see human intelligence as the power of knowledge creation?

10.5 Do you think that you need new knowledge of your leadership and management?

References

Beck, K., Beedle, M., Van Bennekum, A., Cockburn, A., Cunningham, W., Fowler, M., Grenning, J., Highsmith, J., Hunt, A., Jeffries, R., and Kern, J., 2001. Manifesto for agile software development. http://agilemanifesto.org/. (Accessed December 14, 2015).

Buckingham, W., King, Peter J., Burnham, D., Weeks, M., Hill, C., and Marenbon, J., 2011. *The Philosophy Book*. Dorling Kindersley Limited, London.

Dietz, J. L. G., 2006. *Enterprise Ontology*. Springer-Verlag, Berlin.

Effingham, N., 2013. *An Introduction to Ontology*. Wiley, Hoboken, NJ.

EMPROSS, 2002. The Ariadne methodology. http://www.empross.com/en/the_ARIADNE_Methodology. (Accessed December 14, 2015).

EMPROSS, 2003. The Ariadne methodology. http://www.empross.com/en/methodological_approaches. (Accessed December 14, 2015).

Evolute, 2016. Evolute.com. https://www.evolute.com.

Hanhisalo, T., 2017. *Agile Practices and Their Development in a Technology Company*. MSc. Thesis, Tampere University of Technology, Pori, Finland.

Kantola, J. 2016. *Organizational Resource Management, Theories, Methodologies, & Applications*. CRC Press, Taylor & Francis Group, Boca Raton, FL.

Markopoulos, E., 2008. I.C.T. process development and evolution models and the first financial Bank of Montenegro case. *Bankar: Montenegro Bank Association Journal*, 1 (1).

Markopoulos, E. and Bilbao, J., 2006. An evaluation, correlation, and consolidation of information technology project management processes. In: 1st International Conference on Engineering and Mathematics, Bilbao, Spain.

Markopoulos, E. and Panayiotopoulos, J.C., 2005. A project management methodology selection approach based on practical project and organizational constraints. *WSEAS Transactions on Computers*, 4 (8), 934–942.

Markopoulos, E., Bilbao, J., Bravo, E., Stoilov, T., Vos, T.E., Talamanca, C.F., and Reschwamm, K., 2008. Project management stage mutations within agile methodological framework process transformations. *WSEAS Transactions on Information Science and Applications*, 5 (5), 776–785.

Oberle, D., Guarino, N., and Staab, S., 2009. What is an ontology? In: *Handbook on Ontologies*. Springer, New York.

Osterwalder, A., 2004. *The Business Model Ontology a Proposition in a Design Science Approach*. Doctoral dissertation, Université de Lausanne, Faculté des hautes études commerciales.

Vanharanta, H. and Kantola, J., 2012. Strategy needs structure–structure needs ontologies: Dynamic ontologies carry meanings. In: International Conference on Knowledge Management and Information Sharing, SCITEPRESS, Barcelona, Spain. 2, 261–264.

THE COMPANY DEMOCRACY MODEL

3

Chapter 12

The Company Democracy Model for Organizational Management and Leadership Strategies: Democratic Innovation for Competitiveness and Extroversion

Executive Summary

Democracy is one of the most powerful words. It is a word that indicates freedom, equality, rights, fairness, respect, justice, development, prosperity, and many other significant concepts. It is pronounced very similarly in many different languages, expresses the same meaning. However, managing, leading, achieving, and sustaining democracy in its true meaning can be challenging, if not almost impossible. This chapter presents the researched and developed democratic company culture model and reveals its principal components with the Co-Evolutionary Spiral Method. Such a democratic culture creation approach helps organizations develop new data, information, knowledge, and wisdom to initiate, innovate,

DOI: 10.4324/9781003158493-15

understand, perceive, and apply management and leadership results to achieve innovation, competitiveness, and extroversion. The overall process adopted in this model is based on previous works on human and company performance improvements. First, the actuality is viewed in detail through the current democratic behavior, and then, the capability and potentiality of the organization are examined. In this process, indicative critical concepts are being addressed and answered, such as actuality, potentiality, and capability. What could we plan to do for our company's democratic behavior? What could we do to develop our organization's democratic behavior? What could we achieve by developing democratic behavior in our organization? This chapter presents answers to these questions with an approach that identifies and defines the degree of Company Democracy.

12.1 Introduction

Understanding democracy requires, first of all, situational self-awareness. The essential Delphic maxim is 'Gnothi Seauton,' i.e., know yourself. Second, it requires humble and honest knowledge, whether applied at the governmental, organizational, or individual levels. Third, having the ability to create, perceive, and adequately interpret knowledge requires a culture that promotes self-knowledge, self-control, commitment, motivation, cognitive capacity, competence, and social skills. Finally, situational awareness is expected on the knowledge, information, and data triptych that creates meaning among people. Creating such a culture with an excellent fundamental ontology requires initially a robust strategy to manage and implement it, but also powerful and wise leaders and managers to execute it. Being democratic or applying democracy to an organization is a very challenging goal for managers and leaders.

The Company Democracy Model is based on a framework through which an organizational, evolutionary, level-based Spiral Method is used to create and execute knowledge-based democratic cultures for effective organizational management and leadership strategies. Through such a Co-Evolutionary Spiral Method, an organization can identify and achieve the capacity, capability, competence, and maturity needed to move through the Company Democracy levels (from the lower to the higher levels). In this context, the spiral process is based on managing the degree of democracy in organizations. The levels in the model correspond to the elements and steps of organizational democracy development. When all of these are fulfilled, the organization can verify that organizational democracy can be applied, and has been applied efficiently, effectively, and rewardingly. The Company Democracy Model integrates engineering, management, leadership, and social science disciplines to provide both the opportunity and the challenge to redefine the concept of democracy within organizational operations.

Organizations must first understand the current degree of democracy in their operations and work to improve it over time with a democratic self-grown process, product, or project innovations. This significant change can be achieved in any organization's culture by changing the organization's people with the appropriate education and learning activities and measuring the progress of the democratic coexistence inside the organization that can enable the desired changes (Vanharanta, Markopoulos, 2013).

The Company Democracy Model can be effectively applied in all organizations in any sector and of any size. It is a unique method that promotes the human being as the center of organizational development achieved through ethos and knowledge, elements that develop a knowledge-based organizational culture, sustains leadership and innovation, and delivers competitiveness and extroversion. The Company Democracy Model is a holistic model. It can be expanded to include Company Micro and Macro Democracy, Company Democracy, Corporate Democracy, Business Democracy, Organizational (Institutional) Democracy, Enterprise Democracy, Intrapreneurial Democracy, Corporate Entrepreneurial Democracy, Government/Public sector Organizational Democracy, but also Entrepreneurial Democracy for SMEs and Family Business.

12.2 The Capability and Maturity to Change

Before targeting new organizational goals and expectations, it is vital to understand the organization's needs and current state. This kind of proactive vision, which can be created with the people inside the organization, creates an environment where organizational democracy grows with the harmonic collaboration of all employees, managers, executives, and leaders. The development of any organizational culture, and even more an organizational democratic culture, must be driven by maturity stages (levels) that verify the accomplishment of specific goals based on the organizational or individual capability and capacity (Markopoulos, Bilbao, Christodoulou, Stoilov, Vos, Makatsoris, 2008a). Any democracy, and especially an organizational democracy, depends on the organization's maturity to achieve the capability and competence needed to move democratically from one level to another. Achieving this capability and maturity requires a co-evolution environment and a spiral-staged evolutionary co-development approach as the prime elements of democratic organizational culture development.

However, it must be noted that such an approach expects strong leadership on the development and maintenance of a democratic organizational culture.

It also requires innovative and strategic management with proactive planning on reaching the organizational maturity degree that can utilize organizational knowledge in a sophisticated way and create this democratic culture for organizational development. The company democracy paradigm presents a framework that combines such requirements, supported by fuzzy logic as the necessary technique to handle and control the fuzziness of such management methods, models, and practices. As common sense is not that common, concepts such as democracy have been proved to be quite fuzzy when understanding and applying them in leadership and management.

12.3 Research Foundations

The research methodology used in the Company Democracy Model combines various methods to obtain a fundamental situation-aware construct for identifying and defining the degree of Company Democracy. The methodology is focused on covering both past and current data and information to get the idea of how people evaluate democratic development in their own company at present and in the future (Figure 12.1).

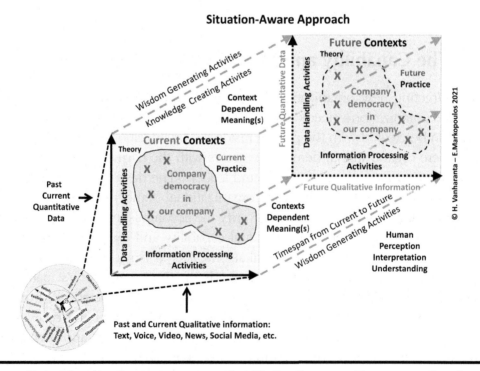

Figure 12.1   The situation-aware approach with the Company Democracy Ontology.

The basic principle of the Situation-Aware Approach is to see how people view their company in their minds (Vanharanta, 2005). If they see it as 'just a job,' then there is no need to go further since they do not care much about it. However, if people see their work as part of their life, as a community, and an environment in which they live and grow, then Company Democracy has more chances to succeed. Therefore, by analyzing people's behavior patterns in their work, meetings, decisions, and other activities, significant information can be obtained about their past to justify their present situation and forecast their future.

The Holistic Concept of Man consists of Corporeality, Consciousness, and Situationality (Vanharanta, Pihlanto, Chang, 1997), where a person sees democratic behavior in their company. By combining this with a broader view, a new dimension is projected of how people can have different concepts of their situation and how they handle them to explain their situation and understand how different concepts build meanings in their brains today and in the future (Figure 12.2).

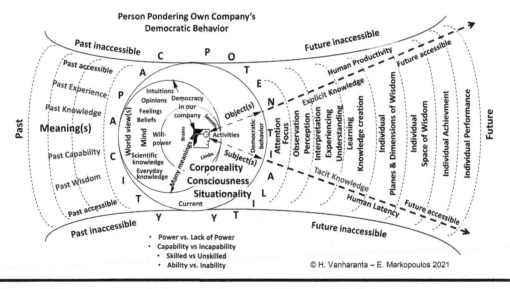

Figure 12.2   Person pondering own Company's Democratic behavior.

It is essential to envisage an accessible future democratic company culture, i.e., 'What does it contain?' and 'How can the degree of Company Democracy be evaluated?' Past, current, and future data, information, and knowledge are, therefore, essential. The company must have scenarios, visions, and plans of how a democratic company culture can be created.

Each company member envisages a democratic company in their own way; however, a collective view gives the initial perception and understanding of democratic company culture, i.e., the current situation and what people would like to see. People must first understand the concept of democracy, then interpret it through the Company Democracy Model, and then perceive their collective view of this critical management and leadership issue.

Before utilizing the research instruments for this methodology, it is crucial to understand the broader construct of company activities that lead to democratic company culture. Thus, the developed Spiral Method for Company Democracy is a significant support process for democratic company growth.

12.4 Basic Principles of the Spiral Method

The Spiral Method is based on the concepts of process agility and mutation, which are defined as the flexibility a process can have toward achieving an organizational goal (Markopoulos, Bilbao, Stoilov, Vos, Reschwamm, 2008b). Process engineering is the prime discipline for agile and mutational process development management. Organizational democracy is a burdensome and fuzzy concept in terms of definition and adoption. As it can be considered a live entity with continuous change, it must be managed with agile practices that support such environments to absorb the ideas and voices from all and not from the few.

Concepts such as organizational reengineering, reconstruction, redefinition, transformation, optimization, etc., cannot be related and aligned with the values of democratic company environments. They are based on a change that cannot easily be 'unchanged' if needed. For such concepts to be practical, organizational change through agile and mutated practices is required. Change is a harsh word for live entities such as humans or organizations. Therefore, the risk of making an unsuccessful or erroneous change is very high, and the consequences can be devastating. The Company Democracy Model, through the Spiral Method, provides a structured path that supports an organization to achieve democratic management, leadership, and operations. Still, on this journey, nothing can be considered predictable and standard. As the goal is Company Democracy, people must learn first to cooperate and coexist before they co-evolve.

12.5 Responsive Environment for Democratic Development in Organizations

The Spiral Method of the Company Democracy Model is used as the core tool for evolutionary organizational development. It contributes to the management of organizational democratic cultures based on organizational knowledge, capability, and maturity of strategic goals. It has been designed in such a way to help organizations democratically evolve by reaching their strategic goals collectively. The method, through its iteration loops or spiral levels, creates an evolutionary framework in which an organization moves from designing a strategy, which in this case is the organization's democratic strategy, to the deployment of the strategy, based on an organization's democratic culture that generates and grows knowledge for that purpose.

This path can be achieved by following the six levels of the Spiral Method for organizational democratic culture development:

- Level 1: Democratic culture knowledge-based strategy
- Level 2: Democratic business methods, structures, and knowledge management
- Level 3: Democratic culture process and project engineering
- Level 4: Democratic culture innovation management
- Level 5: Democratic ecosystems development for competitiveness
- Level 6: Extroversion and internationalization

The Company Democracy Spiral Method levels are represented in a pyramid-like structure (Figure 12.3). The pyramid shape has been chosen to point out the incremental progression of the levels and illustrate that not all knowledge contributors who attempt this route can reach the top without commitment, determination, or an organizational strategy.

THE COMPANY DEMOCRACY MODEL

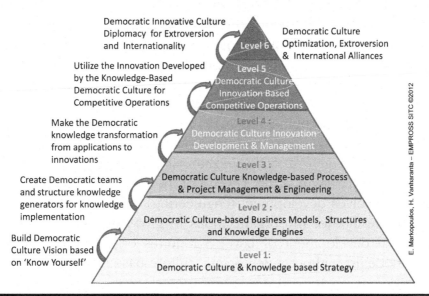

Figure 12.3   The Company Democracy Model.

Level 1 helps an organization define a knowledge-based organizational democratic culture strategy, essential for planning, development, operations, activities, and initiatives. Through assessments, discussions, debates, workshops, knowledge-sharing activities, and initiatives, the organization generates the knowledge that defines and identifies its organizational ability to understand its current position and its capability and maturity to grow. Such activities create a knowledge-based culture where ideas and knowledge are generated democratically toward specific organizational goals and strategies. No organizational culture, especially a democratic one, can develop effective strategies without the internal knowledge derived from its people.

Level 2 contributes to developing the business methods and structures required to execute the organizational democratic culture strategy. Progress is achieved through team-based knowledge management practices, which act as knowledge management engines that validate and verify the knowledge derived democratically from Level 1. The development of democratic and knowledge-based business methods and structures is based on activities and initiatives that need to be implemented to utilize the people's knowledge. In contrast, the organizational structures define the hierarchies to be put in place regarding the human resources and operations management needed to utilize the organization's knowledge. The business method determines 'WHAT' needs to be done, while the business structures define 'HOW' it will be organized and achieved.

Level 3 continues with developing process and project engineering practices, using the knowledge democratically generated in the previous levels, designing, implementing, and applying it in projects and initiatives within the organizational development culture and strategy. The term 'process engineering' integrates and develops organizational management processes and project management processes to implement organizational knowledge and transform it into products or services that can contribute to organizational development. Process engineering creates processes, process management executes them, project engineering creates projects, and project management executes them (Markopoulos, Panayiotopoulos, Bilbao, Makatsoris, Samaras, Stoilov, 2008c). Management of organizational knowledge is required for both process and project engineering. Level 3 of the Spiral Method is very significant since it involves development (engineering) efforts and produces actual and tangible results for the organizations to grow. On the other hand, the organizational development of Level 3 requires organizational knowledge, which cannot exist without a democratic culture-based strategy.

The first three levels of the Spiral Method develop the infrastructure for creating and adapting Company Democracy. The knowledge-based strategy, the business methods and structure, and the process and project engineering cover the necessary and basic operational and organizational development requirements for an organization to operate successfully and effectively. On the other hand, there are, and should be, organizations with higher expectations targeting internationalization through more aggressive and challenging development routes. Such routes can be achieved by developing organizational innovation, competitiveness, organizational ecosystems, international networking, and extroversion. Company democracy is needed much more in organizations that target such development strategies. It is precisely the democratic mentality that can grow innovative cultures through innovative thinking to develop process, project, and product innovations that can lead to competitiveness and extroversion. The democratic culture can utilize everyone's voice, capability, and maturity to successfully achieve internationalization for the benefit of all and not only for the periodic targets of the management.

Level 4 contributes to identifying the real innovation that exists and grows from within the organization. This innovation is what creates the added value needed for the organization to compete in the international arena. To be competitive, organizations need to identify their key areas and opportunities to make a difference and help them stand out in a competitive environment. Identifying innovation and managing innovation are relevant but different activities. Once the organization's innovation has been identified, its strategy must be redefined to integrate the new innovative elements and use them as competitiveness forces. Innovation management is an essential process for all organizations that aim to develop significant competitive advantages.

Level 5 aims to utilize the organization's competitiveness and to promote the organization's international strategy and operations. This can be done by creating organizational business ecosystems that share and disseminate organizational innovation and competencies. It must be noted that not all innovations can be sustainable. Innovations that reach the industry through internal and external organizational networks and ecosystems can return rewarding competitive advantages. Being accepted in the international markets presupposes being competitive, and being competitive requires innovation, and innovation requires development, which requires knowledge. In turn, knowledge requires a democratic culture to grow freely and unbiased. Level 5 is the level that pays the organization back for all the work done in the previous levels. It creates competitiveness through co-opetition and not competition.

Level 6 describes the stage where an organization reaches and stands on the apex of its strategy, i.e., extroversion, international recognition, and all the opportunities that come with the development of international collaborations, worldwide consortia, partnerships, and strategic alliances. Collaborating and participating in global schemas require a high degree of organizational competitiveness, innovation, maturity, and capability. This level is reached with robust and continuous democratic knowledge utilization processes, not only in technical activities but also in communication, teamwork, operations, and production.

The time and effort required for an organization to reach each level in the Company Democracy Model are related to the degree of the democratic and Co-Evolutionary mentality in its democratic culture. In a democracy, people co-evolve for the creation of shared added value. The Company Democracy Model provides an action plan for identifying the degree of Company Democracy through a new pyramid-type representation based on individual and collective evolution dimensions (Figure 12.4).

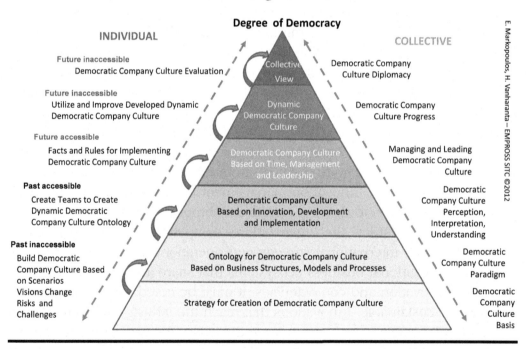

Figure 12.4   Dynamic Democratic Company Culture Co-Evolutionary Method.

The individual side of the pyramid can remember and view the past inaccessible part of the company's democratic process, which may be accessible today and in the future. From a collective point of view, the base of the democratic company culture must be firm. The created paradigm must contain all the available information, and the democratic company culture must be understood, interpreted, and perceived by each company member. Company managers and leaders must know the constructs, concepts, and indicators to manage and lead this fuzzy concept in their company and see how changes happen through critical figures and actions. Implementation continues at each level of the Company Democracy Model.

The overall approach identifies the opportunity to evaluate the current degree of Company Democracy and see how the people inside the organization view democracy. Everyone in the organization can access such research instruments and evaluate their feelings about the company's democracy.

The six levels of the Company Democracy Model and the Spiral Method are supported by several activities executed in loops (Figure 12.5). The first five loops are composed of three prime activities, preferably delivered in the following order:

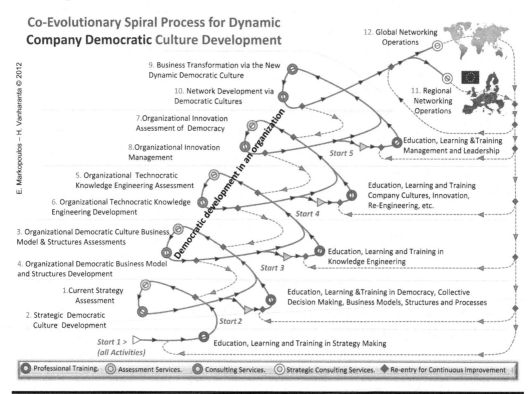

Figure 12.5   Co-Evolutionary Spiral Method for dynamic Company Democracy Culture development.

1. Training: Needed for the organization to define a common language and establish a common understanding of the level requirements.
2. Assessment: Identifies the distance between the 'as is' and the 'to be' in the organizational democratic culture development framework. The

assessment can also define the actions, priorities, effort, cost, and the specific human resources needed to complete a specific level.

3. Implementation actions: Drive the execution of the assessment results to reach the level's requirements and secure the development of the organizational democratic culture strategy and operations framework.

This triplet of activities is implemented at each level of the Company Democracy Model through the Spiral Method, which drives and guides the organization from Level 1 to Level 6. The Co-Evolutionary Company Democracy Spiral Method identifies all the directions and operations an organization should follow in its journey to achieve innovation, competitiveness, and lead extroversion.

It must be noted that the Company Democracy Spiral Method has five (5) entry points. The entry points indicate that the organization is not obliged to go through all the levels if it considered that it has the required expertise and maturity to apply organizational democratic culture from another level, not necessarily from the start (Level 1). It must also be noted that all levels start with training and assessment actions. These actions help the organization identify whether it can begin its journey from the desired entry level without going through the previous ones. If the organization fails to advance to the next level, then the option to move down a level and complete the prerequisites is always available.

Organizations can repeat a level if they want to be confident before advancing to the next one. Once an organization reaches the optimal goal (Level 6), it can redefine its strategy or develop a new one and start the process again for that new strategy. This restart can begin either from the first level or any other level the organization feels confident to enter.

12.6 The Spiral Method for Knowledge Creation of Democratic Behavior

The Company Democracy Model and the Spiral Method is a vehicle for creating an organizational democratic culture for operations and development. The six levels of the method are structured to reflect the Co-Evolute approach and methodology (Kantola, Vanharanta, Karwowski, 2006) and its organizational democratic performance application.

Levels 1 and 2 of the Spiral Method reflect the first fundamental element of the Co-Evolute organizational democratic performance approach: Potentiality. The relationship is based on identifying what needs to be done to develop the organizational democratic culture and what organizational infrastructure needs to exist.

Levels 3 and 4 of the Spiral Method reflect the second fundamental element of the Co-Evolute organizational democratic performance approach: Capability. The relationship is based on developing organizational competencies within an organizational democratic culture framework toward democratic organizational operations and performance.

Levels 5 and 6 of the Spiral Method reflect the third fundamental element of the Co-Evolute organizational democratic performance approach: Actuality. The relationship is based on utilizing an organizational democratic culture once it is in place (Table 12.1).

Table 12.1   Correlation between the Essential Elements of the Co-Evolute and the Spiral Method Methodologies

Co-Evolute Methodology Basic Elements	Company Democracy Spiral Method Methodology Levels	Relationships
Potentiality	Level 1: Democracy culture- and knowledge-based strategy Level 2: Democracy culture-based business models and structures	Identification of what needs to be done to develop organizational democratic behavior.
Capability	Level 3: Democracy culture-based process and project management and engineering Level 4: Democracy culture innovation development and management	Capability and competence development via structured processes and innovation management toward getting the most out of organizational democratic behavior.
Actuality	Level 5: Democracy culture knowledge-based operations Level 6: Democratic culture optimization	Challenge for organizational management based on organizational democratic behavior and culture.

Both organizational development methodologies (Co-Evolute and the Company Democracy Model with the Spiral Method) are based on utilizing the organizational knowledge which defines the organizational capability and maturity, directed at creating an organizational knowledge-based culture

(Paajanen, Piirto, Kantola, Vanharanta, 2006). Both methods are based on identifying a strategy, which will utilize organizational knowledge by developing a knowledge-based culture that continuously contributes to the organization by transforming tacit organizational knowledge into explicit knowledge (Nonaka, Takeuchi, 1995).

This transformation drives a knowledge-based organizational culture and forms the infrastructure for organizational democratic culture development. For an organization to adopt and execute democratic processes, strategies, and leadership, it is essential to master the organizational knowledge and to justify, defend, and support the democratic organizational culture in the best possible way. Therefore, the processes between the concepts of organizational culture, knowledge culture, and democratic culture start from identifying a democratic organizational strategy that will support the development of each one of these three cultures, based on the organization's capability and maturity to learn first and from itself (Figure 12.6).

Culture Evolution within Organizations

Figure 12.6 Democratic Culture co-evolution within organizations.

The Company Democracy Model and the Spiral Method present organizational knowledge within democratic behavior more dynamically. The six levels of the method develop the organizational capability and maturity through an organizational knowledge culture that can be evolved into an organizational democracy-based knowledge culture. Regarding the development of such a culture, the organization can utilize the knowledge generated inside the organization and the external knowledge generated outside the organization by partners, suppliers, customers, etc. (Figure 12.7). This unintentional or targeted knowledge swapping process contributes significantly to the generation of practical experience and its culture outside its operations. Organizations that share common knowledge through standards or open procedures, methods, and practices form intentional or unintentional organizational ecosystems and can develop and support more effective collaboration.

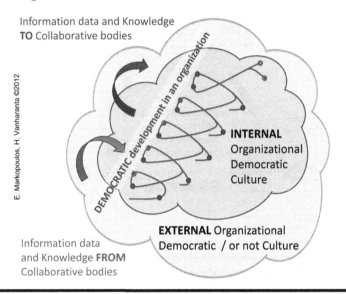

Organizational Democratic Culture Enrichment

Figure 12.7   Democratic culture co-evolution with external organizations.

The direct and indirect, intentional and unintentional exchange of knowledge between organizations can be conceived, valued, and utilized differently if organizational democratic culture is in place. For incoming external knowledge, in particular, the existence of an organizational democratic process can significantly support its best possible assessment and utilization. Instead of inviting selected, even qualified, knowledge management experts or knowledge engineers to access the organization's internal knowledge, environment, and culture and propose solutions to various challenges, changes can be made in other ways. A change can be made more effective if everyone in the organization contributes to the challenges given, based on their role and expertise. Similarly, this concept can be expanded by involving the knowledge of other organizations in resolving a challenge. Corporate networks can develop formal organizational ecosystems if, and only if, common organizational cultures are shared. A wider group of organizations can collaborate in a line of business, shared product or service development, etc., and jointly evolve to utilize each other's knowledge through each organization's organizational democratic culture (Figure 12.8).

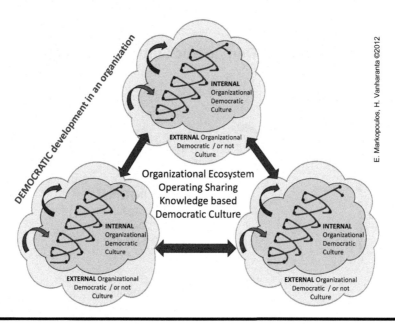

Figure 12.8 Organizational democratic culture ecosystem.

Developing this concept, furthermore, organizational ecosystems based on democratic culture can increase in size. This can form industry management and operations standards based on open democratic culture principles that promote the exchange and utilization of knowledge between organizations with similar operating processes, goals, and visions.

Such wide organizational ecosystems with a co-evolutional democratic culture concept as a common denominator can significantly impact any industry, sector, or region, on the way of doing business, conceiving knowledge, developing strategies, utilizing human resources, promoting innovation, defining and redefining profitability, productivity, performance, efficiency, and much more.

12.7 Methods for Qualitative Analysis of Organizational Democracy

The analysis of the Company Democracy Model can be conducted with the help of ontologies and fuzzy logic. The relevant concepts of the Company Democracy levels and their relationships can be modeled by using ontologies. The degree to which each concept is present on each company's democracy level can be modeled using fuzzy sets and fuzzy logic (Klir, Yuan, 1995).

A fuzzy set can be defined mathematically by assigning each possible individual in the universe of discourse a value representing its grade of membership in the fuzzy set. This grade corresponds to the degree that an individual is similar or compatible with the concept represented by the fuzzy set (Zadeh, 1965). In this work, the perception of democracy in an organization becomes a degree of membership in fuzzy sets, representing different perceived democracy ontology concepts.

Fuzzy logic is reasoning with imprecise concepts and has two principal components. The first component is a translation system for representing the meaning of propositions and other semantic entities. The second component is an inferential system for reaching an answer to a question related to the information resident in a knowledge base (Zadeh, 1983). In the Company Democracy Model, the meaning propositions refer to the semantics of democracy in organizations. Therefore, the knowledge base refers to a collection of presented meanings important in different management and leadership concepts (here: democracy in organizations). Fuzzy logic provides Decision Support Systems (DSSs) with powerful reasoning capabilities. Vagueness in linguistics can be captured mathematically by applying fuzzy sets. The ability to make precise and yet significant statements about a system's behavior diminishes as its complexity increases (Zadeh, 1973). Therefore, it is not easy to make accurate observations on complex systems such as democracy-oriented methods and procedures.

Conventional mathematical methods require several preconditions to be met before they can be utilized, especially when there are concerns about the independence of the factors used. Fuzzy logic allows us to ignore these preconditions due to linguistic variables (Zadeh, 1973). In the Company Democracy Model case, where human behaviors and interactions are intense, 'conventional' mathematical methods can face difficulties when applied to such complex and living systems.

12.8 Summary

The integrated Company Democracy Model supports an interdisciplinary approach (management strategy, knowledge, innovation, human resources, technology, production, leadership, quality, processes, design, research and development, etc.). This integration is based on the degree of wisdom created with data handling, information processing, and knowledge creation activities. It creates the understanding needed to unite people through freedom of expression and generates the required knowledge that drives an organization to innovation, competitiveness, and extroversion (Figure 12.9).

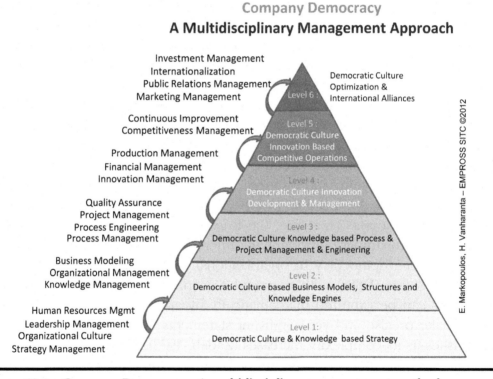

Company Democracy
A Multidisciplinary Management Approach

Investment Management
Internationalization
Public Relations Management
Marketing Management

Level 6 : Democratic Culture Optimization & International Alliances

Continuous Improvement
Competitiveness Management

Level 5 : Democratic Culture Innovation Based Competitive Operations

Production Management
Financial Management
Innovation Management

Level 4 : Democratic Culture Innovation Development & Management

Quality Assurance
Project Management
Process Engineering
Process Management

Level 3 : Democratic Culture Knowledge based Process & Project Management & Engineering

Business Modeling
Organizational Management
Knowledge Management

Level 2 : Democratic Culture based Business Models, Structures and Knowledge Engines

Human Resources Mgmt
Leadership Management
Organizational Culture
Strategy Management

Level 1: Democratic Culture & Knowledge based Strategy

E. Markopoulos, H. Vanharanta – EMPROSS SITC @2012

Figure 12.9   Company Democracy: A multidisciplinary management method.

The Company Democracy Model and the Spiral Method can be considered tools that set up the required infrastructure to support an organizational knowledge-based democratic culture. The Spiral Method levels can be viewed as the staged arena in which democracy can be measured based on the organizational culture's effectiveness. The loops/levels of the Spiral Method are the organizational development and operational challenges that need to be tackled democratically. There are areas where organizational democracy needs to be extensively demonstrated to ensure that the organization can apply such management methods which can be accepted, followed, and executed by all and not by the few.

Taking, for instance, the Spiral Method's innovation level (4th level), it is crucial to understand that no innovation can be developed unless there is a democratic culture in the organization where every idea can be presented by anyone, at any time, and on any subject. The process engineering level (3rd level) of the Spiral Method behaves similarly. Process and project engineering methods and practices need to be developed in a democratic environment where they can be accepted and used. In this content, each Spiral Method level contributes to democratically achieving strategic organizational development milestones. Lack of democracy in executing such significant organizational development stages can have limited or no rewarding results. The Co-Evolute theory and methodology work supportively inside and around the Spiral Method to developing an organizational culture that can exist and succeed in democratic environments. A step-by-step development approach is required, for all organizational assets, including organizational knowledge, to be utilized in an incremental and agile way.

Without an organizational democratic culture with educational ethos, organizational learning cannot be created. In turn, without organizational knowledge, there is no innovation. Without innovation, there is no development. Without development, there is no competitiveness, and without competitiveness, the organizational extroversion required in today's globalized society cannot exist.

Questions for Review and Discussions

The Company Democracy Model is based on a framework through which an organizational, evolutionary, level-based Spiral Method is used to create and execute knowledge-based democratic cultures for effective corporate management and leadership strategies. Through such a Co-Evolutionary Spiral Method, an organization can identify and achieve the capacity, capability, competence, and maturity needed to move through the Company Democracy levels (from the lower to the higher levels). In this context, the spiral process is based on managing the degree of democracy in organizations. The levels in the model correspond to the elements and steps of organizational democracy development.

The situation-aware approach supports the development of democratic company culture.

What is the situation of your company's democratic culture? Do you have enough resources to develop a democratic culture in your company today and support its development in the future? What is needed to make the change happen in democratic thinking inside your company?

Think and discuss these issues and answer the following questions:

1. Does your company have a democratic culture similar to the Company Democracy Model (CDM)?
    1.1 How can you compare the organizational culture your company has against the CDM? What are the similarities and differences?
    1.2 Critically analyze them by giving examples.
2. What is the difference between the individual and collective degree of democracy?
    2.1 Please point out the key differences and critically analyze them.
    2.2 Can you combine any?
    2.3 Can you come up with a hybrid model?
    2.4 If YES, how would that work?
3. What is needed to create a responsive environment for democratic development?
    3.1 How can you incentivize employees to participate in a democratic culture?
    3.2 What is in for them? List ten incentives.
    3.3 Prioritize the incentives and explain how each motivation works.
    3.4 Give examples for each incentive.
4. What could be the criteria/conditions to enter a spiral process level if the progression is not sequentially made?

    4.1 How can a company or project descent levels in the spiral methodology?

    4.2 What impacts the advancement to the next or the descent to the preceding level?

    4.3 Justify your answers by giving examples.

5. If there were a seventh level in the CDM, what would that be?

    5.1 Can you think of an extension of the model?

    5.2 How would you restructure the levels to include the seventh level?

6. Identify the essential elements of the Co-Evolute and the Spiral Method methodologies.

    6.1 List five elements of each methodology.

    6.2 Compare the elements and critically analyze them.

7. If you could improve the co-evolute methodology, what would you add, delete, or change?

    7.1 Present a new version of the methodology based on your recommendations.

8. If you could improve the Spiral Method, what would you add, delete, or change?

    8.1 Present a new version of the methodology based on your recommendations.

9. How do external organizations impact the democratic culture co-evolution with each other?

    9.1 How do external organizations co-evolve with your organization under the democratic culture principles?

10. How can you define an organizational ecosystem?

    10.1 What is an organizational democratic culture ecosystem?

    10.2 Compare the two types of ecosystems.

    10.3 What differentiates them?

11. Go through the chart Figure 12Q below and discuss what kind of traditions you have in your company, and is it possible to discuss them collectively, change the habits, and strengthen your company that way?

    11.1 Is it possible to discuss democratic company culture this way?

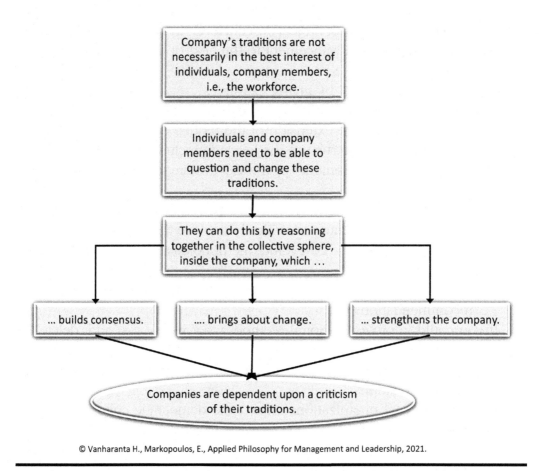

© Vanharanta H., Markopoulos, E., Applied Philosophy for Management and Leadership, 2021.

Figure 12Q Chart for Question 11 (c.f., ref. Buckingham, et al., 2011, Jurgen Habermans, p. 307).

References

Buckingham, W., King, Peter J., Burnham, D., Weeks, M., Hill, C., and Marenbon, J., 2011. *The Philosophy Book*. Dorling Kindersley Limited, London.

Kantola, J., Vanharanta, H., and Karwowski, W., 2006. The evolute system: A co-evolutionary human resource development methodology. In: Karwowski, W. (ed.) *The International Encyclopedia of Ergonomics and Human Factors*. CRC Press, Boca Raton, FL, 2nd Edition.

Klir, J. G. and Yuan, B., 1995. *Fuzzy Sets and Fuzzy Logic, Theory, and Applications*. Prentice Hall, Inc., Hoboken, NJ.

Markopoulos E., Bilbao J., Christodoulou E., Stoilov T., Vos T., and Makatsoris C., 2008a. Process development and management: Towards the maturity of organizations. *International Journal of Computers*, 4 (2), 361–370.

Markopoulos E., Bilbao J., Stoilov T., Vos, T., and Reschwamm, K., 2008b. Project management stage mutations within agile methodological framework process transformations. In: WSEAS International Conference on Circuits, Systems, Communications, and Computers, Beijing, China.

Markopoulos E., Panayiotopoulos J-C., Bilbao J., Makatsoris C., Samaras G., and Stoilov T., 2008c. Project management process framework for developing and managing I.T. systems. In: 12th WSEAS International Conference on Computers, Heraklion, Greece.

Nonaka, I. and Takeuchi, H. 1995. *The Knowledge-creating Company: How Japanese Companies Create the Dynamics of Innovation*. New York, Oxford University Press.

Paajanen, P., Piirto, A., Kantola, J., and Vanharanta, H. 2006. FOLIUM: An ontology for organizational knowledge creation. In: 10th World Multi-conference on Systemics, Cybernetics, and Informatics, Orlando, FL.

Vanharanta, H., 2005. Co-evolutionary design for human-compatible systems. In: Conference on Computer-Aided Ergonomics and Safety, May 25–28, Technical University of Košice, Slovakia.

Vanharanta, H. and Markopoulos, E. 2013. Creating a dynamic democratic company culture for leadership, innovation, and competitiveness. In: 3rd Hellenic-Russian Forum, September 17, Athens, Greece.

Vanharanta H., Pihlanto P., and Chang, A.-M., 1997. Decision support for strategic management in a hyperknowledge environment and the holistic concept of man. In: HICSS '97 Proceedings of the 30th Hawaii International Conference on System Sciences, Hawaii.

Zadeh, L., 1965. Fuzzy sets. *Information and Control*, 8 (3), 338–353.

Zadeh, L., 1973. The concept of a linguistic variable and its application to approximate reasoning. *Information Sciences*, (8), 199–246.

Zadeh, L., 1983. Commonsense knowledge representation based on fuzzy logic. *Computer*, 16, 61–65.

Chapter 13

The Levels of the Company Democracy Model: A Spiral Co-evolution

Executive Summary

The Company Democracy Model is characterized by its pyramid structure and the number of levels that compose it. The pyramid indicates that the journey to the top is a challenge that cannot be achieved without commitment, dedication, and hard work. It also signifies the journey of knowledge creation. The lower levels mostly generate information rather than actual knowledge. However, as the levels rise, the information is transformed into knowledge, products/services, innovations, competitive advantages, and extroversion strategies. The pyramid also indicates the effort required for each level to be reached. The lower levels are time-consuming as they set up the base and infrastructure for the model to be applied. In contrast, the upper levels are less time-consuming since they utilize the previous levels' output. Another way to see the pyramid is the involvement of the people concerned. The lower levels are open to all company employees, while the upper levels are continuing with those who have evolved through the Company Democracy Model processes. There are many ways to interpret the Company Democracy Model structure related to effort, benefits, participation, complexity, and goals. Still, the most critical way to see this

DOI: 10.4324/9781003158493-16

evolutionary path is its openness to the participation of all the employees in a company. Democracy provides the opportunity, not the outcome. Both the employees and the company should work together to co-evolve toward achieving the best, but this cannot happen unless the opportunity is given to everyone, unbiased and unconditionally.

13.1 Introduction

The Company Democracy Model has been structured in sequential stages, to be executed serially once each level's goals are achieved. The model's levels are knowledge-related and not company-related, meaning that the evolution from one level to the next is based on the evolution of a specific knowledge contribution and not from the company's evolution itself. A company cannot be characterized or rated by a Company Democracy Model level. Such a company rating derives from the overall knowledge contributions that it has successfully developed at various levels of the model.

It is the knowledge that moves through the levels, from the first to the sixth, and not the organization itself. The model follows a knowledge-driven development, meaning that the levels start from the individual goals and end up with company goals with the institutionalization of the knowledge during the process. The Company Democracy pyramid presents the evolution and institutionalization path of knowledge and not the evolution of the individual or the company.

Therefore, there can be many pyramids within an organization whose number is equal to the amount of knowledge, ideas, and insights identified by each employee. In other words, there is one Company Democracy Model pyramid for every piece of knowledge presented. This allows employees to build more than one pyramid if they can.

The model empowers and motivates employees to build their Company Democracy Model pyramid based on the quality of the knowledge they can produce. Suppose a knowledge contribution lacks quality, validity, and reasoning. In that case, no pyramid can be built, and the process stops for the specific person at the first level where the idea was introduced as it was not strong enough to continue.

Employees work together with the company for mutual benefit when building these pyramids. Some pyramids will stop on the second level, others on the third or fourth, and so on, as not all can reach the sixth level. This is also the reason why the pyramid shape was selected to represent the model.

One way to see the entire company, and not a specific knowledge contribution, with a pyramid is to associate with the degree of democratic organizations value created from the sum of its pyramids. Organizational value is related to the number of pyramids being built over a period of time, based on the size of the organization in terms of employees (knowledge engines), and the impact of each pyramid on the development and operations of the organization (i.e., increase in sales, customers, innovations, contracts, partnerships, new products, etc.).

Another way to see the company with a pyramid is to calculate the average level of the pyramids divided by the number of employees and the impact on organizational development. This can be supported by the ratio of the pyramid level per employee, the ratio between pyramids and employees, and the ratios between pyramids and impact.

If, for example, an organization with 50 employees initiates 70 pyramids over a period with an average pyramid level of three, this organization is more competitive on intellectual capital production and utilization than another organization with 100 employees that initiated 70 pyramids of the same average level in the same period.

Therefore, the degree of Company Democracy in an organization and the Company Democracy value can be calculated through the intellectual capital value produced per employee. The organization provides the knowledge utilization framework, and the employees offer the knowledge. This co-evolution requires outstanding leadership skills and a well-defined democratic organizational culture in place. The rest is driven by the Company Democracy Model and its levels.

13.2 The Six Levels of the Company Democracy Model

The six levels of the Company Democracy Model (CDM) are presented narratively in a theoretical context and supported by an imaginary case where four members are involved with the following roles:

Paul: Company manager; Panos: Employee; Jane: Engineer; George: Economist.

13.2.1 CDM Level 1: Democratic Culture and Knowledge-Based Strategy

Theoretical Approach: The organization provides all employees the opportunity to share knowledge, ideas, and insights in any form, area, subject, or organization's need. An employee's knowledge or information that may benefit the organization can be a structured proposal, written notes, figures, sketches, videos, pictures, algorithms, and anything that can demonstrate the main idea, need, functionality, or benefit. This knowledge does not have to be technical, innovative, radical, or disruptive. It can be a simple procedure for rearranging the parking slots in a garage for more cars to fit, a safety procedure, a new product idea, a new technique or method to fix a machine/device, or any other intellectual contribution. This knowledge is recorded as a contribution of the employee to the organization. The employee gets the opportunity to present it or defend it once the organization finds interest or value in it.

It must be noted that this is an ongoing process and not a one-off event or project delivered from an 'ideas day' or 'ideas week' event. The limitless and timeless adaptation of knowledge elicitation practices turns sporadic knowledge-based activities into an organizational knowledge-driven culture where employees feel free and secure to continuously present their intellectual contributions. Freedom is related to fair and non-discriminative opportunities for all. Security is associated with the fact that any employee's contribution to the organization is recorded as the employee's contribution. Therefore, any opportunity that arises from this knowledge obliges the organization to recognize, involve, and give credit to the employee, if still in the organization, before and during the utilization of this intellectual capital.

Example: Panos (employee), who works in the logistics department, briefly reports a new way to increase truck loading and off-loading productivity with a gamified training process. Paul (manager) shows an interest in Panos's idea, requests more information, and invites Panos to present it in more detail.

13.2.2 CDM Level 2: Democratic Culture-Based Business Models, Structures, and Knowledge Engines

Theoretical Approach: The contribution of ideas and knowledge from the organization's employees turns them into organizational knowledge engineers, regardless of their actual work. They are the ones who start with a simple idea and generate additional knowledge around it by integrating their experiences, desires, expertise, visions, and even their potential career objectives. However, this might not be possible for all employees due to their workload, education constraints, or specific skills needed to think and work like this. Therefore, the company provides temporary adjustments to support the employees with promising knowledge contributions work furthermore on them. Such adjustments may impact the organization's structure and the business operations model to help the employee validate the initial knowledge contribution and generate the extra knowledge required to transform it into practical project requirements whose implementation can benefit the organization. This temporary organizational structure adjustment provides the space needed for the employee to work individually or collectively toward the validation and transformation of the knowledge contribution into a potential organizational asset.

Example: Paul has evaluated Panos's idea after a detailed presentation and found that there might be something interesting in it. He advises Panos to answer further questions such as: How will the idea be implemented? What is the time needed? What budget is required to produce the first results? What is the target group? etc. However, Panos does not have the technical business and financial expertise to reply. Therefore, Paul decides to assign George to help Panos. George is a finance and entrepreneurship expert who can assist Panos with the business plan. Paul also assigns Jane, a software engineer, to assist Panos with the technical part. To help Panos work on his idea, Paul temporarily removes 20–40% of Panos's workload. Panos, Jane, and George work together to develop the preliminary business plan requested by Paul. Paul treats the case under the Corporate Entrepreneurship or Intrapreneurship theories that promote innovation within the organization. Paul practically invests in Panos's idea, Panos's, Jane's, and George's time, plus any other expenses needed, such as hardware, software, or various other assets. This investment may be lost if the business plan does not indicate any potential, but there is no other way to explore the opportunity. The democratic dimension, in this case, is that anyone with a good idea can receive this support. Employees do not need to have any particular technical and management skills, but they are expected to comprehend and justify what they are proposing.

13.2.3 CDM Level 3: Democratic Culture Knowledge-Based Process and Project Management and Engineering

Theoretical Approach: Knowledge and ideas that have been matured in the second level of the model and indicate potential application in the organization as new projects that can optimize organizational operations or become new products and services, move to the third level of the Company Democracy Model ready for their actual implementation to take place. The project requirements are fully identified at this level, and project, product, or service engineering activities occur. This is the stage where the actual new product or service derives from the employee's idea, which was presented at level 1, matured at level 2 with the related team, and gets now implemented at level 3.

It must be noted that not all ideas or knowledge contributions reach this level. This is where the organization invests in developing the prototype or the whole product and launches it in the market to test it and hopefully further develop it into a complete new product or service. Any potential failure in this level impacts only the organization but not the employee who proposed and designed the new product or service with organizational approval and support.

Example: Paul is satisfied with the business plan developed at the second level and proposes the idea to the company's senior managers. In the case of a negative response, the project will be kept in a file. However, if the answer is positive, the team of Panos, George, and Jane will receive further support from the related engineering and business development departments to develop the actual project requirements and deliver, launch, and market the complete product or service. In this case, Panos remains on the project as the project owner and deputy project manager, while Jane and George supervise the project implementation and commercialization process.

13.2.4 CDM Level 4: Democratic Culture Innovation Development and Management

Theoretical Approach: Very few knowledge contributions reach this level. It is the level where the company decides to invest heavily in the product developed in level 3 and turn it into innovation based on which the organization will generate a new business strategy or enhance the existing one. Most of the new products or services developed in level 3 stay in level 3 for two reasons. The first reason is that the product or service did not perform as expected. Therefore, it will be removed from the market or from the company's operations sooner or later. The second reason is that the product or service performed well. It contributes significantly to revenue or operations management. Still, it does not have the innovative elements needed to justify further investments that can give a substantial competitive advantage in the future.

In this case, the product or service's behavior in the market determines the need for further research and development efforts and investments to move it into an innovation exploration space. This is a costly and time-consuming process; therefore, the company must be very selective with the ideas and knowledge funded beyond level 3 and supported with research and innovation funds.

Example: Paul sees the new product or service's success at level 3 and identifies some unique points that could turn it into innovation if further research can be done. He consults with George and Jane and proposes a research fund request from the organization's leadership or exploring various funding instruments such as the European Union Research and Innovation Programs or other national, regional, or international funding schemes. Panos stays on the project as the originator of this idea with good knowledge on the subject. This can be a time-consuming process as receiving research funding either internally or externally might take time. Nevertheless, Paul insists on moving the product or service into the innovation development space where researchers will further develop, integrate, and test its state-of-the-art potential concepts. Once funding is secured, Panos, Jane, and George continue with the project supported by researchers.

13.2.5 CDM Level 5: Democratic Culture Innovation-Based Competitive Operations

Theoretical Approach: Innovation brings competitiveness. Organizations can be competitive only if they are innovative. Over time, various practices have been used to boost competitiveness, such as cost reductions, salary reductions, increased working hours, layoffs, rightsizing, downsizing, reengineering, redesign, refinance, redundancies management, lean management, etc. However, the competitiveness problem is not a cost issue but an innovation issue. If a product or service is not innovative, it will never be competitive, no matter how low the production or operations costs are. Innovative products and services are sold by themselves. They don't need special marketing efforts as their innovation uniqueness leads them straight into blue oceans. They create a competitive advantage that stands above all other efforts to achieve competitiveness, reshuffling the marketing practices without offering anything new.

The fifth level of the CDM explores innovation competitiveness from the marketing and communication point of view. The power of presenting and marketing innovative products or services is tremendous enough to create monopolies, set prices, and create significant financial and reputational profit margins. This is the level where marketing and communication take the lead on identifying, promoting, and disseminating the power of new products or services. This is also the level where organizational strategy is redesigned to utilize the innovation's competitiveness by targeting new markets, locally, regionally, territorially, or globally.

Example: Paul is pleased to see that the research and innovation initiatives had positive results and introduced a new innovative product or service that can disrupt the markets. Panos, Jane, and George, the initial team involved in this creative project from day one, collaborate with the marketing strategy team to reveal the story behind this success and participate in the marketing and communication activities. They are also part of the new innovative product management teams and part of the international product marketing campaign, as knowledge holders and initiators. The Company Democracy Model provides the freedom and opportunity to any employee, with a valid knowledge contribution, reach the company's higher organizational ranks, build a new career, or lead intrapreneurship or Corporate Entrepreneurship initiatives.

13.2.6 CDM Level 6: Democratic Culture Optimization and International Alliances

Theoretical Approach: An effective marketing and communications campaign is strong enough to create 'blue oceans' or attract international investors, partners, or even competitors, toward establishing strategic alliances for the benefit of all. It is a 'winner takes it all' state when the organization can impact the markets alone or create joint strategies that can bring long-term success. In either case, what matters is the organization's ability to move internationally without considering any local or international competition. The sixth level of the Company Democracy Model eliminates competition and creates new and uncontested markets.

Level 6 achieves the extroversion all organizations seek in a globalized world but cannot succeed due to the high costs and risks in strategies not led by innovation competitiveness. The utilization of the innovation competition in level 6 can be managed by creating a new spin-off company to deal with the innovation globally or keep this innovative product or product line within its portfolio, making it part of its international products and operations.

Example: Paul managed to take an idea from level 1 and turn it into a blue ocean or an innovative competitive advantage for the organization. The rewards for Paul will be reflected in his career development. On the other hand, Panos, Jane, and George can manage the innovation or the board of directors of the new entity established to address the invention separately as part of the organizational business ecosystem.

13.3 Reading the Company Democracy Levels

To describe the Company Democracy levels in just one paragraph.

The description of the Company Democracy levels can be briefly presented in just one paragraph.

Create a democratic culture by giving everyone the freedom and the opportunity to express themselves by sharing knowledge, ideas, and insights. Support those who have useful knowledge with teams that can help them mature it. Develop matured knowledge into new products or services for organizational operations optimization or new market creation. Support further research on the products or services that have innovative elements and potentially turn them into innovations. Identify innovation competitiveness and establish an aggressive marketing and communication strategy that will lead to 'blue oceans.' Utilize competitiveness to develop strategic alliances and partnerships that will achieve extroversion, internationalization, global exposure, operations, and opportunities.

To describe the Company Democracy levels in just one sentence.

The description of the Company Democracy levels can be briefly presented in two sentences by reading the levels from top to bottom (Level 6 to Level 1) or from bottom to top (Level 1 to Level 6).

Top-Down (Level 6 to Level 1): To achieve extroversion, strategic international alliances, and 'blue oceans,' you need to have competitiveness derived from your innovative products or services after they have been developed within your organization and tested in the markets by internal teams of employees, who validated and matured the idea that came from the individuals who proposed it, thanks to the opportunities and freedom of speech offered in a Company Democracy culture.

Bottom-Up (Level 1 to Level 6): You need to have a democratic corporate culture where people can freely speak, share knowledge, insights, and be supported with internal resources to develop their ideas into new products or services and test them in the markets before helping them with innovation research efforts to achieve innovative competitive advantages that can lead to strategic and international alliances, corporate extroversion, and 'blue oceans.'

Describing the Company Democracy levels in just one short sentence.

The Company Democracy levels can be presented in two short sentences by reading the levels from top to bottom (Level 6 to Level 1) or bottom to top (Level 1 to Level 6).

Top-Down (Level 6 to Level 1): To go international, you must be competitive, which requires you to be innovative, after having built something successful in the markets which were designed with knowledge from employees empowered by your company's democratic culture.

Bottom-Up (Level 1 to Level 6): You need to have a Company Democracy Culture to develop and design new products or services that can stand in the market and turned into innovation, giving you the competitiveness to go international.

13.4 Level Categories

The Company Democracy levels can be categorized into three prime groups that reflect the evolution of the knowledge which exists in the organization from its early identification stages up to its international utilization.

The three categories are as follows: Knowledge Identification, Knowledge Implementation, and Knowledge Optimization (Figure 13.1).

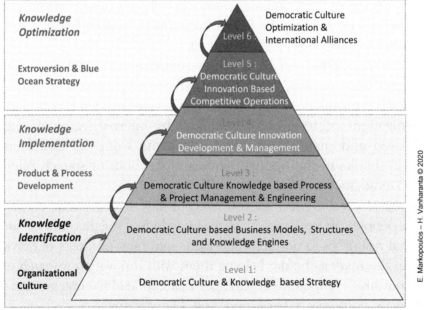

Figure 13.1 Company Democracy level categories.

13.4.1 Knowledge Identification: Levels 1 and 2

The knowledge identification category consists of the first two levels, targeting developing the democratic organizational culture, knowledge elicitation, screening, and maturity. The prime goal of this category is knowledge elicitation. Knowledge can be available; if it can not be gathered, it does not exist. The knowledge that resides in people's experiences, ideas, and expertise must be transmitted to the organization through a democratic culture that allows everyone to express their knowledge in any form.

Knowledge elicitation is used to identify the original knowledge before it gets analyzed in terms of validity, completeness, and coherence. Invalid knowledge is information but not knowledge. Of course, analyzing information, its source, and the frequency it is presented can provide other organizational knowledge types that can also be significant.

The identification of knowledge is achieved with collective efforts from teams constructed to support this process and those who provide the knowledge. This systematic process matures the collected knowledge and identifies its qualities and characteristics that can be turned into products, services, projects, or process requirements for further development.

13.4.2 Knowledge Implementation: Levels 3 and 4

The knowledge implementation category realizes the knowledge identified, analyzed, and approved in the first category of the Company Democracy levels. The implementation of knowledge passes through two stages: basic and advanced execution. Basic implementation transforms the product, service, project, or process requirements into new market-oriented products, services, internal projects, or processes that optimize the performance of the organizational operations.

Advanced implementation is the extended development of the product or service developed with the requirements derived from the first two levels into an innovation that can differentiate the organization and lead toward new development opportunities and strategies.

The two knowledge implementation categories determine the organizational strategy from sustainable to extroversion. This is why not all levels in this category, even under the development concept, are necessarily executed. It is very likely for an organization to stop on level 3 (basic implementation) and not extend to level 4 (advanced implementation).

13.4.3 Knowledge Optimization: Levels 5 and 6

The knowledge optimization category is composed of knowledge utilization activities in the organization's operations and markets. The last group of the Company Democracy Model is not reached by many in an organization or by all organizations. The optimal utilization of organizational knowledge can lead to 'blue oceans' based on the innovativeness identified in past levels. This innovation degree determines the organizational competitiveness and defines the marketing strategy, which further establishes the extroversion strategy.

This competitiveness-driven extroversion strategy can then move the organization into international markets and can be used to form strategic alliances. The confidence driven by the organization's innovation and the marketing strategy on effectively communicating the invention can help enter global markets or establish international partnerships that can lead to market dominance or 'blue oceans.'

13.5 Company Democracy Model Strategies

The Company Democracy Model structure and its level activities offer two strategic development paths for an organization to follow.

The first three levels of the model lead to the practical development of products, services, or procedures that can benefit an organization either in its operations or in its target markets. However, those products, services, or processes do not have to be radically innovative or include state-of-the-art concepts or functionality. The last three levels of the model primarily target research innovation, competitiveness, and extroversion toward developing products and services that can become 'blue oceans.'

It must be noted that the Company Democracy Model is not applied only for innovation management. It can still be used effectively to develop and improve the company in its existing market space and sphere of operations. Therefore, not all organizations are expected or must pass beyond level 3, which leads to innovation management and extroversion. Success can be significant if organizations reach the third level, which is the practical application of the knowledge and ideas identified in the first level in the market or within the organization.

Figure 13.2 presents the Company Democracy Model's six levels divided into two organizational strategies: sustainable organizational and organizational extroversion.

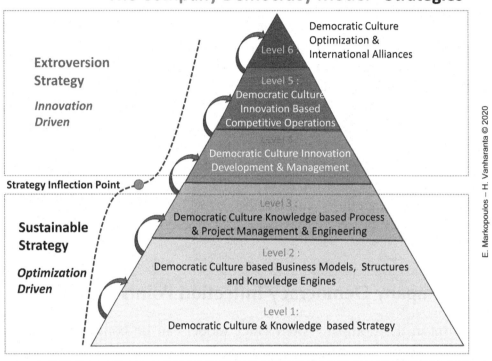

Figure 13.2   Company Democracy strategies.

13.5.1 *Sustainable Strategy*

The first three levels define the organizational sustainability strategy to keep the organization within the continuous improvement of its operations, products, and services or develop new ones. This strategy does not require significant investments other than investing in developing the organizational culture, generating the intellectual capital needed to generate knowledge and ideas. The goal is to transform this knowledge and ideas into products or services to support the existing market space or internal organizational needs.

There are no obligations to invest in research and development to turn this knowledge into innovation for two reasons. The first one is that not all knowledge or ideas can reach level 3. The second reason is the uncertainty about the organization's ability and strategy to support projects and initiatives above the third level. Therefore, organizations can strategically decide not to go above level 3. The cost of innovation and extroversion might be even more than they can be afforded or outside the organizational development strategy.

13.5.2 Extroversion Strategy

The last three levels define the organizational extroversion strategy, which demands innovation, sets high competitiveness expectations, and expects internationalization and 'blue oceans.' This is a more demanding strategy. It requires significant funding and investments in knowledge and ideas to be turned into innovative projects, products, or services after level 3. The last three levels rely heavily on the first three. Nonetheless, they require more organizational commitment, resources, and strategic planning, which it might not be possible for all organizations to provide or satisfy. An organization that attempts to move upward from level 4 targets international markets, responds to international competitors, and creates extroversion strategies through innovations, which can be pretty expensive and time-consuming.

13.6 Company Democracy Inflection Points

Every level in the Company Democracy Model can be considered a significant milestone in an organizational transformation strategy. Establishing, for example, a democratic organizational culture requires enormous leadership and management skills, transparent procedures, and an unpredictable schedule. Therefore, the achievement of setting up such an organizational culture is a significant organizational milestone.

The same applies to all the levels, and as the levels rise, the effort to aim for the next and maintain what has been achieved in the past increases with geometric progression. Therefore, it is easy for an organization to fall back a level or two if the level activities are not maintained and sustained effectively. The place where an organization changes the progression route either negatively or positively is defined as a progression inflection point.

Figure 13.3 presents the progression of organizational efforts' inflection points on a specific knowledge contribution to achieving the final level of the Company Democracy Model. The inflection points shown in the figure are indicative and could be as many as the achieved levels in a given time frame. An organization that can reach the first level, for example, at a specific time, can lose this achievement if the effort and activities needed to be in place for democratic culture, in this case, are not followed persistently. Therefore, the organization can move in and out from level 1 until the actions are stabilized and mature enough to support at level 2 the knowledge gathered at the first one.

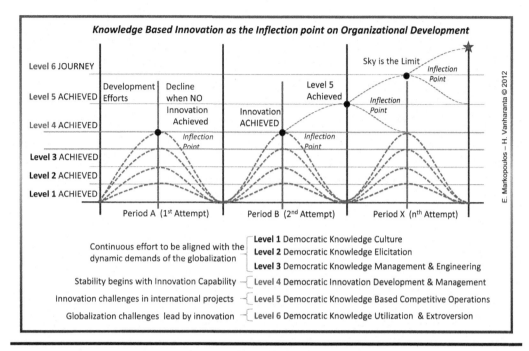

Figure 13.3 The Company Democracy journey inflection points.

The same applies to all levels. An organizational initiative at level 2 can drop to level 1 and get back to the second level after rectifying the mistakes that led to that descent. This up-and-down phenomenon can occur from any level to any level. An organizational initiative can drop from level 3 to level 2, and then to level 1, and/or even to level 0, if the Company Democracy Model is abandoned.

The periods in which the organization is measured to indicate the effectiveness of a specific level's activities reveal the inflection point and the route being followed, either positive (upward) or negative (downward). The second period (Period B) shown in Figure 13.3 indicates a positive progression route from level 4 to level 5 and then to level 6. These continuous positive inflection points could have also been successive negative inflection points (from level 4 to level 3 and then to level 2).

It must be noted, once again, that a critical milestone on the Company Democracy Model is the achievement of level 4, which is the Innovation Management level. This level advances the organizational strategy from Sustainable to Extroversion. Achieving the fourth level in the Company Democracy Model is the most challenging and most rewarding. The maturity of the investments made on transforming the organizational culture into a democratic knowledge-based culture can now lead to innovations.

The space between levels 3 and 4 is the strategy transition period that organizations select to either enter or avoid. Avoiding the fourth level of the model can be a strategic decision to stay within a sustainable strategy and not advance to the extroversion strategy.

The same applies to all of the levels. Stepping down from level 3 can be a decision and not a failure. Organizations might need to reshuffle their human resources and redirect their product and service development efforts toward other markets or sectors. In this case, new and more targeted ideas toward new organizational goals might be necessary, and to achieve that, the organization might need to restart from a different point. However, it is not recommended to restart at level 1, as the first level is the base for all the others to be developed upon.

13.7 Effort-Based Effectiveness

Unorthodoxly, the Company Democracy Model's effectiveness is not related to the effort placed into achieving a level. There is an inverse relationship between the action placed and the results achieved at each level. This relationship has a logical explanation and can stand out if the organization institutionalizes the processes and activities delivered to complete each level. The risk of falling back into old habits or easing up on the effort, commitment, and determination to sustain what has been achieved reflects the effort needed to maintain a level and negatively impacts any progression plans.

Figure 13.4 presents the Company Democracy Model's benefits with an inverse pyramid to the Company Democracy Model levels. This indicates that the effort needed to reach level 1 is tremendous, although the benefits are not quite visible.

Creating an organizational culture or changing organizational culture is the most complex and challenging strategy for any organization. It requires strong organizational and leadership skills and adaptive human resources. It also requires people to understand the new culture's benefits and how to work and function. Time is also needed to develop trust in this unique culture and the required momentum to convince the few whose participation will ignite the process.

If time is money, then only two types of organizations can succeed in level 1 of the Company Democracy Model. The rich ones and the smart ones. The first type is the organizations with financial capital that can support the development of democratic company culture. The second type is the organizations whose intellectual capital accelerates significantly faster than the time needed to establish a democratic culture. Of course, an organization may possess

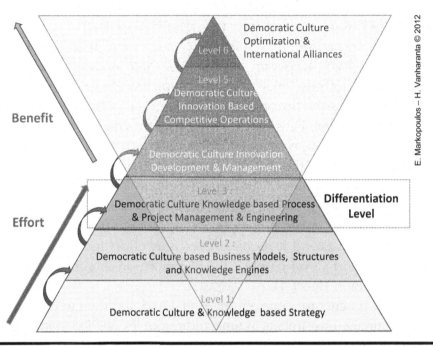

The Company Democracy Model –
Effort – Benefit Relationship

Benefit

Effort

Democratic Culture
Optimization &
International Alliances

Level 6 :

Level 5 :
Democratic Culture
Innovation Based
Competitive Operations

Democratic Culture Innovation
Development & Management

Level 3 :
Democratic Culture Knowledge based Process
& Project Management & Engineering

Differentiation
Level

Level 2 :
Democratic Culture based Business Models, Structures
and Knowledge Engines

Level 1 :
Democratic Culture & Knowledge based Strategy

E. Markopoulos – H. Vanharanta © 2012

Figure 13.4 Company Democracy benefit–effort relationship.

both financial and intellectual capital wealth. In that case, the results will be visible sooner than expected, but in either case, the benefits will not exceed the costs incurred to achieve level 1 at the least.

Moving to level 2, the effort needed is reduced, and the benefits are increased. At the first level, an influential culture helps the teaming required to mature the organizational knowledge that keeps coming at level 2. The benefits increase at this level once the valuable ideas, knowledge, and innovations are identified at level 2. They become the organizational assets for further development at level 3.

At level 3, the benefits are even more substantial as the first products, services, or processes derived from the knowledge of levels 1 and 2 are visible. However, the cost of implementing them and bringing them to market remains, making this level the cost–benefit breakeven point of the Company Democracy Model. Figure 13.4 indicates fewer benefits than effort, but the figure does not present the long-term benefits from the product or service being developed. The cost of creating a new product or service that derived from level 2 might be more than the benefit that can initially be gained at level 3, but when the benefit from such a new product is long term, repeated year after year, or for a while, the development costs that occurred only once are depreciated. The effectiveness of level 3 relies on the acceptance of the delivered output from the market or the organization itself.

From level 4 and above, the benefits are much more than the effort placed without calculating any long-term impact. Achieving innovation is a significant milestone in any organizational strategy or timeline. Innovation is the inflection point that returns the investments made from the point where innovation is reached and beyond that. Furthermore, the efforts to achieve innovation require a specialized team that does not need much support other than financial.

The benefits against the effort increase even more as the organization advances from level 4 to level 5 and from level 5 to level 6 due to the momentum an innovation brings to the overall development and operations process. It needs less effort to create a competitive advantage (level 5) once an organization is innovative, and it requires even less effort for an organization to achieve extroversion (level 6) once the organization is competitive (level 5) due to its innovation (level 4).

To stay on a progressive course from level 4 to 5 and then to 6, organizations have to maintain the investments in time and resources needed to keep the lower levels going. If level 1 fails or stops function properly, this will soon impact the organization's operations as the pipeline of knowledge and opportunities will stop or indicate gaps that can make the organization incompetent. The same applies to all the other levels. The higher the benefits are at the top levels, the more attention should be given to the lower levels to maintain what has been achieved.

13.8 The Effort–Benefit Relationship of the Model

According to McShane and Von Glinow (McShane, Von Glinow, 2019), in their work on organizational behavior, conflict management is approached with a theory indicating that a fair dose of conflict creates awareness and the momentum necessary for a company to perform at its best.

When there is no conflict at all, the creativity and passion needed to achieve a goal deteriorate in the relaxation of everything being right. On the other hand, passion and creativity are lost if conflict exceeds the average, driving people into continuous and long-lasting disputes and arguments. Therefore, some competition level energizes debate, reevaluates assumptions, improves responsiveness to external environments, and increases team engagement and cohesion.

The same can be considered for the use of democracy. Reduced democracy by restricted freedom of thinking and acting blocks innovation, creativity, vision, and goals (Amabile, 1998). On the other hand, unlimited and uncontrolled democracy can lead to demagogy (Eliassi-Rad, Farrell, Garcia, 2020, Hobbs, 2017), chaos, and anarchy (Raekstad, 2020). In contrast, controlled democracy within a specific framework of values and targets can bring the desired results and rewards for all involved.

Figure 13.5 presents the innovation–democracy relationship with an effectiveness curve. A lack of limited democracy can still lead to innovation as humans by nature seek solutions that improve their lives and environment. However, these innovations cannot reach high levels as they are not supported by the infrastructure and maturity needed to achieve significant results. Likewise, extensive and uncontrolled democracy can decrease innovation, as ideas and knowledge are driven by overconfidence, unconditional freedom to act, and limited or no criticism. This results in innovations that lack the strong judgment or critical evaluation required to consider whether they are credible and valuable or not.

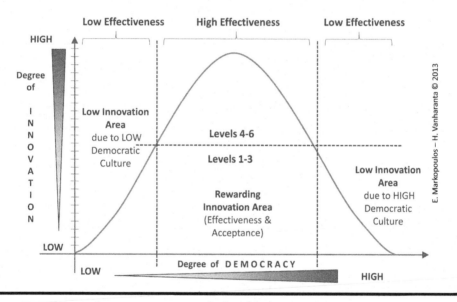

Figure 13.5   Innovation–Democracy relationship.

On the other hand, the right level of democracy, which is enough to provide freedom of thinking with a scope supported by judgment, criticisms, and challenges in a targeted domain, can deliver practical and concrete results, avoiding chaotic brainstorms, fuzzy planning, and careless investments. Balanced organizational democracy is needed to achieve the Company Democracy Model's higher levels where innovations are achieved with a particular scope and strategy.

This Aristotelian golden mean is reflected in the effort–benefit relationship of the Company Democracy Model (Figure 13.6).

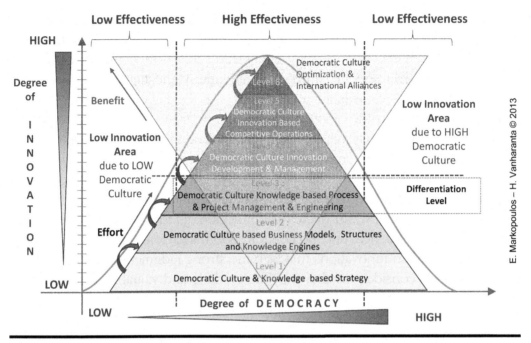

Figure 13.6 Effort–benefit relationship with the degree of democracy.

The maximum benefit in using the model is achieved within moderate democratic freedom. Limited or unconditional democracy is quite unlikely to achieve significant results from the Company Democracy Model as innovative thinking can be either restricted or unstructured due to lack or excess of democracy.

Levels 4, 5, and 6 on the Company Democracy Model need to function in a much more defined democracy space with specific boundaries as they form the organization's innovation extroversion strategy. This space should be controlled within the strategic goals and objectives without deterioration and deficiencies. This restricted area of democratic freedom can inherit the benefits of the lower levels of the model that operated in a more expansive democratic space for unlimited and unrestrictive knowledge creation and elicitation. On the other hand, it will be difficult, if not impossible, for innovations achieved in unlimited or unconditional democratic spaces to attain excellent benefits due to a lack of focus, concentration, support, and organizational strategies.

Thus, limited democracy cannot support the effort needed to achieve higher benefits due to the lack of organizational support and infrastructure; in the same way, unconditional democracy cannot support the necessary actions to achieve higher benefits due to the lack of organizational criticism and judgment that has to be directed toward the organizational strategy, commitments, resources, and markets.

13.9 Company Democracy Model Indices

According to Plato, the beginning is half of every action (Plato, 1961), and this applies precisely to the adaptation of the Company Democracy Model. The first three levels are the most demanding levels, where the organization must set the democratic culture in action and promote democratic teaming within Co-Evolutionary thinking and mentality. To achieve this, several indices need to be monitored in each of the first three levels, in contrast with the limited indices that may be sufficient to track the effectiveness of the last three levels.

Each level in the Company Democracy Model can be related to several organizational indices that direct the effective use of the model at each level and contribute to the progression from one level to the next. Figure 13.7 presents the 40 Company Democracy Model indices, spread over four categories and four dimensions, reflecting the model's six levels.

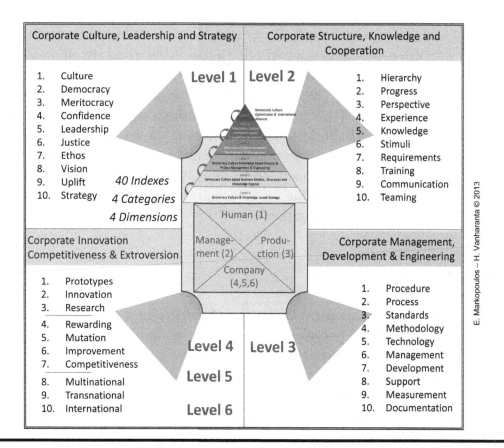

Figure 13.7 The Company Democracy Model indices in categories and dimensions.

The first level of the Company Democracy Model is tracked with ten indices under the category of 'Corporate culture, Leadership, and Strategy' under the dimension of 'Human.' This refers to the leadership skills and effort needed to achieve a democratic organizational culture that can drive and motivate people to participate and share knowledge, ideas, and insights.

The second level of the model is tracked with another ten indices under 'Corporate structure, Knowledge and Cooperation' under the dimentsion of 'Management.' It is the human resource management efforts needed to build teams and execute effective team management under collaborative and Co-Evolutionary thinking and mentality that can turn the experience into knowledge, and knowledge into project requirements and design.

The third level of the model is tracked with ten indices under the category of 'Corporate management, Development, and Engineering' under the dimension of 'Production.' It implements the knowledge derived from level 1 and matures in level 2. It transforms this knowledge into products, services, and initiatives that require product or process engineering and development management to be implemented.

The fourth, fifth, and sixth levels of the Company Democracy Model are tracked with three, four, and three indices, respectively. They are all under the category of 'Corporate innovation, Competitiveness, and Extroversion,' under the dimension 'Company.' The first three indices reflect the innovation management activities of level 4; the next four reflect the competitiveness management activities of level 5, and the last three reflect the extroversion activities of level 6. They are all under the 'Company' dimension as the previous three levels of the Company Democracy Model directly impact the company. Their strategic goals are reshaped due to the competitive innovation that brings extroversion and internationalization.

13.10 Summary

The six levels of the Company Democracy Model form a serial execution of activities that advance an organization's maturing into democratic management and leadership culture. However, each level has a distinct philosophy on implementing its activities, pre- and post-conditions, and deliverables from the strategy and output. The levels can be seen under various prisms grouped under different strategies, measured with different indices, and approached under different dimensions.

Organizations need to study and understand each level's structure and role in the Company Democracy Model. The simplicity the levels initially indicate can create significant complexity if not understood well enough by the organizations before allocating the required time, effort, and resources to complete each level. The simplified complexity of the model can trick or mislead implementation commitments, expectations, and results. The model's pyramid shape has been intentionally selected to indicate the evolution of knowledge from abstract to concrete, from theoretical to practical, and from broad participation and knowledge contributions to the few who reach the top.

The Company Democracy Model levels provide the structure, metrics, and output that an organization requires to plan and execute the model without restricting its implementation to specific activities that could limit the model's effectiveness between organizations with different capabilities and maturity levels.

Questions for Review and Discussions

The Company Democracy Model is characterized by its pyramid structure and the number of levels that compose it. The pyramid indicates that the journey to the top is a challenge that cannot be met without commitment, dedication, and hard work. It also signifies the journey of knowledge creation. The lower levels primarily generate information rather than actual knowledge. However, as the levels rise, the information is transformed into knowledge, products/services, innovations, competitive advantage, and extroversion strategies. The pyramid also indicates the effort required for each level to be reached. Each level of the Company Democracy Model has a theoretical approach and can be described easily with a practical example.

Follow the six different levels from level to level and find examples from your company that might fit this new thinking.

1. What kind of discussions happen in your company concerning a new product or service idea?
   1.1 Who reports to whom the idea?
   1.2 How does the idea owner keep track of whether it is accepted and evolved into a new product or service?
   1.3 Provide examples of cases in your company.

2. How clear, well communicated, documented, and simple are your company's methods of dealing with the workforce's intuitions, insights, ideas, or innovations derived from the employees?
    2.1 Do you document, communicate, and train the employees on such methods?
    2.2 Provide examples of cases in your company that used such methods.
3. How are employees encouraged, motivated, and supported to discuss and present new ideas?
    3.1 What processes are followed? Provide examples.
    3.2 If there are not any such processes, what is the reason for their absence?
4. Level 2 of the CDM talks about 'knowledge engines,' meaning the employees. Why is this metaphor used?
    4.1 How is democracy related to this metaphor?
    4.2 What are the business models and the structures needed to support these knowledge engines?
    4.3 Does your company follow such thinking? If NO, why not? Justify your answer and provide examples.
    4.4 If YES, how? Justify your answer and provide examples.
5. What type of knowledge is created in your organization?
    5.1 Is it controlled around a need or specific requirements, or is it free where employers can think and generate knowledge on anything they feel can benefit the organization?
    5.2 List five benefits and drawbacks of each type of knowledge creation?
    5.3 Critically analyze the benefits and drawbacks.
    5.4 Which approach would you choose? and why?
6. Do you think that the level of thinking with specific content and scope can help your company evaluate intuitions, ideas, insights, and innovations?
    6.1 If YES, why?
    6.2 If NO, what do you propose as an alternative or intermediate process?
7. Why is the third level of the CDM (product development) before the fourth level (innovation management) and not vice versa?
    7.1 Do you think that product development comes before innovation management or the other way around? Justify your answer.
    7.2 How would you read the CDM if you make that switch?
8. Different level categories of knowledge help the evolution of knowledge for specific purposes. Do you have this kind of thinking in your company, i.e., knowledge for identification, knowledge for implementation, and knowledge for optimization?

8.1 How does knowledge evolve in your organization?

8.2 What are the levels you follow?

8.3 What progresses knowledge from one category to the next?

9. How do your company's employees, as knowledge initiators, follow or are part of your company's knowledge evolution process?

9.1 Do you link the evolution of knowledge with the development of the employee who initiated it? If NO, why not?

9.2 If YES, how is this link achieved and maintained in each evolution level?

10. Describe your company's past performance with product or service development through different phases. Can you identify performance inflection points in this journey?

10.1 What makes the difference in your existing process that turns failure into success, or stability into improvement? Provide examples.

11. Discuss and ponder how the effort–benefit relationship could change innovation activities with low and high Company Democracy degrees?

11.1 Is it possible to move your company from the current position to the described actions' high effectiveness position?

11.2 How can this be achieved?

11.3 What processes should be changed?

11.4 Go through all the indices of the Company Democracy Culture and prioritize the indices on each level.

11.5 What are the most critical indices in your company?

12. The effectiveness of CDM can be tracked with 40 indices in four categories and four dimensions, human-related, management-related, production-related, and company-related. Can you think of a fifth or sixth category or dimension?

12.1 If NO, why not?

12.2 If YES, what would these categories or dimensions be, and what indices will each category have?

13. Consider the change process with CDM not to lead to a final assumption. Think about how your business can change continuously and how its structures, concepts, and Situationality undergo continuous historical development.

14. Ponder with the chart Figure 13Q below the basic assumptions in your business.

15. How do you see the current and future reality of your company's performance when applying the CDM?

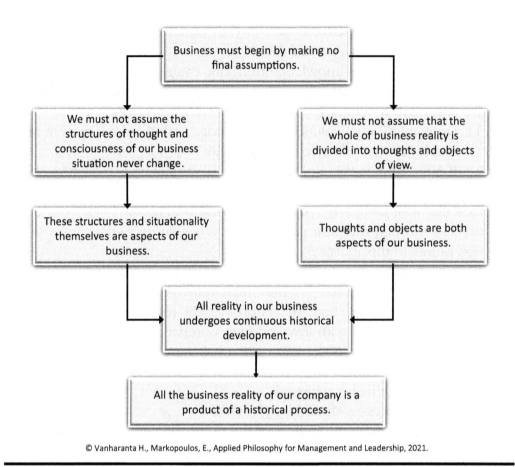

© Vanharanta H., Markopoulos, E., Applied Philosophy for Management and Leadership, 2021.

Figure 13Q   Chart for Question 13 (c.f., ref. Buckingham, et al., 2011, Georg Hegel, p. 181).

References

Amabile, T., 1998. How to kill creativity. *Harvard Business Review*, September-October Issue. Access on October 19, 2020. https://hbr.org/1998/09/how-to-kill-creativity.

Buckingham, W., King, Peter J., Burnham, D., Weeks, M., Hill, C., and Marenbon, J., 2011. *The Philosophy Book*. Dorling Kindersley Limited, London.

Eliassi-Rad, T., Farrell, H., and Garcia, D., 2020. What science can do for democracy: A complexity science approach. *Humanities and Social Sciences Communications*, 7, 30. https://doi.org/10.1057/s41599-020-0518-0.

Hobbs, A., 2017. The rise of the demagogue: A warning from Plato. Published on Angie Hobbs' blog. Access on October 20, 2020. https://www.sheffield.ac.uk/news/nr/rise-of-demagogue-plato-angie-hobbs-1.675492.

McShane, S. L. and Von Glinow, M. A., 2019. *Organizational Behavior.* McGraw-Hill Education, New York.

Plato, H., 1961. Symposium. In Cairns H. (ed.) *The Collected Dialogues of Plato.* Princeton, Princeton, University Press, pp. 526–574 https://doi.org/10.1515/9781400835867-019.

Raekstad, P., 2020. The new democracy: anarchist or populist? *Critical Review of International Social and Political Philosophy*, 23(7), 931–942. doi: 10.1080/13698230.2019.1585151.

Human Perception, Interpretation, Understanding, and Communication of Company Democracy: Building Co-opetitive Ecosystems

Executive Summary

New trendy buzzwords come up every few years in management and leadership, attempting to refresh and maintain old practices. In fact, management and leadership progress frequently ends up in significant failure or zero contributions by those who manage and lead with old constructs and concepts, unable to research and innovate. Modern management gurus and consultants are fast on making up new buzzwords to reinventing old practices for immediate, quick, and measurable organizational profitability and productivity. The rapid changes in the business environments impact organizational management to follow the markets effectively. This leads to failure from not understanding global business situations properly. Organizational change is made possible by knowledge workers who succeed in today's environments

DOI: 10.4324/9781003158493-17

and shape the future ones. They demonstrate knowledge-driven leadership and accept responsibility, provided that the organization adequately supports them. They are people with experience and expertise, seeking only a responsive environment to perform, create ideas, innovate, implement, test new products and services, and run the business efficiently and effectively. When identifying and utilizing knowledge-driven employees with modern management and leadership skills, capabilities, and competencies, democratic company culture must be in place to help and protect their freedom of thought and speech and help them contribute with their knowledge and insights.

14.1 Introduction

Sustainability, co-evolution, progress, development, and extroversion indicate progressive targets, objectives, goals, and visions for any organization. To fulfill these challenging requirements, organizations and companies must utilize their human intellectual capital as the most essential and significant resource. Effective use of organizational intellectual capital extends knowledge creation by transforming information into knowledge and knowledge into wisdom. Knowledge can exist in every person and anywhere within an organization. It can be offered by anyone as long as there is a Co-Evolutionary and cooperative operational environment that can support knowledge under human perception, interpretation, understanding, and communication.

The Company Democracy Model offers an environment where more 'co' concepts can be developed by introducing new management and leadership culture. Success can be achieved with the unity of all rather than the charisma of the few. The Company Democracy Model has three distinct activity areas to show this path: the pre-condition stage, the operations stage, and the post-condition stage. The pre-condition stage of the model contains an ethical and moral base. The operations stage includes the cooperation and co-evolution processes. In contrast, the post-condition stage contains the reward and success processes that lead to higher levels of Company Democracy, increasing the adaptation of the Company Democracy Model.

The pre-condition stage focuses on communicating the concepts of cooperation and co-evolution, understanding human behavior, developing ethical governance, management, and leadership where each employee can apply, contribute, and share the message of getting results together.

The operations stage is based on executing the Company Democracy Model. It is the stage that moves the ethical advantage from theory to practice.

This stage offers an opportunity for anyone who has any knowledge or idea to implement it and reach their personal and professional goals.

The post-condition stage sustains the company's democratic culture and expands it to other employees, organizations, and cooperative entities. This is the stage where success is recognized, rewarded, distributed, and communicated to all who have contributed with knowledge from within or outside the organization. It is also the stage of setting new tasks, objectives, goals, strategies, and visions.

14.2 Analyzing the Phenomenon of Company Democracy

The Company Democracy Model (Markopoulos, Vanharanta, 2014) is more than a modern technocratic strategic management methodology. It is a philosophy and a way of living. Some people can adopt the Company Democracy Model, but many cannot. The model is about co-evolution in a democratic environment where ego, selfishness, and insecurities cannot exist. Today, many are in favor of democracy, while others are against it. This depends on people's capability or incapability, confidence, insecurities, and on many other concepts and life philosophies each person has on giving, taking, or sharing.

The Company Democracy Model can be useful if it can be seen as an Applied Philosophy rather than a neo-management attempt to reinvent or rename existing practices. Emphasis must be placed on the model's human perception as this plays the central and most critical role. The model is based on people, as knowledge derives only from them and the environment in which they operate. If the value of people is neglected, no management model can be applied effectively. Working mechanically is a different approach than working emotionally. Progress and success can only be achieved when people work together for a common goal with common and sincere intentions. History has many examples of powerful nations losing wars because their armies were fighting as machines without a human purpose, obeying the rules without leaving any room for emotions to create the passion needed for intuition, knowledge, creativity, and vision.

Regardless of color, race, sexual orientation, ethnicity, and any other characteristic, people will always be born equal. What differentiates the good from the bad and the winners from the losers is the environment they have developed in and the opportunities they have been given. This can be applied in companies in which the Company Democracy Model represents modern management and leadership. Knowledge is everywhere and can be created by anyone. All it needs is an open mind for it to grow, for both individuals and organizations. People can achieve anything they can dream of, but first, they must be free to dream. The human perception of Company Democracy is the most crucial challenge of the model, as people are trained to think and not believe. Impossible is nothing for those who dare and seek the dream, but space and freedom are essential requirements.

A second challenge of the Company Democracy Model is to interpret its fuzziness reasonably due to its philosophical background. Deciding what freedom is and what is not is a significant issue for those who do not understand democracy or do not want to understand and pretend they do not understand. Democracy has so many enemies today because it offers opportunities to all who have eyes to see, all who have mouths to speak, and all who have ears to listen (Conzelmann, Lindemann, 1999). On the other hand, this troubles the few who want people to have eyes but not see, mouths but not speak, and ears but not listen.

In a world mad for power, organizations cannot be the exception, and democracy is certainly not a system that helps. In this case, there are two paths to follow. The first is to interpret the Company Democracy Model as the only way to stand united in a Co-Evolutionary environment for growth, sustainability, and prosperity. The other way is to interpret Company Democracy as a romantic theoretical model far from the reality of current business practices, which seeks for leaders to lead with acts but not with promises. In a democratic world, each organization is free to select which path to follow.

However, regardless of the path chosen to understand and adopt democracy and the Company Democracy Model, it is essential to define a communication strategy to justify selecting a specific route. Of course, there is always the option not to explain anything. Still, as organizations care about their image and profits more than anything else, they must defend their decisions. Henry Kissinger once said it is not what is true that counts but what is perceived to be true (Cote, Allahar, 2011). This drives the public perception of what people must believe.

Communicating the Company Democracy Model is necessary for the internal and external publicity of the organizational efforts to adopt such management methods, but this requires a good understanding of the model. Organizations might announce their Democratic Culture to the media to gain publicity without being really committed to apply the Company Democracy. Therefore, to justify the gap between the good intentions and the reasons for failing to implement them is crucial to develop the arguments of why democracy and co-evolution are not suitable for the organization, at that given time, or not good enough in general. If, on the other hand, the organization truly decides to adopt the Company Democracy Model, then the communication strategy must defend why it is worth applying the model. Even though many people think it must be easy to prove why Company Democracy can benefit the organization, it may still be hard to execute such a communication strategy successfully. It is not only the management of the organization that needs to support such revolutionary models, but also the middle management, the unions, and probably other internal and external groups of people who do not fear democracy and wish to co-evolute with their fellow employees and colleagues for the benefit of all (Figure 14.1).

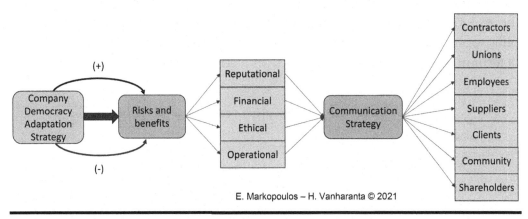

E. Markopoulos – H. Vanharanta © 2021

Figure 14.1   The Company Democracy adaptation and communication strategies.

Handling human perceptions, interpretations, understanding, and communication for or against the Company Democracy Model needs an effective communication strategy that considers the model's pre- and post-conditions.

14.3 Pre-conditions, Operations, and Post-conditions for Innovation

The Company Democracy Model is designed to promote knowledge utilization for innovation. Without knowledge, there is no innovation, and without innovation, there is no development. With no development, there is no future, and therefore no point in investing in such organizations.

For many organizations, innovation is still considered a luxury, failing to understand that innovation today is a necessity. In this fully globalized business environment, with tremendous changes in all markets and sectors, Charles Darwin's words are more relevant than ever 'it is not the strongest of the species that will survive, nor the most intelligent, but the most adaptable to change' (cf. www.goodreads.com). On the other hand, adaptation cannot be achieved without innovation, as only new ideas can conquer new environments.

If innovation is perceived as a cost center by an organization, then there is no need to consider any application of the Company Democracy Model. Even if innovation is not seen as a profit center but at least as a vehicle for adaptation and, therefore, for survival, the model can still contribute significantly to the company's development.

In this context, the pre-conditions of the Company Democracy Model deal with 'HOW' innovation can be achieved, while the post-conditions deal with 'WHY' innovation needs to be sustained (Figure 14.2). In between, there is the execution of the model per se. The 'WHY' to innovate has more of a philosophical than practical meaning. The profits of an organization are not determined by the markets but by its philosophy.

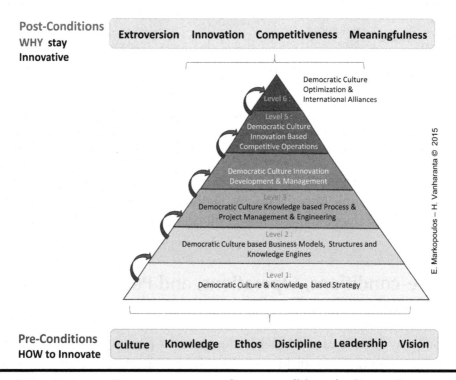

Figure 14.2 Company Democracy pre- and post-conditions for innovation.

The post-conditions for innovation in the Company Democracy Model are associated with the strategy, logic, spirit, reasoning, and interpretation of the benefits gained along the way. Being on top requires more strategy than leadership, and reaching the top requires more wisdom than management. This is why it is challenging to explain the 'WHY' before the 'HOW.' 'WHY' refers to what to do to stay on top once this goal has been reached. However, the 'WHY' refers to the question that must be asked before any initiative starts its journey to the top. Answering the 'WHY' requires wisdom driven by virtues on how this 'WHY' can benefit all.

14.4 Staged Pre-conditions, Operations, and Post-conditions of the Company Democracy Model

Another way to define the pre- and post-conditions in the Company Democracy Model is not by focusing on what is needed for the journey to success and what is needed once this goal has been reached, but thinking more collectively about applying a co-opetitive and Co-Evolutionary philosophy. During the implementation conditions, the pre- and post-conditions can be defined as Success, Rewards, and Share.

The staged pre-conditions form the human-ethical infrastructure, while the staged post-conditions form the distribution of success to all involved. In between the pre- and post-conditions is the execution of the Company Democracy Model under the co-opetition and co-evolution philosophy (Figure 14.3).

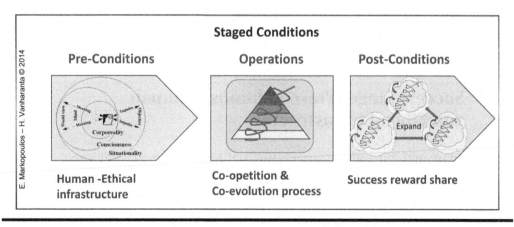

Figure 14.3   Company Democracy Model stages of human perception, interpretation, understanding, and communication.

The staged interpretation of the pre- and post-conditions of the Company Democracy Model is mostly team-oriented, emphasizing the team concept and its benefits instead of how and why the journey should be undertaken. However, the operations process in the staged pre- and post-conditions of the model is related to how to do the 'HOW' and why to do the 'WHY' in a co-opetitive, Co-Evolutionary way. Another way to see these conditions is to divide the model's levels between each conditional stage.

> *The first and second levels* of the Company Democracy Model form the pre-conditions defined by 'success.' This success is related to the generation of valuable ideas that can grow within the model. Lack of helpful knowledge that can justify the purpose of investing in it keeps the model inactive. Therefore, this stage successfully initiates the process.

> *The third and fourth levels* of the model reflect the intermediate stage between the pre- and post-conditions defined as 'rewards.' This is related to the rewards the organization receives by implementing an idea and leading it to innovation. It is the stage where the market accepts the knowledge created in the first two levels.

> *The fifth and sixth levels* of the model reflect the post-conditions defined as 'share.' This is the sharing of the added value created by the organizational knowledge in the previous stages with the society and the market to be generating shared added value for the organization.

The staged pre- and post-conditions give a more in-depth definition of the requirements needed to start the journey, live the journey, and utilize its benefits. It is another way of viewing the same goal with a different added value approach.

14.5 Success Stage (Pre-conditions): Human and Ethical Infrastructure

The human and ethical infrastructure (i.e., staged pre-conditions) is based on communicating the co-opetition and co-evolution concept, understanding human behavior, developing the ethical base to contribute, and communicating the message of getting results together. The approach used in this stage is the Circles of Mind metaphor developed from the Holistic Concept of Man metaphor (Vanharanta, Pihlanto, Chang, 1997).

The Circles of Mind metaphor is the basic model for a detailed analysis of people's behavior patterns in their occupational roles and other roles. Essential information can be obtained about the employees' past, justifying their present situation, and forecasting their future progress in the Company Democracy. Conscious experience comes through the internal and external senses of the human being. The unconscious part of the human brain contains the previous experience in the memory system, the motivational system, interpreting systems, and automatic systems, affecting how the current understanding and the ideas and activities of future experiences are perceived. A strong focus on Company Democracy can help people interpret how democratic behavior can bring new methodologies and methods to current and future activities. This collective approach gives a further democratic action to company members. In this process, individuals are the focus. They need to learn this new way of behavior.

Consciousness is a very effective process when people move from a particular situation to another. A person moves from a mechanical way of working to a conscious one, which involves beliefs, feelings, emotions, and intuition. People that apply their minds in their work are far more effective than people who do not. The Circles of Mind metaphor takes the entire concept into more profound dimensions.

With democratic behavior, employees reveal and unleash everyday knowledge, blending it with the scientific knowledge in their conscious experience, giving the best they can give to themselves and the company. Employees can see the democracy in their company and use this democracy to create a world in which they have the chance to develop themselves. The most important thing is that new meanings emerge in the human mind, the conscious, and the unconscious parts of the human brain.

Organizations had undoubted possibilities and inaccessibility to create a democratic company culture under different leadership and different circumstances. Likewise, there are, in their current stage, opportunities to increase their democratic culture, and there can be more future opportunities and future accessibilities to develop a democratic company culture in the future. However, this process is complicated and takes time as it is difficult to see how to increase the degree of democratic company culture. When people first understand its possibilities and perceive them in their daily lives, they can improve their democratic company culture. Everything is based on the situation people live in and the meanings generated from the current situation.

14.6 Rewards Stage (Execution): Co-Opetition and Co-Evolution Process

Company democracy offers a unique environment for development and growth through a co-opetitive philosophy and a Co-Evolutionary process. This process and philosophy for the Company Democracy Model conditions can be considered the journey stage in the innovation-based conditions for applying the model.

Once the Company Democracy Model has been accepted to be used and the proper infrastructure has been set, the model's execution can be a relatively straightforward and pleasant process for all. As the model is based on a co-opetitive philosophy, there are no rivalries between the employees and the organization's management. It is impressive what can be achieved once people are united under shared drives and goals. The degree of Company Democracy has a significant conscious and unconscious effect on the employees. This affects the way and ease of implementing and executing the Company Democracy Model.

The Co-Evolute methodology integrated with the Company Democracy Model is an incremental spiral-based progressive path that drives the organizational journey through the Company Democracy levels (Figure 14.4).

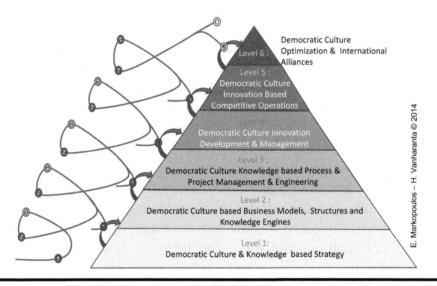

Figure 14.4 The co-opetitive and Co-Evolutionary philosophy of Company Democracy.

To demonstrate the evolutionary journey in the Company Democracy Model, the word 'Spiralmyd' has been invented. It is a compound word from 'spiral' and 'pyramid' with the 'y' referencing the collective Y-theory represented in the pyramid, instead of the individualistic 'I.' It also indicates the spiral process that leads from one level of the pyramid to the next, either upward or downward. Knowledge and ideas will always move the pyramid upward, but they can also move downward if they cannot achieve a specific competition requirement at a particular level.

The "Spiralmyd" Co-Evolutionary model and methodology reveal the Applied Philosophy in the Company Democracy Model. It represents what democracy is, offering the chance for all to grow together in the model's levels as capability and maturity become more robust, more reliable, and effective over time.

14.7 Share Stage (Post-conditions): Shared Added-Value Networks

The post-conditions of the staged requirements of the Company Democracy Model target the utilization process of the results and benefits gained from the journey of applying the model. The post-conditions deliver and share the added value created by the Company Democracy Model's innovations.

Shared added value refers to utilizing the benefits after completing the journey with the industry, society, and the organization's collaborative entities. The shared stages are at the top of the pyramid. With direct (entrepreneurial benefits) or indirect benefits (job security, pride, satisfaction), the post-condition requirements aid all those who worked to achieve this goal. This pre-condition group targets the sustainability of the thriving Company Democracy culture and its expansion to more organizations, people, and other cooperation entities.

Being at the top requires the wisdom, vision, and strategy to stay at the top. Once Company Democracy has been successfully achieved, it is not difficult to maintain it, share the process and results, and expand the process broadly within the organization (if the model has been used as a pilot in one organizational unit first) or to other collaborative organizations that form the organizational ecosystem (Figure 14.5).

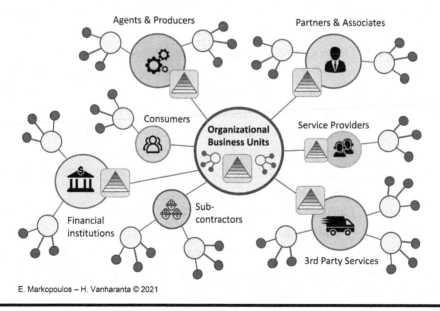

E. Markopoulos – H. Vanharanta © 2021

Figure 14.5   Company Democracy in organizational ecosystems.

Organizational ecosystems indicate the death of direct competition (Moore, 1993, 1996). They tend to be management-driven by the lean organization concept that offers flexibility, reduces organization costs, and increases operational value. They are groups of organizations complementary to each other, not necessarily with the same shareholders or owners. These organizations share common corporate cultures, knowledge, participate in projects, and develop an unofficial Co-Evolutionary philosophy as one contributes to the other's progress for the benefit of all.

Such organizational ecosystems are found mainly in the construction industry, manufacturing, logistics, and lately in technology. The practical application of the Company Democracy Model in one organization within an ecosystem can be adopted in other ecosystem organizations. This enhances and supports the philosophy of trust, a foundation of the co-opetitive and Co-Evolutionary Company Democracy theories.

14.8 Summary

The Company Democracy Model can be characterized as a product of multidisciplinary science, which integrates many disciplines such as management (strategy, leadership, etc.), engineering (process knowledge, innovation), sociology (human societies, social change, behavior of humans, ethos, etc.), finance (investments, extroversion, etc.), communication (marketing, branding, etc.), and others. The model's uniqueness is its capability to integrate them in a transparent, logical, reasonable, and complementary way.

The Company Democracy Model is not a classic, ordinary organizational model, strategy, process improvement, quality assurance, or another type of business management or operations model to be used by all-purpose type business consultants. It is a people-centric management and leadership philosophy with processes and system synergies built around it in a democratic organizational environment. It provides opportunities for everyone to share knowledge, connect, and collaborate for personal and organizational development and growth.

The Company Democracy Model requires a significant degree of organizational maturity, primarily in leadership, to overcome selfishness, ignorance, insecurities, and the personal interests of executives, senior management, and middle-level management, who tend to oppose and inhibit democratic organizational operations.

All organizations in any sector and of any size, scope, and financial standing can be effectively applied to the Company Democracy Model. The model has customizable features and a mutational and agile structure under a Co-Evolutionary philosophy, which can be adjusted to all types of organizations that understand its principles and see the value of implementing them. Since 2008, the world has entered into a global financial crisis driven by economic, health, and political accidents that have made the future of the economy, society, and the people quite uncertain. A possible way to escape from this depressing situation is to think about coexisting, co-evolving, and co-innovating for the people and companies' common good.

The Company Democracy Model is a holistic model that can also be seen as Company Micro Democracy, Company Macro Democracy, Company Democracy, Corporate Democracy, Business Democracy, Organizational (Institutional) Democracy, Enterprise Democracy, and also Entrepreneurial Democracy for Small and Medium Size Enterprises Democracy, Young Entrepreneurs Democracy, and Inventors Democracy.

The human perception, interpretation, understanding, and communication of Company Democracy toward successful implementation is challenging but feasible if organizations understand the model's pre- and post-conditions, allowing and assuring a rewarding journey to success and progress.

Understanding Democracy, Company Democracy, and the Company Democracy Model does not require advanced scientific skills but only common sense. Unfortunately, it seems that common sense is not that common after all.

Questions for Review and Discussions

Organizational change is made by knowledge workers who succeed in the present and shape the new future. They demonstrate knowledge-driven leadership and accept responsibility, provided that the organization adequately supports them. They are people with experience and expertise, seeking only a responsive environment to perform, create ideas, innovate, implement, test new products and services, and run the business efficiently and effectively.

When identifying and utilizing knowledge-driven employees with modern management and leadership skills, capabilities, and competencies, the democratic company culture must be in place to help protect their freedom of thought and speech and help them contribute with their knowledge and insights. Please go through the following questions and answer them according to your experience from practice.

1. Do you think the leaders and managers in your company apply to extend the Company Democracy Model?
   1.1 If NO, why? Should they? And how?
   1.2 If YES, how is this done?
   1.3 What processes do they follow?
   1.4 How can the existing processes be compared with the Company Democracy Model?
2. Do you see that it is possible to learn Company Democracy with the Company Democracy Model?
   2.1 Can the Company Democracy Model help establish an organizational learning culture in a company?
   2.2 If NO, why not?
   2.3 If YES, how does the Company Democracy Model culture suit the organizational learning culture?
   2.4 Explain this alignment (2.3) in general and level by level.
3. Do you think your company needs a particular change management strategy, such as the ADKAR model (Hiatt, 2006), Kotter's model (Gupta, 2011), or others, to help the communication and adaptation of the Company Democracy?
   3.1 If NO, why not? What is the effective strategy used today?
   3.2 If YES, what is the change management model used to support this communication and adaptation?
   3.3 Explain your answer and provide examples.
4. How challenging is it for your company to keep the innovation process continuously active?
   4.1 What methods or actions are currently used?
   4.2 What do you think is still needed?
   4.3 Justify your answer and provide examples.
5. Innovation management and the Company Democracy Model rely on several pre-conditions before its application. What kind of resources does your company need in the pre-conditioning phase of the Company Democracy Model?
   5.1 Who innovates in your company?
   5.2 What are the innovation incentives?
   5.3 What is the innovation support?
   5.4 How does the innovation need gets communicated?
   5.5 How are people encouraged and trained to think innovatively?

5.6 Identify the conditions for innovation and explain what your company does to fulfill each one.

6. How would you define the term 'innovation ethos'?

   6.1 From your point of view, how would you describe the following statements?

      6.1.1 Ethical thinking

      6.1.2 Ethical innovation

      6.1.3 Ethical idea

      6.1.4 Any other point of view on innovation ethics

      6.1.5 Any combination of the given statements

   6.2 How would you relate ethical and social innovation?

7. What is the innovation ethos in the Company Democracy Model ?

   7.1 What ethical values of the Company Democracy Model promote innovation? And why?

   7.2 What ethical values of the Company Democracy Model support innovation? And why?

8. Can ethical innovation lead to be highly profitable?

   8.1 If no, why not?

   8.2 If YES, how can this be achieved?

9. What does the term 'co-opetition' mean?

   9.1 Is it an activation or deactivation issue?

   9.2 How is it different from the competition?

10. Should organizations strive for competitiveness or co-opetitiveness, and why?

    10.1 What is the degree of co-opetition in your company?

    10.2 How do you identify co-opetition in your company? Please justify your answers and give examples.

11. Does your company fairly share the innovation results with all the company members and its large company ecosystem?

    11.1. If NO, why not? Should they? Why and how?

    11.2. If YES, how is this done?

12. What are the benefits and drawbacks of sharing innovation within the company's business ecosystem?

    12.1 Can this be extended to the company's competitors?

    12.2 What are the advantages and disadvantages of sharing innovation with the company's competitors and their ecosystem?

13. Freedom covers self-determination, your hopes, and intentions, as well as those purposes you have in your company and your own life.

    13.1 Please ponder the fundamental sense of freedom in your company and life with the chart Figure 14Q.

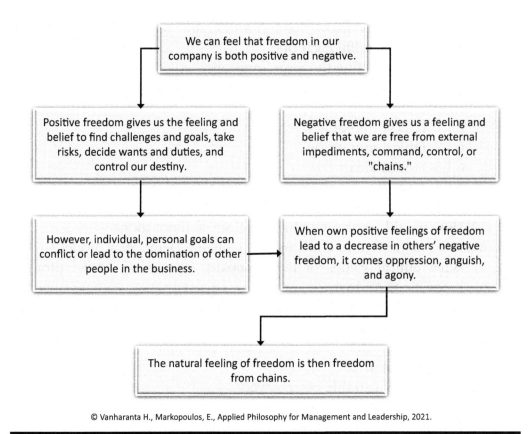

Figure 14Q   Chart for Question 13 (c.f., ref. Buckingham, et al., 2011, Isaiah Berlin, p. 280).

References

Buckingham, W., King, Peter J., Burnham, D., Weeks, M., Hill, C., and Marenbon, J., 2011. *The Philosophy Book.* Dorling Kindersley Limited, London.

Conzelmann, H. and Lindemann A., 1999. *Interpreting the New Testament: An Introduction to the Principles and Methods of New Testament Exegesis.* English translation. Peabody, MA: Hendrickson.

Côté J. E. and Allahar, A., 2011. *Lowering Higher Eéducation: The Rise of Corporate Universities and the Fall of Liberal Education.* University of Toronto Press, Toronto, Canada.

Gupta, P., 2011. Leading innovation change: The Kotter way. *International Journal of Innovation Science*, 3 (3), 141–150. https://doi.org/10.1260/1757-2223.3.3.141

Hiatt J., 2006. *ADKAR: A Model for Change in Business, Government, and Our Community.* Prosci Learning Publications, Loveland, CO.

Markopoulos, E. and Vanharanta, H., 2014. Democratic culture paradigm for organizational management and leadership strategies: The company democracy model. In: Proceedings of the 5th International Conference on Applied Human Factors and Ergonomics AHFE 2014, Kraków, Poland.

Moore, J. F., 1993. Predators and prey: A new ecology of competition. *Harvard Business Review*, May/June, 75–86.

Moore, J. F., 1996. *The Death of Competition: Leadership & Strategy in the Age of Business Ecosystems*. Harper Business, New York.

Vanharanta H. and Markopoulos E., 2013. Creating a dynamic democratic company culture for leadership, innovation, and competitiveness. In: Hellenic-Russian Forum, Athens, Greece.

Vanharanta, H., Pihlanto, P., and Chang, A.-M., 1997. Decision support for strategic management in a hyperknowledge environment and the holistic concept of man. In: Proceedings of the 30th Annual Hawaii International Conference on Systems Sciences, IEEE Computer Society Press, California. 243–258.

www.goodreads.com

Chapter 15

The Company Democracy Model for Human Intellectual Capitalism and Shared Value Creation: Toward Added Value and Circular Economies

Executive Summary

People face difficulties in understanding and applying democracy and Company Democracy in practice. Democracy, as such, is difficult to define because it is so laborious to understand and perceive. Incomplete definitions, democratic rules, and regulations can have catastrophic results leading to anarchy, populism, and demagogy. Therefore, democracy and Company Democracy need protective and applicable frameworks, although too much protection runs the risk of making it less democratic. 'Metron Ariston' (moderation is best), a Delphic maxim, may contribute to a reasonable definition of democracy and give better options for applying it effectively in practical contexts like Company Democracy. Democracy and Company Democracy in speech, actions, and different practical contexts can be demonstrated based on the shared added value produced. Shared value in business has been defined as the balance of economic value creation for the company. The target and the

DOI: 10.4324/9781003158493-18

ultimate goal is to achieve financial success through company activities for all stakeholders. Such shared value can be seen as a creative means for meeting social requirements and a tool to develop Company Democracy. However, this activity needs continuous initiatives, insights, ideas, and innovations to respond to the risks, challenges, and requirements of a fast-changing world. Shared value is the added value created inside companies that reaches society. This chapter combines the ideas of shared added value with the Company Democracy Model to present the company–society synergistic effects in a business context.

15.1 Introduction

As everything happens for a reason, it is essential first to understand and evaluate what *has happened* to predict what *could happen*. Organizations today strive for sustainability in critical and unstable economic environments worldwide. They need to make radical changes in management and leadership to survive the devastating periods when the consumers' buying power, habits, and society's prosperity are diminished. Instead of figuring out why sales or productivity has decreased, it may be wiser to face the truth, understand, accept the reality, and seek ways to create shared value that can reboot the economy and society (Porter, Kramer, 2011).

The creation of shared value for the society is based on added value for the organizations (Duncan, 1985). Added value requires human capital utilization through management and leadership models and practices that promote ideas, insights, and innovations. In turn, innovation activity requires freedom of mind and speech, which can be found best in vibrant company democracies. The rescue chain for the economy can start from organizations' ability to generate shared value for societal needs, which will return its benefit to them directly or indirectly sooner or later if giving precedes receiving.

15.2 The Value of Sharing

Shared value has been defined as the value creation inside a company and value creation for society according to societal needs and challenges (Porter, Kramer, 2011). Shared value can also be seen as a creative means for meeting social requirements. However, this activity needs continuous insights, ideas, initiatives, and innovations to respond to the changing world's risks, challenges, and conditions. The shared value should be seen more as added value creation with that added value to be delivered as a shared value for both the economy and society (Kay, 1993). In this new way of thinking, there are two issues. The first is to identify the organizations and individuals that can create added value in the market. The second issue is to identify the organizations or individuals who need the shared added value.

In both cases, the answer is the society itself, which forms the market. The challenge then shifts to the individuals' motivation to be directly or indirectly involved in a shared value creation process. One approach to this issue is to start gradually from the organizational workforce since employees form both the organization and society. By treating the employees' needs as societal needs, employees can feel valued, respected, and committed to their work, giving them higher degrees of motivation. It is also vital for the organization to be involved by urging individuals to be part of such shared value creation.

People must understand the business better and contribute together through democratic processes to meet the shared value requirements that originate outside the organization. The relationship between employees, organizations, and society is based on co-evolution. Co-opetitive personal and organizational development principles can lead to new organizational productivity levels, profitability, and performance (Kantola, Vanharanta, Karwowski, 2006, Markopoulos, Vanharanta, 2014, Vanharanta, Markopoulos, 2013, Eklund, Paajanen, Kantola, Vanharanta, 2012).

15.3 The Circular Economy

The term 'Circular Economy' has become a trend in sustainable development. It is defined as a production and consumption model, which involves sharing, reusing, leasing, repairing, recycling, and refurbishing existing materials and products as much as possible. In the Circular Economy, products' life cycle is extended through waste minimization (European Parliament, 2018). Thus, when a product reaches the end of its life, its materials are kept within the economy wherever possible to be used again productively to create additional value.

However, this circulation can be approached from a different perspective, not necessarily associated with resource reusability for sustainable development. A new dimension can be given from a financial perspective, which is what society needs the most. The theory of Green Capitalism emphasizes the people's need to sustain themselves first before delivering any good that can help the planet (Markopoulos, Gann, Kirane, Vanharanta, 2020a). This financial sustainability can be achieved when the organizational value is first shared with the society before it returns to the organization for another iteration of shared value creation.

The number of iterations can define the strength of the economy and the effectiveness and success of the circularity. However, the number of iterations is also determined by the number of innovations implemented for new products and services to be created, the unique value to be generated, and the new socioeconomic circles to be achieved. Diving deeper into this relationship is the quality of knowledge needed to develop innovations that will be implemented in new products and services that can be shared with society to boost the economy.

Following this chain of elements that compose the circular financial economy, it is understood that the most critical factor in this process is knowledge elicitation to identify and resolve societal needs. In that case, knowledge does not contribute to the resolution of a societal need. Whether it is a product or a service, the output of this knowledge will not be entirely successful due to its distance from society, which is the pillar of a sustainable economy.

By viewing the circular economic issues from this perspective, the need for democratic organizational cultures to generate practical knowledge related to societal issues is more in demand now than ever. Figure 15.1 presents the organizational value chain elements and their place in the shared value Circular Economy. These elements are Corporate Democratic Culture, Human Intellectual Capital, Innovation, and Added Value. They all need to be in place and work together to deliver a society driven by shared organizational value. This shared value generation process does not have a specific starting point. It can start from any element and provide the same results.

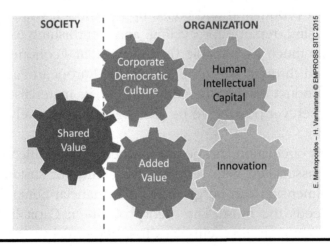

Figure 15.1   The Shared Value Circular Economy Chain.

There are three execution approaches to the value generation process, which are briefly described in Figure 15.1.

15.3.1 Democratic Culture Driven

This is the classic approach where an organization that has adopted the Company Democracy Model receives inspiration from the society for the generation of knowledge at the first level of the model. This results in the creation of new human intellectual capital, which brings innovations to resolve societal needs. These innovations create added value for the organization, primarily a reputational added value, as such efforts and activities that can be promoted under the ESG (Environmental, Social, Governance) index elements contribute to the organizational strategy for well-developed and well-defined ethical, environmental, social, and governance operations (Markopoulos, Kirane, Gann, Vanharanta, 2020b). The delivery of social-driven innovation that resolves societal needs and addresses societal challenges creates shared value between organizations and society. Society receives solutions to fulfill its needs, and the organizations make a market by investing in and resolving these societal needs.

15.3.2 Human Intellectual Capital Driven

This process is similar to the Democratic Culture-driven approach. In this case, the elements are not initiated by the society but by the employees within an organization that has adopted the Company Democracy Model. As employees are part of society, their concerns may be societal concerns if evaluated according to their social impact. Therefore, without being inspired by a specific event, movement, challenge, or other societal issues, the organization's employees can still come up with shared value knowledge if a democratic culture is in place. The rest of the process is the same as presented in the Democratic Culture-driven approach.

15.3.3 Added Value Driven

In this approach, the shared value process is generated totally outside the organization without involving any employees or citizens. The organization can observe and analyze the needs that people have. These needs can derive from the society's responses or reactions to social, political, environmental, or economic issues or circumstances, or even from the people's demands for equality, justice, diversity, and opportunities. By observing the society's behavior and its responses to various situations, knowledge is gathered to pass through the Company Democracy Model in the organizations that apply the model with an established democratic culture. This knowledge acts as food for thought, helping employers to think about how this knowledge can best deliver solutions that address related issues. Such an approach creates new organizational human intellectual capital, which can be turned into innovations that generate added value by addressing real societal challenges and delivering solutions to society.

As indicated, there is no specific starting point in this Democratic Circular Economy for shared and added value. It can start from any of its elements, but it certainly requires a democratic culture in place. Such a culture can be achieved through the Company Democracy Model, the people's model. Wherever people are involved and support a process, plan, strategy, or initiative, the result can only be successful.

15.4 The Shared Value of Democracy

In the external and internal business world, organizations and companies have become aware of the benefits, challenges, and risks of democracy. In the organizational context, democratic culture is not an easy concept to understand and demonstrate. It relies on how people inside and outside companies and organizations think about democracy and how they act.

Generally speaking, democracy has been seen as the only construct and concept of a living system and a vehicle that can successfully cope with contemporary civilizations' changing demands in managerial and governmental contexts. It has been said that the message of democracy is irresistible, and its progress is inevitable (Slater, Bennis, 1990). This means that, sooner or later, management and leadership will have to pay more attention to it.

Today, more than ever, the need for creating space for Company Democracy is obvious. For such an important concept, a real and non-virtual space must be communicated, operated, controlled, and maintained to benefit the organization, the economy, and society in a shared value framework. A thriving democracy in speech and actions can be demonstrated based on the shared value concept. As democracy can be for all the people, exercising democracy must also be for all the people.

The Company Democracy Model is based on utilizing organizational knowledge through democratic methods and practices in knowledge culture, creation, extraction, and sharing toward shared added value goals and objectives. The model promotes the concept of 'one person – one vote for shared value,' but it expects democratic reasoning, documentation, and justification for each vote.

Organizational failure does not occur due to an inability to solve problems but due to the inability be recognize and identify them. Problem identification and exploitation of possible solutions are approached in the Company Democracy Model by offering democracy to everyone. The generation of the shared added value is achieved when their solutions support the people's problems, needs, ideas, beliefs, and even their wishes.

15.5 From Company Democracy to Human Capitalism

Besides being a model for innovation-based organizational development and management, the Company Democracy Model can also be considered a model that promotes human capital creation. Since all people are equal, then all people have the same capability to build and develop their intellectuality. The degree of intellectual capital creation possibilities varies between the environments that people are into. Structured and constructive organizational environments can contribute more to the creation of human intellectual capital, while unstructured and volatile ones may be less successful.

As all people can think, they can all be considered human capitalists to a degree. Intellectual power is human capital, and any capital can be monetized or utilized to benefit the people, the organization, and society. Under this prism, the Company Democracy Model, based on the people's freedom to produce information, ideas, knowledge, and grow through them, turns people into human intellectual capital owners. This makes intellectual capital another type of wealth people can possess if given the democratic freedom to produce it. Therefore, all people can be rich in intellectual capital and potentially rich in financial (monetary) capital based on their intellectual savings.

Innovation, a core element in the shared value generation process, derives from the human intellectual capital grown in democratic, progressive, responsive, and meritocratic company environments. Figure 15.2 presents the evolution of democratic human capital.

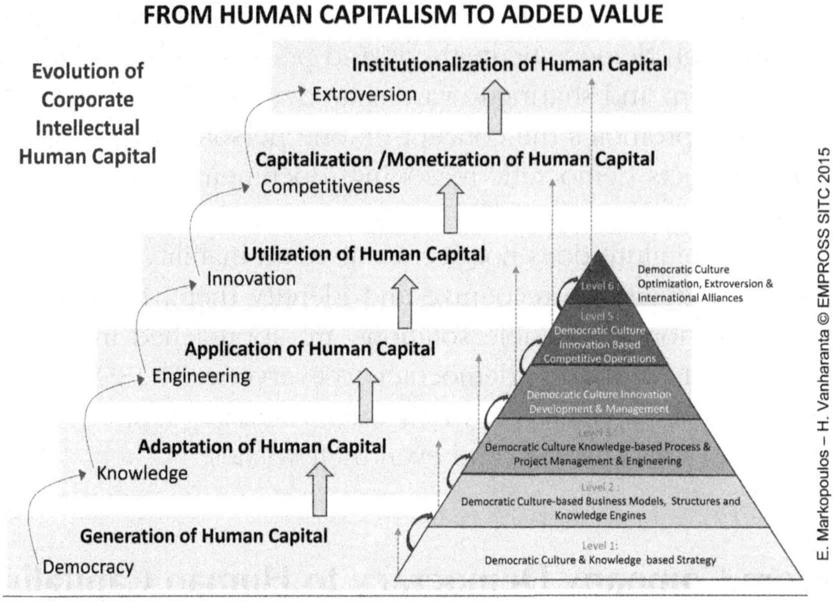

Figure 15.2 Evolution of corporate human intellectual capital in democratic environments.

The first level of the Company Democracy Model sets the infrastructure for the creation of human capital. Responsive democratic environments offer people the opportunity to express their thoughts, insights, ideas, visions, and beliefs. For knowledge to be generated and turn into human capital, it is crucial to allow the people to develop it, regardless of its quality or quantity. The quality of knowledge determines the value of human capital, and the amount of experience defines the organization's degree of human capitalism. Together they reveal the degree of organizational growth toward achieving, maintaining, or improving the desired results.

The second level of the model utilizes people by allowing them to benefit from the model's operations. Level 2 offers an opportunity to those who know how to turn their knowledge into intellectual capital. This level provides an environment where the right people receive the proper chance to stand out, present their knowledge, and apply it in practice. Level 2 reshuffles the deck of human resources in an organization. As organizations are living entities in a competitive world, nothing and no one can be taken for granted or be considered irreplaceable. Employees should not see organizations as givers of the monthly paycheck but as the stage to perform and secure those paychecks. The second level of the model rewards those who see democracy as an opportunity and not a threat. This level formulates organizational and individual human capital.

The third level of the model practically transforms each employee's human capital into new products, services, projects, procedures, initiatives, and other deliverables. It is the level where intellectual capital is tested for its applicability. The results of this level impact the careers of those involved in it. Employees who have significantly contributed to creating new products and services with their intellectual capital are part of the success and, therefore, part of the benefits. Still, those who failed to learn from this experience have the opportunity to try again.

The fourth level of the model defines the actual value of the human intellectual capital at a personal and organizational level. Innovation is nothing more than the justifications of valid, trustworthy, and applicable human intellectual capital beyond the current market space. Innovators are human capitalists who benefit from their capital in monetary, reputational, and other ways. Level 4 is the most challenging as it pays off and demonstrates the different levels' success, especially for the effort placed in level 1.

The fifth and sixth levels of the model determine the leaders among the intellectual capitalists regarding people and organizations. In level 5, the model considers the competitive advantages of the people's contributions. It is the broader commercialization of their collective effort to deliver new products and services that offer competitiveness. On the other hand, in level 6, extroversion is considered an organizational-driven process since strategic synergies and globalization strategies are done at the organizational and individual levels. The achieved extroversion helps organizations maintain operations and continue offering Company Democracy where their employees can grow and harvest their intellectual capital. Both levels utilize the human intellectual capital of the previous international commercialization (level 5) and global institutionalization (level 6) activities.

15.6 From Human Capitalism to Added Value

Human capitalism can only be successful if it can generate added value to those who have such capital. People and organizations must utilize human capital to create added value and justify their intellectual capital and capitalism.

The Company Democracy Model generates human capital by empowering the people to utilize their potential, initiative, willpower, skills, and capability actively and proactively. On the other hand, skillful and charismatic people who have evolved through democratic company environments do not necessarily assure the creation of added value from their intellectual capital unless this added value is generated in a controlled way that can produce intellectual capital.

Level 1 of the model generates added value for an organization through its people's motivation to work in co-opetitive and collaborative processes that generate knowledge which becomes human intellectual capital. The added value in this level comes from people's alignment with a process that can benefit them and the organization. Anything that derives from this process can give added value. Similarly, level 2 of the model considers the proper utilization of every person in the organization based on their capability to generate intellectual capital as added value. Assigning the right people in the right places can generate organizational added value from their efficient operations. Likewise, level 3 of the model generates added value from the new products, services, processes, projects, and initiatives selected for implementing human organizational capital.

Organizations cannot have any added value unless they take the initiative to develop something new. Level 4 of the model generates the specific, measurable, and concrete added value for the organization by identifying the innovation derived from the actions implemented in level 3. Level 5 directs the added value generated in the organization to a competitive advantage, which is what added value promotes. Level 6 moves the organization's added value to new application areas through extroversion and internationalization (Figure 15.3).

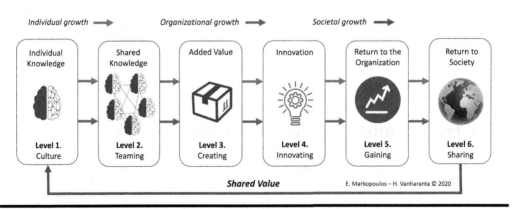

Figure 15.3 Shared value evolution of the Company Democracy Model.

Added value is what organizations need to survive and prosper. This added value may derive from the organization's innovations powered by the intellectual capital people developed in the organization's democratic environment. The organization still requires the degree of organizational commitment to be at a high level by sustaining current achievements while aiming for future development (Einolander, Vanharanta, Kantola, 2010, 2011).

15.7 From Added Value to Shared Value

The Company Democracy Model structure can be seen as a responsive environment, which supports organizations to create added value. This responsive environment is an essential requirement for the creation of shared value. The added value triggers shared value creation.

The Co-Evolutionary management and leadership paradigm has been illustrated using the concept of capital productivity and market productivity. Capital productivity indicates how much capital is invested in all the added-value operations inside the system, i.e., the company. Market productivity means external business performance when the added value is evaluated and bought by customers. All added-value activities only yield profit.

Inside the company system, capital productivity is the added value divided by total capital (total assets). The ratio does not indicate any difference between physical and intellectual capital, so profitability is calculated, dismissing the human capital side. In the typical manufacturing industry, the capital side consists primarily of physical capital. In the new postmodern industrial world, especially in the service industry, however, the intellectual capital side is the most important. In the service industry, companies 'invest' mainly in intellectual capital, and the proportion of physical capital is low. Nevertheless, organizational efficiency calculations follow the usual way to calculate company productivity, profitability, and performance.

The combination of all the created added value inside a company reveals the total added value, which is the company's driving force, i.e., the system itself. Part of the added value must be reserved for new investments inside the company, and part of the created added value goes to the shared value for the society and its people. When the added value changes into monetary form through the markets, the company receives capital. This can support new investments to create more jobs, pay more taxes to the government, and return more social dividends. Figure 15.4 presents this critical equation in moving from added value creation to shared value creation within a company.

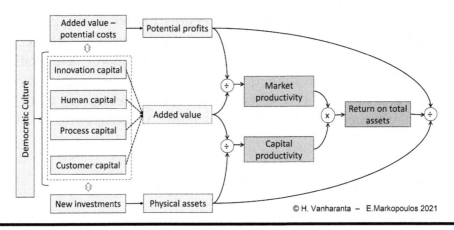

Figure 15.4   Equation for return on total assets through capital and market productivity concepts.

The effective use of the Company Democracy Model helps a company target and manage the equation's ratios. It is critical and necessary to keep high capital productivity, together with physical capital and intellectual capital. The market productivity ratio should also be kept high to secure the profits needed to be used inside the company and given back to society.

15.8 Summary

Shared value is what drives the new economy. Organizations must give to receive. Giving does not mean only offering their products and services but also addressing social needs through their added value, which indirectly generates new revenue streams for the organizations by servicing social needs. The challenge in creating shared value for an organization is to gain the added value that can be used to address social needs through shared value initiatives.

Organizations with no added value cannot participate in this new global change and demand and remain trapped in conventional, if not selfish, operations, strategies, or habits. Creating added value for shared value, on the other hand, is an ongoing process that monitors and addresses society's demands. To reach this maturity, organizations need to continually utilize their human resources as the best way to contribute to this goal through their operations and environment. Environments that use democratic practices to identify those with intellectual human capital potential, promote the right people to the right place, and transform their human capital into new products and services whose innovation creates added and share value with less effort and higher results.

Questions for Review and Discussions

Democracy and Company Democracy in speech, actions, and different practical contexts can be demonstrated based on the shared added value produced. Shared value in business has been defined as covering the value creation inside a company and the value creation for society according to its needs and challenges. The targets and the ultimate goals are to achieve financial success through company activities so that all stakeholders get their share.

Please go through the following questions for review and discussion.

1. What is Shared Value?
   1.1 Can a company share its product or service value with the people and society?
   1.2 How can this practically be done?
   1.3 Do you believe that it can happen, or is it simply a communication strategy?
2. Does your company apply the Shared Value Circular Economy Chain?
   2.1 If NO, why not? Should they? And how?
   2.2 If YES, how is this achieved?
   2.3 How does your company keep an active relationship with society?
3. Prioritize the main components of shared value. Explain your thinking.
   3.1 If you were to add, change, or remove something from the Shared Value Circular Economy Chain, what would that be?
   3.2 How could you make the Shared Value Circular Economy Chain more effective and more rewarding to the people, the company, and society?
   3.3 Redesign the Shared Value Circular Economy Chain concept with your changes and provide examples of its operations.
4. The Company Democracy Model helps build human intellectual capital for a company. How is this done?
   4.1 How does the human intellectual capital grow from level to level?

4.2 How can the human intellectual capital value be turned into a new organization and business entity?

4.3 Can human intellectual capital be quantified, measured, and valued in a monetary currency?

4.4 Justify your answer and provide examples.

5. Does your company have a human intellectual capital mechanism?

    5.1 How is knowledge created, evolved, and reflected in your company's value?

    5.2 Is there any process for this? If NO, why not? Could there be any? And how?

    5.3 If YES, what are those processes, and how are they executed?

    5.4 How does your company measures human intellectual capital, and in what terms?

6. What are the challenges to increase the evolution and maintain continuity of human intellectual capital in a company?

    6.1 List five challenges, prioritize them and explain them. Does your company face any of such challenges?

    6.2 If NO, what has been done to avoid them?

    6.3 If YES, which ones, and how does it cope with them?

7. Do your company measure market productivity and capital productivity ratios?

    7.1 If NO, what alternative metrics does it use? How do they work?

    7.2 If YES, how are these metrics calculated?

    7.3 What is the process, and how effective are they?

    7.4 Please justify your answer and use examples.

8. What is the difference between added value and shared value?

    8.1 What are the relationships between these two values?

    8.2 Does your company measure added and shared value? If NO, why not?

    8.3 If YES, how is it done? Is this done continuously?

    8.4 Please justify your answer and use examples.

9. What are the motivations and attitudes to work in your company?

    9.1 How do you see the possibilities to increase employee happiness and commitment inside your company?

    9.2 Please see the chart of Figure 15Q below and ponder happiness, motivation, and commitment to work in your company.

Figure 15Q   Chart for Question 9 (c.f., ref. Buckingham, et al., 2011, Bertrand Russell, p. 237).

References

Buckingham, W., King, Peter J., Burnham, D., Weeks, M., Hill, C., and Marenbon, J., 2011. *The Philosophy Book*. Dorling Kindersley Limited, London.

Duncan Kidd, A., 1985. Productivity analysis for strategic management. In: Guth, W. (ed.) *Handbook of Business Strategy*. Warren Gorham & Lamont, Inc., Boston, MA, 17.1–17.25.

Einolander, J., Vanharanta, H., and Kantola, J., 2010. Managing organizational commitment: Constructs and concepts for a computer application. In: Wlodarkiewicz-Klimek Hna (ed.) *Entrepreneurship and Innovations*, Vol. 1, 1–12. Elsevier, Amsterdam, Netherlands.

Einolander, J., Vanharanta, H., and Kantola, J., 2011. Managing commitment through ontology-based evaluation: Basics of new decision support system. In: Proceedings of the World Congress on Engineering and Technology, C.E.T. 2011, Shanghai, China. 167–171.

Eklund, T., Paajanen, P., Kantola, J., and Vanharanta, H., 2012. Knowledge creation and learning in organizations - measuring proactive vision using the co-evolute methodology. *International Journal of Strategic Change Management*, 4 (2), 190–201.

European Parliament, 2018. Circular economy: Definition, importance, and benefits. https://www.europarl.europa.eu/news/en/headlines/economy/20151201STO05 603/circular-economy-definition-importance-and-benefits

Kantola, J., Vanharanta, H., and Karwowski, W., 2006. The evolute system: A co-evolutionary human resource development methodology. In: Karwowski, W. (ed.) *The International Encyclopedia of Ergonomics and Human Factors*. CRC Press, Boca Raton, FL.

Kay, J., 1993. *Foundations of Corporate Success*. Oxford University Press, Inc., New York.

Markopoulos E. and Vanharanta, H. 2014. Democratic culture paradigm for organizational management and leadership strategies: The company democracy model. In: Proceedings of the 5th International Conference on Applied Human Factors and Ergonomics AHFE 2014, Kraków, Poland.

Markopoulos E., Gann E. L., Kirane I. S., Vanharanta H., 2020a. Green capitalism: Democratizing sustainable innovation by recycling intellectual capital energy. In: Ahram T., Taiar R., Gremeaux-Bader V., and Aminian K. (eds.) *Human Interaction, Emerging Technologies, and Future Applications II. IHIET 2020. Advances in Intelligent Systems and Computing*, Vol. 1152, Chapter 77. Springer, Cham, 507–519.

Markopoulos E., Kirane, I. S., Gann E. L., and Vanharanta, H., 2020b. A democratic, green ocean management framework for environmental, social, and governance (E.S.G.) compliance. In: Ahram, T., Taiar, R., Gremeaux-Bader, V., and Aminian, K., (eds) *Human Interaction, Emerging Technologies, and Future Applications II. IHIET 2020. Advances in Intelligent Systems and Computing*, Vol. 1152, 4. Springer, Cham, 21–33.

Porter, M., and Kramer, M., 2011. How to fix capitalism and unleash a new wave of growth. *Harvard Business Review*, January-February 2011, 61–77.

Slater, P. and Bennis, W., 1990. Democracy is inevitable. *Harvard Business Review*, 68 (5), 167–176.

Vanharanta H., and Markopoulos, E., 2013. Creating a dynamic democratic company culture for leadership, innovation, and competitiveness. In: Hellenic-Russian Forum, Athens, Greece.

Chapter 16

Maturity Spaces for Company Democracy: The Seven Clouds of Glory

Democratic Space

Space is a vitally important element in a system for developing any business initiative. It defines the freedom needed for knowledge to mature, evolve, and be applied. Organizations are living systems obliged to give space to new management and leadership initiatives, theories, and practices; otherwise, they will not see any progress. The Company Democracy Model provides the space in which people can act in a democratic environment. This space can lead to meritocracy, valid knowledge, innovation, competitiveness, extroversion, and other organizational and personal advantages and development. Democracy, in turn, can be annoying to those who resist it by reducing its space, freedom, and the opportunities people deserve to have. This chapter presents a comprehensive approach to why organizations fail to learn from their mistakes. It provides a democratic Co-Evolutionary and co-opetitive framework that can significantly contribute to organizational development, as long as the minimum space is given for freedom of speech and action.

DOI: 10.4324/9781003158493-19

16.1 Introduction

New management concepts frequently pop up in a fast-changing world, which is nothing more than rephrasing or repackaging methods, models, and past practices to suit the current business, economic, societal issues, needs, and trends. Ethical management, sustainable development, social engineering, greenware, etc., are some of the hundreds of new terms, commercially produced and sold overpriced to those who want to comply but not apply these new terms.

Many neo-management gurus and upcoming consultants tend to make up new trendy words. They creatively avoid essential management and leadership pillars to be different and the first ones to satisfy the market needs for fast and measurable productivity and performance targets. The faster–cheaper–better methodology continues to be in high demand by those who fail to understand that this triptych cannot and will never deliver the desired results without a long-term financial commitment to knowledge investments. However, in a dynamic business environment, time is relevant. Organizational targets become short-term oriented as long-term predictions do not fit the fast pace that the world desires to move today.

In this sense, 'quality' today is called 'just-in-time delivery,' 'cost' is called 'efficiency,' and 'time' is called 'effectiveness.' By the time the client understands the incompetence of a product or service, other requirements will have been introduced. The improved versions will be ready before the demand appears.

The fast pace organizations follow in their attempt to get ahead of the competition often results in developing products or services that might not be needed and certainly do not create the environment for organizational democratic cultures to grow. Regardless of what many companies announce publicly, new and impressive terms, most of them hire employees to deliver and not think. Thinking takes time, and time is a luxury not everyone can afford.

16.2 The Neo-manager Buzzword Phenomenon

The recent management literature has become a space for management and leadership buzzwords to continuously change due to their failure to deliver what they promise.

Words like 'down-sizing,' 'right-sizing', 'total quality', 'win-win', 're-engineering', 're-structure', 're-ignition', 're-design', 're-invent, 're-organize', and others have been used primarily to cover up past and recent failures due to the faster–cheaper–better methodology. Such words also support the human resources redundancy programs or layoffs necessary to balance losses from making the wrong decision in the first place, primarily due to a lack of long-term and well-thought-out strategies.

All the 're-…' words and other similar concepts developed in the last 20 years give the impression that success is difficult to achieve and that failure dominates the outcomes of any activity and effort. It is always wise to have room to think and a backup plan ready, even if it is not fast, not cheap, and not necessarily managed by the existing managers.

Such concepts, especially ones like 're-organize,' 're-think,' 're-ignite,' 're-invent,' etc., act as a shield for the insecurity, incapability, and immaturity of management and leadership. Every few years, a new 're-' term comes up to save the neo-managers' continuous failures who seek success through announcements but not through action. Such buzzwords keep on giving a second, third, fourth chance, and so on to all neo-managers who claim that they did everything right, but the markets failed to understand them. Furthermore, such buzzwords are portrayed and communicated to look logical, and as the new management and leadership trends, everyone should follow. Unfortunately, such movements have been adopted by neo-managers who fail to learn from their mistakes and from old-fashioned managers who feel the need to compete with the neo-managers by adopting anything the mainstream management media offers without knowing what it is or how it can be applied. It seems that, at the end of the day, what counts is who makes the first announcement and who uses the media more effectively.

16.3 Innovation Paradox

Innovation seems to be the latest victim of neo-managers and neo-management. As it has turned out to be, this significant concept and science is treated as just another misconceived pseudo-knowledge buzzword for pseudo-development strategies where many talk about. Still, very few invest in applying them. The disastrous .com bubble (Figure 16.1) indicates the results of the neo-manager speculative practices (Johansen, Sornette, 2000). The world, however, continued to innovate massively and cautiously, at least in theory, as the term has been misused. It is spread to make people believe that innovative organizations will survive while others will die or that innovative people will succeed while others will fail. Innovation and 'creative innovation'

Nasdaq
Points

Source: Bloomberg

Figure 16.1 Dotcom bubble burst: Ten years on. (BBC, 2010).

specifically seem to be the new carrot neo-managers use to push employees to achieve more with less infrastructure, time, support, and incentives. It is used to increase productivity, profitability, and performance rates without the support, commitment, and serious investments for innovators to think and for innovations to grow.

Unfortunately, today's real innovation is approached primarily as a cost center rather than a profit center through research and development. Innovation in most corporations turns out to be a stressful race for profit and competitiveness, a marketing and communication tool for glamorous corporate press releases and announcements, and an obligation under time pressure with unrealistic deadlines that allow no time to think, research, experiment, develop, test, produce, and, why not, to dream.

Such approaches are likely to fail as they are usually adopted by those who have never innovated but are called to manage innovative minds without an organizational culture for knowledge development, strategy, human capital, and the overall space needed to innovate. In such cases, well-paid pseudo-gurus and neo-managers who failed due to their superficial knowledge of critical concepts seek other management 'buzzwords' to cover up their incompetence. In business management and economics, there is always a way to blame a disaster on an unpredicted geo-socio-techno-cultural-economic-polit ics-x-y-z situation that unfortunately triggered loss and failure, instead of admitting poor management decisions and insufficient strategies. Such buzzwords offer trendy excuses to failure and several chances to re-structure, re-organize, re-plan and re-design, re-think, and re-innovate on what failed to get structured, organized, planned, design, thought, and innovate.

The way innovation is treated and suddenly promoted must trouble the real thinkers. For neo-managers who see the tree but not the forest, innovation is an attractive buzzword for today. Tomorrow, and after failing, they will find another buzzword to be experts on. After the term 're-invent' was loudly introduced in 2006 (Merriam-Webster, 2016, Bertoni, Duncan, Waldeck, 2015, Linkner, 2014) and continues to be used even stronger, the word 're-innovate' (Koulopoulos, 2009, Cheng, Shiou, 2008) began to appear in the international management communities as a newer trend, associated with concepts such as 're-innovate innovation,' 're-innovate for success,' etc. Such alternative neo-terms do not help innovation. On the contrary, they harm it. What is invented cannot be re-invented, and what is innovated cannot be re-innovated unless they were never invented or innovated in the first place.

Unsuccessful invention and innovation initiatives and investments are reported widely. In most cases, failure was not caused by a lack of skills but by poor management, lack of resources, funding, and lack of time needed to generate the intellectual capital and deliver the expected results. Innovation is not a mass production process. Everyone can think, but not everyone can innovate. It takes time, commitment, devotion, hard work, resources, and support. Neo-managers fail to understand this as they have never been in such a position in their fast-paced career development, only among others like themselves.

Innovation indeed contributes to long-term goals and is certainly not the strategy for fast results, profits, or fast and fancy exposure marketing and promotion announcements. Moreover, innovation requires education, expertise, high technical and scientific skills, strategic thinking, risk management, contingency planning, change management, well-defined visions, goals, leadership, patience, funding, and space to grow.

16.4 Understanding Innovation

Not all managers, of course, are neo-managers. After demonstrating significant careers and contributions in their areas of expertise, those who have evolved in management know that inventing and innovating require a long-term investment in intellectual capital and an innovation culture to host, promote, and support innovative thinking.

However, neo-managers systematically dismiss the most challenging part of the work that has to be done to achieve innovation as either very theoretical and wishful thinking or as very costly (Young, Shields, 1994). What is worse is that neo-managers and neo-leaders exist today in all types of organizations. With cost-cutting-oriented thinking and mentality toward innovation, they hinder those who could innovate and transform their companies, if not the world.

Innovation is purely a process that only motivated people can follow. It requires outstanding human resource management to identify, empower, and manage the brilliant minds who can innovate. Innovation forms new management and leadership operational strategies and new measures of corporate and individual success. Organizations who seriously consider innovating must answer the question, 'Can space for innovation be given?' This answer determines the organizational innovation culture and predicts the success or failure of any decision taken.

Achieving innovation success requires tremendous self-awareness and effort. Management and leadership should rely more on information and knowledge creation through their people. Innovation can only be achieved from within. It is a continuous quest for those who can think and continuously identify more thinkers than believers. Innovation needs to be understood from a holistic and strategic point of view. It requires dedicated and accomplished managers, not neo-managers. It grows within a culture and not within a project. It is a philosophy, an ideology that needs time, budget, human capital, and above all, space.

16.5 The Power of Knowledge

Today, knowledge is one of the most democratic sources of power. Innovation is nothing more than fundamental knowledge, although knowledge alone is not enough. Knowledge is handled like a tool, and like any tool, it can only be helpful in the hands of a person who holds it properly and uses it wisely. Knowledge can contribute creatively but also destructively unless developed within ethical and not only legitimate principles. People need the freedom to create what they can envision through their knowledge. This freedom can be offered through a democratic corporate culture. Respect for the individual and the freedom to express ideas and feelings can return the most to both the people and the organization.

Despite the .com bubble, innovation for many still remains the success recipe for all types of organizational challenges in a local, regional, national, or global environment. However, very few mention the need for developing a responsive environment for innovation creation and learning before initiating innovation programs and initiatives. Significantly, few managers and scholars have stressed the strategic importance of innovation cultures in developing corporate data, information, and knowledge. Responsive organizational cultures are still considered theoretical ideologies, costly and time-consuming initiatives, hard to establish, adapt, accept, and communicate.

Truth and knowledge can be achieved in a culture that promotes and supports self-awareness, discipline, integrity, and honesty. Innovation is based on facts and knowledge. Organizations that ignore such values and ideals can never be innovative. They can be progressive but not creative and innovative. Innovation culture development requires more philosophical thinking than management practices and a humble communication strategy.

16.6 People's Knowledge

There have been various methods for identifying organizational knowledge by bringing people together for a common purpose that could lead to success. One such approach is the X and Y theory of McGregor (1960).

According to McGregor, people are divided into two categories, combining two different principles. The first category includes the people that can be productive under rules, controls, and rigor. In contrast, the second category consists of those who can be effective and productive in an atmosphere of trust, confidence, and encouragement. Both types represent a kind of unity. From the X-theory point of view, people are united through fear, while from the Y-theory point of view, this unification is achieved through kindness. In both cases, people become connected under different practices in a binary model.

In McGregor's theory, any person can produce knowledge that can deliver any type of benefit, from simple products or services to highly innovative ones. The difference, in this case, is the momentum and efficiency of the knowledge and its deliverables. Suppose knowledge production is done in a supportive environment. In that case, this knowledge will be driven primarily by personal goals for the 'me' and not for the 'us.' People's knowledge contributions and success are highly influenced by the culture and the environment in which they work and operate. In organizations where competition overrules co-opetition, real innovation cannot be generated, as actual knowledge cannot be shared even if it exists.

There are several approaches to the generation, interpretation, and utilization of organizational knowledge. However, the Company Democracy Model is a new approach for achieving the aspects mentioned above through a co-opetitive unity. The model creates a business culture based on corporate ethos and unity principles, allowing organizations to develop innovation, competitiveness, and extroversion through real knowledge from their people regardless of their status, rank, or education. It identifies and precisely captures people's experience in a new responsive innovation culture.

16.7 Emphasis on People

The Company Democracy Model supports an interdisciplinary management approach (management strategy, knowledge, innovation, human resources, technology, production, leadership, quality, processes, engineering, research, development, etc.). It is a union of scientific, theoretical, technical, and practical approaches that directs all management and leadership practices toward uniting people through the freedom of expression to share and work with the raw materials of innovation such as data, information, and knowledge.

The model provides a dynamic adaptation space that gathers these raw materials for successful innovation and organizational development from the employees' knowledge. This knowledge has no cost. It flows freely within the organization. The challenge is how the organization can acquire it from all its members and without any exception.

Another challenge of such a Co-Evolutionary space is how this knowledge is assessed, analyzed, and redirected into the organization to generate further knowledge. Organizational knowledge has to be integrated into the business operations and production to create innovation that can enable the organization to achieve competitive advantage and the subsequent extroversion. It must be understood that innovation has pre-and post-conditions regardless of the process used to achieve it.

In the case of the Company Democracy Model, the innovation pre-condition requires developing an ethical infrastructure that will generate knowledge or real knowledge to be more precise. Innovation cannot be bought, imported, or copied in an organization. The post-condition of innovation creates shared added value and expands the innovation throughout the organization and its corporate ecosystem (Markopoulos, Vanharanta, 2014a, Markopoulos, Vanharanta, 2014b, Vanharanta, Markopoulos, 2013).

Innovation without a specific purpose and target will lead to re-innovation. Regardless of the neo-managers' efforts to consider re-innovation as a strategic decision, it remains a second chance to a failure.

16.8 The Dynamic Company Democracy Space

The Company Democracy Model needs the space first to be understood, evolve, and contribute to the development of an organization. To obtain such a space, a certain level of organizational maturity, primarily in management and leadership, is expected. People usually resist such processes to conceal their sense of insecurity and inadequacy. The same people also avoid performing with the necessary humbleness needed to bring people closer and help them contribute their knowledge, which is the most critical asset of any organization.

This needed space provides the Company Democracy Model the foundation to promote co-evolution and co-opetition rather than competition. Space is required for unity rather than rivalry, for in-depth knowledge and not superficial knowledge, innovation and not banality, and intellectual freedom rather than intellectual slavery.

People can be more innovative if they are free to work together. Freedom in a safe working space changes people's thinking habits, increases knowledge creation, initiates, implements, inspires, improvises, imagines, improves, ignites, invests, interacts, and incubates small things into big ideas, generates respect and enjoyment, and cultivates insights.

Within a corporate democratic space, people influence their attitudes and values. They make Company Democracy work for all and introduce stepwise innovation and knowledge creation processes. It is essential for an organization first to create the Dynamic Company Democracy Space (DCDS) that will allow the model to be applied effectively. Space also allows the model to measure the current degree of Company Democracy, create the democratic company culture needed, and generate many organizational capability and maturity metrics critical to developing a successful organizational strategy.

Such metrics can reveal what is needed by the employees, contribute to adjusting the management and leadership styles, and facilitate progress with new concepts and content derived from the Company Democracy methodology. Many other goals can be achieved via continuous education and learning and by perceiving business processes based on an ongoing strategy. Respect for all employees at all levels is the basis for this new way of company performance development. Their latent potential will be utilized, and their productivity will be used to get the most out of company performance. Thus, the created space is dynamic. The company's democratic culture enables new dynamic business dimensions and operations to be attained by utilizing existing resources thoroughly and fairly (Figure 16.2).

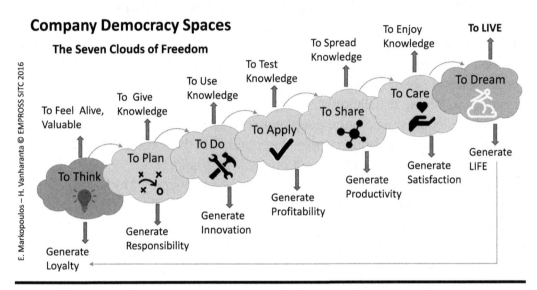

Figure 16.2   Spaces in the Company Democracy Model.

16.9 The Company Democracy Space Levels

The seven spaces of the Company Democracy Model are associated with the model's six levels (Figure 16.3). There is direct space-to-level mapping, with only the seventh space standing alone as it extends beyond the organizational operations.

> *The first space* is related to the time needed to create a democratic organizational culture. This is the most critical space for the time and requires the support of the employees to trust the model and open up. The challenges of the Company Democracy Model in the first level are not the lack of knowledge but the lack of time for employees to trust the model, learn it, and understand it. The size of this space is similar to the criticality of the level. If the first level of the Company Democracy Model is not implemented well, then all the levels after that will not run effectively, or they will not run at all. Therefore, the first space of the Company

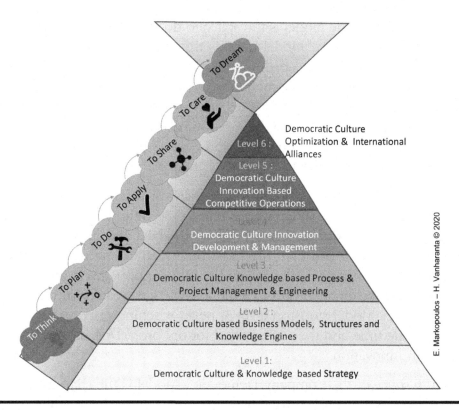

Figure 16.3   Spaces in the Company Democracy Model levels.

Democracy Model is the space to think. It is the thinking space people need to put their thoughts together and generate valuable knowledge. If people cannot believe the model and share their thoughts, the model will not proceed.

The second space in the Company Democracy Model is related to the second level of the model, characterized by teaming toward maturing and understanding the knowledge generated. This is a space to plan, as knowledge validation is related to planning efforts. Incomplete knowledge impacts planning and implementation due to insufficient requirements. Furthermore, the planning space provides the leeway needed to identify the proper teams to plan and understand its implementation. Space, and therefore time, is also required to determine the available experts to work together on the idea's evolution. Teaming is a time-consuming process as it results from a well-thought-out process since people cannot be randomly picked to form a team.

The third space of the model is the space to do what has been planned. The Company Democracy Model defines the third level as the implementation level. In this case, space is needed to deliver the knowledge from plan to action. The development process and effort can vary based on the support and resources employees have to implement their knowledge. The implementation can be done part-time, in different periods, or at full capacity. This organizational decision defines the space and the support given to the employees to implement their plans.

The fourth space in the Company Democracy Model overlaps between level 3 and level 4. This overlapping is due to the time needed for the developed service/product to mature in the markets and indicate innovation signs. This space can take the most time as the time a product/service stays on the market is also related to the support given for its promotion and dissemination. Most of the knowledge created in the Company Democracy Model stops on level 3, never reaching or completing level 4 due to the time and the cost needed for the project/product to be turned into an innovation.

The fifth space of the Company Democracy Model is the sharing space and is related to the competitive advantage organizations gain when reaching level 5. Identifying the competitive advantage requires time to share the results with clients, users, or others involved in the developed service/product to determine its competitive characteristics. Organizations driven by confidentiality agreements and defensive practices need more time and space to communicate their competitiveness since knowledge is not shared and not adequately evaluated to understand its real potential and value of the innovation.

The sixth space of the model is the caring space. It is time that the project/product developed within organizational knowledge reaches the sixth and last level of the Company Democracy Model. At this level, the organization returns Part of the project/product's value and success to the knowledge holders and shares its added value with the project initiators and the society. The time needed for the organization to reach this level and provide this recognition can vary due to knowledge extroversion procedures and operations. However, the Company Democracy Model considers this recognition and shared value as a crucial governance practice necessary for the model to continue reaching similar future success.

The seventh space is not related to any specific level of the Company Democracy Model. This is the space where acts do not matter or are not needed. Employees who reach the sixth level of the model are in the space of ultimate job satisfaction and personal achievement independently. Starting from an idea and transforming it into an international success places these employees in a career opportunity sphere where the sky is the limit.

16.10 Space for Human Capital and Shared Value Innovation

Company Democracy in speech and actions can be demonstrated based on the shared added value produced. The creation of shared value for society requires creating added value for the organization (Duncan, 1985). The Company Democracy Model, once appropriately conceived and given the space to evolve, can significantly contribute to the development of human capital. This capital is needed to generate the added value that can be turned into shared value and benefit both the organization and society.

Human intellectual capitalism can only be successful if it can generate added value from those who have such capital. People and organizations must utilize human capital by creating added value that proves its value and produces human intellectual capitalism (Markopoulos, Vanharanta, 2015). The Company Democracy Model generates human capital by actively empowering people to utilize their potential, willpower, skills, capability, and competence. Furthermore, it extends to creating shared value, providing economic value creation inside a company, and creating value for the society (Porter, Kramer, 2011). The Company Democracy organizational spaces can be extended in the second set of spaces, beyond the organization, to include the society for shared added value creation (Figure 16.4).

The two sets of spaces can be interconnected, forming several subspaces where the Company Democracy Model is applied to satisfy the industry–society relationship.

The first subspace is related to the knowledge creation space, dealing primarily with the interaction between the organization and the society to identify societal needs and create business requirements that can ignite organizational knowledge and experiences toward resolving them. The

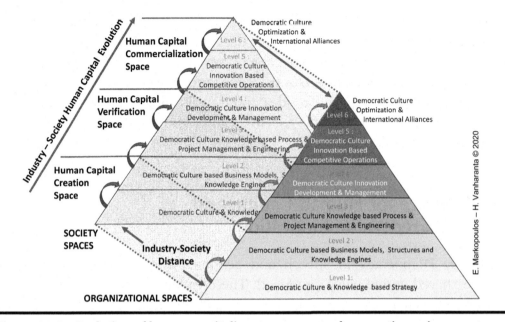

Figure 16.4 Evolution of human capitalism to corporate democratic environments.

essential characteristic of this space is knowledge validation with observations and external organizations' potential involvement to clarify and optimize societal needs. This can be a time-consuming process to provide the time necessary and identify the organizational knowledge that could create innovations for these specific needs.

The second subspace is related to the testing process on verifying the organization's implementation status and effectiveness to address a societal need. This space is a testing space where innovations are tested with the direct or indirect participation of society. The solutions can operate in the society with pilot projects or with external organizations representing specific social groups related to the innovation. These groups can take part in the solution with testing and optimization processes. The space needed for the maturity of a solution in society is related to the openness that space has for externals to contribute to this process.

The third subspace is related to the commercialization and utilization benefits by the organization and the society. Joint commercialization efforts can be achieved via various schemas such as public–private partnerships (PPP), operations licensing methods, or governmental authorities' participation that can offer free innovations to the citizens in return for tax increases (council tax, income tax, etc.). This space can also grow other strategic partnerships at national and international levels between societal entities and organizations. Besides the three main spaces for shared value creation, more subspaces can be generated based on the model's adaptation.

Democracy can generate knowledge-based innovation, which is the most significant innovation of all. The transformation of people's knowledge into innovation through democratic processes aligns corporate targets with real needs, which are usually the needs of both the economy and society.

16.11 Summary

Innovation is undoubtedly a trendy term, but it is not sure if all those who take the lead in defining innovation, especially in a quantitative sense, consider the investments needed for setting up effective organizational cultures that can provide space for innovation. Innovation needs democratic organization cultures that can offer everyone the opportunity to deliver their share of ideas, vision, and wisdom. It is not the smartest who can innovate, but those who have the knowledge and character to share it with others. Innovation is a philosophy and not a practice, process, project, or initiative. Innovation needs freedom, democracy, justice, and above all, time and space to grow.

As democracy is irresistible, and its progress is inevitable, the management and leadership will have to adopt democracy sooner or later (Slater, Bennis, 1990). Therefore, today, more than ever, there is a critical need to create space for Company Democracy and to let such structures be communicated, operated, controlled, and maintained systemically for the benefit of the people, the organizations, and the society. Companies need to educate and teach the basic methods to their employees at every level, but as a corporate shared value philosophy and not as a management practice. Such an approach would allow companies to understand how their employees perceive, understand, and interpret their everyday experiences and utilize them through the spaces of Company Democracy.

Organizations fail because they cannot identify their problems, not because they cannot solve them. Attempting to solve the wrong problem with the best practice is a waste of effort and time. The Company Democracy Model can contribute to the generation of business knowledge that can be utilized in achieving added value in the markets and shared value in society. This chapter's overall thinking is based on an Applied Philosophy for Management and Leadership via the development of the appropriate responsive dynamic space in which democratic cultures can offer innovation the needed room to breathe, grow, and return added value to organizations, the economy, society, and the people.

Questions for Review and Discussions

This chapter presents a comprehensive approach to why organizations fail to learn from their mistakes. It provides a democratic Co-Evolutionary and co-opetitive framework that can significantly contribute to organizational development, as long as the minimum space is given for freedom of speech and action.

Please see the questions below and review Chapter 16 and discuss the issues inside.

1. Do you see that many buzzwords in management and leadership don't deliver what they promise?
   1.1 Can you list five buzzwords that made an impact but did not deliver what had been expected?
   1.2 Why each one of them failed?
2. List five of today's buzzwords that you don't understand their context or contribution and might lead to wrong management decisions. Explain the risk of each one.
3. Does your company use management and leadership any buzzword(s) to promote a strategy, goal, or vision? If YES, what is this word(s)? In what context is it/are they used?
   3.1 If NO, how special/strong messages are communicated across the company's ecosystem?
   3.2 Who uses these buzzwords most in the company? How often?
   3.3 Do you think people know what those words mean and what it takes to apply them? Please provide examples.
4. Can you relate a face to the term 'neo-manager,' the people that moved up the hierarchy so fast and became management and leadership gurus and influences?
   4.1 List five neo-managers.
   4.2 What do you think about their success path?
   4.3 How much do they influence you, and in what terms?
5. What does the word 'Space' in the term 'Space for Company Democracy' mean?

5.1 What type of space? Space to think, to experiment, to express yourself, to breath?

5.2 How each of the spaces is needed for the Company Democracy Model to be applied effectively?

5.3 Why is space in general essential for the development of the human being?

6. Do you have 'space' in your company to work and live?

6.1 Do you think it could be better for you and the company to have this 'space'? If NO, why not?

6.1.1 Do you need space or more space?

6.1.2 What type of space do you need, and how can the company offer it to you?

6.2 If YES, how does the company provide you the space you need?

6.2.1 What kind of space is available for you?

7. "The Seven Clouds of Glory" present the benefits of space. Each space is a cloud of freedom to perform different types of activities.

If you could change the seven clouds, which ones would you have added or deleted to make the process more effective?

8. How does the 'space' in a company help its employees extend from added value to shared value innovation?

8.1 Can both types of innovation values be achieved if space is available?

8.2 Can people think more for the society when they look and see more for themselves?

8.3 Does your company apply such an approach? If NO, why not? Should they? And how?

8.4 If YES, how is it done, and what are the results?

9. In the Company Democracy spaces, we have to define and specify many text format concepts and deliver this information to our company members. We have to concentrate on what we say and try to be as exact in our sayings as possible. Too many words lead quickly to misunderstanding; however, the target is to deliver data and information to create the knowledge needed in the work roles.

9.1 Please ponder your company's communication so that the Company Democracy spaces are clear to everyone in your company.

Think that the created information suits the different levels of the Company Democracy Model.

9.2 Also, consider the problem in your company "How many iterations are needed in your company communication?" with the help of the chart of Figure 16Q.

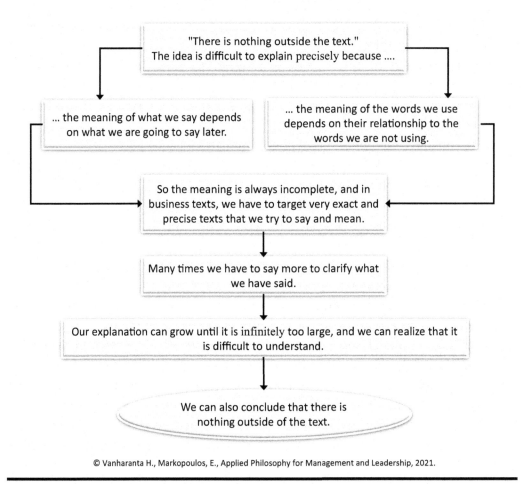

© Vanharanta H., Markopoulos, E., Applied Philosophy for Management and Leadership, 2021.

Figure 16Q Chart for Question 9 (c.f., ref. Buckingham, et al., 2011, Jacques Derrida, p. 311).

References

BBC, 2010. Dotcom bubble burst: 10 years on. http://news.bbc.co.uk/1/hi/business/8558257.stm

Bertoni, M., Duncan D., and Waldeck A., 2015. Knowing when to re-invent. *Harvard Business Review*, December.

Buckingham, W., King, Peter J., Burnham, D., Weeks, M., Hill, C., and Marenbon, J., 2011. *The Philosophy Book*. Dorling Kindersley Limited, London.

Cheng C. J. and Shiou E. C. C., 2008. Re-innovation: The construct, measurement, and validation. *Technovation*, 28 (10), 658–666.

Duncan Kidd, A., 1985. Productivity analysis for strategic management. In: Guth, W. (ed.) *Handbook of Business Strategy*. Warren Gorham & Lamont, Inc., Boston, FL. 17.1–17.25.

Johansen, A. and Sornette, D., 2000. The Nasdaq crash of April 2000: Yet another example of log-periodicity in a speculative bubble ending in a crash. *Eur. Phys. J. B*, 17, 319–328. https://doi.org/10.1007/s100510070147

Koulopoulos, T., 2009. *The Innovation Zone: How Great Companies Re-innovate for Amazing Success*. Davles-Black Publishing, Mountain View, California, USA.

Linkner, J., 2014. *The Road to Reinvention: How to Disrupt Your Organization before the Competition Does*. Jossey-Bass Publications, San Francisco. California, USA

Markopoulos E. and Vanharanta, H., 2014a. Democratic culture paradigm for organizational management and leadership strategies: The company democracy model. In: Proceedings of the 5th International Conference on Applied Human Factors and Ergonomics AHFE 2014, Kraków, Poland.

Markopoulos, E. and Vanharanta H., 2014b. Human perception, interpretation, understanding, and communication of company democracy. In: 14th International, and Interdisciplinary Conference of the Research Cooperation. European Culture s in Business and Corporate Communication (EUCO14), Turku, Finland.

Markopoulos, E. and Vanharanta, H., 2015. Company democracy model for development of shared value. In: 6th International Conference on Applied Human Factors and Ergonomics (AHFE), Las Vegas, NV.

McGregor, D., 1960. *The Human Side of Enterprise*. McGraw-Hill, New York.

Merriam-Webster Dictionary, 2016. http://www.merriam-webster.com/dictionary/reinvent

Porter, M. and Kramer, M., 2011. How to fix capitalism and unleash a new wave of growth. *Harvard Business Review*, January-February 2011, 61–77.

Slater, P. and Bennis, W., 1990. Democracy is inevitable. *Harvard Business Review*, 68 (5), 167–176.

Vanharanta H. and Markopoulos, E., 2013. Creating a dynamic democratic company culture for leadership, innovation, and competitiveness. In: Hellenic-Russian Forum. Athens, Greece.

Young, S. and Shields, M., 1994. Managing innovation costs: A study of cost conscious behavior among R&D professionals. *Journal of Management Accounting Research*, 6 (1), 175–176.

Chapter 17

The Dynamics of Company Democracy Culture: Enlightening the Black Hole in Knowledge Management

Executive Summary

Democracy offers the freedom for knowledge and opinions to be expressed unbiasedly, with justice and equality. However, this knowledge must be accurate, well-thought-out, and justified with facts, logic, common sense, and truth. The adaptation of the Company Democracy Model creates dynamic democratic cultures that identify and utilize the knowledge people have. More than that, it contributes to understanding what knowledge is, what true knowledge is, and how the proper knowledge grows and evolves through the Company Democracy Model levels. The model, however, can fail not due to lack of organizational knowledge and ideas or improper use of its processes, but due to the lack of correct understanding or ideas and knowledge with unreasonable expectations and justification. This chapter extends beyond the Company Democracy Model and attempts to define what true knowledge is in the knowledge management discipline in which the Company Democracy Model belongs and operates.

DOI: 10.4324/9781003158493-20

17.1 Introduction

The distance from democracy to anarchy can be very long or very short, allowing between those two systems various interpretations such as oligarchy, socialism, dictatorship, monarchy, liberalism, communism, and others. Today, being democratic in theory does not necessarily mean that democracy is also applied in practice. Democracy is often confused with theocracy, which gradually gathers and consolidates power in the hands of people driven by religion, where God is the people and, therefore, the people's voice and will. In other cases, democracy is also characterized by democratic overconfidence, over-optimism and neoliberalism, and political correctness serving the noisy few against the silent mass, violating the true democratic values and ideas.

These, however, are not the only cases that indicate loss of democratic meaning in thought and action. Throughout history, democracy has completely lost its original purpose, a purpose that people are either unaware of or unwilling to accept.

Understanding democracy requires knowledge, true knowledge with situational self-awareness ("Gnothi seauton") whether applied at a governmental, organizational, or individual level. It also requires meaningful understanding for all the people involved. Finally, it requires the ability to create, perceive, and adequately interpret knowledge within a culture where self-knowledge, self-control, intellectual capability, motivation, and social skills are promoted. Creating such a knowledge-driven organizational culture needs a deeper understanding of what knowledge is. Being democratic or applying democracy to an organization is not an easy task. Democracy that produces fake and invalid knowledge leads to anarchy and significantly impacts management decisions and leadership strategies.

Therefore, it is crucial for an organization to first understand the current degree of validity of its existing knowledge before applying democracy. Change in organizational democratic culture can be achieved with practical education, learning activities, and continuous training, which measure the employees' democratic culture progress. However, this is a slow development process and depends on the ways people understand the value of their knowledge contributions in this process.

Successful dynamic democracy cultures rely on successful knowledge management practices applied in the organizations to separate knowledge from information, thoughts from guesses, and truth from lies.

17.2 Knowledge and Knowledge Management

Knowledge management is one of the most significant management disciplines. It integrates nearly all management dimensions and practices and forms a pathway to success, development, prosperity, achievement, progress, and creativity.

Knowledge is a critical requirement in strategic management, organizational management, production management, financial management, quality management, etc. On the other hand, knowledge is a fuzzy concept, and it seems that there is a hole, a black hole, in the knowledge management discipline exactly on the definition of what knowledge is.

Although knowledge is undoubtedly a recipe for success, it has always been challenging to define what knowledge is and what it is not. Once such a distinction can be achieved, even to some degree, then anything related to knowledge can be significantly improved, starting from the knowledge elicitation process to the knowledge utilization, commercialization, etc.

True knowledge, which is what knowledge should be, cannot be obtained by human-made models, practices, algorithms, and processes. True knowledge should originate from the people themselves, who are the generators of knowledge. It shall derive from their experiences and expertise, regardless of the value and impact of the knowledge on specific organizational goals or preferences.

Today, all knowledge management models recognize people's role in the knowledge management discipline, mainly from the knowledge management perspective and less from the knowledge creation perspective. Big data, business intelligence, decision support systems, artificial intelligence, and other technologies tend to replace, if not remove, humans from knowledge creation, validation, verification, and utilization processes.

17.3 Knowledge Definitions

The definition of knowledge is based on the perception of reality, on the truth, on the clear and specific mental apprehension, and on the state or fact of knowing. *"Knowledge is a familiarity, awareness, or understanding of someone or something, such as facts, information, descriptions, or skills acquired through experience or education by perceiving, discovering, or learning. Knowledge can refer to a theoretical or practical understanding of a subject."* Knowledge can be implicit (as a practical skill or expertise) or explicit (as the theoretical understanding of an issue); it can be more or less formal or systematic [librarianshipstudies.com] (Oxford, 2016). In philosophy, the study of knowledge is called epistemology; the philosopher Plato famously defined knowledge as "justified true belief," though "well-justified true belief" is a complete definition as it accounts for the Gettier problems (Gettier, 1963).

There are undoubtedly many ways to define knowledge and how knowledge can be developed (Turri, 2012). Once knowledge is defined, according to the definition that suits better the one seeking knowledge, it can go through many and different management, development, and utilization practices. Knowledge acquisition is a crucial knowledge engineering process that involves complex cognitive processes such as perception, communication, and reasoning. At the same time, knowledge is also related to the capacity of acknowledgment in human beings (Stanley, 2002). Knowledge elicitation is a scientific definition based on explaining the domain-specific knowledge underlying human performance and reviewing the cognitive issues surrounding this practice. Knowledge elicitation is a sub-process of knowledge acquisition, i.e., a sub-process of knowledge engineering (Cooke, Durso, 2008). Knowledge creation is another term for knowledge that emphasizes the continuous transfer, combination, and conversion of different knowledge types, as users practice, interact, and learn (Nonaka, Toyama, Konno, 2000). Cook and Brown distinguish between knowledge and knowing and suggest that knowledge creation is a product of the interplay between them (Cook, Brown, 1999).

Knowledge analysis states conditions that are individually necessary and jointly sufficient for propositional knowledge (Stanford Encyclopedia of Philosophy, 2001). Propositional knowledge should be distinguished from knowledge of "acquaintance." Propositional knowledge, which is also called descriptive knowledge or declarative knowledge, is the type of expertise expressed primarily in indicative propositions or declarative sentences. This differentiates descriptive knowledge from what is known as "know-how," or procedural knowledge (on how a task can be delivered best), and "knowledge of," which is the knowledge by acquaintance (knowledge on something that exists).

Knowledge, however, is different than beliefs. A belief is internal memory or thought in someone's mind, and if it is right and well justified, it can be considered by many people as knowledge. The Gettier problem in philosophy is whether there are any other requirements before a belief can be accepted as knowledge.

Similar terms have been evolved to become modern management and engineering methods to deal with knowledge, once defined and utilized in various ways according to the individual or professional case. There are many definitions given for each term, and even more, words have been used to describe and analyze knowledge. Figure 17.1 presents an indicative structure of knowledge mapping, the process of surveying, assessing, and linking the information, knowledge, competencies, and proficiencies held by individuals and groups within an organization (Hyerle, 2008, Jafari, Akhavan, Bourouni, Amiri, 2009).

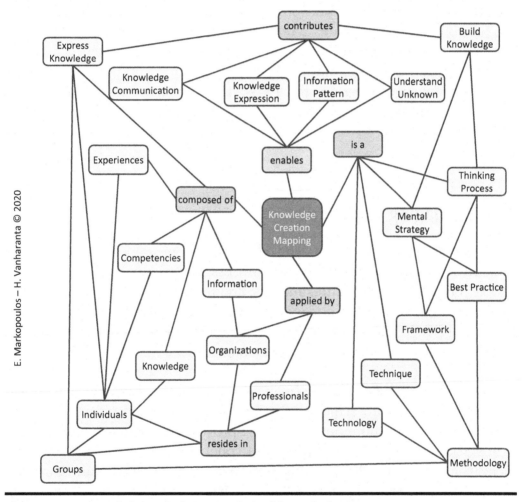

Figure 17.1   Knowledge creation mapping with a mind map.

Once knowledge has been defined, other knowledge terms arise to determine knowledge as knowledge, regardless of the knowledge type. Knowledge utilization in research is concerned with factors that explain the utilization of scientific and technical knowledge by decision-makers and those in professional practices, including research, scholarly, and programmatic intervention activities, to increase the ability to solve human problems. Knowledge utilization is a complex process involving political, organizational, socioeconomic, and attitudinal factors in addition to knowledge (Larsen, 1986).

Similar to knowledge management, knowledge transfer intends to capture, create, organize, and distribute knowledge. It is much more than a communication challenge, as emails, memorandums, or meetings would also be considered knowledge transfer practices. Knowledge transfer is more complicated for two reasons. First, knowledge resides in organizational members, tools, tasks, and sub-networks (Argote, Ingram, 2000), and second, most of the knowledge in organizations is tacit or hard to articulate (Nonaka, Takeuchi, 1995).

Defining and managing knowledge has been taken up under the title of knowledge management since the 1990s. The definitions of knowledge and the methods and models developed to master this effort are endless. They will keep on growing as long as people try to quantify and define knowledge individually.

17.4 Managing Knowledge

From the definitions, the terms, and the practices given, knowledge can be primarily considered a people-centric process. Knowledge not only exists in people, but it is all over nature, animals, and the physical phenomena, which can be defined, interpreted, and utilized by people, hopefully with good intentions. Knowledge management combines the definition of knowledge and its utilization process. Today knowledge management can be defined as the process of capturing, developing, sharing, and using organizational knowledge (Davenport, 1994). It is a multidisciplinary approach based on effective knowledge utilization toward achieving organizational goals and objectives (UNC, 2013) such as innovation, performance improvement, competitive advantage, extroversion, sharing best practices, and continuous organizational improvement (Gupta, Sharma, 2004). Knowledge management efforts can be related to organizational learning, differentiated, however, from their greater focus on managing knowledge as a strategic asset and encouraging sharing knowledge (Maier, 2007). Furthermore, they can be seen as a concrete mechanism for continuous organizational learning (Sanchez, 1996).

Human beings' quest to define and extract knowledge toward its utilization has become one of the most challenging management issues. If knowledge management can be applied successfully, many development opportunities can be revealed. New products, new services, quality management, project management, product management, innovation management, strategy management, organizational management, and many more initiatives, activities, and processes can be addressed or developed in depth and precisely. Once knowledge exists, it can be explored effectively and handled even more effectively. There are no limits to what can be achieved with knowledge and where it can be applied.

17.5 Modeling Knowledge

Since knowledge and knowledge management have been presented as a new management trend, several models have been developed to emphasize different knowledge management perspectives, approaches, methods, algorithms, systems, and practices.

The Nonaka and Takeuchi knowledge management model focuses on knowledge spirals that explain the transformation of tacit knowledge into explicit knowledge and then back again as the basis for individual, group, and organizational innovation and learning (Nonaka, Takeuchi, 1995).

The Skandia Intellectual Capital Model of Knowledge Management was developed by a Swedish firm called Skandia to measure its intellectual capital. The model focuses on the importance of equity, human, customer, and innovation in managing the flow of knowledge within and externally across partners' networks. The model emphasizes the human, that is, the customer, and uses structural metrics for tight organizational control (Karl, 1997).

Demerest's knowledge management model emphasizes the construction of knowledge within an organization. This construction is not limited to scientific inputs but extends to the social construction of knowledge. The model assumes that constructed knowledge can then be embodied within the organization, not just through explicit programs but also social interchange (Lank, 1997).

Frid's knowledge management model is a knowledge management maturity assessment framework based on the following five knowledge management implementation levels: knowledge-chaotic, knowledge-aware, knowledge-focused, knowledge-managed, and knowledge-centric (Caganova, Szilva, Bawa, 2015; Frid, 2003).

Stankosky and Baldanza's knowledge management framework addresses enabling factors such as learning, culture, leadership, organization, and technology. This framework presents knowledge management as encompassing a wide range of disciplines that include cognitive science, communication, individual and organizational behavior, psychology, finance, economics, human resource, management, strategic planning, system thinking, process reengineering, system engineering, computer technologies, and software and library science (Stankosky, Baldanza, 2001).

Kogut and Zander's knowledge management model is based on the concept that knowledge is created and transferred better within organizations than in the markets. Knowledge, which consists of data, information, and know-how, is held by individuals and expressed in regularities by which members cooperate in a social community. Like social communities, firms act as capabilities repositories determined by the social knowledge embedded in enduring individual relationships, structured by organizing principles. These principles refer to the process of organizing knowledge that establishes the context of coordination and discourse between individuals with contrasting expertise. Furthermore, it recreates the organization over time in response to its members' revised expectations and identity (Kogut, Zander, 1996).

From the indicative literature, most of the knowledge management models treat knowledge as something that can be considered standard, correct, and valid. Therefore, they emphasize how knowledge can be managed with practices and techniques based on proactive and reactive analysis, computations, and statistics. Knowledge management models are primarily about management, neglecting, in a way, the knowledge engineering process which precedes knowledge management.

Knowledge engineering is a highly people-centric discipline, and where people are involved, the degree of uncertainty is significantly increased. Managing a valid set of information is different from managing a vague collection of information. If knowledge is wrongly collected and constructed, then no management practice can interpret it successfully.

17.6 The Black Hole

Knowledge is considered power, and power is freedom compared to the slavery of ignorance. Socrates claimed that one thing he knows is that he knows nothing. Any increase of the circle of knowledge also increases the circumference of the darkness around it (Fine, 2008). Aristotle believed that all men, by nature, desire to learn, but the question is if it is possible to learn without learning themselves first (Cantor, Klein, 1969).

A human cannot possess anything that s/he does not understand. However, knowledge is not enough as it is nothing more than a tool that can be useful only to those who use it wisely. Knowledge is the optimal democratic source of power, but not using knowledge legitimately and ethically can bring devastating results. Therefore, is it a duty of the free and enlightened to reach for the truth and create through the truth (Markopoulos, 2013).

Countries grow and prosper based on the knowledge they produce. A society that fears knowledge fears itself. The worst enemy of knowledge is ignorance, the illusion of knowledge, and imperfect knowledge, as people are trained primarily to 'believe' and not to 'think.'

Most of the knowledge engineering and management models fail today to tackle knowledge creation for two reasons. The first one is based on people's ability to learn from themselves as knowledge creators, and the second is the degree of truth in the knowledge created. These challenges form a black hole in the knowledge management and engineering discipline as lack of identifying the science and defining the term properly results in chaos.

To tackle these challenges, a responsive innovation culture needs to be established to support the ethos and the bravery of those who dare to learn to know themselves first. The ancient Hellenic Delphic maxim "Gnothi seauton" (Know thyself), one of the oldest quotes about knowledge, is directed to the human soul. It is a maxim derived from the Delphi oracle teller Pythia, words of wisdom that could behave sent by any God (Parke, Wormell, 1956). Gnothi seauton is half the equation on understanding knowledge. The other half is the generation of the true knowledge that derives from Gnothi seauton.

Thus, people can have Gnothi seauton, know themselves, but still generate false knowledge. This seemingly impossible but probable case is the black hole in the discipline. People know themselves in the wrong way, which they think is the right way. They want to help but don't know how, obsessed with passions, selfishness, ego, anger, ambition, greed, and other feelings that negatively impact their character, generate the wrong self-awareness and therefore wrong knowledge.

It is not people's fault if wrong knowledge is generated despite their hard efforts to generate true knowledge. People cannot know the outcome of their knowledge since they do not know themselves. They feel that they know themselves and give their best without being aware that they are mostly controlled by their passions and less by their minds. Plato describes this black hole with the cave's allegory in his work *The Republic*, a classic literature masterpiece (Losin, 1996).

This problem, however, cannot be resolved by any human-engineered process model. Even the Company Democracy Model, which honors and respects all the people in an organization by offering freedom and the opportunity to stand out and work united in a co-opetitive and not competitive environment toward knowledge generation, can fail. People get the chance to speak out democratically and produce valuable knowledge, but this does not make their knowledge authentic or valid, even if they think they know themselves or learn to know themselves. It turns out that in most cases, people don't know themselves at all, and even if they think they do, the gap between the actual and the perceived reality can be chaotic.

It seems that the creation of true knowledge cannot be resolved with management, engineering, or even medical disciplines, neither with the use of innovative prediction systems or meditation treatments. True knowledge is more of a spiritual issue than a social one. True knowledge is composed of elements people can use to think and generate knowledge only if they open up their hearts first and then their minds.

True knowledge is the only requirement considered valuable and constructive for all management disciplines. No knowledge management model, or management model in general, can succeed without true knowledge. Lack of true knowledge makes management models function within Plato's cave, in an illusion, in theory, weak, fragile, powerless, and useless.

Without true knowledge, all decisions, results, strategies, and anything derived from modern and advanced management processes, algorithms, methods, and technologies are directed toward a false result. Nothing can light the way. Nothing can deliver quality, success, and effectiveness unless it is developed with true knowledge. Management and knowledge management models based on uncertain knowledge affect significant organizational decisions and lead to risky results regardless of the efforts made to make specific, confident, concrete, correct, and wise knowledge contributions.

On the other hand, acquiring true knowledge is and will always be the biggest challenge in management. It is the black hole that automatically destroys any management theory and initiative before it even starts. The black hole makes all those called management gurus and neo-managers look incompetent, making risky and dangerous decisions for the economy and humanity by following from ignorance the wrong methods and practices in a correct way.

17.7 True Knowledge

True knowledge is composed of the elements of 'Knowledge,' 'Love,' and 'Ruth.' True knowledge can be generated if love (care) is in place to create the trust needed for the truth to come out. The sequence or the order in which these three elements are carried out cannot be determined. Their order is related to each person's philosophy and the situation they apply it to. Each order gives a different interpretation and strategy toward identifying true knowledge. 'Love–Truth–Knowledge,' 'Knowledge–Truth–Love,' 'Love–Knowledge–Truth,' or 'Truth–Knowledge–Love,' and so on can be some of the various combinations with the right knowledge elements, giving different approaches and perspectives but the same result. Regardless of how these elements are placed, they must all coexist with the same value. There cannot be, for example, a lot of knowledge with some love and limited truth. Since the degree of defining and measuring true knowledge elements can be considered a fuzzy variable, this degree can only be defined conceptually as the elements of truth, love, and knowledge have the same value to all people. Therefore, no further definitions or metrics are required.

Truth and good (from love) complement each other for the creation of wisdom. To love, people must know what is right. In *The Truth of All Things*, Josef Pieper writes: "The good is essentially dependent upon and interiorly penetrated by knowledge" (Pieper, 1962).

Knowledge derives from the relationship of the intellect to what is known. Therefore, a fundamental unity must exist between knowledge and love. Knowledge needs love to act effectively, and love requires the knowledge to understand things right. Similarly, Sophia and Phronesis can function properly only when joined, just like the will (desire) and the intellect, which cannot be separate functions either. This corresponds to the transcendental attribute of "one," which denotes integrity, inner, and wholeness. This dynamic unity manifests itself in intelligent and ordered life. Ultimately, knowledge and love are impacted by the same unity source and element: the truth.

Creating true knowledge can be easy for a few and impossible for others. True knowledge is not obtained through hard work, experiences, management discipline, or academic studies. As true knowledge is based on the triptych of Love, Truth, Knowledge, knowledge cannot be true if not delivered with truth through love. Lack of love, on the other hand, cannot create true knowledge. Likewise, no knowledge is valid if it is not given with truth. Keeping or hiding knowledge delivers false or incomplete knowledge. Love cannot be considered only as emotional love but also as a love of care, a sense of respect, and sincere feelings. People are honest with each other if they respect those who deserve their genuine feelings. Under the same concept, the knowledge that is given without care is not knowledge. Likewise, knowledge is not knowledge if not shared with the truth.

In any case, all three elements that compose true knowledge need to be aligned and analyzed separately as each combination gives a different path toward achieving the same result, which is true knowledge.

Innovation, for example, is nothing more than true knowledge. Anything developed with true and original knowledge can be innovative and successful. Still, in this case, the questions are: 'Where is the right knowledge in an innovative initiative?' and 'Who has it?', 'How can such a response to knowledge creation for an innovation environment be developed, maintained, and co-evolved?'

A know-it-all attitude demonstrates ignorance and fear. The power and value of true knowledge cannot be questioned. It is the only knowledge that leads to growth and prosperity through people's union toward a common goal, vision, and perspective. The triadic unity of love, truth, and knowledge can lead to absolute freedom. Freedom from the darkness of ignorance and imperfection. Freedom to create what one can create. Freedom leads to unity, and unity leads to freedom.

Love can transform knowledge into a blessing, the blessing of creation. True knowledge is a blessing that requires spiritual knowledge to grow internal knowledge that can identify, receive, interpret, and practice true knowledge. Acquiring true knowledge does not need only an open mind but mainly an honest soul. Souls can only be opened with love. Love must precede knowledge. Love unites people and creates conditions for compound development through the creation and exploitation of knowledge.

17.8 Knowledge and Knowledge Management Driven Company Cultures

Knowledge management and managing knowledge is what monopolizes and attracts the interest of modern businesses and organizations. Power has always been a means for effectiveness, high productivity, and good profitability. Successful management in any area can result in various types of effectiveness, with each one contributing to organizational profitability, productivity, and performance. On the other hand, what is missing from this equation to success is that knowledge must preexist before managed. No product management can exist without product engineering, and no product can be engineered without the knowledge to conceive it, plan it, and develop it. Therefore, no knowledge means no product, and no product means no sales, no financial management to exercise on the revenues, no profit management, and of course, no business management. Knowledge management cannot exist without knowledge engineering; knowledge engineering cannot exist without people; people cannot deliver knowledge without freedom of speech. Freedom of speech cannot exist without democracy.

Not many knowledge management models emphasize the utilization of the people and the people as sources and centers for knowledge creation. Such models need a sense of democratic freedom and certain leadership support to all diverse groups personally and professionally. It is democracy within a dynamic organizational culture that can empower the broad participation of the employees' knowledge creation that defines its intellectual capital. Organizational development efforts should be directed to developing its people's human capacity and intellectuality first before considering how they will manage products and services for financial sustainability and market dominance. Knowledge engineering is a complex discipline to be understood and even more complicated to be executed. It is a people-oriented process within a dynamic democratic culture that balances leadership and management on all company assets.

17.9 Knowledge Creation and Wisdom Generation

Chapter 9 presented four important activities to knowledge creation and wisdom generation: data handling activities, information processing activities, knowledge creation activities, and wisdom generation activities. The chapter broke down the activities into several sub-activities and showed a supply and demand relationship between them. There were 22 different data handling examples, which describe the overall collection of data from various activities, starting from accumulating data and ending with data storage. The demand for these concrete ways of human activities comes from information demand. Humans need information, and it is processed with different human activities. This demand exists and possesses a considerable number of various information processing activities.

In the example given, the formed information in different categories, starting from acquainting information and ending to transferring information, is a feed to knowledge-creating activities. This human knowledge creation maintains the demand through information demand down to data demand. Knowledge creation activities, in turn, start in this example from achieving objectives and ending with understanding objectives, patterns, relations, and interrelationships. In the following knowledge creation flow chart, 40 different knowledge creation activities have been picked, understanding that the list is not complete. Figure 17.2 shows the relationships between data handling activities, information processing activities, and knowledge creation activities. The flowchart also shows the wisdom generation activities, which belong to the demand side of knowledge creation activities.

Wisdom generating activities are the 'products' of this flow chart and describe the idea that humans are behind the data handling activities, information processing activities, and knowledge creation activities. Twenty-four (24) different activities have been initially categorized under wisdom generation, understanding that there are many different ways to create wisdom. The balanced leadership and management model presented in the Management Windshield shows the main activities and indicates how a balanced way can serve the employees and the company.

Figure 17.2 indicates how people can be active in data handling, information processing, and knowledge creation to increase collective wisdom in the company. The creation of true knowledge always starts with people, the workforce. This created knowledge serves the company's added value creation and supports the company workforce to behave according to the ideas presented in the Company Democracy Model. All the human activities are needed to fulfill the requirements to reach higher and higher levels in the Company Democracy Model.

17.10 The Company Democracy Model on Knowledge Engineering and Management

The discipline closest to the Company Democracy Model is knowledge management. The Company Democracy Model can be characterized as a knowledge management model. It can also be defined as a model for innovation management, human resources management, strategic management, leadership, and any other discipline related to its operations. Still, knowledge management is the core and most precise discipline that the model serves and represents.

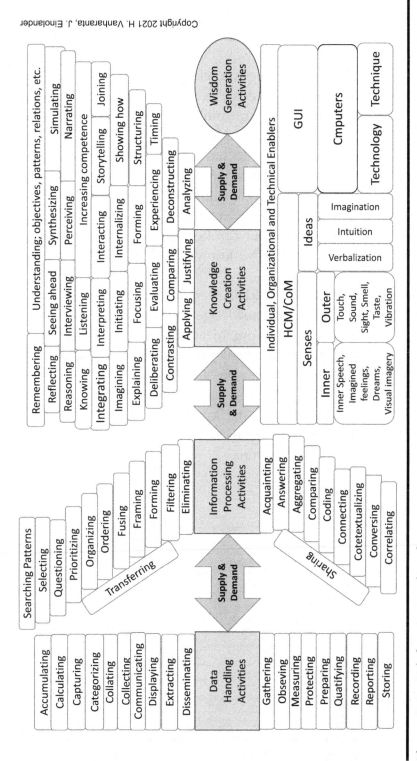

Figure 17.2 Wisdom generation chart.

All the Company Democracy Model levels serve the evolution of knowledge to achieve various organizational goals at each level. Those goals and the effectiveness of the model depend on the quality of knowledge produced and conceived.

The need for original and true knowledge is what the first level of the model targets. Guesses, abstract ideas, not reasonably documented thoughts and opinions are welcomed but are unlikely to reach the second level and certainly impossible to get to the third level.

Even though the model seems to have profit-driven organizational goals for growth through people's knowledge, it also supports strong educational purposes. It teaches the employees to think and express their knowledge reasonably, clearly, and in a well-justified manner. The quality needed for an idea to evolve from one level to another can be considered the motive employees have to generate less but qualitative knowledge instead of more quantitative information.

The Company Democracy Model, if applied effectively, offers the space in all levels for the employee's knowledge to mature and develop. Space for Company Democracy is vital for organizational culture. It provides the time needed for the information to be transformed into knowledge, the knowledge to be transformed into true knowledge, and the true knowledge to be transformed into innovation that will bring competitiveness and extroversion to the organization. Figure 17.3 presents the knowledge maturity process for both the people and the organization that adopt the Company Democracy Model within a dynamic democratic culture.

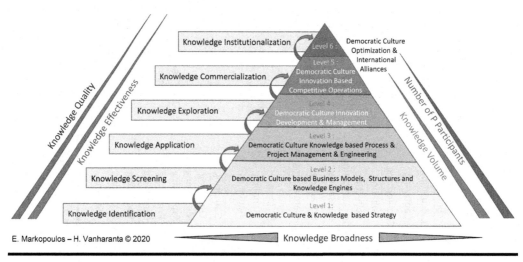

Figure 17.3 Knowledge maturity within the Company Democracy Model.

The model's pyramid shape can be interpreted as the evolution of knowledge based on its value and validity. The lower levels produce more knowledge than what is found at higher levels. Knowledge analysis, screening, and evaluation restrict the evolution of false and invalid knowledge in the model's higher levels. The dynamic democratic culture is an environment that supports the continuity of the Company Democracy Model operations.

Regardless of the organizational goals in adopting the Company Democracy Model, no results can be achieved unless a dynamic democratic culture is in place to support, educate, and motivate the people to identify the true knowledge that each employee has and contributes to personal and organizational development. The success of the Company Democracy Model is related to the truth in the organizations' knowledge. This truth impacts all uses of the model. It is either the validity of the human intellectual capital or the added and shared value innovations created to support the organization, the economy, and society.

Knowledge engineering and, even more, knowledge management cannot be performed effectively unless true knowledge is generated and managed under the right knowledge elements (truth, love, knowledge).

17.11 Summary

In today's world, applying fundamental knowledge elements can be considered impossible as people are trained to believe and not to think. The knowledge derived from true knowledge has no size, degree of importance, value, impact, or characteristics that people use to give the attention needed for various types of knowledge. True knowledge is one and only, and regardless of whom it comes out, it has the same significance and contribution as any knowledge derived from any wise person.

As all people have been created equally and therefore can think equally, democracy provides the freedom needed to generate knowledge equally. In company environments, the Company Democracy Model adopted within a dynamic democratic culture extends democratic freedom for knowledge creation and expression. Furthermore, it educates people to deliver true knowledge and benefit from its opportunities.

However, true knowledge seems to be a black hole in the knowledge engineering and management discipline for two reasons. The first is that people demand opportunities without knowing themselves, lacking Gnothi seauton, and the second is that people do not love or care enough for one another.

Therefore, they don't appreciate the opportunities given or don't believe in them. Even though loving and caring for each other is a fundamental principle in all religions of the world, people fail to follow and apply their fundamental faith: if it is impossible to love or care for each other, it is impossible to work constructively, effectively, and successfully with each other.

Without true knowledge, no engineering, and even more, no management science or discipline can progress. Management cannot move with false knowledge as a lack of true knowledge destroys any strategy. Therefore, before developing advanced management models, theories, metrics, algorithms, processes, artificial intelligence, and environments that promise to generate knowledge from nothing, it is more important to turn these efforts toward developing similar practices that could help people and the society come closer and generate the desired knowledge themselves for themselves. Such Gnothi seauton will create the true knowledge needed for the technology to process it and further deliver beyond any expectation.

True knowledge cannot be generated by everyone today, but the few who can attempt it are enough for a start. It needs more than a single individual. It requires an exchange of giving and taking for true knowledge to be created. It is a collective, not an individual process. It needs the 'we,' not the 'I.' This unity needs more than one to be built. True knowledge is everywhere and in everything, but it needs an open heart first to see it, listen to it, and say it. Those who have eyes to see let them see, those who have ears to listen let them listen, and those who have a mouth to speak let them speak (Conzelmann, Lindemann, 1999). The complexity derives from simplicity. Things are simple, but people make them complex due to their incapability or insecurity. Simplicity may be the next management keyword for the global economy, but it is tough to achieve it. The simple things are also the most extraordinary, and only the wise can see them (Coelho, 1998). Simplicity requires love, truth, knowledge, and a dynamic democratic organizational culture to grow within. Those who have that can change the world.

Questions for Review and Discussions

The model does not fail due to lack of organizational knowledge and ideas or improper use of its processes, but due to the lack of right understanding and ideas with unreasonable expectations. This chapter extends beyond the Company Democracy Model and attempts to define what true knowledge is in the knowledge management discipline to which the Company Democracy Model belongs.

Please answer the following questions and review and discuss the issues inside.

1. True knowledge is composed of the elements of 'Knowledge,' 'Love,' and 'Truth.' How would you prioritize these elements and why?
   1.1 What is their sequence that can produce true knowledge based on your experience and beliefs? Explain your answer and provide an example.
2. What is the understanding of true knowledge in your company?
   2.1 Do you think true knowledge is generated better than typical or superficial knowledge?
   2.2 If YES, how is this being achieved? How are employees treated to deliver true knowledge?
   2.3 If NO, what blocks the generation of true knowledge? Please provide examples.
3. Can an organization measure the degree of knowledge?
   3.1 If YES, how can this be done?
   3.2 What are the elements that compute the degree of knowledge?
   3.3 If NO, why not?
   3.4 What needs to be measured to calculate true knowledge, and how feasible is it to measure such elements?
4. Does your company measure true knowledge?
   4.1 If YES, how is it estimated?
   4.2 If NO, why not?
5. Can knowledge maps help you reason where the knowledge comes from and how valid can it be?
   5.1 Draw a knowledge mind map on the sources of knowledge in your company.
   5.2 Examine the mind map, group the knowledge sources, and critically analyze them.
   5.3 What type of knowledge do you think each group of knowledge sources generate?
   5.4 Why did you reach this conclusion?
   5.5 What can you do to develop and generate more true knowledge?
6. To what extent do you believe that people are knowledge engines? Explain your answer.
   6.1 Do you think that your company sees people as knowledge engines?

6.2 If NO, why not? Where does your company seek knowledge engines, and what process does it follow for that?

6.3 If YES, what function does your company follow to keep those knowledge engines running?

7. If knowledge can be generated from the people in a company, does this makes it true knowledge?

7.1 If YES, explain your thinking.

7.2 If NO, why do people not necessarily produce true knowledge?

7.3 What impacts their ability to see and deliver the truth?

7.4 Describe your thinking and provide examples.

8. What methods and processes can be used to increase the amount of knowledge in your company?

8.1 Does your company use such techniques or approaches?

8.2 If YES, which ones, and what are the results?

8.3 If NO, why not? Provide examples.

9. What are the relationships between data, information, knowledge, and wisdom?

9.1 How is wisdom generated?

9.2 Explain these relationships with examples. Is your company data-driven, information-driven, knowledge-driven, or wisdom-driven?

9.3 Explain your answer by relating the type with your company's activities and strategy.

9.4 If it is more than one type, please explain which part of the company is which type.

10. How fast new knowledge penetrates your company? And how fast wisdom is created in your company?

10.1 What mechanisms, if any, accelerate knowledge input, acceptance, and utilization in your company?

10.2 What are the related tools, if any, that transform this knowledge into wisdom?

11. To what extent does technology create knowledge?

11.1 What technologies exist in your company that generate knowledge?

11.2 What operations do they support?

11.3 How does your company utilize this knowledge?

11.4 Explain your answer and provide examples.

12. The Company Democracy Model is considered a model that discovers, matures, utilizes knowledge, and turns it into wisdom. Furthermore, is it considered to be able to produce true knowledge?

12.1 How is this happening?

12.2 Explain the process of knowledge evolution in the Company Democracy Model, from the discovery to wisdom.

12.3 Explain how true knowledge can be produced or not through the Company Democracy Model.

13. Please follow the thinking inside the chart of Figure 17Q below. Try to describe the two different business worlds and the knowledge creation with different business constructs and concepts. Find help also from Figure 17.2.

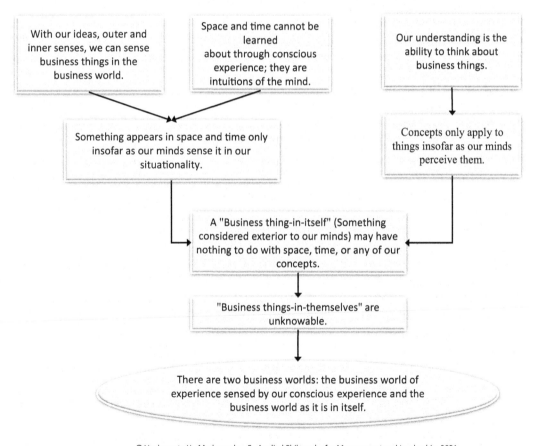

With our ideas, outer and inner senses, we can sense business things in the business world.

Space and time cannot be learned about through conscious experience; they are intuitions of the mind.

Our understanding is the ability to think about business things.

Something appears in space and time only insofar as our minds sense it in our situationality.

Concepts only apply to things insofar as our minds perceive them.

A "Business thing-in-itself" (Something considered exterior to our minds) may have nothing to do with space, time, or any of our concepts.

"Business things-in-themselves" are unknowable.

There are two business worlds: the business world of experience sensed by our conscious experience and the business world as it is in itself.

© Vanharanta H., Markopoulos, E., Applied Philosophy for Management and Leadership, 2021.

Figure 17Q Chart for Question 12 (c.f., ref. Buckingham, et al., 2011, Immanuel Kant, p. 167).

References

Argote, L. and Ingram, P., 2000. Knowledge transfer: A basis for competitive advantage in firms. *Organizational Behavior and Human Decision Processes*, 82 (1), 150–169.

Buckingham, W., King, Peter J., Burnham, D., Weeks, M., Hill, C., and Marenbon, J., 2011. *The Philosophy Book*. Dorling Kindersley Limited, London.

Caganova, D., Szilva, I., and Bawa, M., 2015. Application of Frid's knowledge management model to an industrial enterprise. *AMM*, 795, 16–23. https://doi.org/10.4028/www.scientific.net/amm.795.16

Cantor, N. F. and Klein, P. L., eds., 1969. *Ancient Thought: Plato and Aristotle. Monuments of Western Thought 1*. Blaisdell Publishing Co., Waltham, MA.

Coelho, P., 1998. *The Alchemist*. Harper San Francisco, San Francisco.

Conzelmann, H. and Lindemann A., 1999. *Interpreting the New Testament: An Introduction to the Principles and Methods of New Testament Exegesis*. English translation. Hendrickson, Peabody, MA.

Cook, S.D.N. and Brown, J.S., 1999. Bridging epistemologies: The generative dance between organizational knowledge and organizational knowing. *Organization Science*, 10 (4), 381–400.

Cooke, N. and Durso, F., 2008. *Handbook of Applied Cognition*. Wiley, Hoboken, NJ, 2nd Edition.

Davenport, T. H., 1994. Saving I.T.'s soul: Human-centered information management. *Harvard Business Review*, 72 (2), 119–131.

Fine, G., 2008. Does Socrates claim to know that he knows nothing? *Oxford Studies in Ancient Philosophy*, 35, 49–88.

Frid, R., 2003. *A Common K.M. Framework for the Government of Canada: Frid Framework for Enterprise Knowledge Management*. Canadian Institute of Knowledge Management, Ontario, Canada.

Gettier, E., 1963. Is justified true belief knowledge? *Analysis*, 23 (6), 121–3.

Gupta, J. and Sharma, S., 2004. *Creating Knowledge-based Organizations*. Idea Group Publishing, Boston, MA.

Hyerle, D., 2008. Thinking maps®: A visual language for learning. In: *Thinking Maps®: A Visual Language for Learning*, ISBN: 978-1-84800-149-7. [Online] http://www.springerlink.com/content/x57121720731381j/

Jafari, M., Akhavan P., Bourouni A., and Amiri, R. H., 2009. A framework for the selection of knowledge mapping techniques. *Journal of Knowledge Management Practice*, 10 (1), [Online] http://www.tlainc.com/articl180.htm

Karl, M. W., 1997. Integrating intellectual capital and knowledge management. *Long Range Planning*, 30 (3), 399–405.

Kogut, B. and Zander, U., 1996. What firms do? Coordination, identity, and learning. *Organization Science*, 7 (5), 502–23.

Lank, E., 1997. Leveraging invisible assets: The human factor. *Journal of Long Range Planning*, 30 (3), 406–12.

Larsen, J. K., 1986. Critical variables in utilization research. In: G. M. Beal, W. Dissanayake and S. Konoshima (Eds.) *Knowledge Generation, Exchange and Utilization*. Westview Press, Boulder, Colorado, 345–367.

Losin, P., 1996. Education and Plato's parable of the cave. *The Journal of Education*, 178 (3), 49–65. http://www.jstor.org/stable/42741825

Maier, R., 2007. *Knowledge Management Systems: Information and Communication Technologies for Knowledge Management*. Springer, Berlin.

Markopoulos, E., 2013. The Kapodistrian principles for freedom through knowledge and education. In: Ioanis Kapodistrias Conference. Athens, Greece.

Nonaka, I. and Takeuchi, H., 1995. *The Knowledge-creating Company: How Japanese Companies Create the Dynamics of Innovation*. Oxford University Press, New York.

Nonaka, I., Toyama, R., and Konno, N., 2000. SECI, Ba, and leadership: A unified model of dynamic knowledge creation. *Long Range Planning*, 33, 5–34.

Oxford, 2016. http://oxforddictionaries.com/view/entry/m_en_us1261368#m_en _us1261368

Parke, H. and Wormell D., 1956. *The Delphic Oracle*, Vol. 1. Basil Blackwell, Oxford, 389.

Pieper, J., 1962. *Guide to St. Thomas Aquinas*. Pantheon, New York.

Sanchez, R., 1996. *Strategic Learning and Knowledge Management*. Wiley, Chichester.

Stanford Encyclopedia of Philosophy, 2001. The analysis of knowledge. First published February 6, 2001; substantive revision November 15, 2012. http://plato.st anford.edu/entries/knowledge-analysis/

Stankosky, M. and Baldanza, C., 2001. *A Systems Approach to Engineering a KM System*. Unpublished manuscript.

Stanley, C., 2002. *Knowing and Acknowledging, Must We Mean What We Say?* Cambridge University Press, Cambridge, 238–266.

Turri, J., 2012. Is knowledge justified true belief? *Synthese*, 184 (3), 247–259.

University of North Carolina (UNC), 2013. *Introduction to Knowledge Management*. The University of North Carolina, Chapel Hill.

Chapter 18

Applying the Company Democracy Model: From Theory to Practice

Executive Summary

The Company Democracy Model comprises six levels, and its adaptation follows the Spiral approach in a staged evolutionary process. However, the model can be adopted in several other ways based on organizational capability, maturity, management, leadership, strategy, priorities, and commitment. Therefore, the Company Democracy Model cannot impose or strongly suggest a specific adaptation process but can only recommend several from which an organization can select or combine the one to follow. Regardless of the chosen adaptation approach, it must be noted that the Company Democracy Model creates and impacts the organizational culture. Therefore time, commitment, and support are needed to build this new culture or enhance the existing one. Change management practices can be applied in the adaptation of the Company Democracy Model but are not required. It is the leadership's power and charisma to deliver effective and inspirational management that will motivate the people and the organization toward building and functioning in a democratic organizational culture for the benefit of all.

DOI: 10.4324/9781003158493-21

18.1 Overview of the Company Democracy Model

The Company Democracy Model is the methodology and technique to create organizational information and knowledge that contributes to developing insights, ideas, and innovations, making the competitive advantages needed to achieve extroversion. It is a model for managing and leading innovation initiatives within a company under individual and collective approaches (cf. www .evolute.fi). The model is based on its ability to identify the data, information, and knowledge within a company and transform it into new projects, products, or services either for internal use in the optimization of organizational operations or for external help to identify new markets and opportunities.

What is the model? The model is a combination of management practices and technologies (strategic management, knowledge, innovation, human resources, technology, production, leadership, processes, etc.), through which a human-focused, people-centered framework of freedom for expression enables the production of knowledge as the raw material for personal and organizational development and growth. It starts as an individual process and soon becomes a collective effort. Through the model, employees learn, support team-working, participate, and innovate by expressing ideas, insights, and knowledge. It is a systemic way of activating individuals to knowledge creation and sharing, a very significant activity inside an organization (cf. www.evolute.fi).

What the model is NOT: The model is NOT a classic and straightforward model of business reorganization, reengineering, strategy, process improvement, quality assurance, and such practices they are being repeated over the years by the non-specialized and general type of business consultants, neo-managers, and gurus. It is not a silver bullet or a magic recipe, and it will not save a company unless the company accepts and adopts a democratic organizational culture in practice.

18.2 The Company Democracy Model Spiral

The Company Democracy Model is implemented through the execution of its six levels. The levels seem to follow a serial path, which does not necessarily start from level 1. Achieving each level does not secure the organization and the projects supported through the model, presence at the achieved level, or advancement to the next. The organization can descend a level unless the criteria to stay in the achieved level and grow to the next are applied effectively. The evolution of knowledge through the Company Democracy Model can be seen as a spiral-oriented process that advances knowledge from one level to the next and descends it if the current level activities are not delivered effectively. The level requirements are not sustained or fulfilled.

The spiral diagram presented in Figure 18.1 illustrates this relationship and points out two critical activities at each level. The first is the organization's maturity assessment before entering a level, and the second is the actual execution of the activities that compose the level. The following example presents the ups and downs a knowledge contribution can have in the Spiral process. The example given is for level 4, which is related to innovation management.

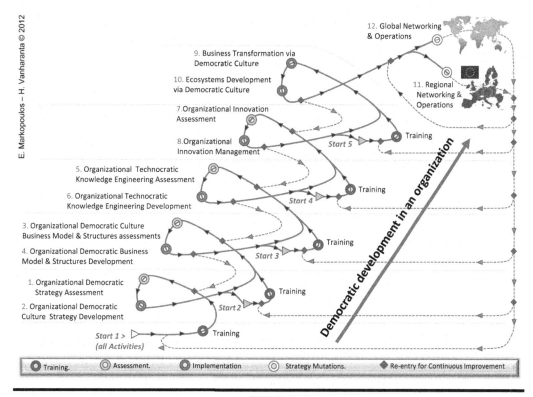

Figure 18.1   The Company Democracy Model spiral evolution.

For a knowledge contribution to move from level 3 to level 4, the organization must ensure that the knowledge which has been transformed into a product or service in level 3 has matured enough in the market, innovation elements have been identified, and this new product/service is now ready for further research and development. Before leaving level 3 and attempt to enter level 4, the organization is assessed on its ability to deliver activities and commitments needed to turn the current level 3 product/service into an innovative product/service in level 4. This assessment covers the availability of human resources, budget, organization support, and other key elements needed to move from a red ocean (existing market) to a blue ocean (uncontested market).

Without researchers (human resources) or research funding, there is no reason for organizations to enter the fourth level with the specific project/service since it is not possible to execute the expected and scheduled activities of that level and deliver the results that can advance the project to the next level, level 5 in this case, for the identification of blue oceans with the utilization of the innovation's competitiveness. In such a case, the organization does not attempt to move toward the next level until the previous level (level 3) has been mastered and the preconditions of the next level (level 4, in this case) are satisfied.

However, even a successful pass through the upcoming level assessment does not ensure that the organization can stay on the next level until the level activities have been completed. Staying, for example, at level 4, the organization must secure the funding needed to turn the product of level 3 into innovation through research and innovation activities. The organization must also guarantee that the implementation of these activities will not be disrupted by many issues such as poor fund management, lack of necessary expertise, teaming conflicts, intellectual property rights conflicts, etc. Suppose such problems arise and are not resolved in a reasonable period. In that case, the organization descends back to level 3 to preserve the project at this level, if possible, and try ascending again to level 4 at a later stage. It must be noted that stepping back one level does not assure that the organization will keep that project/service (level 3 in this example). In case the organization experiences unsuccessful attempts to return to level 4, it might be wise to descend even one more level, down to level 2, to redesign the project and attempt the progression route back to level 3, and from level 3 to level 4 with something new or enhanced.

The example given of a project/service in the transition process between level 3 and level 4 applies to all other stage transition efforts. To minimize the risk of an unsuccessful assessment, the project team goes through a training period to understand the upcoming level's expectations and prepare for the next level assessment and requirements.

The democratic development route for organizational knowledge does not end at level 6. Once reaching this optimal stage, the innovation developed can return to level 1 to be enhanced with new ideas and reenter the process for a second and more enhanced journey. This is a cyclical development process that continuously transforms an innovation over a series of evolutions.

It must be noted that organizations can return to any level within the spiral path if the organizational strategy is such. For example, an organization that has reached level 6 can go back to level 4 to integrate new functionality on the innovation developed and then go back to level 2 to reassign a new project team if needed.

18.3 Level Implementation Approach

The implementation approach and strategy of a level can vary between organizations. The Company Democracy Model does not impose any specific implementation process. This can conflict with the organization's capability and maturity to execute a particular function, provide another round of funding, the proper human resources, expertise, time, alignment with the strategic goals, expected outputs, etc. Nevertheless, a proposed approach is presented in Figure 18.2, explaining a conditional transition process from one level to the next.

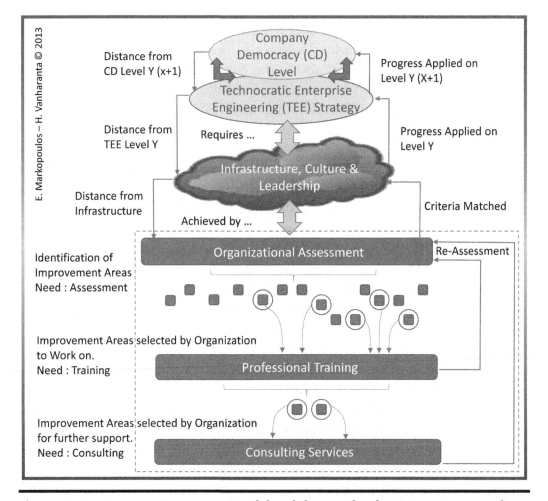

Figure 18.2 Company Democracy Model and the next level assessment approach.

The Company Democracy Model levels are noted as X and Y (which is X+1). The level is implemented through a technocratic enterprise engineering perspective, which requires the expected leadership, infrastructure, and culture to be in place before, after, and during each Company Democracy level. The organizational culture expected from each level is different from the democratic organizational culture developed at the first level of the model, promoting and supporting democratic knowledge elicitations from the base (employees). The technocratic enterprise engineering process is based on practical, concrete, and well-defined activities that engineer a process's execution in a technocratic and realistic way. This ensures that leadership, culture, and infrastructure in practice, and not in theory, are in place to support a level's implementation activities.

Leadership can be a very fuzzy concept with very theoretical and vague interpretations. It is not easy to remain continuously available, committed, supportive, and present. The proposed approach expects the leadership to be available before executing a level's activities practically. The same applies to the required infrastructure and also to the culture at the level that is targeted. For example, level 4 expects an innovative culture, while level 5 expects a communication culture, and level 6 an extroversion and international strategy culture.

The process begins with assessing existing activities and their compliance with the targeted level's activities. This assessment identifies the organization's status on the level's activities and the organizational capability, maturity, and infrastructure that satisfy them. It also highlights problematic activities that need attention or missing activities that need to be adopted before entering the next level. To minimize this risk, the proposed process suggests the isolation of the problematic or missing activities and the delivery of a training program to the employees involved in the transition progress from one level to the other. This training will clarify the needs and will propose a way to resolve the challenges that are indicated.

Following the training, organizations can also provide consulting support with internal or external resources. In this case, consulting works effectively as the challenges identified are addressed with practical studies, actions, and recommendations or with the development of different processes or tools that can be used to fulfill the specific level requirements. To ensure that there is no risk for the organization to move from one level to the next, the organization is reassessed after the training process and after the consulting process. This assessment loop can be repeated until the organization can be considered mature enough to enter the next level.

Once the reassessment indicates full compliance with the next level expectations, the organizational infrastructure, leadership, and culture are restructured to manage the implementation of the next level activities.

18.4 Model Implementation Approaches

The Company Democracy Model has no restrictions on the type of organizations of any business sector willing to adopt it. However, the best implementation can be achieved in:

■ Manufacturing organizations (engineering, heavy industry, shipping, defense, construction, development, etc.).
■ Organizations that have significant contact with people/clients (financial, commercial networks, tourism, sales, etc.).
■ Organizations that have or require specialized knowledge (technology, energy, health, environment, etc.).

The organization's or the department's (within an organization) minimum size for implementing the model is 30 to 50 employees.

The model can be adopted in many ways within an organization, such as:

■ Horizontally (directly across and throughout the entire organization).
■ Vertically (in a selected department, division, or business sector of the organization).
■ Pilot (in a selected group of people only, primarily for acquaintance or trial purposes).

The overall, gradual, tiered, or targeted adaptation of the model requires limited commitment on financial resources, human resources, and operations management to generate the benefits and support a subsequent expansion of the model to other strategic business areas across the organization.

This section presents two implementation approaches for the Company Democracy Model:

■ Organizational link approach (for SMEs)
■ Bottom-up approach (for Large-Scale Organizations)

18.4.1 Organizational Link Approach (for SMEs)

Implementing the Company Democracy Model requires organizational capability and maturity in leadership, management, and openness to adapt to new operational practices. Small and medium-sized enterprises (SMEs) are under pressure from their daily operations, which does not leave much room to experiment with new management models. The survival mode SMEs are into, and their daily routine, driven mostly from cost-efficiency goals, imposes primarily conservative and safe business transformation strategies.

To bypass this challenge, it is suggested that such organizations identify the most creative department or business unit, which can be considered a pilot project to adopt first the Company Democracy Model. Such departments are usually the ones related to creative or technical activities. They both have high demands for new ideas, either in designing new products or solving technical challenges. They also have tremendous technical knowledge and expertise residing in their employees. Figure 18.3 presents a simple organizational structure for identifying one unit that can run first the Company Democracy Model for a given time.

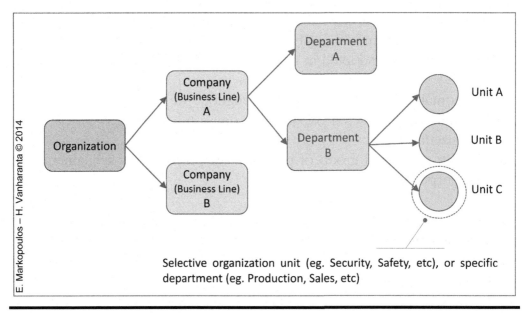

Figure 18.3 Pilot organizational unit for adopting the Company Democracy Model.

Applying the model in a small organizational unit has benefits but also risks. The advantage is that the risk of failure and the implementation costs are reduced to the minimum. If the organization is not convinced that the model can be helpful, the considered damage in personnel cost and time loss is restricted to the pilot organizational unit.

However, there are other risks associated with minimizing the model's adaptation, and these are related to the possibility of achieving poor results. Applying the model without really committing to it and believing in it does not enable the model's organizational culture to flourish. Lack of commitment also

impacts the leadership skills needed to support the model and the employees. Therefore, even if an ideal business unit has been selected to apply the
Company Democracy Model successfully, the possibility of failure is very high
if the leadership team won't strongly support it and embrace it.

Once an organization decides to apply the model, even as a small-scale
project, there should be full faith in this initiative, especially in creating a
democratic culture. Without conditional support, the model will be treated as
an experiment and will not motivate, empower, and support the employees to
go through the first two, critical for its success levels.

18.4.2 Bottom-Up Approach (for Large-Scale Organizations)

Large-Scale Organizations (LSOs) do not face the operational challenges
of the Small and Medium size Enterprises (SMEs). Due to their size, they
face other challenges that can restrict a decision to adopt the Company
Democracy Model throughout the organization at once. This hesitation
makes sense as the Company Democracy Model impacts the organizational
culture, which is not easy to change in large or multinational organizations.
In such cases, the model can be applied in a bottom-up approach by identifying several business units, subsidiaries, or company divisions to adopt it
first. This way, Large-Scale Organizations can follow a process similar to the
one suggested for SMEs.

However, the difference in this approach is the suggestion to adapt the
model in more than one sub-organization or business unit in parallel. This is
needed to achieve comparisons, benchmarking, and metrics on the impact
the model can have on various operations (business units) within the same
large-scale or multinational organization. Without the parallel adaptation
of the model across multiple business units, there is a risk for the overall
attempt to pass unnoticed. In a similar context, the need for more than one
business unit to apply the model in parallel can generate the creative competitiveness needed between them and achieve the best results from this
experiment.

Figure 18.4 presents the proposed approach for the adaptation of the
Company Democracy Model in Large-Scale Organizations. The specific
approach is divided into six stages.

The first stage covers a training program in selected business units
with the most relevant culture for the model to succeed. The training results will identify the business unit with a higher possibility of

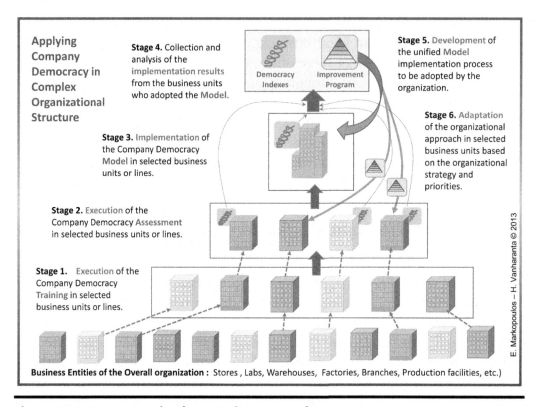

Figure 18.4 Bottom-up implementation approach.

implementing the model successfully. The decision to start with training programs reduces the costs of a training initiative. It also makes
it easy to execute it in many business units without impacting their
operational workload. This stage can be presented as a training program only and not as an assessment process for a long-term project
to avoid resistance.

The second stage is selecting the business units with the best training score
to go through the Company Democracy Model assessments and identify
the ones most suitable to adopt the model in practice.

The third stage is implementing the Company Democracy Model in the business units that successfully passed the assessment with the highest score.

The fourth stage is collecting the adaptation results from all the business units
who participated in the Company Democracy Model adaptation experiment and consolidated this information for the central management. The
selected data can be analyzed to identify the best practices used, the
implementation faults, the knowledge created, the results achieved, the

human resources used, the employee participation and satisfaction, and in general, all the information gathered from this initiative.

The fifth stage analyzes the information collected at stage 4 and creates the final and most suitable adaptation process. This way the organization can extend the model's adaptation. The adaptation process considers organizational restrictions, strategies, opportunities, and other elements that need to be aligned with the model's expected results.

The sixth stage determines the organization's decision to adopt the model entirely or continue its gradual adaptation with a similar process used until the entire organization adopts it over a period of time.

The proposed implementation approach manages the adoption risk of failing to align the organizational strategies and priorities with the democratic organizational culture requirements for changing the existing organizational culture. Furthermore, it provides the pilot adoption results based on which the organizations can align the new adoption processes with their current operational processes and culture, reducing their organizational culture change.

18.5 Alternative Implementation Processes

The implementation of the Company Democracy Model can be executed in many ways according to the organizational strategy, resources, and priorities. The most common approach is presented in the Spiral Method and is composed of the triptych of training, assessment, and consulting. However, other alternatives combine these activities without the Spiral process. Three of these implementation alternatives are the following:

- Plan-driven process (assessment based without immediate action).
- Assessment-driven process.
- Training-driven process.

18.5.1 Plan-Driven Implementation Process

The plan-based implementation process does not implement the Company Democracy Model. However, it delivers a business plan based on which the organization will implement the model when ready or decide to do it (Figure 18.5).

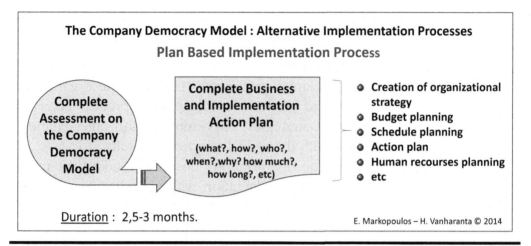

Figure 18.5 Plan based implementation approach.

The process is based on a holistic assessment of the organization against the six levels of the Company Democracy Model to identify the state of readiness and infrastructure the organization needs to adopt the model. For example, suppose there is a collaborative knowledge-sharing culture but no effective teaming practices in place. In that case, the first-level readiness assessment score will be higher than the second-level readiness score. In both cases, feedback, recommendations, and action plans are given.

The deliverable of the assessment is a complete business plan that answers questions (what?, how?, when?, how much?, why?, who?, etc.) related to the adoption process plan of the Company Democracy Model.

This approach is selected by organizations that do not have the time, resources, or the readiness to initiate an organizational culture change initiative and prefer to understand their commitments better before deciding to implement and adopt the Company Democracy Model.

The delivered business plan helps them secure the resources needed, possibly refresh their human resources, select the best period to execute the model, decide who will be assigned to run this initiative, receive organizational approval if needed, secure implementation funding, and in general, understand and plan the adoption of the Company Democracy Model before they start any adoption initiative.

18.5.2 Assessment-Driven Process

The assessment-driven approach is similar to the Spiral approach on implementing the Company Democracy Model, with the difference that the adoption effort is focused on one level only.

If, for example, an organization needs to emphasize or target specifically only the fourth level of the Company Democracy Model (innovation management) thinking that this will be its entry point, and feeling confident enough to comply with the process, leadership, and infrastructure level requirements. The organization can try entering the model directly from this specific level. Such a decision means that the organization is fully mature, experienced, with a democratic culture in place, and capable of complying and satisfy the requirements of the previous levels of the model (levels 1, 2, and 3 in this case).

The process begins with assessing the leadership, culture, and infrastructure expected from the organizations on the assessed level, which in this example is level 4. The assessment results will indicate the organization's distance from the requirements of the Company Democracy Model level 4. After the assessment, the necessary action plan is delivered. The organization works with internal resources or external consultants to adopt the Company Democracy Model level 4 practices and runs a couple of projects (Figure 18.6).

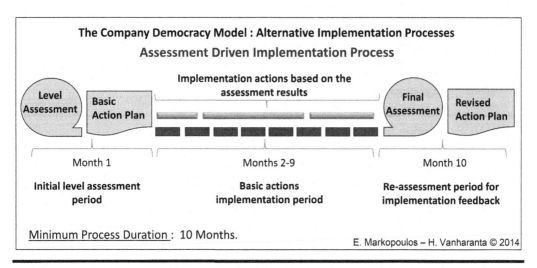

Figure 18.6   Assessment based implementation approach.

This specific process ends with a second assessment that assesses the development and adoption of the Company Democracy Model's process requirements for the targeted level. The second assessment's deliverable verifies the organizational readiness to adopt the specific level and provides a scorecard on the achievements against each level requirement or a revised action plan to complete the level requirements that were not satisfied.

There is always the risk in this approach that no adoption processes will start at all. Suppose the first assessment indicates that the organization is overoptimistic and far from the desired level entry requirements. In that case, it is recommended to perform another evaluation on a lower level and probably start from that level.

18.5.3 Training-Driven Implementation Process

The training-based approach is similar to the assessment-based method, whereby the first assessment is replaced with an extensive training program that acts as an indirect assessment (Figure 18.7).

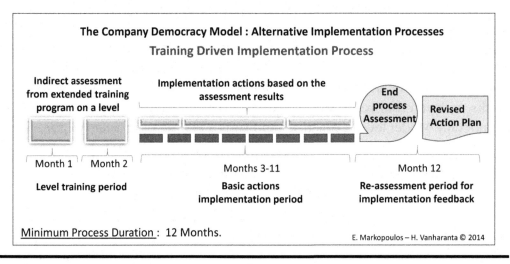

Figure 18.7 Training based implementation approach.

This approach can be selected for the more practical and hands-on type organizations that prefer to replace the initial assessment with an extensive training process that teaches the requirements of the desired levels and, at the same time, assesses the readiness and compliance of the organization against them.

A disadvantage of this approach is that an extended training period might not be followed consistently by all the trainees. This will affect the indirect assessment done through the training as those who are absent from a training session will not provide the required feedback when needed. If, however, attendance can be guaranteed, then this specific approach can deliver better results.

It must be noted that this approach is also focused on a specific level of the Company Democracy Model and not on the whole model. It is recommended to implement the full model only through the Spiral implementation methodology, starting from level 1 and progressing level by level after that.

18.6 Supporting Software Applications

In addition to the process and methodological frameworks offered for the implementation of the Company Democracy Model, the model is also supported by software technologies, situation-awareness information systems, artificial intelligence and fuzzy logic systems, and other technologies that contribute to the best possible adoption and enhance business operations to deliver more successful and rewarding results.

The Evolute applications support knowledge elicitation and organizational assessments toward identifying the organizational capability and maturity needed for the practical adoption strategy of the Company Democracy Model (Evolute, 2020). The applications are executed individually or in groups, based on the Company Democracy Model implementation level and its implementation strategy. They generate metrics and knowledge that supports and guides the implementation efforts.

Evolute technology is a platform that computes and visualizes the meaning of the knowledge input collected from various stakeholders and participants in the Company Democracy Model. The Evolute system's computing is based on soft-computing methods and algorithms to cope with the imprecision and uncertainty embedded in natural language and human knowledge inputs. Management uses the computed current and future meanings to analyze its organizational resources to enhance its organizational analysis for a development strategy. The analysis can be made for the whole group of participants but also subgroups. Stakeholders can be involved in this management step, according to a modular delivery process.

Today, 40 Evolute applications have been developed covering Work commitment, Occupational role competencies, Innovation culture, Sales culture, Time management culture, Customer's conscious experience, Safety culture, Knowledge creation, Organizational learning, and others. The development of these applications is an ongoing process.

Several others are under development, and others have reached the beta testing phase. The upcoming technologies cover Added value, Shared value, Competitive advantage, Customer service culture, ICT culture, Leadership culture, Management culture, Corporate governance culture, Ethical management, Sustainable management, Democratic company culture, Nanufacturing excellence, Learning culture, and Reengineering culture.

The technologies can be found on the www.evolute.fi, a strategic partner of the Company Democracy Model inventors.

The following examples present a brief description and indicative results of three applications.

18.6.1 Software Application Accord

Name: Accord. Version: 2.0

Purpose: Management and Leadership

Area of Application: Democratic Organization Culture

Brief Description: The application measures democratic culture inside an
organization regarding its current state and future vision (cf. Tuomainen,
2014). The Accord application framework is presented in Figure 18.8.

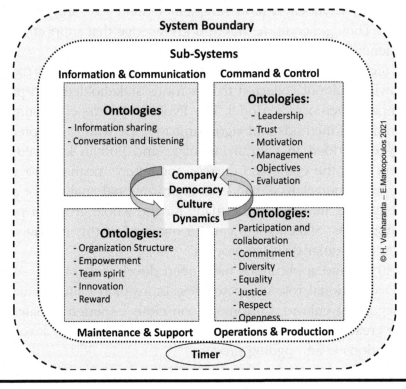

Figure 18.8 Accord application framework (cf. Chapter 4).

The Accord 2.0 version supports the collective evaluation of the democratic organization culture. The ontology covers 20 different democratic
organization culture features embedded into a systemic view of the organization. Accord has been tested in a real company environment in Finland
(Figure 18.9).

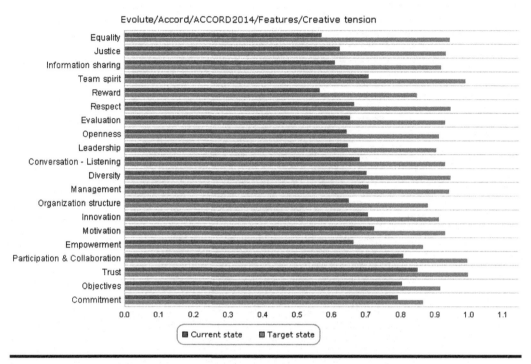

Figure 18.9 Accord results in a Finnish company (Tuomainen, 2014).

18.6.2 Software Application Pursoid

Name: Pursoid. Version: 1.0

Purpose: Management and Leadership

Area of Application: Innovation Competence of Human Resources

Brief description: The Pursoid application has a robust ontology behind it, which describes the many innovation competencies needed to measure the test subject's degree of innovation competencies. The ontology contains two main categories:

Personal competencies: Thinking habits, attention, experiences, working habits, self-awareness, self-regulation, motivation, expertise, and development.

Social competencies: Empathy and eelationship management.

The results in Figure 18.10 show in more detail the particular competence characteristics. It is interesting to see that the application shows relatively high research results and that creative tension, i.e., the future view of the test subjects compared to the current situation is optimistic. The test subjects are

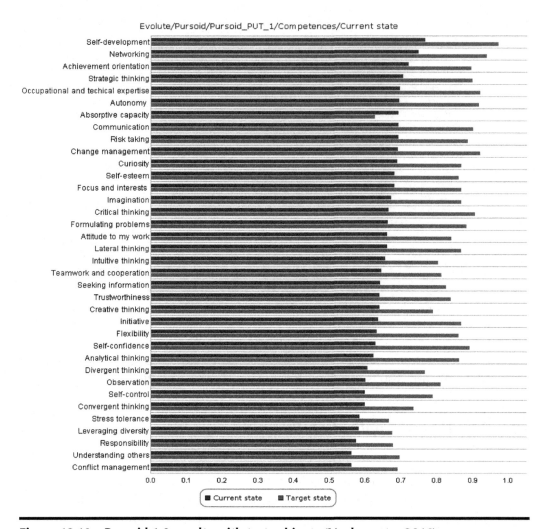

Figure 18.10 **Pursoid 1.0 results with test subjects (Vanharanta, 2016).**

eager to improve their innovation competencies. The absorptive capacity may have been a problematic competence, and it shows a declining activity in the future.

18.6.3 Software Application FOLIUM

Name Folium. Version: 1.0

Purpose: Management and Leadership

Area of Application: Organizational Knowledge Creation

Brief Description: Folium is used to evaluate features that describe activities, functions, and practices in organizational knowledge creation (Table 18.1).

Table 18.1   Organizational Knowledge Creation Ontology (cf. Paajanen, 2012)

Features (Sub-classes)	Main Classes	Organizational Knowledge-Creating Activities
Sharing of experiences	Socialization	
Observation of others' work		
Spending time and doing things together		
Articulation of tacit knowledge	Externalization	
Translation of tacit knowledge into an understandable format		
Adoption of new knowledge and combination with existing knowledge	Combination	
Spreading new knowledge in the organization		
Evaluation of new knowledge		
Making knowledge visible in operations and practices	Internalization	
Exploitation of training and simulation		

The application follows the framework by Ikujiro Nonaka and Hirotaka Takeuchi (Nonaka, Takeuchi, 1995). The application has been tested in a natural company environment in Finland (Figure 18.11).

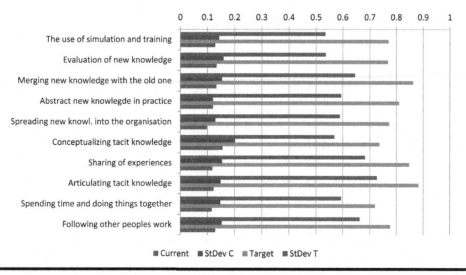

Figure 18.11   Folium results in an organization – Histogram (cf. Paajanen, 2012).

A more detailed analysis of the Folium features can be seen in Figure 18.12. The results are shown with Evolute Index.

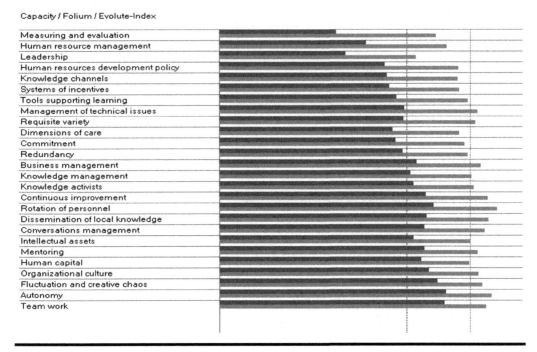

Capacity / Folium / Evolute-Index

Measuring and evaluation
Human resource management
Leadership
Human resources development policy
Knowledge channels
Systems of incentives
Tools supporting learning
Management of technical issues
Requisite variety
Dimensions of care
Commitment
Redundancy
Business management
Knowledge management
Knowledge activists
Continuous improvement
Rotation of personnel
Dissemination of local knowledge
Conversations management
Intellectual assets
Mentoring
Human capital
Organizational culture
Fluctuation and creative chaos
Autonomy
Team work

Figure 18.12   Detail analysis of Folium features in a Finnish company (Evolute, 2020).

18.7 Benefits of the Company Democracy Model for Innovation Management and Leadership

The benefits from using the Company Democracy Model can be categorized into personal benefits for the employees involved in the process, organizational benefits in terms of operations management and optimization, and organizational impact benefits in terms of strategy, profitability, and impact on the society and the economy.

18.7.1 Individual Benefits

From the management and leadership dimension, the Company Democracy Model supports and enhances:

- Protection and registration of everyone's knowledge under their corporate knowledge account.
- The weighting of ideas, innovation, and knowledge via the Company Democracy Contribution Impact algorithm.

- Ontology-based management and leadership in innovation culture and innovation competencies.
- Individual growth development and performance with productivity and latency dimensions.
- Co-opetition, inclusiveness, and cooperation in the decisions, plans, and acts of the organization.
- Co-Evolutionary, co-operative, co-opetitive, and NOT competitive relationships between employees, business units, and departments.
- Responsibility and NOT irresponsibility among the employees on taking initiatives and sharing knowledge.
- Display of high individual commitment and motivation levels in the organization.
- Dynamic, continuous, and democratic production of business knowledge for the benefit of all.
- Shared value thinking for the benefit of the whole organization.
- Understanding the Delphi maxims' principles, the Holistic Concept of Man and Circles of Mind metaphors, and the overall Applied Philosophy that drives the model.

18.7.2 Organizational Benefits

From the innovation management and leadership dimension, the Company Democracy Model creates an organizational culture to achieve:

- Dynamic and continuous tracking, monitoring, and evaluation of organizational data, information, and knowledge.
- Optimal management and leadership of human resources based on the continuous development of skills, capabilities, competencies, and knowledge management experience.
- Knowledge analysis and processing as raw material for developing new organizational services, products, projects, processes, and initiatives.
- Identification and management of competitiveness that derives from organizational insights and innovations.
- Identification and management of extroversion through the utilization of organizational competitiveness.
- A self-awareness-driven organizational business strategy.
- Identification of the right people for the right place, at the right time, and for the correct period.
- Development of new products, services, and processes based on the knowledge generated.

- Increased corporate loyalty and job satisfaction by providing all the opportunities to succeed.
- Reduced employee turnover and identification of the processes for a stable workforce.
- Identification of team players, knowledge givers, ideas, and innovation generators.
- Fast, reliable, and qualitative results from the utilization of intellectual capital toward organizational goals.
- Identification of profit centers and value centers in areas where that knowledge is identified.
- Safe and effective business transformation based on the capability, maturity, and capacity of the personnel.
- Identification of business transformation areas where knowledge exists to support such initiatives.
- Effective processes, programs, and program management through knowledge and people utilization.
- Knowledge-based projects and program creation and management.
- Creation of data analytics regarding the intellectual capacity of the organization.
- Creation of knowledge for market data analysis and relationships.
- Business intelligence based on intellectual capital information.
- Dynamic knowledge-based data models for mapping the intellectual capital, profit, and value centers and their overall value against the organizational strategy. Establishment of a Blue Ocean Strategy on management and operations.
- Establishment of a Green Ocean Strategy (sustainable development) on management and operations.
- Establishment of a Pink Ocean Strategy (social development) on management and operations.

18.7.3 Economic Impact

From the socioeconomic dimension, the Company Democracy Model contributes to the:

- Optimization of organizational operations, production, and performance.
- Reduction of losses, errors, accidents, and avoidance of inefficient practices and procedures.
- Strengthened innovation, competitiveness, and extroversion.

- Development of new services, products, projects, processes, and initiatives.
- Creation of organizational knowledge by human resources utilization management.
- Development and implementation of feasible business strategies with widely accepted leadership.
- Increased revenue via corporate entrepreneurship and intrapreneurship operations.
- Sustaining the best talents, gain from their willingness to create.
- Reduced workforce turnover costs that impact the organization's operations and customer relations.
- Reduced hiring costs and effort for mid to top management positions as they are covered from within.
- Setting organization goals and strategies as the areas for knowledge creation.
- Reducing consulting costs for knowledge that can be obtained internally.
- Promotion of the concept of the Democratization of Innovation as a new corporate public relations strategy.
- Execution of knowledge with impact and return for society, the community, and other areas can improve its image and increase its acceptance, awareness, and democratic culture.
- Achievement and promotion of ethical governance can score on the ESG (Environmental, Social, Governance) organizational sustainability index.

18.8 Summary

The implementation of the Company Democracy Model can be delivered in many ways based on organizational maturity, capability, and strategy.

The model itself seems quite challenging for immediate adoption in an organization and can be misconsidered as another change management model. Effective changes need the support of the entire organization. Serious organizational commitment is required for the Company Democracy Model to be presented as an organizational strategy rather than an experiment. Lack of support allows second thoughts and criticism for the model, which does not help it deliver its best as people, by nature, do not like changes. Therefore, the employees need to believe first in the Company Democracy Model more than the leadership.

The way the Company Democracy Model is implemented does not matter as long as it *is* implemented. Whether this is via the Spiral Method, the assessment-based approach, or the training-based approach, or any combination of them or with a sequential staged approach (from level 1 to level 6) or with a focus on a specific level, it is the leadership of the company that will define the implementation strategy. Such a decision comes after evaluating the people's readiness, capability, competence, and maturity, marking the organization's readiness, capability, competence, and maturity.

The organization's management can also decide the timing, the support, the resources, the budget, and anything else needed to adopt the model and its impact on the organizational operations. Therefore, the Company Democracy Model does not impose or strongly recommend any specific way to implement it. The recommendations proposed in this chapter via different approaches are optional for the organizations to analyze and select the best with nothing else in mind other than faith in the model, commitment, and determination to support its adoption process. If the leadership does not believe in a change, no change can ever happen.

Although the Company Democracy Model is about freedom of speech, equal opportunity, justice, and ethical management, it seems that many people do not like to have the chance for equal opportunities as this can expose their emptiness, incompetence, or unwillingness to go the extra mile, to work harder, and raise the bar of their personal development and organizational contribution.

The Company Democracy Model fights attitudes and feelings of injustice and inequality, exposes free riders, and gives people self-respect. It provides people with real democratic opportunities to prove themselves and demonstrate their abilities, skills, and charisma when treated fairly, equally, and free to express their ideas, insights, and knowledge.

However, where there is freedom, there is responsibility. The Company Democracy Model is for those who do not fear freedom and can accept responsibility and accountability for their thoughts and actions. Freedom without responsibility is anarchy, leading to chaos rather than social and economic development and prosperity.

Therefore democracy and Company Democracy are for the doers, not the followers, for the responsible, not the irresponsible, and the thinkers, not the believers.

Democracy is inevitable, and Company Democracy is indispensable for corporate, social, and personal development.

References

Evolute, 2020. www.evolute.fi

Nonaka, I. and Takeuchi, H., 1995. *The Knowledge-creating Company: How Japanese Companies Create the Dynamics of Innovation.* Oxford University Press, New York.

Paajanen, P., 2012. *Managing and Leading Organizational Learning and Knowledge Creation.* Ph.D. Thesis, Tampere University of Technology, Finland, Publication 1062.

Tuomainen, M., 2014. *Measuring the Degree of Company Democracy Culture.* Master of Science Thesis, Tampere University of Technology, Pori Campus, Finland.

Vanharanta, H., 2016. Pursoid: Innovation Competence of Human Resources. In: Kantola, J. (ed.) *Organizational Resources Management: Theories, Methodologies, and Applications.* CRC Press, Taylor & Francis Group, Boca Raton, FL, 79–89.

Chapter 19

Repetition Is the Mother of Studying, Learning, and Internalization: Concluding Remarks for the Company Democracy Model and Applied Philosophy for Management and Leadership

19.1 Introduction

At the beginning of the book, we concentrated on introducing humans as part of the living system and showing with examples how it is possible to use their capacity in the best possible way. Our target has also been to show the reader the challenges and possibilities that the Company Democracy Model (CDM) can give first for individuals, groups, teams, and the whole organization.

We understand that the Company Democracy Model has its potential when companies apply it continuously, as presented in Chapters 1–18. The CDM is based on our thinking with the Applied Philosophy for Management and

DOI: 10.4324/9781003158493-22

Leadership. The model itself is constructed as a visual tool that contains many methods of using it and how to utilize it in practice.

Many of the questions at the end of each chapter may be challenging to answer. It would be good if the reader of this book has a current practical situation to interpret the company's challenges and possibilities to use the Company Democracy Model inside the company. It would be even better if a project team has the right to apply the Company Democracy Model inside the company first as a pilot project and then in an actual project. We have demonstrated the benefits of using the systematic approach and applying it in practice. We have also thought that it may be an excellent way to learn if the team members go through all the three sections, ponder all their collected answers once again, and then see how new ideas emerge in their current company situation. We rely a lot on the team-based working methodology together with the Company Democracy Model.

In the following, we have presented six different ways to start thinking the Applied Philosophy way, and we have followed the same principles as we have shown at the end of each chapter – this Chapter 19 is our bonus chapter for the reader.

Section 1. Applied Philosophy in Management and Leadership

Business Situationality specifies the use of Applied Philosophy thinking in management and leadership. Our target has been to open the Applied Philosophy in many different ways and bring ancient and contemporary philosophers' ideas close to modern business management and leadership. Describing Applied Philosophy in management and leadership opens up the visions we have had while writing this book to our readers.

A.1   The situation in your company

Business situation is critical to understand both quantitatively and qualitatively. Often, the quantitative situation assessment reveals the past and current financial situation and gives management essential data and information about the possibilities to progress in the current state and see the prospects to invest in the future. Qualitative information, in turn, needs a lot of processing before it is helpful as a feed to knowledge creation and wisdom generation.

Our vision is that qualitative and quantitative data and information are needed to get practical knowledge for decision-making. Perceiving the past and current business situation gives good possibilities to find new paths for business development and growth.

Please see the thinking inside the diagram of Figure 19.1. Please describe the Situationality in your company with the questions A.1.1–A.1.8.

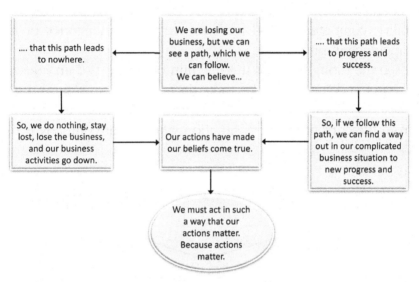

Modified: c.f., ref. Buckingham et al., 2011, William James, page 207.

Figure 19.1   Company situations think chart (c.f., ref. Buckingham, et al., 2011, William James, p. 207).

A.1.1   Do you have this kind of situation in your company that you are losing business?

A.1.2   Do you have many options in that specific business situation to choose from?

A.1.3   Are you ready to present different alternatives for decision-making?

A.1.4   Do you have difficulties deciding which path you should follow?

A.1.5   Are you a believer, or is it better to say that you understand and know your business Situationality?

A.1.6   Are you optimistic or pessimistic with your ideas?

A.1.7   Do you act positively or negatively?

A.1.8   Do you use any systematic processes to develop your company?

A.1.9   How do you see the Company Democracy Model? Does it have good action paths to follow?

A.1.10 Do you think that the Company Democracy Model has a solution to progress in this kind of philosophical situation?

A.2   Managers and leaders in your company

In Chapter 2, we presented the Delphic maxims' classification, which can be used in many ways to evaluate the characteristics of leaders and managers. Taking some maxims from specific ontology can give rise to and guide business management thinking, acts, and decisions. Personal Situationality, capacity, capability, competence, and mastery are the cornerstones of individual work competence improvement.

Please see the thought inside the diagram of Figure 19.2 and describe how your managers and leaders make their decisions in practice and what kind of traits they use in different business situations. Evaluate also the demands coming from the current business situation where your company is right now.

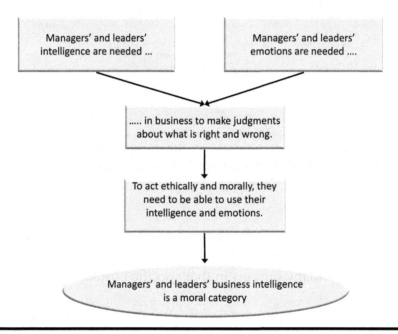

Figure 19.2   Company's managers and leaders think chart (c.f., ref. Buckingham, et al., 2011, Theodor Adorno, p. 266).

A.2.1   Do your company leaders and managers use their rational and emotional side of their brain capacity in decision-making?

A.2.2   Do your company managers and leaders understand well what is right and wrong during their decision-making?

A.2.3   Are your company managers and leaders able to act ethically and morally?

A.2.4   Do you have charismatic leaders in your company?

A.2.5   How do you categorize business intelligence?

A.2.6   What are the traits you appreciate a lot in managing and leading your company, personnel, groups, and teams?

A.2.7   How close are your managers and leaders with your company organization's members in different business situations?

A.2.8   How do you like your managers and leaders treat you and other company members?

A.2.9   How emotional and rational are your managers and leaders?

A.2.10   Do you see the possibilities each company member has to develop personal work-related competencies?

A.2.11   What would be the ways to improve the individual work-related competencies and mastery?

Section 2. Human Focus in Living Systems

Systems science is the base for understanding living systems and especially humans in work-related situations. Humans are systems, and so in organizations, we have to have a focus on humans. Knowing yourself is the most crucial starting point to develop human growth up to high competence and mastery. Nothing in excess gives the basic understanding of how the systemic view, feedback, and variety enable business processes to follow low entropy, low material, and energy consumption. These activities, in turn, lead to sustainable growth, agile business processes, added value creation, and share value generation. Moderation is best when we concentrate on human development to knowledge creation and wisdom generation. With small continuous activities, we end up with sustainable individual growth.

B.1.   Individuals in the business situation

Individuals are the core of business knowledge and wisdom. Human capacity gives opportunities to human growth, and human growth enables work-related competence development. We have shown that skills are needed, and learning and understanding business concepts and competencies are based on education and learning in practice. Scientific, theoretical, and technical education is required in everyday business, but how to convert business understanding to simple, practical knowledge needs experience.

Positive business culture is necessary and also a democratic way to understand different people in different roles. With the help of systems thinking and systems practice, there are possibilities to find business knowledge and wisdom.

Please see the thought inside the diagram of Figure 19.3 and answer the following questions after the flow diagram.

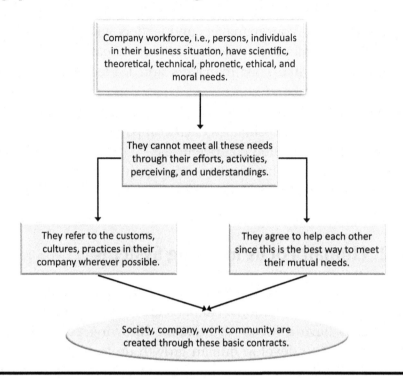

Figure 19.3 Individual's situations think chart (c.f., ref. Buckingham, et al., 2011, Edmund Burke, p. 173).

B.1.1 How well are your company personnel motivated and committed to your company's challenges and goals?

B.1.2 Do all the employees in your company have fair contracts?

B.1.3 What kind of contracts has your company made with society, with other companies, personnel, and communities where your company is active?

B.1.4 Do you consider the people in you company as team players? Do you think they are willing to help each other and that they like to work together?

B.1.5 How do the customs, company culture, and ordinary practical work help people understand and perceive the company situation?

B.1.6 Is it clear for everyone that wisdom generation needs good data handling, information processing, knowledge generation so that sound wisdom generation is possible inside your company?

B.1.7 Do you see that individuals have specific ethical and moral needs in their business activities?

B.2   Supply and demand in the business situation

Supply and demand define the business situation in many ways. The current business situation strengthens the green business, global circular economy, sustainable growth, low entropy, and energy consumption, forces companies to carefully look at energy consumption, save energy, and find new ways to be without fossil raw materials. The current markets operate this way, and companies try to find new strategies to find new paths to follow.

Opinions are not relevant and not either belief. Business situations need facts and true knowledge to find new knowledge and wisdom to guide the new business. Supply and demand can be fast or slow, but the change opportunities must be found all the time. New initiatives, new scientific discoveries, new theories, new technologies change our current living fast.

Please see the thinking inside the diagram for Figure 19.4 and try to find out answers after the flow diagram. Please also find new questions which come to your mind.

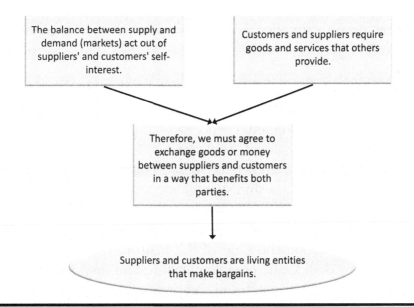

Figure 19.4   Business's supply and demand situations think chart (c.f., ref. Buckingham, et al., 2011, Adam Smith, p. 161).

B.2.1   A free-market economy gives a lot of possibilities to balance supply and demand. Many times the balance comes out with suppliers' and customers' self-interests. How do you see supply and demand in your business area?

B.2.2 A supply network serves customers' interests. However, it is not so clear how supply and demand emerge in the markets. What are your ideas on how business is created in your business sector?

B.2.3 Living systems theory supports the idea that suppliers and customers are living entities that make bargains with each other. How do you see this against the living systems theory?

B.2.4 New business systems follow the ideas of a green economy and sustainable growth. How in your company are these essential areas discussed and put into practice?

B.2.5 Do you have new ideas, innovations, and insights flows in your business network?

B.2.6 Do you have thoughts about how the added value creation should be understood in your business network?

B.2.7 How are the supply and demand seen from the business network viewpoint?

B.2.8 Do you need in the new business new contracts?

B.2.9 How do your customers understand the new green economy demands?

B.2.10 How do your suppliers see the new demands in the green economy?

Section 3. The Company Democracy Model

This book presents the Company Democracy Model in detail as a framework through which an organizational, evolutionary, level-based Spiral Method is used to create and execute knowledge-based cultures for effective organizational management and leadership strategies.

The model can be effectively applied in all organizations in any sector and of any size. Its unique method promotes the human being as the center of organizational development. One of the main targets of the technique is to create a positive democratic company culture and then see the company's development and growth through the company's active members.

We consider that without an organizational democratic culture, organizational learning cannot be created with an education ethos. In turn, without organizational knowledge and wisdom, there is no innovation. Without innovation, there is no development, and without development, there is no competitiveness. Without competitiveness, the extroversion required in today's globalized society cannot exist. This is why we understand that the base is connected to developing a democratic company culture that needs the systemic CDM approach to reach the required level.

C.1   Company Democracy Model in theory

The democratic approach in a business situation needs a lot of scientific, theoretical, and practical experience. Managers and leaders have this kind of education and practical experience, but some tools are required to make this kind of Company Democracy Model active in live organizations.

This book has given the methodology, methods, and tools to enable the model's adoption to active projects inside the company/organization. What the adoption needs are cognitive capacity, capability, competence, and good business experience.

Please see the thought inside the flow diagram of Figure 19.5 and answer the following questions after the flow diagram. Please invent new questions and try to answer them in your company's business context (Cf. Figure 19.1).

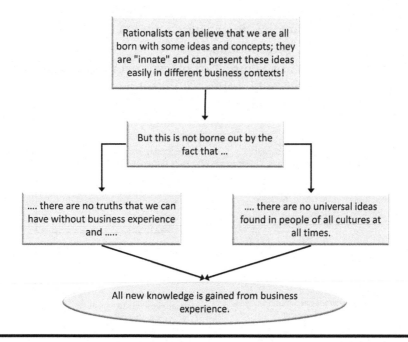

Figure 19.5   Business's knowledge think chart (c.f., ref. Buckingham, et al., 2011, John Locke, p. 131).

C.1.1 Do the leaders and managers of your company have enough critical intelligence?

C.1.2 Do you support the tabula rasa thinking? Or do you think that we are all born with some ideas, insights, and concepts in our minds?

C.1.3 How do you understand tacit knowledge?

C.1.4 Business experience is vital in business situations. Do you believe that universal ideas in people are found in different cultures at all times?

C.1.5 How can we be sure that we work with facts in our business?

C.1.6 Do you rely on your business experience?

C.1.7 Do you think that all business knowledge is created from the business experience?

C.2 Company Democracy Model in practice

Company Democracy Model in practice needs first understanding of the democratic company culture. After that, it is possible to start applying the democratic approach in a business situation. There is a need to find out practical examples and find detailed procedures for making the model operational. Teaming in a project context would be a promising start-up and then find a relevant project to start this new endeavor. Many applications are already available, but each company has its business context and so to copy any other project might not lead to good results.

Based on the diagrams of Figure 19.6 please invent new questions and try to answer them in your company's business context.

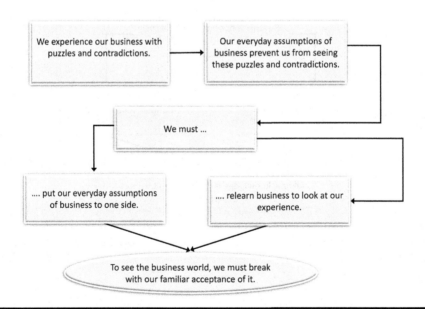

Figure 19.6 Individual's knowledge think chart (c.f., ref. Buckingham, et al., 2011, Maurice Merleau-Ponty, p. 275).

C.2.1   Do we experience our business with puzzles and contradictions?

C.2.2   Do we have assumptions that prevent us from seeing current business problems?

C.2.3   Do our employees easily find current business problems?

C.2.4   Do we have possibilities to throw away our assumptions?

C.2.5   Do we rely on our business experience?

C.2.6   How active are our people to find and solve our business problems?

C.2.7   Do we have enough constructs and concepts to deal with these problems?

C.2.8   Do we have reasonable assumptions of our business situation?

C.2.9   Do we see our business situation with new eyes?

C.2.10 How do you see Company Democracy Model in practice?

C.2.11 Does this book give enough information and knowledge on how to turn and run the model into practical tasks and activities?

C.2.12 Do you see that the Company Democracy Model is too theoretical? Or do you think that this model gives new possibilities for your company to survive in the challenging competition?

Reference

Buckingham, W., King, Peter J., Burnham, D., Weeks, M., Hill, C., and Marenbon, J., 2011. *The Philosophy Book*. Dorling Kindersley Limited, London.

Conclusions

The Company Democracy Model presented in this book has followed the systemic view of inputs, processes, and outputs. The input side contains many different scientific, theoretical, technical, and practical data, information, and knowledge that have converted the authors' scientific and practical experience into a model with a human-centric approach. Each of the main inputs has several sub-inputs. The processes inside the system, in turn, have several sub-processes that make the model realistic and dynamic. The outcoming streams or outputs have several new combinations of the data, information, and knowledge used, generating a pearl of new wisdom for the reader.

The first inputs to the system comprised philosophical issues in the form of metaphors. From the beginning, Plato's cave allegory was the essential guiding metaphor we wanted to channel through the book. It made us think more profoundly about carrying the ancient philosophical message to the modern world. Following this, the metaphors we presented were the Holistic Concept of Man, the Workspace of Mind, and the Circles of Mind. The combination of past ideas and meanings with contemporary notions of the business world's current situation led us to create the term:

Applied Philosophy of Management and Leadership

As our intuitive thinking started from these fundamental issues and methodologies, it was relatively easy to connect our ideas to the Delphic maxims, a timeless philosophical wisdom and inspiration source. In turn, the Delphic maxims gave us an understanding of how people should know themselves, how they should behave in different situations, and how they should practice moderation in all their activities. Furthermore, they help our values and ethos that people need to coexist in peace and prosperity. All these views, content, and issues were fuel for the development of:

The Company Democracy Model

It was a real turning point when we realized that we could combine Aristotelian thinking with our intuitive thinking. By using the unconscious part of our brain capacity, thinking a lot, and using inner speech, visual imagery, and verbalization, we could find ways to construct the Wisdom Cube with its four crucial dimensions and planes of wisdom: Episteme, Sophia, Techne, and Phronesis. This process led us to develop the Data Information Knowledge Wisdom (DIKW) Table and the Collective Wisdom and Machine Wisdom constructs.

All the previously mentioned approaches, methodologies, methods, constructs, and concepts have helped us create the base for our innovation model, i.e., the Company Democracy Model. The model needs a company culture to operate, so we were challenged to develop such a culture that could provide the necessary space for knowledge to be created and used effectively in the innovation process. The created dynamic democratic company culture works similarly in a systemic way. It contains different sub-concepts: Information and Communication, Command and Control, Operations and Production, Maintenance and Support. In this created space, our Company Democracy Model operates as one of the systems inside the organization.

The Company Democracy Model is a knowledge management model. Knowledge derives democratically from everyone in the company regardless of rank, education, social status, race, color, sex, religion, or lifestyle. The democratization of knowledge in the Company Democracy Model is inspired and empowered by Socrates, especially the Socratic method for knowledge elicitation. The Company Democracy Model provides the opportunity for all who improve the company's operation to speak and act freely. As companies are living entities, operating as living systems, the people's knowledge is the fuel of life, not only for the company but also for the economy, society, and humanity.

From the organizational perspective, it is essential to understand how companies can be viable in different periods, conditions, and circumstances. The chapters of this book have shown how the company performance dimensions operate and how knowledge democratization can create and sustain good company performance with its financial and intellectual assets. We have also demonstrated how we can connect the company performance, human performance, and democratic company performance through a co-evolution framework driven by a co-opetitive rather than a competitive environment. All these activities target the creation of human-centric thinking in the Company Democracy Model realization and implementation process.

The next section of the book concentrated on management and leadership issues. The presented model helps managers and leaders focus first on "time issues" to manage time from several different perspectives, i.e., the chronological, experienced, preparation, recording, managing, and discretionary standpoints. The visual "Management Windshield" metaphor and model, in turn, gave important ontologies for leadership and management with the following sub-ontologies: activities, style, focus, and purpose. Altogether, these sub-concepts contain a total of 38 different management and leadership issues.

The Holistic Concept of Man and the Circles of Mind metaphors' content describes the human-centric view of the Company Democracy Model. It is interesting to see how dynamic usage of the Circles of Mind metaphor allows us to understand how our brains can operate and how this individual aspect can also rely on the metaphor's concrete model. With the concrete model's help, it is relatively easy to see the vast combination possibilities of the content and how we can be unique and think differently in a specific conscious on-stage experience. We also showed how to improve individuals' networking performance, focusing on networking productivity and latency dimensions. We also presented how large the ontology of personal mastery is and how important it is to develop the unique traits and characteristics to build work-specific capabilities, task-specific competencies, and role-specific competencies. The Circle of Mind metaphor can help us find these essential traits and attributes continuously.

The chapters contain our efforts to harness modern knowledge systems to help apply the metaphors used and show the importance of obtaining essential collective wisdom from data, information, and knowledge. We started a new way of thinking about how machine learning, and therefore Machine Wisdom, can be part of knowledge creation and support human decision-making. When human decision-making operates from a situational perspective, and when data, information, and knowledge creation are part of the available computer systems, we end up with the co-evolute process, a cross-scientific approach with modern decision-making artificial intelligence tools. The co-evolute processes and fuzzy system computer applications show how it is possible to obtain relevant current information and how company personnel can deliver their creative tension to analyze problematic ontologies through linguistic statements and heuristics. The examples with the Evolute applications showed how such qualitative and quantitative measurements could be achieved.

After presenting the background of our efforts to create the Company Democracy Model, we were ready to describe in detail the innovative Company Democracy Model itself. The model contains six different activation levels: the first level represents a democratic culture and knowledge-based strategy; the second level includes democratic culture-based business models, structures, and knowledge engines; and the third level contains process, project management, and engineering activities. The fourth level is the core of the democratic culture innovation, development, and management level. The fifth level has activities around innovation-based competitive operations, and the sixth level extroversion and international activities. The Company Democracy Model comes into operation with the spiral co-evolution process applied at each model level. In the end, we have overall indices in categories and dimensions.

Co-opetitive ecosystems have to be built to apply the Company Democracy Model in practice. First, there has to be an adaptation and communication strategy to sell the Company Democracy Model to the organization and stakeholders. It is also necessary to understand the required staged conditions of the model implementation, i.e., preconditions, operations, and post-conditions. One crucial issue is the co-opetition requirement in the implementation phase. The Co-Evolutionary process incorporates the need for co-opetition. Only then can managers and leaders see how the Company Democracy Model operates in practice and peace without the obstacles of human competition. At the end of the implementation phase and during the operational phase, it is possible to see how the different business units that implemented the model behave, function, and contribute within their organizational ecosystem: agents, producers, partners, associates, consumers, financial institutions, subcontractors, service providers, and third-party service companies.

With the Company Democracy Model, it is possible to look more carefully at shared and added value economies and analyze the related issues. For this purpose, we created the Shared Value Circular Economic Chain. Activation happens with the human intellectual capital first opening innovation activities which generate added value that brings shared value. One way to apply the spiral process in the Company Democracy Model is the evolution of corporate human intellectual capital in democratic environments. The generation, adaptation, utilization, competitiveness, and extroversion of human capital follow the spiral approach's idea. The end phase marks the institutionalization of human capital in the organization. The evolution of shared value in the Company Democracy Model follows the systemic approach. It starts from individual knowledge, continues to shared understanding in teams, is manifested as added-value creation and innovation. In the end, it follows the path to organizational activities as social growth and contribution to society. The creation of added value with different human-based capital components in a democratic culture supports market productivity and capital productivity in return on total assets calculations.

The seven clouds of glory describe the spaces needed for the Company Democracy Model to mature, understand, and apply effectively and successfully. The metaphorical clouds are: to think, to plan, to do, to apply, to share, to care, and dream. This process has links to different levels of understanding. First, to have the feeling that I am valuable, a living entity, followed by various knowledge activities like giving, using, testing, spreading, enjoying, and, in the end, inclining to continue living in this new way. Different activity states have, in turn, links to the generation of responsibility, innovation, profitability, productivity, satisfaction, and a sense of generating 'life' at work and in the workplace. These spaces reflect the Company Democracy levels.

The dynamics of company democracy culture enable knowledge and knowledge management. The many different definitions somehow reveal the large ontology of knowledge and its creation. Knowledge creation mind maps show clearly how vast the concept of knowledge creation is. In the previously presented Data Information Knowledge Wisdom (DIKW) Table (in Chapter 9), knowledge creation consisted of 40 different knowledge-creating activities. However, it is essential to pick the most critical concepts of knowledge creation, i.e., true knowledge, a triptych of knowledge, love, and truth. We believe that the lack of real experience, knowledge, and wisdom in management and leadership makes management models function as in Plato's cave allegory; they are more like illusions, weak, fragile, powerless, and useless. One way to understand knowledge creation is to see this from a systemic viewpoint where data handling, information processing, and knowledge creation generate wisdom. The most crucial aspect of this is that we end up with a certain level of maturity in knowledge creation inside the Company Democracy Model.

If we move from theory to practice, the target in the company context is to show how the model works through different implementation approaches and processes. The main methods are the organizational link and the bottom-up approaches, which are implemented through the plan-driven, assessment-driven, and training-driven implementation processes, or any combination of them. We have given one example with the Accord application. This Evolute fuzzy application evaluates how well the company personnel understands the democratic company culture and how their collective creative tension describes how actively they are ready to improve on the current degree of Company Democracy in the future. Folium, a second Evolute application, evaluates organizational knowledge creation in current and future perspectives in a real company context. A third application, Pursoid, assesses the innovation competence of human resources.

We have found that the Company Democracy Model offers several benefits for individuals, organizations, and society, and we have tested the model in several different ways. We can also say that the whole model's innovation and development process has been a test. We hope that the model will give something new and valuable to all our readers, their organizations, companies, and societies, mainly those searching for new intuitions, ideas, insights, innovations, and practical implementations.

At the end of this book, we feel that our book fulfills the initial idea.

"One Voice and Many Insights"

Evangelos Markopoulos   **Hannu Vanharanta**

Glossary

BMLOs	Business Management and Leadership Objects
CDM	Company Democracy Model
CoM	Circles of Mind
DCDS	Dynamic Company Democracy Space
DIKW	Data, Information, Knowledge, Wisdom
DSS	Decision Support System
EU	European Union
GUI	Graphical Computer Interface
HCM	Holistic Concept of Man
ICT	Information and Communication Technologies
IoT	Internet of Things
KPI	Key Process Indicator
KS	Knowledge system
LOOs	Leadership Object Ontologies
LS	Language system
MLOs	Management and Leadership Objects
MOO	Management Object Ontologies
PPP	Public–Private Partnerships
PPS	Problem processing system
PS	Presentation system
ROE	Return on Equity
ROI	Return on Investment
SME	Small and Medium-sized Enterprise
SWOT	Strengths, Weaknesses, Opportunities, Threats
UN	United Nations

====== ANALYTIC PER CHAPTER ======

Section 1. Applied Philosophy

Chapter 1. Science and Theory Precede Practice: Scientific Framework for the Applied Philosophy Approach in Management and Leadership

BMLOs	Business Management and Leadership Objects
CDM	Company Democracy Model
CoM	Circles of Mind
HCM	Holistic Concept of Man
MLOs	Management and Leadership Objects

Chapter 2. Delphic Maxims' Ontology-Based Taxonomies for Applied Philosophy: An Interpretation of the Ancient Hellenic Philosophy in Business and Governance Management

None

Chapter 3. Visualization of the Wisdom Cube: Wisdom Space for Management and Leadership

None

Chapter 4. The Company Democracy Culture: Understanding Culture and Dynamics

None

Chapter 5. Dimensions in Company Performance: The Power of Co-evolution

EU	European Union
ROI	Return on Investment
ROE	Return on Equity
UN	United Nations

Chapter 6. Managing and Leading Democratically: Achieving Democratic Balance

None

Section 2. Human Focus in Living Systems

Chapter 7. The Holistic Concept of Man in the Business Environment: The Concepts We Live By

None

Chapter 8. The Circles of Mind Metaphor: Actors on the Stage of Consciousness

SWOT   Strengths, Weaknesses, Opportunities, Threats

Chapter 9. Harnessing Modern Knowledge Systems: Applying Knowledge Frameworks

DIKW   Data, Information, Knowledge, Wisdom
DSS   Decision Support System
GUI   Graphical Computer Interface
KS   Knowledge System
LS   Language system
PPS   Problem Processing System
PS   Presentation System

None

Chapter 10. The Cross-Scientific Approach for Human-Compatible Systems: Acting with Modern Decision Tools

IoT   Internet of Things
LOO   Leadership Object Ontologies
MOO   Management Object Ontologies

Chapter 11. Agility Application, Ontology, and Concepts in a Technology Company Context: Agility Boosts Collective Wisdom

ICT   Information and Communication Technologies
KPI   Key Process Indicator
TPM   Total productive maintenance

Section 3. The Company Democracy Model

Chapter 12. The Company Democracy Model for Organizational Management and Leadership Strategies: The Innovative Company Democracy Model

SME   Small and Medium-sized Enterprise

Chapter 13.The Levels of the Company Democracy Model: A Spiral Co-evolution

None

Chapter 14. Human Perception, Interpretation, Understanding and Communication of Company Democracy: Building Co-opetitive Ecosystems

None

Chapter 15. The Company Democracy Model for Human Intellectual Capitalism and Shared Value Creation: Toward Added Value Economies

None

Chapter 16. Maturity Spaces for Company Democracy: The Seven Clouds of Glory

DCDS   Dynamic Company Democracy Space
PPP   Public–Private Partnerships

Chapter 17. The Dynamics of Company Democracy Culture: Enlightening the Black Hole in Knowledge Management

None

Chapter 18. Applying the Company Democracy Model: From Theory to Practice

None

Index

Printed in the United States
by Baker & Taylor Publisher Services